Teaching Children Who Find Reading Difficult

FOURTH EDITION

Timothy V. Rasinski
Kent State University

Nancy D. Padak
Kent State University

Gay Fawcett
Kent State University

Allyn & Bacon

Boston   New York   San Francisco
Mexico City   Montreal   Toronto   London   Madrid   Munich   Paris
Hong Kong   Singapore   Tokyo   Cape Town   Sydney

To all children who struggle in learning how to read,
and to the dedicated and caring reading teachers who help them.

Executive Series Editor: *Aurora Martínez*
Series Editorial Assistant: *Jacqueline Gillen*
Executive Marketing Manager: *Krista Clark*
Production Editor: *Gregory Erb*
Editorial Production Service: *Lynda Griffiths*
Composition Buyer: *Linda Cox*
Manufacturing Buyer: *Megan Cochran*
Electronic Composition: *Publishers' Design & Production Services, Inc.*
Interior Design: *Publishers' Design & Production Services, Inc.*
Photo Researcher: *Annie Pickert*
Cover Designer: *Elena Sidorova*

For related titles and support materials, visit our online catalog at www.pearsonhighered.com.

Between the time website information is gathered and then published, it is not unusual for some sites to have closed. Also, the transcription of URLs can result in typographical errors. The publisher would appreciate notification where these errors occur so that they may be corrected in subsequent editions.

Printed in the United States of America

10 9 8 7 6 5 4 3 2 1 RRD-VA 13 12 11 10 09

Allyn & Bacon
is an imprint of

www.pearsonhighered.com

ISBN-10: 0-13-233718-5
ISBN-13: 978-0-13-233718-2

❧ About the Authors

Timothy V. Rasinski is a professor of literacy education at Kent State University. He has written over 200 articles and has authored, coauthored, or edited over 50 books or curriculum programs on reading education. His scholarly interests include reading fluency and word study, reading in the elementary and middle grades, and readers who struggle. His research on reading has been cited by the National Reading Panel and has been published in journals such as *Reading Research Quarterly, The Reading Teacher, Reading Psychology*, and the *Journal of Educational Research*. Tim is currently writing the fluency chapter for Volume IV of the *Handbook of Reading Research*.

Recently Tim served a three-year term on the Board of Directors of the International Reading Association and from 1992 to 1999 he was coeditor of *The Reading Teacher*, the world's most widely read journal of literacy education. He has also served as coeditor of the *Journal of Literacy Research*. He is past-president of the College Reading Association and has won the A. B. Herr and Laureate Awards from the College Reading Association for his scholarly contributions to literacy education.

Prior to coming to Kent State, Tim taught literacy education at the University of Georgia. He taught for several years as an elementary and middle school classroom and Title I teacher in Nebraska.

Nancy D. Padak is a distinguished professor in the Department of Teaching, Leadership and Curriculum Studies at Kent State University. She also directs the Reading and Writing Center at KSU and teaches undergraduate and graduate courses in the area of literacy education. Prior to her arrival at Kent State in 1985, she was a classroom teacher and district administrator (language arts, reading, Title I) for the Elgin (Illinois) Schools.

Nancy has authored and edited books and monographs, has contributed book chapters, and has written more than 100 articles on topics related to literacy development. She is a frequent presenter at professional meetings and an active consultant for school districts within Ohio and in other parts of the Midwest. Nancy has also served in a variety of leadership roles in professional organizations, including the presidency of the College Reading Association and (with others) the Editor of *The Reading Teacher*, the *Journal of Literacy Research*, and the *Ohio Journal of English Language Arts*.

Gay Fawcett has been in education for over 35 years as a teacher, principal, language arts consultant, curriculum director, and adjunct professor. She has also directed Kent State University's Research Center for Educational Technology. She currently teaches face-to-face and online graduate and undergraduate courses in literacy and school psychology. She also consults with schools and school districts regarding curriculum issues.

Gay has authored and coauthored over 80 articles, books, and book chapters for educational publications and has served as associate editor for *The Reading Teacher*. She currently serves on the editorial review boards for several professional organizations. Her dissertation on literacy in middle school classrooms received three awards, including ASCD's Outstanding Dissertation Award and NCTE's Promising Researcher Award.

❧ Contents

CHAPTER 5

Preventing Reading Problems through Early Literacy Experiences   73

CHAPTER 6

Overcoming Difficulties in Word Recognition   89

CHAPTER 7

Developing Fluent Reading in Struggling Readers   *117*

CHAPTER 8

Building Deep and Wide Vocabularies in Struggling Readers   *139*

CHAPTER 9

Developing Comprehension with Narrative Text   165

❧ *Preface*

WE HAVE BEEN WORKING TOGETHER FOR OVER 20 YEARS, teaching and thinking; talking with children, teachers, and parents; conducting research; providing professional development; and discussing reading and instruction with each other and with others—sometimes heatedly. We have struggled with many questions: What are the best ways to provide instruction for children who struggle as readers? How should their instruction differ from instruction for children who progress more typically? What insights can we glean from research? What are the proper roles of teachers and parents in instructional efforts? And how can we best communicate our ideas about corrective instruction to teachers—those in training and those already working with children?

This edition of *Teaching Children Who Find Reading Difficult*, like the three that preceded it, is our best current response to those questions and many others. We describe instructional strategies for helping children in an informal, easy-to-read, yet scholarly, approach. The ideas presented here have been tried and tested in studies of effective instruction and, more important, in our own classrooms and tutoring rooms and those of teachers we have known and worked with over the years.

Our Framework for Helping You with Struggling Readers

Many books offer ideas for helping struggling readers, often with a highly diagnostic-prescriptive approach that results in a detailed recipe book of prescribed activities designed to remediate specific skills and subskills. These books include lists of skill activities aimed at remediating everything from medial vowel sounds to homonyms, to sequential comprehension difficulties. But such books pay little attention to the instructional context or how various activities might interact to form a coherent, logical, and effective whole.

Our book breaks with this traditional model. The instructional strategies and activities are arranged around general areas of focus, such as phonemic awareness, fluency, vocabulary, and comprehension. Additional chapters describe curriculum development, assessment, working with parents, and more. Because we built the framework of this book around these broad areas, you now have a framework for organizing your own under-standing and approach to remedial and corrective reading instruction.

GENERALIZED STRATEGIES

The strategies can be generalized to many situations so that informed teachers can mold and modify them for their own teaching and learning contexts. As you work with these strategies, you will find they offer supported opportunities to experience reading success. We like to think of our descriptions of the instructional strategies as the raw material. Teachers use this raw material to meet their students' needs without lessening the effec-tiveness of the activities. Indeed, because our presentation assumes that informed, sensi-tive, and caring teachers will mold the strategies to fit their own instructional contexts, we expect the effectiveness of the strategies to be enhanced.

TEACHER VOICES

Because instruction depends heavily on the context in which it occurs, we wanted you to hear the voices of teachers who have tried out these strategies in their own rooms. You will see how they perceive and provide corrective instruction, how they modify the strategies for their own use, what they like about the strategies, and why they choose them. We believe that, by reading about these teachers, your understanding of and insight into the activities will be deepened and enhanced.

CONNECTING STRATEGIES TO MAKE A COHESIVE WHOLE

Teaching Children Who Find Reading Difficult includes another unique feature—our atten-tion to how different strategies might fit together in whole instructional packages or rou-tines. We offer opportunities for wide and guided reading to help you form consistent and complete instructional routines that are predictable, successful, and effective.

New to This Edition

In this fourth edition, we have updated all the chapters by incorporating new research findings and describing new instructional activities. We have continued to address the role of technology in children's literacy learning and have increased attention to issues sur-rounding teaching reading to children whose first language is not English.

Perhaps the most significant addition to this edition, however, is the focus on scientif-ically based research and policy for reading, and learning to read, and working with strug-gling readers. In 2000, the National Reading Panel (NRP) report provided the research foundation for the reauthorization of the Elementary and Secondary Education Act, com-monly called No Child Left Behind. The panel's findings have influenced curriculum and instruction in reading, especially in the elementary grades. In 2004, the reauthorization of the Individuals with Disabilities Education Act (IDEA) introduced a concept called Response to Intervention (RTI). Although intended primarily to guide instructional sup-port for children with disabilities, the RTI concept is currently influencing instruction for all children who struggle with learning in many schools. We have woven information from the NRP and about RTI into a research-based approach that reflects an integrated curriculum with authentic and engaging reading.

Whether you use this book as a course textbook or a handbook for working with children in a classroom or clinic, you will find that it contains ideas, suggestions, and discussions that will help you be the best teacher you can be. This book is for you and for the struggling readers with whom you interact.

Acknowledgments

A book such as this is more than the product of any three individuals. We had help. Among those we gratefully recognize are Linda Bishop, who shared our vision of a new type of book on corrective reading strategies and methods.

Tim and Nancy also wish to thank their mentors, Jerry Zutell at The Ohio State University and Jane Davidson at Northern Illinois University, who have continued to influence our thinking and challenge us to consider persistent problems in new ways. Gay wishes to thank Tim and Nancy, who were her doctoral advisors and have continued to include her in challenging projects such as this throughout the years. We are especially grateful for our own students—those who challenge us in our classes now and those who have graduated and are on their way to becoming conscientious teachers. These students and former students have continually provided us with fresh insights into working with children who find reading difficult.

We would be remiss not to acknowledge all of the teachers, principals, and other educators with whom we have had the privilege to work. Their collaboration provides us with ideas, insights, and inspiration into teaching reading. We wish to thank teachers and administrators from Akron, Canton, Cleveland, Mayfield, Nordonia, Tallmadge, and other locations in Ohio. Around the country, we thank teachers from Chicago, ESU #3, Mobile, Palatine, Sonoma County, and many other districts. Each has contributed greatly to this book, and we sincerely appreciate their part in its development.

Finally, we acknowledge the contributions of our reviewers from this and previous editions for their careful reading and thoughtful comments: Eileen Baker, Holy Family University; Carole L. Bond, The University of Memphis; Hazel A. Brauer, University of San Francisco; Leonard Breen, Sam Houston State University; Mariam Jean Dreher, University of Maryland; Karen R. Cook-Enlow, Rio Linda Union School District; Joyce Kostelnik, Arizona State University West; Harry B. Miller, Northeast Louisiana University; Kouider Mokhtari, Miami University (Ohio); Evangeline Newton, The University of Akron; Barbara Pettegrew, Otterbein College; Lucille B. Strain, Bowie State University; Elizabeth Sturtevant, George Mason University; and Deborah Tidwell, University of Northern Iowa.

We hope that everyone who has influenced our work—especially those teachers and children whose classrooms we have visited and whose stories we have told—will benefit from this book. In many ways, we can say that this is a book for teachers and children by teachers and children.

Timothy V. Rasinski, Nancy D. Padak, and Gay Fawcett

Chapter **One** ∾

Setting the Stage for Helping Struggling Readers

BRIANNA IS AN ENERGETIC LITTLE GIRL who wakes up every morning happy to go to school—so far. However, her teacher reports that Brianna doesn't recognize rhyming words and doesn't know *p* from *d* from *g*. How long will it be until this happy kindergarten child wakes up with dread because she has to go to school?

Jerome is a fourth-grader whose reading is choppy, slow, and expressionless. His teacher is frustrated because Jerome no longer receives Title I support services and everything she has tried hasn't helped Jerome much.

Vitaliy's family immigrated to the United States when he was 11 years old. His teachers are baffled as to why he is not doing well in school. He has made great progress with spoken English and he is a bright boy, but he struggles with the reading assignments in all subjects.

Do you have (or expect that one day you might have) a Brianna, or a Jerome, or a Vitaliy in your class? No doubt you do, along with other children who have reading problems that are different, yet just as perplexing, as the problems of these three children. What can you do? What is the best way to teach students who find reading difficult?

Throughout this book we will share a variety of instructional strategies that have proven successful for scores of teachers who work with struggling readers. However, we lay claim to no magic bullets. We believe there is no method, no materials, and no program more powerful than informed and caring teachers. Indeed, we believe that despite nearly daily attacks by the media on U.S. schools, you are doing a great job.

In the 2007 Progress in International Reading Literacy Study, U.S. students in low-poverty schools outperformed the top-ranked Swedes. Even in schools with a rate of poverty up to 50 percent, students attained an average score that, had they constituted a nation, would have ranked fourth. Only U.S. students attending schools with more than 75 percent poverty scored below the international average of the 35 participating countries (Bracey, 2007).

Even the actions of test-makers themselves serve as a testimonial to the good work teachers do. Test restandardization, which takes place regularly, has consistently made pas-

1

sages at every grade level more difficult because today's test-takers are better readers than those of the past.

Yet we know there are students who still struggle with reading and teachers like you who continue looking for ways to help them. Our hope is that this book will provide you with food for thought and some concrete ideas as you consider how best to meet the needs of students who find reading difficult.

Key Ideas Underlying Literacy Development

Despite great progress in understanding how children acquire literacy and in methods for teaching reading and writing, the field of literacy education continues to be dominated by multiple perspectives and approaches.

Although we do not wish to enter into the debate over best theories and theoretical orientations to teaching reading, the authors of any book that attempts to describe and advocate certain approaches to reading and writing instruction must begin by providing the orientation that frames the book. The approach we advocate in this book derives from three key ideas that underlie many theories of literacy development and approaches to literacy education: authenticity, engagement, and essentials.

We know from the theories and work of John Dewey that learning is most powerful when it is connected to the world that exists outside the classroom. When teachers make their classrooms and the work that occurs in their classrooms reflect students' lives outside the classroom, students are more likely to want to learn. This is what we mean by *authenticity*—what students read, how they read it, and how they respond to what they read (and write) must connect to the children's interests and lives, to the real world, and to other curriculum areas. After all, literacy is essentially a vehicle for enriching one's life and for helping one learn about the world in all its wonderful facets.

It's not enough, however, for reading and writing to be authentic. Students need to approach literacy tasks eagerly; they need to be *engaged*. Too many students live passive school lives. They allow school to happen to them. These students are less likely to take the initiative to employ reading and writing for their own purposes and pleasure.

Progress in becoming literate depends largely on the amount of time that students spend engaged in literate activity. If students struggle in reading and writing, one of the best ways to move them forward is to engage them in the literacy act. The teacher's job, then, is to engage students fully and completely in the task of learning to read—moving students away from responding in a passive and mechanical fashion and toward responding thoughtfully and with understanding and enthusiasm.

Authentic reading leads to engaged reading. Engaged reading results in improved reading. And improved reading leads to more authentic reading. The teacher's job is to provide authentic reading and writing experiences so students will engage themselves in the task and bootstrap their way to full literacy.

A focus on the *essential* elements in reading suggests that specific competencies must be developed for students to experience the success of full literacy. The National Reading Panel (2000) identified five essential elements: phonemic awareness, phonics or word recognition, reading fluency, vocabulary, and comprehension. To be successful in reading, students must be competent in each of these areas. We agree. We argue that there is more to reading success than what is embodied in these five competencies, but we do recognize that these components are incredibly important. Moreover, students who struggle in reading usually experience difficulty in one or more of these areas.

Throughout this book you will see the ideas of authenticity, engagement, and essentials come through over and over. When essential reading strategies and skills are taught within a context of authentic reading for authentic tasks and in a context that challenges students to fully engage their cognitive and creative selves, those strategies and skills are likely to be internalized quickly and find use in students' school tasks and in their lifelong reading.

We begin, then, with the belief, almost a cliché nowadays, that people learn to read by reading. Several studies have documented that good readers read substantially more than less able readers during reading lessons and free reading time in school and at home. Findings from the National Assessment of Educational Progress (NAEP) for 1992, 1994, 1998, and 2000 (National Center for Education Statistics, 2001) show that fourth-grade students who read the most in school and home tended to be the highest-achieving students in reading. Students who read the least were the lowest achievers. In both 2001 and 2006, the Progress in International Reading Literacy Study (PIRLS) (Mullis et al., 2007) found a positive relationship between fourth-grade reading achievement and the number of children's books in the home and the amount of time parents engaged their children in reading.

Lewis and Samuels (2003) reviewed a number of studies on in-school independent reading and found "clear causal evidence that students who have in-school independent reading time in addition to regular reading instruction, do significantly better on measures of reading achievement than peers who have not had reading time" (p. 1). Furthermore, noted ESL researcher and writer, Stephen Krashen, maintains that free voluntary reading enhances language acquisition for students like Vitaliy (*Free Voluntary Reading*, online). Clearly, reading success can be achieved only when students practice the reading skills, strategies, and competencies taught them—and this can be done only through reading.

Our next assumption is connected to the first. We believe that children are most likely to engage in reading when they perceive it as meaningful, instrumental, and/or enjoyable. When students see that reading is useful, playful, or interesting, they are more likely to pull out books, newspapers, and other written materials and read with purpose and passion.

Proceeding from this assumption, we believe that teachers, principals, schools, and parents must help students find meaning and joy in reading. Teachers need to help students master and make sense of the written symbols on the page. Equally important, they need to help students develop a passion for reading—to see that reading can be as engaging as video games, watching sports on television, talking on the telephone, camping in the woods, playing soccer, collecting stamps or baseball cards, or any other activity in which students take pleasure and delight. In other words, students need to see reading as worth doing. Teachers can foster this attitude by sharing their own passion for reading—for example, by talking about their own reading, reading to students, recommending books, and listening with interest to students talk about personal reading.

In authentic, engaging, and essential reading classrooms, teachers create conditions and develop activities that inspire students to read wholeheartedly and enthusiastically. When students read willingly and teachers provide necessary instruction, assistance, modeling, and encouragement, students become more proficient readers. Because instruction is aimed at students' needs and interests, they see the importance of reading and remain active and engaged readers beyond the boundaries of the classroom. The teacher who subscribes to this authentic, engaged, and essential orientation, therefore, aims not simply to develop students who *can* read but those who *want* to read and *choose* to read.

The Essentials of Reading Instruction

Proficiency in phonemic awareness, word recognition, reading fluency, vocabulary, and comprehension are necessary competencies for success in reading (National Reading Panel, 2000). As such, these areas must be the focus of instruction. Students need direct, thoughtful, organized, and regular instruction in these competencies in order to become readers.

Phonemic awareness refers to the ability to think about and manipulate the sounds of language. Proficiency in phonemic awareness is necessary to profit from phonics and word recognition instruction. *Word recognition* is the ability to turn a written word into its oral representation. Clearly, reading requires word recognition. *Fluency* is a bridge between word recognition and comprehension. It is the ability to read accurately, expressively, meaningfully, with appropriate phrasing, and at an appropriate rate. Fluent readers need not think about each word as they decode it or sound it out; rather, they recognize words in print automatically and so can devote their attention to the most important part of reading: comprehension. *Vocabulary* refers to the ability to know the meaning of words encountered in print. *Comprehension* refers to the ability to actively construct appropriate meaning from written text.

We think these competencies are critical to reading success and must be taught. That is why we devote a chapter to each of the first four essential reading components and two chapters to comprehension. We believe, too, that writing is an essential part of reading success. Thus, we devote a chapter to writing. But reading success entails more than these essential elements. In the next section we describe other components critical to successful reading instruction.

Authentic and Engaged Reading Classrooms

Teachers who create conditions that make students want to read are avid readers themselves and they share their enthusiasm with students, telling them about what they are reading, why they choose certain books, and how reading affects them. They also communicate this enthusiasm by reading to their students every day. In effect, they are saying: Reading is so important that I am willing to take the time to share with you some of the best stories and poems that I know. I want you to know about and enjoy these stories and poems, too. Students are much more likely to develop an enthusiasm for reading in an environment in which reading is treated as special and important.

A considerable amount of research supports this point. In his review of the Reading Panel Report, Michael Pressley (2001) cited study after study showing that dents in authentic and engaging classrooms read independently more than children in skills-driven classrooms, use comprehension strategies more effectively, are more academically curious, and better understand the structure of stories.

Authentic and engaging classrooms share certain characteristics, regardless of whether the grade level is primary, intermediate, or secondary. After a decade of studying effective reading instruction, Allington (2002) identified common features of effective literacy instruction that he calls the "six T's":

1. *Time:* Children spend more time reading and writing across the whole school day and less time doing "stuff" (all the other things teachers have children do instead of reading and writing).

2. *Texts:* Children more often read texts that are at just the right level.

3. *Talk:* There is more authentic dialogue between teachers and children as opposed to "interrogation" of students by teachers.

4. *Tasks:* Teachers assign substantive, challenging work that allows students choices.

5. *Teach:* Teachers provide direct instruction with explicit demonstrations of strategies that good readers use.

6. *Testing:* Teachers evaluate student work based more on effort and improvement than simply on achievement.

The way these features of effective literacy instruction play out in the classroom is necessarily different between grade levels. In the primary grades, instruction focuses on introducing students to the printed word and stories. Because many activities at this level are group oriented, we would expect to find the teacher reading aloud and talking to the class about books every day. Groups of students would be reading oversized (big) books together. Usually the content of these books is patterned or predictable, which makes them easy and fun to read and read again. Bill Martin's *Brown Bear, Brown Bear, What Do You See?* is one of the best examples of a patterned book. After several group readings in which the teacher points to words as they are read, most children can read the story on their own and begin to identify specific phrases, words, and word parts in the text and in isolation.

Language experience activities are also a large part of reading instruction at this level. In language experience, students share an experience—for example, a field trip to a supermarket, a visit with the school principal, or a math or science activity. After a brief discussion of the experience, students dictate a text that summarizes what they learned or reflects their perceptions of the shared experience. As the children dictate, the teacher acts as a scribe, writing students' words on a large sheet of paper that hangs from the chalkboard. When the text is finished, students read and reread it, first with the teacher's help and later independently. Children read this text successfully because it is about an experience they have all shared, talked about, and composed. Once students are familiar with the text, the teacher may begin pointing out individual words and letters.

...pect many opportunities for children to read and look at
...eers; write their own stories and make entries in personal
... to and with the teacher, classroom aides, parent volunteers,
...srooms and grades. When students begin to develop an affin-
...oficiency in fluent reading, the teacher gives them even greater
...bout their reading.

...students may engage in what many reading educators call readers'
...87; see Chapter 8). In readers' workshop, most instructional time
...books, primarily ones that students have chosen. Students' responses
...are important in this approach. They may respond in their personal
...to their teacher and peers. In addition, they may recast the story in a
...it, or visual art form. Students also have many opportunities to discuss
...vith peers and teacher in an informal, accepting environment.

...her's role in authentic, engaged, and essential reading and writing classrooms
is in... traditional. Authentic, engaging, and essential teachers are encouragers and
explicit models of what it means to be a literate person. Just as students write books using
the model of a book written by a distinguished author, students also model their development as literate people by watching and listening to their teachers. Teachers who love
reading and demonstrate this passion to their students allow students an important view
at what an engaged literate person looks like in the flesh.

In addition, effective literacy teachers constantly seek to improve themselves and their
schools through staff development and support from administrators (Gaskins, 1998).
Through self-improvement activities, teachers take ownership of their instructional programs and become more willing and able to make them work.

Corrective Reading in an Authentic and Engaged Context

We now have a good picture of authentic, engaged, and essential reading and writing
instruction in regular classrooms. Less clear is how it works with students who experience
considerable difficulty learning to read and require some adaptive instruction. Some people claim that this approach may be fine for students who learn to read in a normal manner and at a normal rate but will fail with those not making it. According to this way of
thinking, these children need a more structured environment in which reading is divided
into small, digestible units. Educators who subscribe to such an approach assume that
students can better master smaller segments of reading as they work alone or in groups
with other children who also have reading problems. This approach is called a *diagnostic–
prescriptive model:* Identify the specific skills in which the student exhibits the most difficulty, provide intensive remedial instruction in the deficient skill(s), often in the form of
mindless drill and incessant worksheets, and (according to the theory that underlies this
model) the student will achieve proficiency in reading.

The idea may sound good on paper, but in reality it doesn't work. Richard Allington
and his associates have studied remedial, special, and compensatory reading instruction
for several years (Allington, 1987, 2000; Allington & McGill-Franzen, 1989; Allington,

Stuetzel, Shake, & Lamarche, 1986; Allington & Walmsley, 1995). They report that current approaches to remedial reading do little for struggling readers. Instruction tends to rely heavily on skill, drill, and worksheet activities focused on isolated words, sounds, and letters. Students have few opportunities to read materials of their own choosing. What they do read is usually chosen for them according to perceived reading level. Children work by themselves or with other struggling readers, and little of what they do in these special reading classes has any connection to what they are learning in their regular classrooms. Remedial instruction usually emphasizes word-perfect oral reading of uninteresting texts rather than acquisition of meaning from the text or development of attitudes and habits that will draw students to reading throughout their lives.

Students placed in such special programs rarely leave or improve sufficiently. They tend to remain behind classmates who achieve at more normal rates. What usually changes in these students are their attitudes toward learning, reading, and themselves. They begin to see themselves as failures and to view reading as a meaningless and frustrating task—something to be avoided. Allington and others say that it is time to reinvent remedial reading.

Those taking a broader perspective on educational reform share a similar view. The Commission on Chapter I (now Title I) was formed to investigate the strengths and weaknesses of current Title I programs in order to recommend changes in the legislation. The commission's report describes typical remedial instruction: "Children in Chapter I learn and relearn discrete low-level skills. They rarely know what it is like to attempt interesting content or to use knowledge creatively. Rather than experiencing the joy of wrestling with ideas, children are more likely to spend their time circling m's and p's on dittos" (Commission on Chapter I, 1993). The Commission argued for remaking the federal program for remedial reading.

One way to reinvent remedial reading is to make instruction look, feel, and be more like authentic and engaged classrooms than skill-and-drill emporiums. The ideas and activities in this book are innovative and exciting approaches for helping students overcome their difficulty with and dislike of reading. Moreover, they are organized around components essential for reading success, areas that are often the source of difficulty for struggling readers.

Our university reading center gives children this kind of instructional experience. They read books of their own choosing as well as exemplary trade books and other material chosen by the teacher. They respond to their reading in creative ways—for example, by recasting their stories as scripts and performing them in readers' theater for their families. These children write every day in school and at home about topics of interest to them. While developing competency in the essential components of reading, they learn to like reading, understand that reading is enjoyable, and discover that it can help them in their own lives.

Parents see the difference this instruction makes for their children, and they are universally pleased. They tell us how their children hated to read before enrolling at our center. Today, those children not only look forward to the center sessions but also insist on reading to and with their parents at home. Parents tell us that students who had previously refused to pick up a book, even when Mom or Dad told them to, now choose to read on their own.

Good instruction is good instruction, whether it's for children reading four levels above grade placement or for those who struggle with reading. If children learn to love reading and make good progress in learning to read in regular classrooms with an authentic, engaged, and essential orientation, then it makes sense that instruction with the same basic characteristics will work just as well for children who have trouble learning to read. Certain adaptations may be necessary, but we believe the principles that drive high-quality instruction in regular classroom settings are equally applicable in settings that address the needs of struggling readers.

Throughout this book we will describe various instructional strategies aimed at overcoming specific areas of difficulty in reading (such as attitude and motivation, phonemic awareness, word recognition, reading fluency, vocabulary, comprehension, and writing). Rather than precisely defined skills, these are broad areas essential to growth in reading. Difficulties in reading can often be attributed to problems in one or more of these areas.

Although we describe and recommend instructional practices, let us be clear at the outset that such instruction must occur within a larger framework of authentic literacy education. The strategies and practices we describe are generic and can easily be adapted and applied to nearly any instructional setting, including math, social studies, and science classes; with students of all levels of achievement; and with texts of any level of difficulty.

Principles of Authentic, Engaged, and Essential Corrective Instruction

These principles apply directly to corrective reading situations and establish a general framework for corrective reading.

USE AUTHENTIC TEXTS AND OTHER READING MATERIAL

If the goal is to have children read real books and other reading materials, they need plenty of opportunities to read such material in their corrective reading instruction. Texts should center on children's own language and focus on communicating for real purposes. The language in books should sound as natural as it would in conversation. As Alfie Kohn (2008) wryly observed, "No child cares whether Pat's rat has a hat" (p. 58). By reading real stories, poems, and essays, students learn that reading is enjoyable and has meaning in their lives.

The workbooks and skill sheets of traditional remedial reading offer little enjoyment and satisfaction for students, and they certainly have questionable applicability to students' real-life reading. Skill sheets, if used, are best developed by the teacher and aimed specifically at whatever difficulty the student is experiencing.

FOCUS ON THE ESSENTIAL COMPONENTS OF READING

Struggling readers most likely experience difficulty in one or more of the essential components of reading: phonemic awareness, word recognition, reading fluency, vocabulary, and comprehension. Corrective instruction needs to focus squarely and rigorously on these essential components of reading. Successful teachers of struggling readers develop intensive instructional routines that focus on the essential component that is the source of students' reading difficulty, while at the same time providing independent and guided opportunities for students to put the essential component to use through real reading.

MAXIMIZE READING OF CONNECTED TEXT

Students in traditional corrective reading programs often read little connected written discourse. Certainly, they read less than students in regular classrooms. Yet we know that quantity of reading is directly related to reading growth. We must create situations that make students want to read real books on their own, both in and out of school.

PROVIDE FOR HIGH LEVELS OF ENGAGEMENT

Not only do students need to read a lot, but the nature of that reading should encourage high-level thinking. This requires that students read for their own purposes or purposes determined within the classroom community. Students need to read and write to solve their own problems and to satisfy their own hunger for enjoyment and learning.

FOCUS ON STUDENTS' MOTIVATION AND INTEREST IN READING

Most students who have difficulty learning to read also dislike reading. They have experienced pain and frustration in their reading instruction and associate reading with unpleasant experiences. Corrective instruction must help students develop more positive images of reading and of themselves as readers. Teachers accomplish this by helping students achieve success in reading, by encouraging them to read real and personally satisfying materials, and by developing authentic and enjoyable instructional activities.

MAKE CONNECTIONS

Purposes for reading and writing lie in the world around the students—their lived-in world and their school world. Students must read and write so as to make connections to their own world and the various content areas in the school curriculum. Students need to see that they can apply literacy to all areas of the curriculum and life.

LET STUDENTS LEAD THE WAY

In traditional corrective reading classrooms, the teacher makes all the decisions about lessons for individual students, sometimes basing lessons on diagnostic test results or packaged instructional materials. Students have little voice in this process and often have difficulty making sense of lessons or connecting lessons to real reading situations. Consequently, motivation and interest can decline.

We can best foster motivation and interest when students are involved in reading and learning that they care about. By encouraging students to select their own reading material and inviting them to react, ask questions, and seek answers, we can help students control the purpose, content, and direction for their literacy experiences. Learning is easiest and most efficient under these conditions.

PROVIDE SUPPORT WHEN NEEDED

Students in corrective reading placements cannot read material with the same degree of fluency as more normally progressing students. Effective teachers are ready and able to provide support (or scaffolding) to make reading manageable and meaningful for students. This may mean reading to or with students before asking them to read the text on their own, ensuring that they have sufficient background knowledge to understand the text, checking that the text is sufficiently easy for them to read, or asking them to practice reading a passage at home with their parents before reading it at school. Readers should never struggle to the point of failure or frustration in any reading task or activity.

Sometimes support involves instruction in specific skills or strategies. But this instruction is neither the focal point of the curriculum as in traditional corrective reading programs, nor provided for all readers. Instead, teachers provide skill or strategy instruction as needed—only if they see that lack of a particular strategy or bit of reading knowledge is hampering a student's progress. That is, teachers make no assumptions about student need; rather, they take their cues from student performance.

FOCUS ON SUCCESS

Traditional corrective reading programs are predicated on a deficit view of students. They assume that something is missing or wrong with a student, that instruction should fill in what's missing or correct what's wrong. This view focuses on weaknesses among readers—on what they *can't* do. To the contrary, we believe that teachers need to focus on what students *can* do. Rather than think about students as remedial or view teaching as fixing what is wrong with learners, teachers should view students from a developmental perspective: They should believe that all students can learn and expect that they will. Such teachers base instruction on what students know and are interested in and what they can do.

EVERYBODY'S A TEACHER; EVERYBODY'S A LEARNER

Authentic and engaged classrooms look little like traditional classrooms—no desks in rows, no isolated individual learners, no teacher behind a desk monitoring activity. Instead, students are learning from and with each other. Variety and choice are evident. And the teacher is a learner, too. Teachers learn about students by listening to and observing them in action; they value students and are genuinely interested in their thoughts and opinions. Together, teachers and their students strive to create a learning community where everybody's a teacher and everyone learns.

INVOLVE PARENTS

Reading is best learned when it is practiced at home as well as at school. Ideally, students read any time, any place. Making parents aware of what is going on in the school and encouraging them to help their children at home in ways that complement school instruction will reinforce and multiply instructional effectiveness. Moreover, involving parents usually makes them greater stakeholders in their children's education and increases their support for and satisfaction in the job that schools do. Effective reading instruction demands that teachers inform parents and involve them in substantive ways in their children's development as readers.

At the same time, effective reading teachers know there will sometimes be parents who cannot or will not be involved. These teachers do not approach children from such homes with a defeatist attitude but continue to do everything, and more, to help these children succeed. One important thing to consider in such situations is that the education of children is society's responsibility, not just that of teachers and parents. Joan, for example, is a high school reading intervention specialist. Her students keep a reader's response journal, and Joan's goal is for parents to write back and forth with their children in the journal. Unfortunately, not all parents do. Joan has enlisted the help of her own retired mother's bridge club. Each time the club meets, they begin by responding to the journals Joan has sent. She reports that they often spend more time reading, discussing, and responding to the journals than they do playing bridge.

KNOW YOUR STUDENTS; TRACK THEIR PROGRESS

Effective teachers know their students. They know their likes and their dislikes. They know what motivates students and they are aware of what tends to turn students away from engaged learning. Teachers should observe their students closely, question their students often, and use this information to guide instruction. In addition, teachers can help their students learn to assess themselves. Not only can student self-assessment provide insight for the teacher but it also leads to more self-directed learning.

Progress in reading should be monitored regularly. Brief but regular assessment aids teachers in determining instructional effectiveness and guides them in altering instruction when necessary. In this book we describe several approaches for helping teachers learn about their students and track their reading progress.

A New Direction for Teaching Struggling Readers

Authentic, engaging, and essential instruction is a legitimate approach for helping children who experience significant difficulty when learning to read. This book was written to introduce classroom and specialist teachers of students with reading difficulties to instructional strategies that fit within this orientation. In it we provide descriptions of instructional strategies and activities. As we suggested earlier, however, these strategies are not aimed at remediating any particular or precise skill such as learning consonant blends, mastering sight words, or determining the main idea of a paragraph. Rather, the strategies we present are organized under general areas of concern that can be diagnosed simply by listening to children read and respond to questions about the reading, observing children within the classroom during instruction and recreational reading times, talking with children about how they perceive and feel about reading, and talking with parents and teachers about how they perceive the children's progress and interest in reading. Our major topics include the broad areas of phonemic awareness and word recognition, interest in and motivation for reading, reading fluency, vocabulary development, and comprehension.

Although teachers will find these strategies useful for helping children learn to read, we do not intend them to be implemented in any prescriptive or lockstep manner. Rather, we recommend that teachers become familiar with the strategies and modify them for use within their own instructional settings. Not all strategies work the same way for all students or teachers. Informed teachers will take the essence of strategies they believe have the greatest potential for success; fit them to the needs and interests of their students; and combine them with other strategies to create complex and integrated lessons that synergistically support children's reading while engaging children in authentic, interesting, and enlightening literacy experiences.

We encourage teachers to use the strategies creatively to develop effective lesson formats, but we recommend implementing them with a high degree of consistency. From one day to the next, the general lesson format should be consistent yet used with a variety of texts. This consistent application of effective instruction will minimize lost time, make lessons secure and predictable for students, and ultimately lead to significant gains in reading.

It is our hope that you use this book as a handbook or reference guide. It is not a book to be read during a university course in corrective reading and then forgotten. It is meant to be read, reread, and consulted frequently as you search for instructional strategies that make reading real for students and help them overcome the difficulties and failures they have experienced in past attempts to become successful readers.

DISCUSSION QUESTIONS

Some of the discussion questions for each chapter ask you to think through your own work as a teacher. If you are not currently a practicing teacher, try to respond to these questions from your own school experience (either from when you yourself were a student or from visits to schools that you have made in your teacher education program).

1. In this chapter we state there is more to good reading instruction than the five components identified by the National Reading Panel (phonemic awareness, phonics/word recognition, fluency, vocabulary, comprehension). What would you add to the list and why?

2. As cited in the chapter, Allington and colleagues report that current approaches to remedial reading do little for struggling readers. Describe the remedial reading program in your school. Do you agree with Allington? Why or why not?

3. Form a "consultation line" with your colleagues. Place two rows of chairs in lines facing one another so that people sitting in the chairs are knee to knee. People on one side are speakers; people on the other side are consultants. The speaker tells the person directly across from him or her about a one of his or her struggling readers. The consultant makes suggestions, asks questions to help the speaker think it through, shares stories of personal experiences with a similar student, and so on. After three minutes, the consultants move down one chair. The person from

the end of the line will fill in the empty chair that is created at the other end. Speakers stay in the same seat. Repeat the process so that the speaker gets consultation from another person about the same student. After three consultations, switch the roles of consultant and speaker.

4. Chose one of Allington's "six T's" of effective literacy instruction and give specific examples of what it looks like in a classroom.

5. How do you choose "just right" texts for children?

Chapter Two

Determining Instructional Needs

ASSESSING READERS IN ACTION

SALLY BURTCH'S ELEMENTARY SCHOOL created a pre–first-grade class for students thought to be at risk for success in first grade. Sally volunteered to teach the class. During the summer before the new program began, she gathered the children's readiness test scores. As Sally examined the records, she realized she had a problem—she didn't really know any of her students as readers or people. She worried about creating a classroom environment that would respond to children's needs with no idea of what those needs might be.

Sally considered what she needed to know about the children and how best to learn it. She wanted more than test scores because "when we contrive a reading or writing task, setting the topic and the purposes for reading or writing, what we observe may bear little resemblance to students' natural reading and writing behavior" (Rhodes & Dudley-Marling, 1988, p. 36). Sally, interested in these natural literacy behaviors, turned to the kindergarten teachers' anecdotal notes. She valued her colleagues' opinions but knew that her classroom would be different from theirs and that classroom contexts influence children's actions as readers. She also knew her students would change over the summer.

Sally finally decided to create a reading portfolio for each student. An artist's portfolio is a sample of work collected to demonstrate the artist's breadth, depth, and flexibility. Likewise, a reader's portfolio is a sample of information about the reader. During the first few weeks of school, Sally began by observing, talking with children, and collecting reading and writing samples for each child. During choice time, for example, she made notes of who chose to read or write. During read-aloud time, she noted who paid attention and appeared to enjoy the story. She talked with children to discover their interest in books; these conversations also allowed her to evaluate their oral language development. She combined the insights she developed with the kindergarten teacher's notes and standardized test scores. In this way, she gained an in-depth and valuable perspective about each student as a reader and a person, which helped her develop a literacy program responsive to children's needs and interests.

Sally's situation was a bit atypical; after all, she was planning a new program. In many ways, however, her problem is one we all face. We need ways to find out about students as readers—what kinds of instructional opportunities to provide for them, what progress they are making, and what that progress means in terms of future instruction. These are important issues for all students but are particularly critical for struggling readers.

Response to Intervention

The 2004 reauthorization of the Federal IDEA law (Individuals with Disabilities Education Act) formalized the process of assessing and teaching struggling learners. The IDEA Response to Intervention model (RTI) calls for tiers of instruction, assessment, and increasingly intense interventions. The first tier consists of research-based instruction in a regular classroom setting accompanied by continual progress monitoring. Students who struggle with the universal curriculum move into the next tier, where they are provided targeted interventions accompanied by progress monitoring. Students who continue to struggle despite receiving research-based interventions are moved to the highest tier, where they are provided special education instruction based on a comprehensive evaluation.

The RTI model offers many valuable opportunities to learn about students as readers, but RTI can be successful only if teachers monitor students' daily progress. In determining the appropriate tier of instruction for a struggling reader, teachers should assess factors that influence reading, such as background knowledge, perceived purpose, instructional expectations, and type of materials or activities. All these factors vary among children, of course. But even for one child, they may vary throughout the school day or from one day to the next. This variation provides a strong rationale for basing assessment on daily routines.

In this chapter we develop that rationale. We also describe several informal, classroom-based assessments for determining the RTI level for struggling readers. Our overall goal is to present several systematic assessment and evaluation strategies that can serve as alternatives or additions to formal and informal tests. Rich descriptions of children involved in the day-to-day business of being readers can yield useful instructional insight.

Making Use of Standardized Tests

Most of this chapter is devoted to informal teacher assessments because we believe those who are with students day-in and day-out are the ones who should determine how those students are achieving. However, because of the prevalence of standardized tests in today's schools, we would be remiss if we did not address the issue.

In the past decade, politicians and the general public have increasingly demanded "proof" that students are receiving a quality education. The response to this demand has been to give more and more tests. With the passage of No Child Left Behind (Public Law 107-110, 107th Congress), standardized testing has taken on an increased significance with test results often figuring into "high-stakes" decisions such as student promotion or graduation, teacher merit pay, and school sanctions. For these reasons, many teachers help students prepare for the type of comprehension they must demonstrate on standardized tests, which feature shorter (and often less engaging) text selections than students are accustomed to and questions aimed toward "one right answer."

The test results aren't terribly useful for planning instruction for individual children. Suppose Jeremy earned a stanine score of 3 on a standardized reading test or a percentile rank of 40. What should his teacher do to promote his reading achievement? Furthermore, standardized test results are often returned near the end of the school year when any useful information they might have provided is too late.

However, standardized tests may give an overall snapshot of how a class of students is doing in reading, and that is information a teacher can use if tempered with professional caution. By studying class results over several years, teachers may identify areas of programmatic strengths and weaknesses. For example if a teacher notes that year after year her classes score low on nonfiction selections, she may want to incorporate more nonfiction texts and strategies. Or if a teacher sees that his students' scores in writing conventions are weak year after year, he might meet with other teachers at his grade level whose classes score well and ask them to share what they are doing. If all the school's scores are low in certain areas year after year, teachers can develop a plan for program changes and undertake action research to determine whether the new plan is successful using standardized scores as well as other measures.

Many children today feel pressured by parents and the media to do well on standardized tests. We do not advocate "test prep" that moves children away from authentic reading and writing, but we do believe teachers should help their students prepare for high-stakes tests by teaching them how to fill in bubble sheets, how to eliminate answers on multiple-choice questions, and how to pace themselves to finish the test.

As we stated earlier, though, standardized tests have little value for planning daily instruction for individual children. Many teachers and reading researchers (e.g., Harp, 1994; Rhodes & Shanklin, 1993; Tierney, 1998) question the assumptions that underlie standardized tests. They ask: If the reading process is fluid, and growth in reading ability idiosyncratic, how can a single measure designed to compare students with each other (or to some prescribed set of expectations) provide useful instructional information? Like many others seeking to understand at-risk readers, we think the answer is simple: Standardized tests alone cannot help teachers understand and assist struggling readers.

The Classroom as Setting, the Reader as Informant

More and more, teachers are turning to informal, in-process assessment and evaluation to help them understand and plan instruction for struggling readers. This shift partly reflects advances in understanding the processes of reading and learning to read. Teachers know the reading process is fluid and flexible rather than static. Teachers also know children become readers in a variety of ways, with different learning tempos, and by using different strategies and styles when interacting with text. Thus, teachers need a plan for assessing these differences.

The first step in developing an assessment plan involves deciding where assessment should take place and what kinds of reading tasks children should complete as part of the assessment. We recommend that assessment and evaluation take place *in* the classroom rather than outside it. Moreover, assessment should focus on authentic (classroom-like) reading activities rather than artificial ones. Ideally, assessment and evaluation should be natural parts of the continuous learning process in classrooms. Indeed, good assessment methods maximize instruction and involve children in real reading activities (Tierney, 1998).

The second step is to decide whose opinions to seek. Because they are active participants who know students and activities better than anyone else, knowledgeable teachers are the best evaluators. But in addition to the teacher, struggling readers should have some say in evaluating their own growth. In fact, students' ideas and opinions are crucial information in any assessment or evaluation. Self-evaluation can benefit both students and the teacher. Students can begin to take responsibility for their own learning, and teachers can learn about instruction from their students' points of view.

Assessment and evaluation plans aimed at creating reading portfolios for children who find reading difficult can provide a framework for successful implementation.

The Value of Portfolio Assessment

Portfolios can document what students think and do in situations involving reading. Teachers who use portfolios formulate questions about struggling readers and look to naturally occurring events in their classrooms to provide answers. They value the insights and interpretations that emerge from this process and realize that parents, children's previous teachers, and even friends can be good sources of information about a child.

Successful portfolio assessment takes some initial planning, as the overview in Figure 2.1 shows. First, you should generate questions to be answered. These questions may relate to broad curricular goals or hunches about at-risk readers based on preliminary observations. Questions may be general (What does Janey know about reading? What evidence shows that she is developing as a reader?) or they may be more specific (In what areas is Mike experiencing reading difficulty? What does Ricky do when he encounters an unknown word?)

Questions provide a focus for deciding on the contents of the portfolio. The next step in planning involves deciding what kind of evidence belongs in the portfolio and how to obtain it. A student's reading portfolio might contain anecdotal notes and records of observations, conversations, and interviews; checklists or charts kept by the teacher or the student; and performance samples documenting reading behaviors and abilities. A variety of other documents may also be helpful in understanding the child as a reader: lists of books read, written self-evaluations, notes from parents, report cards or progress cards, records of at-home reading, tape recordings of oral reading, or selections from reading-response journals (Maxim & Five, 1997). All this variety means that teachers and students will create portfolios to fit the environments in which they teach and learn.

FIGURE 2.1   An Overview of Assessment

- **Generate questions based on the following:**

  Broad curricular goals

  Observations

  Hunches

- **Decide on forms of evidence:**

  Observation

  Interaction

  Analysis

- **Develop a systematic and comprehensive plan for gathering information from and with the following sources:**

  Students

  Parents

  Other teachers

  Peers

  Yourself

- **Analyze information:**

  Look for patterns

  Form hypotheses

Whatever the focus and content of portfolios, the plan for gathering information must be systematic and comprehensive. Four broad kinds of activities can provide information for portfolios:

1. *Observation:* Teachers watch what struggling readers do, either independently or with others. The teachers are not directly involved but only observe.

2. *Conversations or interviews:* Informal conversations or planned reading conferences offer opportunities to talk with students in depth.

3. *Performance samples:* Lists of books read or written products such as excerpts from reading logs or notes made during instructional activities can yield useful information.

4. *Assessment activities:* Activities undertaken for assessment purposes, such as evaluating oral reading for fluency or word recognition, can complement other information.

Each of these assessment activities can be formal; for example, teachers might plan specific times or activities for observation. Each can also be informal and incidental as teachers and students naturally come into contact during a school day. They can even occur simultaneously: Observing an interesting situation might lead to a conversation or some diagnostic teaching as the teacher seeks to understand the student more completely.

Standardized tests are often described in terms of their validity and reliability. The value of portfolio assessment can be determined by thinking about the same concepts. An assessment or evaluation is valid if it offers a true picture of the issue under study. Certainly, information gathered in natural classroom settings has the potential to offer true pictures of students as readers. Moreover, teachers ensure the reliability or consistency of portfolio data by developing a systematic and comprehensive plan for developing the portfolio. Thus, the diagnostic insights that emerge through portfolio analysis and interpretation yield valid and reliable conclusions about struggling readers.

The Importance of Observation

The best situations for assessing or evaluating attitudes, thoughts, and behaviors are integral parts of day-to-day instruction. This view of the relationship between assessment and instruction suggests the importance of observation as a tool for understanding struggling readers. Opportunities for observation are abundant. Over the course of any day, effective teachers observe in a variety of reading situations from free-choice activities through informal and incidental encounters with reading to more formal instructional situations. We learn a great deal about students by observing them as they read, write, and respond to instruction.

Yetta Goodman (1985) calls this approach "kidwatching." The informal name is purposeful because kidwatching is an informal but systematic process that aims to record naturally occurring behaviors in reading situations. Effective kidwatchers share a few critical beliefs and skills. First, they believe in observation as a valid and valuable tool for learning about struggling readers. They also believe that their own judgment is critical as they watch what children do, listen to what they say, and make decisions about what these observations mean. In other words, kidwatchers are comfortable as professional decision makers. Finally, kidwatchers are skilled observers who use several means of gathering and recording information.

WHY KIDWATCHING?

Language and concepts grow and develop depending on the settings in which they occur and students' experiences in those settings—including interactions with texts, the teacher, and each other (Goodman, 1985). Kidwatching allows teachers to explore what happens when readers interact with genuine texts for real purposes. Unlike more formal assessment procedures, kidwatching allows a teacher to record these natural and social language events for later examination and analysis. Moreover, the information derived from this sort of observation is easier to apply to instructional situations.

PROFESSIONAL JUDGMENT IN MAKING DIAGNOSTIC DECISIONS

Through kidwatching, you can learn about students as readers and develop insights about the effect of instruction on their growth. Professional judgment allows teachers to translate these observations into instructional improvements. Effective kidwatchers are comfortable making educational decisions. They trust their own professional judgment, even in the face of conflicting information. Unfortunately, many teachers lack this faith in their own judgment.

Sue is one such teacher. Not too long ago, we visited an elementary school for a day. During the lunch hour, we overheard a conversation between Sue and John, two fifth-grade teachers who were chatting about the results of the district-mandated standardized testing they had just received. The conversation went something like this:

Sue: I was really surprised by some of these results.

John: Me too.

Sue: Take Andy, for instance. I thought he was a pretty good reader. It seems as if he's always got his nose in a book. And the things he shares during our discussions are usually good—pretty insightful, actually.

John: So?

Sue: Well, the test says he's reading at the 18th percentile. I wonder if I should ask Ms. D [the Title I teacher] to take a look at him.

Why didn't Sue trust her own observations about Andy? Why did she assume he might need extra help in reading? We suspect that she does not trust her own professional judgment.

We also suspect that Sue is not alone. Where do these professional insecurities come from? Some people believe that researchers, theoreticians, and policymakers have sent negative messages about teachers' professionalism that have caused us to lose faith in ourselves. Professional uncertainty may also relate to an unexamined belief in the truth of statistical information such as standardized test scores. Yetta Goodman (1989) noted:

> Because numbers take on an aura of objectivity, which they do not intrinsically deserve, statistical data are equated with the development of knowledge and are valued more highly than the sense of an informed, committed professional who uses knowledge about the students, the community, and the context to make judgments. (p. 6)

Whatever the causes, teachers who wish to become effective kidwatchers must learn to exercise professional judgment and trust themselves as decision makers (Tierney, 1998). To do so may involve considering, and perhaps altering, two sets of attitudes: attitudes toward themselves and attitudes toward their students.

Teachers who trust their professional judgment are a bit like detectives. They constantly and carefully observe, looking for clues to answer their questions about students. Like detectives, they base observations on the enormous amount of information they already have about students and the classroom community as well as their analyses of students' reading behavior. They are also careful not to jump to conclusions. They continually ask, "What do I think this means? What else might this mean?" They generate hypotheses about students and test them out. Experience with this process helps them learn to trust the results of their efforts.

Evidence of growth is often revealed through students' errors, so teachers' attitudes toward errors are also important. Dictionaries define *error* as "a usually ignorant or unintentional deviation." Wise kidwatchers acknowledge the occasional careless mistake but largely view errors as windows to students' current ways of thinking about language. They look for changes in patterns of errors as signs that students are developing as readers.

Brenda, a Title I teacher at the primary level, is a kidwatcher. Early in each school year, she gathers several samples of her students' oral reading behaviors, which she uses to determine how students deal with unknown words—an important developmental hurdle for young readers. Last year, she found several students who were "phonics bound"—sounding words out seemed to be their only word identification strategy. Their oral reading errors or miscues tended to look and sound like text words but often changed the author's meaning completely. Some children even made up nonsense words.

Brenda did not assume that these miscues were careless. Instead, she hypothesized that children were doing what they knew how to do or what they thought they should be doing. She made a conscious effort to help them broaden their repertoire for identifying words. She emphasized combining context ("What would make sense here?") with what the children already knew about phonics. After several weeks of instruction, Brenda made another informal check of her students' word identification strategies. She found evidence of growth in flexible use of strategies. Children were beginning to correct miscues that made no sense or that changed the author's meaning.

Several of Brenda's actions and decisions are good examples of professional judgment. First, she understood the importance of gathering data about her Title I students in authentic reading situations. She knew that samples of children's oral reading obtained over several sessions could yield insights about their word identification strategies. Second, Brenda viewed miscues as opportunities to explore how the children were currently organizing things (Goodman, 1985). She saw qualitative differences in errors—that is, patterns of graphophonically similar but nonsense miscues told her something different from patterns of self-corrections. She used her own professional judgment to make diagnostic decisions.

Professional judgment is critical to kidwatching, which in turn is key to effective observation. Professional judgment is at its best when teachers combine their concrete knowledge about the classroom and particular students with their theoretical knowledge about how students learn, what language is, and how language develops. This combination provides a useful framework for assessing struggling readers.

OBSERVING THROUGHOUT THE SCHOOL DAY

Effective kidwatchers are experts at recognizing and interpreting patterns of behavior. They differentiate between recurring behaviors and isolated ones. Patterns become evident when teachers observe over time and in various reading and reading-related activities. This, of course, requires a plan. Merriam (1998) describes general aspects of an event or situation that may be important for an observer to record. She also suggests questions that can help focus the observer's attention.

- *The participants:* Who's there? What are they doing? How are they working together? Although the struggling reader's behaviors may be the focal point for observation, it is equally important to note who else is in the general vicinity and what all the participants are doing.
- *Activities and interactions:* What's happening? What's the sequence of activities? How do people interact with the activity and each other? This is a particularly important aspect of an event or situation to note. Most adults have variable attitudes toward reading; we enjoy some reading activities and dislike others. Students are no different. When watching children within the context of particular reading activities, teachers can often discover the circumstances that promote and detract from positive reading experiences.
- *Frequency and duration:* How long does the activity last? Does it happen often? These questions can apply to indicators of student behavior in reading. For example, the teacher might note how frequently students choose to read during free periods or how long they sustain interest in reading on different days in different situations.
- *Subtle factors:* What unplanned, spontaneous events occur? What nonverbal signals can be observed? These aspects can be revealing. Students who enjoy reading books, for example, may be impatient with disruptions when they are reading. Students who enjoy neither reading nor their books may be pleased with disruptions. To help understand subtle factors, talk with a student: "You look puzzled. What's the matter?" Effective kidwatchers are good listeners as well as keen observers.

Attention to all these aspects of classroom reading need not be complex or difficult. Observations can be brief; a few occasional minutes of concentrated effort ought to provide adequate data.

Matt, who offers extra support in the regular classroom for intermediate-grade students with learning disabilities, has been relying on observation for several years. He is particularly interested in watching his students interact with others.

I watch pretty intensively at the beginning of a school year so I can get a feel for what students might need, and then I do "spot-checks" throughout the year. If I see something that surprises me, either good or bad, I observe more carefully again. It took me a while to get the hang of observing, especially organizing what I'd written, but I am convinced that I now know lots more about my students. And that makes it easier for me to help them, so the time and effort are worth it to me.

Techniques and Strategies

In order to make the best use of kidwatching, the teacher needs to keep good records. Good records may take several forms, which we describe in this section. Information gleaned from any or all of these methods, when added to a student's reading portfolio, adds depth and detail to the picture of the student as a reader.

ANECDOTAL NOTES

One way to learn about a struggling reader is to keep anecdotal notes about informal, unplanned observations and the results of instruction. As all teachers know, classrooms are busy places; without making notes, important incidents are easily forgotten. Additionally, anecdotal notes guide instructional planning. We assess instructional impact as we plot students' progress in anecdotal notes and records.

Although any time can be the right time for making anecdotal notes, a plan or framework aids note taking. Using classroom routines as a framework for observation helps yield a representative sample of how children take advantage of classroom opportunities. (See Chapter 3 for more about routines.) Teachers also need to consider the format for their anecdotal notes and records. Ultimately, this is an individual decision. Experiment with formats; fortunately, you have plenty of options.

Some teachers keep notebooks for recording general impressions of children or make brief observations on sticky notes or large adhesive-backed labels. Later, they expand on their notes and transfer them to students' portfolios. Jacobson (1989) uses a three-column sheet of paper for recording significant anecdotal information in her classroom. The columns are labeled "Goals," "Observations," and "Instructional Plans." This format allows her to make both objective ("What do I see or hear?") and subjective ("What do I think this means?") notes, which researchers suggest can yield more useful records (Merriam, 1998; Patton, 1990).

Kelly, for instance, keeps a portfolio for each of her high school students who speak English as a second language (ESL). The portfolios include anecdotal notes as well as more formal assessments. As often as she can, Kelly shares her notes with the students' content area teachers. Many of the teachers collaborate and analyze anecdotal information. For example, during department meetings or on staff development days they meet to discuss ESL students' progress. Colleagues, then, can provide record-keeping assistance, as can video or audio recordings.

Any system or device for recording anecdotal information should first be field-tested to determine the level of specificity to include in notes. Matt, whom we introduced earlier, did this by looking at his notes a couple of weeks after they were taken. In reviewing the notes, he asked himself, "What doesn't make sense any more?" and "What do I want to know more about?" Answers to these questions helped him modify his note-taking strategies to ensure maximum usefulness.

Kidwatchers who are comfortable with their system for recording anecdotal information are convinced of the usefulness of this documentation technique. Teacher Mary Kitagawa puts it this way: "In spite of the after-school time they consume, anecdotal records seem to be the most accurate way to document the full picture of students' language development" (1989, p. 108).

CHECKLISTS AND CHARTS

Many teachers use checklists or charts to keep their observations of struggling readers systematic and organized. For example, they develop charts that reflect state standards or

FIGURE 2.2   Checklist for Results of Mini-Lessons

Class Roster	Dates/Types of Mini-Lessons			
	9/3 Using Context			
Jenny	NE*			
Peter	S			
LaTosha	O			
Jimmy	O			
*NE: not evident during the week after the mini-lesson; O: Outstanding; S: Satisfactory				

specify instructional routines and include blocks of space for recording information about students. As Figures 2.2 and 2.3 show, charts or checklists can be completed with a coding system or brief notes.

Betsy, a first-grade teacher, uses both types of charts to provide a systematic focus for observing her students. Because she teaches reading skills only if her students need them, different children attend different mini-lessons on different days. Betsy uses the mini-lesson checklist (Figure 2.2) to record which students attended skill and strategy lessons and to evaluate lesson impact on children's reading. For this latter purpose, she observes carefully during the week after the mini-lesson when children have opportunities to use the new skill or strategy. She then codes the checklist with her conclusions about the children's use of the skill.

The chart in Figure 2.3 is more open ended. Over several days, Betsy makes brief notes about particular students listed in the boxes on the chart. Later, she elaborates on these notes and files them in students' reading portfolios. She keeps the chart on a clipboard; it is always nearby when she teaches. Betsy also uses the same chart format to

FIGURE 2.3   Chart for Noting Student Activity During Instructional Routines

Routines	Students				
	Mike	Matthew	Emily	Katy	Maria
SSR					
Sharing SSR books					
Small-group instruction					
Read aloud					
Free choice					
Library visits					

explore other aspects of children's behavior and attitudes as readers, such as their engagement with different types of text material or their reactions to different types of activities.

Students can keep checklists or charts about their own reading. They record insights in reading logs or reading journals and keep lists of books they have read. Students also evaluate their own reading habits and behaviors by responding to questions in their logs: "How was my reading today?" and "Why do I think so?" Finally, students track their progress as strategic readers by maintaining a three-column chart: "Things I Can Do Well," "Things I'm Working On," and "Things I Plan to Learn" (Hansen, 1987). Teachers who encourage students to evaluate aspects of their own reading find that this practice has several benefits: Students learn to take control of their reading behavior and become more aware of their growth as readers, and teachers have yet another source of information about students.

CONVERSATIONS AND INTERVIEWS

A few summers ago, we worked with Dale, a student who had just completed his first year in middle school. Dale's parents and some of his middle school teachers were concerned about his textbook reading. His parents were perplexed because he had done all his homework diligently in elementary school. They said he had begun the school year with equal diligence but soon stopped reading assignments from his texts. When they asked him why, he always answered, "I don't need to." They feared the middle school textbooks were too difficult for him.

Terry, Dale's tutor, attempted to determine what aspects of textbook reading were giving Dale trouble. He seemed quite capable of reading and studying middle school texts independently. Somewhat exasperated, Terry decided to talk to Dale about the situation. Here's how the conversation went:

Terry: Your parents are concerned because you didn't read your textbook assignments last year. Did you read them?

Dale: Well, I did at the beginning of the year, but then I stopped.

Terry: Why did you stop?

Dale: I figured, "Why bother?"

Terry: What made you think that?

Dale: Well, the teachers always told us all the stuff in the book the next day. I figured it didn't make much sense to do all that reading when they were going to tell us all of it anyway.

As you have probably guessed, this brief conversation was as helpful in understanding Dale's reading behavior as all the informal diagnosis that preceded it. The anecdote underscores the importance of conversations and interviews as ways of gathering information. By asking the right kinds of questions in the right ways and listening carefully to how students respond, teachers can learn about students' actions and attitudes as readers. Sometimes, as with Dale, it is the only way to obtain this kind of information.

Other people's perceptions are also important. Parents and previous teachers, for example, often provide helpful information, as do regular teachers for children who receive assistance outside the classroom. By talking with students and their "significant educational others," you can add both depth and breadth to your understanding of children as readers.

Behavior during a conversation or interview influences responses. A good interviewer has rapport with the interviewee but remains neutral about the content of responses. For example, consider these two questions one might ask to determine a student's opinion about a book:

"I really liked this book. Didn't you?"

"What did you think about this book?"

The first question offers cues or implicit suggestions toward a desirable response. Many students would simply agree with the first question, regardless of their true feelings. The second question is content neutral; it sets up neither a positive nor a negative response. Neutral questions help create an environment in which students know they can share freely. Free sharing more often yields useful, accurate information.

A variety of content-neutral questions can enhance the value of an interview or conversation. Researchers who use interviews as a way to gather information have identified several beneficial types of questions (Merriam, 1998; Patton, 1990). The following work particularly well in conversations with children who struggle as readers:

- *Experience/behavior questions:* These questions aim at eliciting descriptions perhaps observable had the interviewer been present. Questions might include "What's something you've learned to do in reading?" or "How did it go with this book?" or "What do you do when you come to a word that you don't know? How do you try to figure it out?"

- *Opinion/value questions:* These questions help determine what people think and what their goals, intentions, desires, or values are. Such questions include "What's the best book you've read this month? Why did you like it?" and "What would you like to learn so that you can become a better reader?"

- *Feelings questions:* These questions elicit readers' feelings: "How do you feel when you run into problems in your reading?" and "Do you like to read? Why?"

- *Hypothetical/future-oriented questions:* These "what if?" questions encourage speculations, including those about the future. Examples include "If you could choose from all the things you read in school, what would you choose?" and "What are your plans for this next month in reading? What do you hope to accomplish?"

- *Ideal-position questions:* These questions relate to readers' notions of perfection, such as "What does someone have to do to be a good reader?" or "Who's the best reader you know? What does this person do as a reader?"

- *Interpretive questions:* These questions generally occur at the end of an interview or conversation. The teacher interprets and summarizes the interview and asks the student to validate the summary: "So, would you say that . . . ?" or "You seem to be saying . . . . Is that what you think?"

Conversations and interviews can be planned or spontaneous, general or focused on a certain aspect of reading. Preparing interview questions beforehand helps ensure that they will be comprehensive, content neutral, and related to the area of interest. In use, however, questions should guide conversation rather than provide a rigid structure.

Some teachers take notes during interviews. Others prefer to record interviews so that they can actually converse with students. In any event, always prepare written summaries of these conferences about reading and add them to students' reading portfolios.

PERFORMANCE SAMPLES

Performance samples, as their name suggests, are samples of students' performances as readers. They also belong in students' reading portfolios. Because performance samples provide tangible evidence, they can complement data gathered through observation and conversations.

Instructional activities can provide performance samples to include in a student's reading portfolio. For example, reader-response entries from students' reading logs can be evaluated holistically, using procedures similar to holistic evaluation of writing, to explore growth in reading comprehension and response to reading. Writing samples can also document reading-related growth. For example, analyzing a young child's spelling strategies can yield important insights about her or his graphophonic knowledge. An early piece of writing can also be dictated back to a child. Then, the teacher, alone or with the child, analyzes the two pieces, looking for evidence of development in spelling and other conventions of written language.

Teachers often obtain valuable information about students' comprehension abilities by listening in as students discuss their reading and by evaluating students' instructional products. Here are 10 quick ways to assess comprehension, some suitable for narrative, some for expository text, some for both:

- Make an *Important Book* page that reflects the content of the text (see Chapter 11)
- Make a Venn diagram to compare and contrast key ideas from a text.
- Describe how something (or someone) in the text is the same or different from something (or someone) else.
- Draw a picture that reflects important content.
- Complete a cloze activity (see Chapter 6).
- Tell "who" and "what happened."
- Write three sentences: beginning, middle, end.
- Make a list or order a list of important ideas.
- Write two sentences: problem and solution, as described in the text.
- Complete a Herringbone chart (see Chapter 9) to represent the text.

These activities can be evaluated with a simple three-point scale: O (Outstanding), S (Satisfactory), or U (Unsatisfactory). Chart the results. None of these assessments alone offers a complete look at comprehension, but patterns may become apparent when you view evaluation results across many of these performance samples.

Performance samples also result from planned, informal reading conferences with students. These conversations between teacher and student revolve around a book that the student is reading. Many teachers easily accept the theoretical value of basing conferences on real books but might be less comfortable about figuring out the real-world logistics. For example, what if the student reads a book unfamiliar to the teacher? In such a case, the teacher can evaluate comprehension and response to reading more generically (for example, "Find the part you liked best, read it to me, and tell me why you liked it") or even read the book at a later time.

Teachers also must consider how much assistance to give students who encounter problems during the reading conference. It is important to discover what the student can do if left to his or her own resources. Frustrating students who encounter unsolvable problems, however, makes little sense. Our best advice is to wait a second or two and help if the student still needs it, noting the student's reaction to the assistance. In reviewing records from the conference, the teacher can ask, "Did the student profit from my help? How do I know?"

Reading conferences that last about 10 minutes every month or so should provide sufficient information about struggling readers, particularly when combined with observational and interview data. Some teachers plan conferences with all their at-risk readers on the same day and invite an adult helper (parent, grandparent, reading specialist, or the principal) to assist in the classroom on conference days.

Reading conferences offer important opportunities to learn how children interact with text and how they feel about reading and themselves as readers. Like other kidwatching techniques, the conference format varies according to the teacher's purpose. The student might read a page or two aloud, for example, or the student and teacher might simply discuss the book. Retelling might be an appropriate activity as well.

ASSESSMENT SITUATIONS

Occasionally, teachers may plan and conduct classroom-based assessments to focus directly on a particular reader's skills, strategies, or behaviors. For example, reading conferences (or any time a child reads aloud) can be used to find out about word identification. Teachers can note on a text copy miscues made during reading, track them on a separate piece of paper, or record the reading. Marking copy of the text a student reads is easiest. Most teachers develop a simple coding system to assist in this process, such as writing substitutions over words in the text, circling omissions, using the editor's caret (∧) for insertions, and so forth.

After the reading conference, the teacher analyzes miscues by comparing them with words in the text. For each pair (i.e., miscue and text word), the teacher asks, "Do they look the same? Sound the same?" "Are they the same part of speech?" "Are their meanings similar?" "Does the child try to correct miscues that change meaning?" Looking for patterns in the answers to these questions allows the teacher to answer the broader question, "What does the reader do when encountering an unknown word?"

When a student rereads a book, comparing the two recorded versions reveals signs of increased fluency or changes in sight vocabulary or word identification strategies. Jacobson (1989) asks students to evaluate changes in their own reading by listening to recordings of the same text made at different times so that they become more aware of their growth as readers.

Curriculum-based assessments or evaluations (CBAs) offer another efficient way to gather several types of assessment information relatively quickly. These assessments use informal reading inventory procedures, which have long been used as a basic diagnostic technique. They differ from informal reading inventories in one important way—administering a CBA takes only one minute per student. Students read orally from a grade-level text. Because CBAs are ordinarily administered several times each year, many teachers select a text for students to read that will not be used in any other way. The teacher records oral reading errors and notes the number of words the student reads in one minute. After the reading, the teacher asks the student to retell the passage. From this information, the teacher can estimate the following:

- *Overall difficulty of the text for the student:* Use this calculation: number of words read correctly (correct or corrected)/total number of words read. For example, if a student reads 145 words but makes 8 errors, the resulting equation would be 137/145, or 94.5 percent. Nearly perfect percentages (99–100 percent) suggest that the material is easy for the student. Those slightly lower (91–98 percent) indicate instructional level performance, and percentages at or below 90 percent show that the material is too difficult.
- *Oral reading fluency:* Compare the student's performance (words correct per minute) to the norms provided in Chapter 7 (Hasbrouck & Tindal, 1992; Howe & Shinn, 2001).
- *Comprehension:* Evaluate the student's retelling.

The three-point scale (O-S-U) works well to record performance in each of these areas. Most teachers keep class charts of all this information, which allows them to efficiently draw several conclusions. For example, you can track one student's reading strengths and weaknesses by examining performance at several points throughout the school year. Likewise, you can determine instructional focus for groups or the entire class by looking across all class records.

Curriculum-based assessments do not provide in-depth information about students, but they do provide a quick "status of the class" overview and a way to look at students' relative strengths and weaknesses in reading over time. As such, they are a powerful addition to the teacher's assessment plans.

Observing, Understanding, and Helping Students

In this chapter we have described both why and how to observe struggling readers in action. We have encouraged teachers to be kidwatchers—to observe and talk with children to understand their behaviors and attitudes as readers in the context of the classroom. The resulting data will help lead to important conclusions about students.

A final question about portfolio assessment relates to the quantity of evidence needed. When we talk with teachers about portfolios, they frequently ask, "How much information should I gather?" Our answer: "Enough to answer your questions." This answer is not flippant, but rather underscores the importance of questions that provide focus for evaluation and assessment and the variable nature of reading behaviors and reading growth.

One way to conceptualize an answer to this quantity-of-information question is to think in terms of three related layers of assessment data described by the Response to Intervention (RTI) model discussed earlier in this chapter and illustrated in Figure 2.4. At the bottom of this triangle belong the assessments to be administered to all students in the class. These techniques are selected to parallel instructional goals—to enhance word iden-tification abilities, comprehension strategies, fluency, and so on. Most of the evaluation techniques described in this chapter would be suitable for all students, perhaps several times each year.

These broad-brush views of students as readers will not provide enough informa-tion about all students, though; teachers may need additional information about some

FIGURE 2.4   A Model for Classroom Assessment

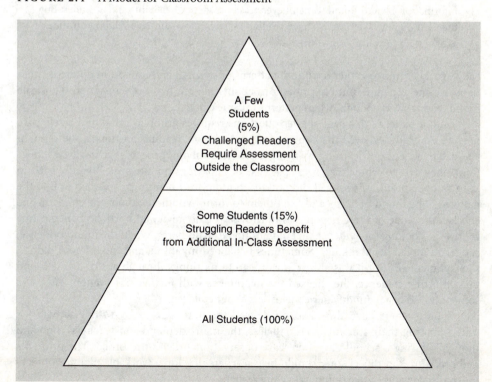

students, particularly struggling readers. For these, you may need additional information, also connected to curricular goals, such as more frequent observations, longer and more detailed oral reading assessments, or additional conversations or interviews. As illustrated in Figure 2.4, approximately 15 percent of your students may need this level of assessment.

Often, a student or two will need an even closer look at reading abilities and behaviors. These few students, about 5 percent, represented by the tip of the triangle in Figure 2.4, may benefit from a diagnosis conducted by a reading specialist or other highly qualified educational professional. Such diagnoses, typically conducted outside the classroom, also focus on curricular goals; they differ from classroom evaluations in depth. Using this classroom assessment model to organize and plan classroom evaluations ensures that you will indeed find enough information to answer questions about students as readers. Moreover, predicating decisions about particular assessment techniques for all levels of the model on curricular goals maintains a close link among the reading curriculum, classroom instructional routines, and evaluation.

Sally, whom we described at the beginning of the chapter, used many of the ideas we have outlined to create a systematic and comprehensive plan for learning about her pre–first-grade students. She says:

> I was interested in both a broad look, so I could get to know the kids, and some specific information that could guide instruction. When I tried to summarize all the information I had, I found some unevenness in students' behaviors and attitudes. But then I thought, "Well, we all have reading behaviors; we all have reading attitudes. Why should the kids be any different?"

Sally's goal became to gather data until patterns of strength and interest in different situations became apparent, until her questions about children had been answered. Thus, she found "enough was enough" when patterns became evident.

To find patterns that will answer questions requires an open mind and a reflective posture. As Sally reviewed the contents of her students' reading portfolios, she thought about the evidence of learning by using a problem-solving process that involved induction—the parts-to-whole search for patterns of behavior and attitudes. "I really tried to keep an open mind," she said. "I didn't want to jump to conclusions. I wanted to find the patterns." She found patterns and used them to form hypotheses about the children. She checked the value of these hypotheses in two ways. Sally reviewed portfolio contents one more time, looking for evidence that did not fit her hypotheses. When she found evidence, she reconsidered her thinking. "Sometimes I changed my mind, and sometimes I didn't," she commented. "But it was always worth it to think things through again." If she found no conflicting evidence, she checked the hypotheses with further observation. This, too, sometimes led her to modify her conclusions about children.

Good teachers have always acknowledged the potential of day-to-day activity for understanding their students. Nevertheless, the many demands on teachers' time and thoughts during a school day often leave observational data unrecorded. The processes and procedures in this chapter should help teachers develop a workable plan for observing, understanding, and helping struggling readers.

DISCUSSION QUESTIONS

Some of the discussion questions for each chapter ask you to think through your own work as a teacher. If you are not currently a practicing teacher, try to respond to these questions from your own school experience (either from when you yourself were a student or from visits to schools that you have made in your teacher education program).

1. Why is it so important for educators to identify the difficulties students are experiencing in reading and monitor students' growth in reading? Why not "just teach"?

2. Evidence of growth is often revealed through students' errors. Give a specific example of a student error you observed and the *growth* it demonstrated.

3. Are standardized tests a necessary evil, an unnecessary evil, a positive force for improving education, or an inconsequential annoyance? Why?

4. Struggling readers should have some say in evaluating their own growth. Discuss with colleagues some ways you could involve struggling readers in evaluating their own growth.

5. Make a list of questions that could guide the portfolio assessment of three of your struggling readers.

6. How would you justify the use of anecdotal notes to a school administrator who was interested only in standardized test scores for struggling readers?

7. What information could you get from parents that might help you in assessing your students' reading performance and in helping you meet the needs of your students?

Chapter **Three** ∾

❧ Creating an Instructional Framework

BETSY, A READING RESOURCE TEACHER, shared with us her views about reading and learning to read: "When I have a student who appears to be at risk, my questions to myself are simple: What does the child know? and What can the child do? Given the answers to these questions, how can I adjust my teaching to support the child's learning? I no longer focus on what's wrong with the child. Instead, I examine my instructional program, the strategies and materials I use." Betsy adapts her instruction to respond to her students' interests and needs rather than expecting them to adjust to her agenda. Her curricular framework, which is intentional and based on students' assessed needs, provides daily opportunities for all children to succeed as readers and writers in meaningful and satisfying ways.

In this chapter we explore several big issues that Betsy and teachers like her encounter in their attempts to foster literacy learning for children who struggle with reading. Figure 3.1 provides an overview of issues that will help you plan an effective instructional environment.

Accommodation

Betsy's comments focus on a critical concept for developing an effective instructional framework: accommodation or environmental responsiveness to students' needs. Accommodation does not involve letting kids off the hook, lowering standards, or anything of the sort. It is simply an acknowledgment that students have their own interests and needs, and that teachers can use these to create successful learning environments.

Suppose you're interested in developing an accommodating instructional environment. The first step, and it's a big one, is to consider how you think about the teaching–learning process. Both successful schoolwide reforms in literacy education (Fisher & Frey, 2007) and successful partnerships between general and special education teachers to support struggling readers (Schnorr & Davern, 2005) depend on the ability to articulate these beliefs.

FIGURE 3.1 Instructional Framework for Working with Children Who Find Reading Difficult

Set Up Literate Environment	Create Community of Learners	Plan for Time on Task	Establish Instructional Routines	Accommodate Individual Needs
• Provide easy access to reading/writing materials	• Encourage cooperation, not competition	• Focus attention on in-depth reading instruction	• Daily read-alouds	• Determine struggling readers' needs
• Set up reading/writing centers	• Plan for joint problem solving	• Allow for practice reading (not skill and drill)	• Independent reading	• Respond to students' conceptual needs and beliefs
• Set up word walls, book displays, spaces for children to share their writing, etc.		• Engage students in an abundance of reading/writing activities	• Choice time	• Respond to students' instructional needs and beliefs
• Use authentic materials—books, magazines, websites			• Mini-lessons	• Monitor students' progress
• Stock the classroom with lots of texts that students can read and want to read			• Flexibility	• Adjust instruction as necessary

Years ago, many people believed that teaching was simply a matter of transmitting knowledge from someone who had it to someone who didn't. Today, experts know that learning involves construction of knowledge, not its transmission. Learning is something you do *with* students, not *to* or *for* them. Gordon Wells (1986) describes constructivism in the literacy learning classroom:

Knowledge [is] constructed afresh by each individual knower, through an interaction between the evidence (which is obtained through observation, listening, reading, and the use of reference materials of all kinds) and what the learner can bring to bear on it. The teacher arranges the situations—or encourages those that the children themselves have set up—and so has considerable control over the evidence that the learners encounter. But teachers cannot control the interpretations the children will make. (p. 116)

Constructivist teachers believe that students must make their own meaning as readers and writers. Rather than tell struggling readers what a story means, for example, they create learning environments that support students as they figure the text out for themselves. This sort of accommodation (or environmental responsiveness) reflects students' conceptual and instructional needs and beliefs.

STUDENTS' CONCEPTUAL NEEDS AND BELIEFS

Since the late 1970s, literacy scholars have done a great deal of talking, thinking, and researching about the importance of students' conceptual schema (what students already know about a topic they are going to study or read about). Experts know that effective teaching–learning environments must accommodate and build on the knowledge students bring with them to the classroom. Therefore, the question isn't *if* accommodations are necessary but *how* to accommodate and what implications such accommodations have for larger curricular issues. When teachers begin thinking about accommodations, they often become concerned about time. It takes time to teach from a constructivist perspective, time for students to think and talk about what they already know, and time for them to embed new learning in their established network of ideas. As a teacher, you will have to decide if your time spent this way is worth it.

Deb struggles with the issues of accommodation and time in her fourth-grade classroom (Watson & Konicek, 1990). She once began a science unit about heat by asking her students to brainstorm a list of things that give off heat. In addition to the sun, stoves, and their bodies, the children mentioned sweaters and hats. (After all, they had been hearing "Put on your warm clothes" for years.) So Deb, sensing a need to address students' conceptual beliefs, said, "What could we do to find out which things give off heat?"

The children decided to wrap sweaters and scarves around thermometers. After 15 minutes, the thermometer readings hadn't changed. But rather than changing their beliefs, the children decided that the thermometers hadn't been wrapped up long enough. They resolved to keep the thermometers wrapped up overnight and predicted three-digit temperatures by morning.

By the next morning, nothing had changed. Deb asked the students to write about the experiment in their science journals. They wrote entries such as, "We just didn't leave them in there long enough," and "Maybe some cold air got in them somehow." So the testing went on, with children hypothesizing, designing ways to find out (including sealing the items in large plastic bags so that cold air couldn't seep in), and reflecting on the results of their experiments.

After three days, Deb realized that the children had given up their old beliefs but had yet to replace them with new ones. So she wrote two summaries on the chalkboard: "Heat can come from almost anything, even sweaters and hats. We are fooled when we measure heat because cold air can get inside," and "Heat comes mostly from the sun and our bodies. Heat is trapped inside winter clothes that keep our body heat in and cold air out." The children decided which theory made sense to them and wrote reasons for their choices in their science journals. Some were still puzzled, so Deb said, "What could we do to find out?" The children went out to recess with thermometers in their hats to test this new hypothesis.

In their commentary about Deb's experience, Watson and Konicek (1990) noted:

> [If Deb had begun the unit] in the usual way, she might never have known how nine long Massachusetts winters had skewed her students' thinking. . . . [Students] would have learned a little about the sources of heat, a little about friction, and how to read a thermometer. By the end of two weeks, they would have been able to pass a simple test . . . but their preconceptions, never having been put on the table, would have continued, coexisting in a morass of conflicting ideas about heat and its behavior. (p. 680)

By viewing teaching and learning as a cooperative construction of knowledge rather than as its transmission, Deb enabled her students to learn about sources of heat. She was satisfied with her decision to accommodate children's conceptual needs, but she worried about the time it took to do so. In her journal she noted, "The kids are holding onto and putting together pieces of what they know of the world. But the time we are taking to explore what kids think is much longer than if I just told them the facts" (Watson & Konicek, 1990, p. 682).

Learning involves conceptual change. To teach for conceptual change, teachers establish instructional frameworks that stress relevance; involve lots of predicting, testing, and confirming; and offer consistent opportunities to talk things through with others. This issue of talk, especially talk supported by a "more knowledgeable other" (the teacher or parent), is critical to establishing effective literacy learning environments.

Exploratory talk helps children learn to use language to aid their thinking. Eventually this talk becomes "inner speech" (Vygotsky, 1962). Supported talk or discussion guides students in the way they think, solve problems, and perform other school-related tasks. With support from peers and the teacher, children perform much more than they can independently (Vygotsky, 1978). The story of Deb and her students illustrates all these principles in action.

Exploratory talk, particularly in small-group settings, is a critical feature of effective literacy learning environments for children who struggle with reading (Gaskins, 2005). Children learning English need this sort of environment as well (Gersten et al., 2007; Haynes, 2007). Fisher and Frey (2007) chronicled teachers at one urban, underperforming school as they attempted to turn achievement around. They concluded that shared beliefs about the following issues were critical to the success of this endeavor:

- Learning is social. As one teacher said, "Learning takes place when humans interact with one another. That means kids with kids, kids with teachers, teachers with teachers, teachers with parents, parents with kids—everything related to learning is social" (p. 33).
- Conversations are critical for everyone's learning but especially for English language learners (ELLs).
- Reading, writing, and oral language must be integrated.
- Learners require gradual release of responsibility.

Authentic experiences, whether in the classroom (such as the ones Deb provided for her students) or outside it (such as field trips), offer students opportunities to develop new concepts and refine old ones. To some extent, the teacher's or students' related readings can achieve the same purpose. In any event, instruction focused on conceptual change should offer students plentiful opportunities to share what they know, think, and have learned. Of course, this takes time. But teachers like Deb have decided that the time spent is worth it because such accommodations allow students to make productive use of what they already know as they try to make sense of or understand how their world works.

STUDENTS' INSTRUCTIONAL NEEDS AND BELIEFS

Surely, creating an instructional environment that accommodates students' academic needs makes sense. Invite your students to read and write, and observe them carefully as they do. Use the results of your observations and assessments to plan instruction that will support students' growth as literacy learners. Also look for ways to challenge students, to offer them opportunities to stretch and grow in an atmosphere that promotes success. These two notions, *challenge* and *support*, describe frameworks that effectively accommodate students' instructional needs.

Students' instructional beliefs, their assumptions about how one "does school," are equally important to the creation of supportive and successful instructional frameworks. Educational anthropologist James Heap (1980) calls these beliefs *cultural logic*. He says that people develop expectations, based on their experiences, about what to do and how to behave in certain cultures (such as classrooms) and use these beliefs to guide future actions. We think he's right. Consider, for example, the story of Johnny:

Johnny came to our summer reading program at the end of second grade because his parents and teachers were concerned about his reading. He had made no progress, they said; he wasn't an independent reader. Johnny's tutor, Janine, verified his lack of independence. He knew what he knew, but he lacked strategies for solving problems in reading. For example, his only word recognition strategy was to make wild guesses based on the first letters of unknown words.

So Johnny and Janine spent some time working on word recognition strategies that summer. She taught him how to use context by asking questions such as, "What word would make sense there?" She encouraged him to skip unknown words when he encountered them and then reread the sentence, looking for familiar words or word parts within unknown words. At the end of the summer program, Janine suggested that Johnny dictate a list of strategies to try when he encountered an unknown word. She hoped the list would remind him of his options as a reader. Here's his dictation:

When I Get Stuck

1. You can skip them and then go back.
2. You can think about what's happened so far.
3. You can look at the pictures.
4. You can sound it out.

After Johnny completed the dictation and Janine read it back to him, they had the following conversation:

Johnny: [points to items 1–3] Did you know about these before?

Janine: Yes.

Johnny: Where did you learn about them?

Janine: At school.

Johnny: You know, [my teacher last year] only knew about how to sound it out.

Janine: Oh.

Johnny: Well, she should learn about them. They work better, and they're easier, too.

We don't know how Johnny drew this conclusion about his teacher, but we suspect that he came to it honestly by constructing knowledge based on his classroom experiences. We have known others like him—students who think that their goal as readers is to say all the words correctly. In fact, a study of intermediate-grade students' perceptions of reading (Henk & Melnick, 1998) found that most children characterized good reading as "automatic, error-free, and rapid" (p. 71). Only one-third of these children mentioned anything about comprehension in their descriptions. Although successful reading is no doubt characterized by automaticity, ignoring comprehension is a mistake.

The point is that students' experiences in school cause them to draw conclusions about "doing school" and about what they should do as readers and writers. It is important for students to understand reading and their roles as readers. If students believe their responsibility is only to produce error-free oral reading, complete assignments, or answer the teacher's questions, the intended learning may or may not take place. Attention to students' conceptual and instructional needs and beliefs can reduce the possibility of their drawing harmful conclusions about reading and themselves as readers.

TEACHERS' INSTRUCTIONAL RESPONSIVENESS

Instructional responsiveness to students' needs—or accommodation—involves conceiving of learning as the construction of knowledge, both content knowledge and procedural knowledge. In many ways, this instructional responsiveness is at the heart of effective teaching. When teachers understand learning as the construction of knowledge, they also understand the importance of instruction that invites students to behave as real readers and writers and to complete tasks that spark genuine student interest in inquiry. Most of all, effective teachers know the importance of signaling that they care about what students know, think, say, and learn. They convey many of these understandings to their students subtly—by the questions they ask, the way attention is focused in the classroom, and their choice of instructional routines. In all ways, teachers signal to students that the classroom is a community of learners.

Develop a Community of Learners

Adults may perceive reading as a solitary activity, but in classrooms, reading is "a very social activity, deeply embedded in interactions with teacher and peers" (Cazden, 1981, p.

118). We know that literacy instruction should foster meaningful interactions with texts and among participants. But we also know that students determine what they should do and how they should participate in lessons by drawing conclusions about the tasks they are asked to perform. Thus, another important aspect of creating an accommodating learning environment for struggling readers involves attention to the nature of children's social interactions, particularly to ways to foster cooperation and student "ownership" and choice.

The instructional environment should promote cooperation, not competition. In competitive situations, difficulties cause distress, particularly if everyone else seems to be coping well. This may lead struggling readers to "believe that reading is a contest they will never win" and to "become more concerned about avoiding failure and embarrassment than with learning to read" (Winograd & Smith, 1987, pp. 307, 308). Moreover, scores, numbers of stories read, or other measures of reading often become more important in students' minds than the actual process of reading, their reactions to reading, or what they are learning as they read.

A competitive classroom atmosphere can actually cause students to make counter-productive decisions about participating in lessons. For example, students whose comprehension instruction consists of providing the right answers to the teacher's questions may decide that silence or "I don't know" responses are safer than risking failure. Having chosen this route, students' minds are free to wander, and little further learning can take place. Over time, all these decisions become part of children's beliefs about being a student.

Activities that foster cooperative involvement and joint problem solving are much better alternatives (Ames, 1992; Turner & Paris, 1995). Students in cooperative situations are likely to view problems as challenges for group consideration instead of indications of their own inability. In addition, cooperation leads to better learning (Marzano, Pickering, & Pollock, 2001; Spurlin et al., 1984). Instruction based on active, cooperative participation among groups of students can support the development of a community of learners within classrooms.

What is a community of learners? Dictionaries say that *communities* are unified bodies of individuals with common interests who share ownership and jointly participate in community activities. Classrooms can become communities if the instructional framework invites learners to participate actively, share responsibility, explore issues of common interest, and interact cooperatively. Here's how Hannah, a third-grade struggling reader, talked about the importance of community as she reflected on her peer discussion groups (literature circles):

> It's better to discuss, maybe . . . 'cause you can talk it out. [It] helps you to be a better reader and to share your thoughts with other people . . . so you can get out what you wanted to say . . . about the book. You can share it with other people and not just yourself. (Potenza-Radis, 2008)

Hannah has pointed toward the important benefits of cooperative communities of learners—opportunities to "talk it out" and share ideas, all in a discussion that children "own." They decide what to talk about; they decide if and how to become involved in the discussion. This ownership aspect of classroom communities is also important.

Classroom communities should also feature choice—children should frequently choose what to read, how to respond to their reading, and whether they wish to work alone or with others. Of course, the teacher has choices, too. In fact, supportive instructional frameworks for literacy learning feature balance between teacher choice and student choice. Classroom routines promote authentic, cooperative interactions among students. Expect active involvement and invite student choice.

Establish Instructional Routines

Accommodation, constructivism, communities—these three big ideas relate to the core message of this book: Struggling readers can succeed if learning is relevant, if they are motivated and successful, and if reading instruction is based on their needs and taught from a student-centered perspective. But how do you create such a literacy learning curriculum? Here, the idea of instructional routines can help. *Routines* are blocks of time during which predictable sets of activities regularly occur. Routines allow teachers to maximize the amount of time spent on instruction and minimize the time spent on giving directions, explaining procedures, and maintaining order. To some, the word *routine* connotes boredom. That is not so in student-centered, constructivist classrooms. The routines we describe in this section—read-aloud, independent reading, mini-lessons, and choice time—are anything but dull.

READ-ALOUD

The benefits of *read-aloud* are many. Listening to an interesting text read well is pleasurable; in fact, both younger and older students report that teacher read-aloud motivates them to read (Ivey & Broaddus, 2001; Palmer, Codling, & Gambrell, 1994). During read-alouds, students encounter new ideas, words, and concepts (National Reading Panel, 2000) as well as interesting characters, situations, and places. Other advantages of reading aloud, especially for struggling readers, are that it familiarizes students with the style and form of written language and it provides a model of fluent reading. (Often poor readers have only other poor readers for models of expressive oral reading.) Finally, a special time for daily read-alouds demonstrates that reading is a worthwhile activity, important enough to include in the busy instructional schedule.

Virtually any interesting material can be read aloud—fiction or nonfiction, picture books or chapter books, poetry, articles, letters, and so on. And read-alouds need not be restricted to story time. Mary Beth frequently reads aloud to her students with learning disabilities. She says,

> We have story time every day. But I also read to students during science and social studies, sometimes just a paragraph or two and sometimes an entire selection. Not just nonfiction either; I look for poetry and fiction related to the concepts that we're working on. Sometimes the kids bring things in. Reading aloud in the content areas is a great way to foster additional learning and to give students access to information that they couldn't read independently.

Mary Beth's friend and colleague, Kelly, has used read-aloud for years, but a few years ago she decided to expand on it occasionally. On Fridays when she reads to her students, she asks them to enjoy the story but also to listen for interesting or unusual words or phrases. After the reading, the students talk about these words. Kelly makes sure she also adds a few words from the story and expands on any words the children may not know well or whose meaning is not totally clear.

During the weekend she thinks about how these words can be used in word sorts, games, and other instructional activities that focus on decoding and understanding the words. Then, on Monday, students put the words on cards. Throughout the week, students spend a few minutes each day practicing, sorting, or otherwise playing with the words. On Friday, the routine begins anew. Kelly explains,

> I only use this different approach to read-aloud on Fridays. By October, students know what to expect. But what's so great about this routine is that the students get wonderful opportunities to study words that come from stories they have experienced. Since they choose the words, they feel a sense of ownership over them. I know that this activity has increased their sensitivity and understanding of how words work. When I see them using the words in their own writing and speech, I know they are developing an appreciation for words.

McGee and Schickendanz's (2007) study of preschool classrooms described another way to focus on words during read-aloud. They found that teachers could provide vocabulary support through gestures or by pointing to illustrations. They also found that children's interaction with read-alouds, whether retelling, dramatizing, or sharing what they're thinking about the story, magnifies the benefit of read-aloud significantly.

The impact of adaptations or extensions of read-aloud should be evaluated, much as Kelly did. She knew the word work was beneficial because she saw and heard the results in her students' word use.

INDEPENDENT READING

To develop feelings of comfort and success as readers, struggling readers need consistent opportunities to behave as readers—to read material of their own choice for their own purposes. Thus, self-selected *independent reading* time should be another regular instructional routine.

Independent reading—in and out of school—relates to reading achievement: The more one reads, the better one reads. Abundant recreational reading has been linked to higher achievement test scores, vocabulary growth, and more sophisticated writing styles (e.g., see Block & Mangieri, 2002). Moreover, as little as 15 extra minutes of reading appears to make a difference, especially for struggling readers (Taylor, Frye, & Maruyama, 1990). In describing their "Hooked on Books" buddy-reading program, teachers Meryl Menon and John Mirabito (1999) report that children's book selection strategies became more sophisticated: "Our students think about what makes any book worth reading, and they comment orally and in writing about characters, events, and the author's writing style. Parents tell us children read more at home. . . . Nonreaders have become readers" (p. 194). Thus, both researchers and classroom teachers have documented the benefits of independent reading time.

Harry introduces independent reading time to his first-graders on the very first day of school. Initially, children read for only 2 or 3 minutes, but by the end of the year, they read for 20 to 30 minutes each day. He begins with such a brief time period because he wants the students to be successful: "Everyone can hang in for a couple of minutes. After a week or so, I gradually increase the time." Two rules govern independent reading time in Harry's classroom: Children must be quiet and they may not leave their seats. Children's desks are arranged in clusters, and Harry puts an extra stack of books on each cluster of desks so that children can easily select other books if they need or want them. Harry often reads during this time as well. "My reading sends the message to the kids that 'reading is so important that I want to do it with you.'"

Independent reading time always concludes with a brief sharing session so that children can read interesting parts of their books aloud, talk about what they have read, and offer evidence that they spent their reading time well. (See Figure 3.2 for other quick response activities.) Harry also tells his students about what he's reading—what he likes, what difficulties he has encountered, and so forth. "I consider myself a model for the children," Harry says. "Just reading is an important part of this, and so is responding to what I

FIGURE 3.2   Quick Activities for Responding to Reading

- Use sticky notes to mark interesting passages, or places where the author describes some aspect of instructional interest (characters, setting).
- Ask several students to "say one thing" or "say something I learned" about their books.
- Ask students to write interesting words on sticky notes. Make a chart for the classroom called "Interesting Words We Read Today."
- Play "Around the Room": Announce some aspect of stories (time, location, protagonist, etc.) and have students tell just this about their books.
- Use large sticky notes to review books from the classroom library. Keep these notes inside book front covers so others can refer to them.
- Ask students to rate their books with a number of "stars" by raising their hands. (Or keep large sheets of chart paper posted in the classroom for this purpose.) Ask them to write a rationale for this rating in their reading journals.
- Create bookmarks for students to use: "This is the problem in the story" or "This is the funniest part" or "This is my favorite character." Students make notes on the bookmarks as they read.
- Ask students to e-mail their pen pals (or parents) about their books.
- Select four students' names. Each goes to a corner of the classroom to talk a bit about his or her book, read a short selection, do a "commercial" for the book, and so on. Other students divide among the four, acting as the audience.
- Ask students to write in their reading journals: "What happened in my book today" or "What's going to happen next" or "My favorite character is . . . ," or other general prompts.

am reading. But sharing tough spots is equally important, I think. The kids need to learn that everyone—even adults—has trouble with reading from time to time."

Of course, Harry's students can choose to read and decide what to read at other times during each school day, too. "But this is a time when we all have our noses in books at the same time," Harry says. "We enjoy it, the kids get good practice, and I think it goes a long way toward helping children develop the 'reading habit.' In fact, I really know they're hooked when they start groaning about having to stop reading. That's music to my ears!"

Some teachers wonder if independent reading time will be frustrating for struggling readers. After all, they are asked to sustain an activity that has proved troublesome for them in the past. We have found just the opposite: Even the most reluctant readers eventually find success. They begin trying to read because they know that reading is their task at hand. As they experience success, their interest in reading grows, as does their confidence in themselves as readers. In other words, success breeds success. Teachers can support this cycle of success by beginning with short time periods, ensuring a plentiful supply of interesting reading materials at a variety of difficulty levels, and clearly communicating that everyone reads during independent reading time.

MINI-LESSONS

Mini-lessons about specific reading-related topics are another useful routine. A mini-lesson is a short, focused instructional session that can introduce a new strategy or help students solve a problem they have encountered recently in their reading.

Topics for mini-lessons often come from what learners need. Morgan and colleagues (2009) note that the best mini-lesson topics are clear and memorable. To ensure clarity and focus, Morgan and colleagues advise developing a one-sentence summary of the mini-lesson. Casting the topic in the form of a question, as seen in Figure 3.3, is another good planning device.

FIGURE 3.3   Mini-Lesson Topics

How can I keep track of the books we read?

What are the classroom library rules?

How do I choose a book that's right for me?

When should I stop reading a book?

What can I do if I don't know a word?

How can I get help with my reading?

Where can I find other books about the same topic (or by the same author)?

The lessons themselves typically begin with the whole, develop into a focus on some part, and then end with a discussion of the usefulness of the new strategy or information. A great thing about mini-lessons is that they can fit naturally within other instructional routines. Suppose, for example, that the teacher makes a significant mistake during read-aloud. This would be a good time to teach a mini-lesson about when and how to employ the strategy of rereading.

Betty makes frequent use of mini-lessons in her Title I instruction. Not long ago, for example, her upper-grade students were conducting library inquiry projects. "I noticed lots of kids just flipping through the pages," Betty says. "At first I thought they were just wasting time, but then I realized that they didn't know how to use tables of contents or indexes." So Betty taught a mini-lesson. She began with the whole—in this case, a brief discussion of students' frustrations about their inability to use the reference books. She then told students about tables of contents and indexes and demonstrated their usefulness by using overhead transparencies taken from a book. Next, pairs of students practiced using tables of contents and indexes in books from the school library. Betty concluded the lesson by asking students how knowledge of tables of contents and indexes might help them. "The whole lesson took no more than 15 minutes," Betty says, "but the students really learned, probably because the topic was immediately useful to them."

Vera teaches strategies through mini-lessons as well. Her routine involves a mini-lesson on Monday followed by the creation of a "Strategy of the Week" poster to hang outside the classroom door. During independent reading time each Tuesday through Friday, children use sticky notes to keep track of times when they use the strategy that Vera has taught—visualizing, inferring, repairing comprehension, and so forth. Then on Fridays, the class assembles all the notes, looks for patterns among them, and prepares the "Strategy of the Week" poster. "Children love sticky notes," she says, "so I use them to help children think about strategies and apply them to their reading."

CHOICE TIME

A third block of daily time should be devoted to choice, a time when students can make their own decisions about what they wish to do as readers or writers. During *choice time*, since students may do whatever they want as long as their activity relates somehow to reading or writing, many different literacy activities occur simultaneously.

Choice time is fun to observe in classrooms because students are so productively busy with such a variety of tasks. Some read or write alone, and others read or write together. Some perform or share their work, and others prepare to do so. "If you don't look carefully, choice time can appear chaotic," says Brenda, a fifth-grade teacher. "And I suppose, in a way, it is. But all you have to do is talk to the kids to see that they are meaningfully engaged and interested. Boy! Talk about time on task!"

Some teachers and students establish informal rules for choice time. For example, they might decide to reserve certain portions of the classroom for children who need silence or establish a procedure for seeking the teacher's assistance. (Brenda's students list their names on the chalkboard, and she works down the list in order.) Other teachers prefer less initial regulation, opting to see if problems arise and inviting students to develop solutions if they do.

Because students are involved in a variety of activities during choice time, the teacher's role varies, too. Bobbi Fisher (1991), a kindergarten teacher, describes her role during choice time:

> I have six primary functions during choice time: (1) to set up the environment, (2) to facilitate the routine, (3) to teach, (4) to act as audience, (5) to kidwatch, and (6) to enjoy the children. . . . Most of the children are practicing independently or with peers, and I work with individuals and small groups of students. . . . During part of each day I watch children and conduct formal or informal assessments, and occasionally I [simply enjoy myself] as a member of the classroom community. (p. 70)

Planning instruction in terms of routines helps teachers focus on what's important and ensures that classroom time will be well spent. Routines also help students; a predictable instructional environment fosters independence. Students can go about the business of reading and writing rather than always waiting for the teacher's directions.

How Much Time on What Kind of Task?

Time is another important factor to consider in establishing a framework for instruction. For example, in the mid-1980s, Anderson and colleagues (1985) reported that students in basal-dominated classrooms spent up to 70 percent of their reading instruction time completing worksheets. That does not leave much time for reading, reflecting, discussing—all the things we know lead to reading growth. Indeed, much research (e.g., Allington, 2002; NAEP, 2000; Postlethwaite & Ross, 1992; Rupley, Wise, & Logan, 1986) indicates that time spent reading correlates highly with reading achievement. A recent research report of classrooms where the Reading First program has been successful indicates that, on average, children are reading for 90 minutes each day (Scott, 2006). So, to grow as readers, students need opportunities to read, and they need to be accountable for how they use this time. Time available for reading and student accountability are important ingredients in instructional planning.

The focus of attention, especially during reading instruction, is another issue related to time. One careful study of two 30-minute reading lessons revealed that students in a high-ability group spent three times as much time on task (that is, reading and discussing what they'd read) as students in a low-ability group (McDermott, 1978). Allington's (1977, 1984) research found a similar dearth of contextual reading for less able readers. Moreover, teachers' discussions with better readers tend to focus on text meaning, but discussions with poorer readers tend to focus on decoding (Allington, 1978, 1980; McDermott, 1978).

These substantial differences must affect reading growth. And students are aware of the differences. In their study of intermediate-grade students' perceptions about "good readers," Henk and Melnick (1998) noted, "Children demonstrate a remarkable sensitivity not only to subtle variations in the way they and others are called upon, but also to the amount of time individuals are allowed for responding to questions or sharing their ideas" (p. 72).

Thus, instructional environments can differ, even for students in the same classroom, with regard to how time is spent. Like others (e.g., Good, 1987), we believe that these differences are cause for concern. Too often, struggling readers participate in lessons that emphasize mindless decoding, rote drill, and meaningless practice. Given our knowledge of the reading process and ways to support reading growth, we believe that this sort of instruction does more harm than good. In fact, it can lead to what Stanovich (1986) calls the "Matthew Effect," a sort of rich-get-richer and poor-get-poorer situation in which the environment supports continued growth for good readers but actually thwarts growth for those who find reading difficult. Instead, instructional frameworks for children who experience difficulty in reading should feature an abundance of time to read and write for meaningful, interesting, student-selected purposes.

Create a Literate Environment

Creating a literate environment involves everything that we have addressed thus far in this chapter. Two other aspects of the physical environment can also affect opportunity to learn: room arrangements and availability of materials. Support, interest, variety, and choice are important concepts to remember when making decisions about either aspect, because environments that reflect these concepts both encourage and facilitate literacy learning.

ROOM ARRANGEMENTS

Think of effective room arrangements as "user friendly." Rooms should be organized so that students can read and write independently and efficiently. This means easy student access to materials and well-defined areas for certain types of activities, such as a classroom library area or a corner where resources and editing supplies are available. Display areas, such as bulletin boards, celebrate children's work and promote books and reading. Even promotional materials should be student designed and made.

Everything about the room arrangement should foster the notion of student ownership of the classroom and their reading. Some of the most exciting and lively rooms we have visited, places in which children engage in real learning, have students' work displayed on tables, walls, and ceilings in the classroom; in the hallway; outside the principal's office; and, in some cases, outside the school itself. What a message this sends to children, parents, and the community about what goes on in school!

Although the specifics of room arrangement may depend on students' ages and curricular issues, the overall organization should promote group inquiry, encourage independence and responsibility, and cultivate student interest. Many classrooms feature reading centers and writing centers as special places. Reading centers have comfortable places to sit, nooks and crannies for curling up with a good book, bookshelves and book displays, and so on. It's amazing what a rug, a few pillows, and a rocking chair can do.

Writing centers have all the materials students need for writing organized for ready access. Classroom computers and writers' reference books are also typically located in writing centers. Other areas of the classroom, such as areas for read-alouds or sharing, may support both reading and writing as well as instruction in other curricular areas.

We believe every classroom should have some form of *word wall*. A word wall is simply a bulletin board, sheet of chart paper, or other portion of a classroom wall dedicated to words the class is studying. Word walls can be composed of high-frequency words, words related to phonics generalizations or word families (e.g., *hat, cat, sat*), content words (e.g., words related to geometric shapes), or interesting words that students select from their reading. Words on word walls are practiced and discussed regularly. Word walls remind students that words are important, that word study can be fun and fascinating, and that the study of words is the work that happens in classrooms. (Additionally, word walls solve for teachers that age-old problem—What do I do with this bulletin board?)

Classroom setups are important because they, too, can support or hinder students' learning. Like so many other decisions teachers make, room arrangements reveal what they believe about how children learn and the best way to support that learning. Bolted-down desks in straight rows reveal one set of beliefs; classrooms arranged as a variety of interest centers where students' interests and work are taken seriously and celebrated reveal another.

MATERIALS

A literate classroom environment offers a wide range of authentic materials for reading and writing. Materials should be conveniently available to allow student readers and writers easy access to what they need. Werderich and Pariza (2007) advise teachers to wander through big bookstores to find ideas for creating warm and comforting atmospheres that invite reading and attention to books.

Reading materials for beginners of any age should support and encourage them in their quest for meaning. Predictable materials are especially effective because it is easy to determine what will come next, both what the author is going to say and how it will be said. Students' own dictations are predictable because dictations contain familiar language and students already know the content. Pattern literature is predictable for a variety of reasons, including repetition, use of familiar concepts, match between illustrations and text, and use of rhythm or rhyme. (A starter list of recommended poetry books is provided in Appendix A.) It provides a familiar, dependable context for beginning readers.

Likewise, materials for developing readers should also be supportive and encouraging. Because reading interests and tastes differ, students need access to a variety of topics, genres, and formats. And because people read for many purposes, reference books, lists, written directions, menus, catalogs, and the like are legitimate materials for the classroom. Figures 3.4, 3.5, and 3.6 offer Web addresses for teachers interested in award-winning books, sources for nonfiction, and children's magazines.

Harste (1989) says that effective literacy learning environments are "littered with print." This is a useful visual image for thinking about both room arrangements and availability of materials. Although organization is apparent, classrooms are arranged and stocked with materials so that students naturally read and write in the process of completing tasks.

FIGURE 3.4   Sources for Award-Winning Books

Batchelder Award (most outstanding book originally published in a language other than English)

   www.ala.org/ala/mgrps/divs/alsc/awardsgrants/bookmedia/batchelderaward/index.cfm

Boston Globe Hornbook Award (excellence in literature for children and young adults)

   www.hbook.com/bghb/default.asp

Caldecott Award (illustrator of most distinguished picture book)

   www.ala.org/ala/mgrps/divs/alsc/awardsgrants/bookmedia/caldecottmedal/
   caldecottmedal.cfm

Children's Choices (children's favorite titles)

   www.reading.org/resources/tools/choices_childrens.html

Coretta Scott King Award (titles that promote unity and world peace)

   www.powells.com/prizes/corettascottking.html

Newbery Award (most distinguished book in U.S. children's literature)

   www.ala.org/ala/mgrps/divs/alsc/awardsgrants/bookmedia/newberymedal/
   newberymedal.cfm

Teachers' Choices (teachers' favorite titles)

   www.reading.org/resources/tools/choices_teachers.html

Young Adults' Choices (young adults' favorite titles)

   www.reading.org/resources/tools/choices_young_adults.html

FIGURE 3.5   Sources for Nonfiction Books

Notable Trade Books for Young People (National Council of the Social Studies)

   www.socialstudies.org/notable

Orbis Pictus Award Winners (nonfiction award from National Council of Teachers of English)

   www.ncte.org/awards/orbispictus?source=gs

Outstanding Science Trade Books (National Science Teacher Association)

   www.nsta.org/publications/ostb/

Reading is Fundamental

   www.rif.org/educators/books/book_list_index.mspx

Society of School Librarians International

   http://falcon.jmu.edu/∼ramseyil/ssli.htm

FIGURE 3.6 Children's Magazines (all Web addresses active as of November 2008)

American Girl
www.americangirl.com/

Boy's Life
www.boyslife.org/

Children's Digest
www.cbhi.org/magazines/
childrensdigest/index.shtml

Children's Playmate
www.cbhi.org/magazines/
childrensplaymate/index.shtml

Cobblestone: The History Magazine for Young People
www.cobblestonepub.com/magazine/
COB/

Creative Kids
www.prufrock.com/client/client_pages/
prufrock_jm_createkids.cfm

Cricket: The Magazine for Children
www.cobblestonepub.com/magazine/
CKT/

Faces: The Magazine about People
www.cobblestonepub.com/magazine/
FAC/

Highlights for Children
www.highlights.com/

Jack and Jill
cbhi.org/magazines/jackandjill/

Ladybug: The Magazine for Young Children
www.cobblestonepub.com/magazine/
LYB/

Merlyn's Pen: Fiction, Essays, and Poems by America's Teens
www.merlynspen.org/

Muse
www.cobblestonepub.com/magazine/
MUS/

National Geographic World
kids.nationalgeographic.com/

Odyssey
www.cobblestonepub.com/magazine/
ODY/

Owl: The Discovery Magazine for Children
www.owlkids.com/

Plays: The Drama Magazine
www.playsmag.com/

Ranger Rick
www.nwf.org/kids/kzPage.cfm?siteid=3

Skipping Stones: A Multicultural Magazine
www.skippingstones.org/

Sports Illustrated for Kids
www.siforkids.com/

Stone Soup: The Magazine by Young Writers and Artists
www.stonesoup.com/

Weekly Reader
www.weeklyreader.com/pubstore/

Zoobooks
www.zoobooks.com/

What Do Teachers Do?

The teacher has an essential role to play in developing and maintaining an effective instructional framework. This role is shaped by beliefs and attitudes as well as instructional skill. Teachers must (1) expect all their students to learn, (2) see the value of everything that students bring into the classroom, (3) believe that it's more important to focus on what students can do rather than on what they can't do, and (4) believe that learning is easiest when students have choices and their instructional opportunities are based on interest and relevance.

Moreover, teachers are models of literate behavior. Through what they do as well as what they say, teachers show students what it means to be a reader, how readers handle problems, what value reading can have in a person's life, and so on. This teacher-as-model role is critical to the development and maintenance of an effective instructional environment.

Other aspects of the instructional environment are equally important. Teachers who recognize the power of talk as a vehicle for learning invite collaboration and encourage children to share with one another and to talk through problems to be solved. In constructivist literacy classrooms, students focus on creating, comprehending, and communicating meaning. The teacher designs instructional activities and supports children's efforts at learning.

Teachers' attitudes toward mistakes are also important. Effective teachers look for what's right about students' work. They encourage students to take risks, try new ideas, learn new skills, and expand their learning horizons. Taking these risks will lead to student errors, but good teachers know that mistakes are an inevitable part of the learning process, part of the human condition. They communicate this attitude to their students through what they say and do.

Reflecting on her 45 years of teaching struggling readers at the renowned Benchmark School, Irene Gaskins (2005) has identified insights that guide her work with children. Three seem particularly apt to this discussion of the teacher's role in creating effective instructional environments:

- Teachers, not materials, determine success in learning to read.
- There are no quick fixes but "there are research-based instructional principles that, if applied regularly, substantially increase the likelihood that students will learn how to read" (p. 245).
- Becoming a teacher is a lifelong process.

We conclude this chapter with reflections about a former student from Jackie, who taught developmental readers in college:

I saw Brian again today. He was driving a campus bus and called to me as I walked across the parking lot. He's confident, majoring in English, and plans to be a secondary teacher. He's a junior, I think, but as a first-semester freshman when he read my comments about his fine writing, he said, "No one ever said that to me before." How could his teachers of 12-plus years not see him as a writer? I think it's because they saw him as "at risk" rather than inviting him to take risks.

Jackie's comments concern a college-age student, whereas Betsy's, mentioned in the introduction to this chapter, depict first-graders. Despite the significant differences in their students' ages, the two teachers share fundamental assumptions about literacy teaching and learning. More important, they believe that their students can learn, and they have developed instructional frameworks based on their assumptions and reflective of their beliefs.

DISCUSSION QUESTIONS

Some of the discussion questions for each chapter ask you to think through your own work as a teacher. If you are not currently a practicing teacher, try to respond to these questions from your own school experience (either from when you yourself were a student or from visits to schools that you have made in your teacher education program).

1. In this chapter we encourage teachers to eliminate competition in the reading classroom. What are some examples of competitive reading activities used in some classrooms and what could replace them?

2. Some teachers wonder if independent reading time will be frustrating for struggling readers. What has been your experience? What can teachers do to assure that such time is not frustrating for struggling readers?

3. Ask your struggling students, "What is reading?" Do their responses reflect a view of reading as constructing meaning or do their responses reflect a skill-and-drill view? Make plans for helping students develop more helpful views of reading.

4. Teachers and students must share assumptions about the purposes and goals of literacy activities and individual literacy lessons. What words would you use to articulate your literacy goals to children? Write your own literacy goal(s) for you and your students as they might appear on a poster that would hang outside the door to your classroom.

5. Everything about the room arrangement should foster the notion of student ownership of the classroom and their reading. Take inventory of your classroom. Make three columns and write a brief description of things like bulletin boards, shelf displays, seating arrangement, books, and so on. What conclusions can you draw?

Student Created	Teacher Created	Commercial

Chapter **Four** ❧

Developing Positive Attitudes about Reading

CHILDREN ARE BORN WITH THE DESIRE TO LEARN. They are curious—interested in objects, people, and events in the world around them. Parents and others encourage this curiosity and, in general, support children's learning. Consequently, almost all children enter school wanting to learn, which includes learning to read, and expecting to do so successfully. Most *are* successful.

When children repeatedly experience difficulty learning to read (or any other kind of learning), however, they may become frustrated or tired of failing. They may lose their enthusiasm and motivation for reading. These negative attitudes can hamper both learning and the desire to learn.

"I learned about the importance of attitudes the hard way," said Barb, who left her third-grade classroom to teach a self-contained group of intermediate-grade students with learning disabilities. "I knew the curriculum, and I had studied ways to accommodate students' learning needs. I thought I was all set. The first few days of school were all right, but something was nagging at me. A week or two into the year, it struck me like a bolt of lightning: I was surrounded by kids who *absolutely hated* reading! As I think back on it now, I guess I should have expected that. But it really took me by surprise. I wasn't prepared for the intensity of their feelings. After all, they're just kids."

This chapter is devoted to principles for developing literacy learning environments in which readers will succeed and want to read. Throughout, we refer to results of a five-year, federally funded research program, which included dozens of separate studies all conducted by scholars associated with the National Reading Research Center (NRRC) (e.g., Baker, Afflerbach, & Reinking, 1996; Baumann & Duffy, 1997; Gambrell, 1996). This research was guided by the "*engagement perspective,* which specifies the goal of reading instruction as developing motivated and strategic readers who use literacy for pleasure and learning" (Baumann & Duffy, 1997, p. 5). Attitudes and motivation are critical, especially for children who struggle as readers. Moreover, NRRC researchers established a synergy between motivation and ability—the two are mutually reinforcing phenomena. The more motivated one is to read, the more strategic one becomes in reading. And greater strategy use results in greater satisfaction and motivation for reading.

Motivation to Read: A View from Children

What motivates children to read? Several large-scale research studies were designed to find answers to this important question. Let's take a look at the results.

Palmer, Codling, and Gambrell (1994) used questionnaires and interviews to explore the reading preferences, habits, and behaviors of 330 third- and fifth-grade students. Their NRRC-sponsored research documented four powerful influences on children's motivation to read:

- *Prior experiences with books:* Children at both grade levels mentioned this category most often. Children reported reading books that their teachers or parents had previously read aloud to them or books based on television programs or movies they had seen. They also frequently mentioned rereading favorite books and reading series books, which may appeal because "the characters, setting, and general story structure remain consistent, but the plot provides new and challenging information" (p. 177).
- *Social interactions with books:* Children placed high priority on reading books that they had heard about from friends, parents, or teachers.
- *Book access:* Easy availability of books, both in the classroom and at home, was important. Most children reported selecting books to read from their classroom libraries.
- *Book choice:* Children were most motivated when they read books they had selected themselves. Often these were books that someone else had recommended, which suggests that choice and social interaction may be related in an important way.

These categories of responses point the way to classroom adaptations that can help struggling readers develop and maintain positive attitudes toward reading. Children need easy access to books and the freedom to choose their own reading material. Moreover, both teacher read-alouds (see Chapter 3) and consistent opportunities to talk about books with others (see Chapter 9) appear critical in developing children's motivations to read. We agree with the researchers that "teachers are in a position to have a positive influence on children's motivation to read through careful planning with respect to the classroom literacy environment" (Palmer, Coding, & Gambrell, 1994, p. 178).

Ivey and Broaddus (2001) explored similar issues in a study of more than 1,700 sixth-grade students' motivations for reading. When asked about the activities they enjoyed most in their language arts classes, students indicated preference for free reading and reading in social contexts, including opportunities to discuss reading with peers and teacher read-alouds, above all other activities. Choice was also important; in fact, students complained about assigned reading and "pointed to difficulties in understanding as the main reason for not liking these texts despite the fact that so much time was spent on activities to help them understand" (p. 368). Students suggested that the classroom literacy environment would benefit from more nonfiction, which they reported reading regularly outside of school.

Sweet and Guthrie (1996), who also explored children's reasons, goals, and motivations for reading, believe that children's motivations are "multidimensional and diverse" and that teachers must learn to recognize the characteristics of these motivations to foster long-term literacy growth. Children in Sweet and Guthrie's NRRC-sponsored research reported both intrinsic and extrinsic motivations. *Intrinsic motivations,* which originate in personal interests and private experiences, include *involvement,* or the phenomenon of "getting lost in a book"; *curiosity,* reading to satisfy personal questions or hypotheses; *social interaction,* which is similar to the Palmer, Coding, and Gambrell (1994) finding; and *challenge,* such as the challenge involved in solving a mystery. Intrinsic motivations have both short- and long-term value. In classrooms, children need strong intrinsic motivations to learn complex strategies, such as summarizing, and to benefit completely from integrated, student-centered instruction. The long-term benefit of intrinsic motivation is that children develop lifelong, voluntary reading habits.

Children in the Sweet and Guthrie study also reported reading for *extrinsic reasons*— that is, for someone else's reasons. Examples of these motivations include *compliance* ("because the teacher said to"), *recognition* ("to get as many points as I can"), *competition,* and *work avoidance* ("I am writing this story so I won't have to read my book"). Sweet and Guthrie believe that extrinsic motivations are powerful because they cause immediate attention and effort but are limited because motivation ceases when the particular task ends. Unlike intrinsic motivations, extrinsic motivations do not regenerate themselves.

Of course, teachers want students to develop and maintain intrinsic motivations for reading. Unfortunately, children who find reading difficult are not typically intrinsically motivated readers. Understanding motivation from a psychological perspective can provide helpful information in solving this problem.

What Affects Motivation?

Psychologists who study people's motivations to achieve recognize two crucial variables. The first is whether a person expects success. An individual is more willing to engage in activities if he or she expects to do well. The second critical variable is the value a person places on success. If someone cares about doing well, he or she will try harder. Both expectations and value affect persistence with any task, including the task of learning to read (Wigfield & Asher, 1984). The teacher's challenge is to create an instructional environment in which students are continually successful so that they learn to expect success, and in which students come to value reading because it meets their needs and satisfies their interests.

Attribution theory attempts to explain how people think about why they succeed or fail at a task. Most people think they succeed or fail for one of three reasons: *ability* ("I am/am not able to do this"), *effort* ("I tried/did not try to do this"), or *luck* ("My success/failure had nothing to do with me"). Research comparing ideas about attribution between students with high and low motivation has found differences that have instructional implications. Highly motivated students tend to believe that they succeed through ability and fail through lack of effort. Poorly motivated students, on the other hand, tend to attribute their success to luck but their failure to lack of ability (Weiner, 1979).

Attitudes affect motivation, and motivation affects people's thinking about why they succeed or fail. Moreover, those who repeatedly fail may begin to believe that they are incapable of success. This is called *learned helplessness* because the feeling of helplessness is learned through repeated negative experiences. People with an attitude of learned helplessness frequently quit trying; they don't see any point in trying because they are convinced that they will fail.

Fortunately, learned helplessness and other negative attitudes can be unlearned; that is, students who believe that they cannot learn to read successfully can begin to believe in themselves as readers. To accomplish this change, one must first understand that motivation is socially constructed (Nolen, 2007). Some scholars believe that motivation begins as situational interest—for example, a child may show interest in a particular situation or a particular book. Eventually, though, this situational interest can change to individual interest—a stable attraction to something, such as reading. In fact, a longitudinal study of children in grades 1 through 3 showed this to be the case. When interviewed about reading interests, first-grade children tended to say that they liked to read a particular book (situational interest). By third grade, children tended to say that they liked to read about certain things (individual interest) (Nolen, 2007).

In other words, the social contexts in which reading and writing occur contribute to children's notions of the nature of reading and writing and of their decisions about the place reading and writing should hold in their lives. An environment in which students come to expect success and in which they learn to value reading can help them overcome feelings of learned helplessness. To develop such an environment, we must first learn about our students' attitudes and interests in reading.

Finding Out about Attitudes and Interests

Struggling readers often associate reading with failure, and this leads to negative attitudes toward reading. Some may view reading as a chore or a waste of time. Many may choose not to read to avoid frustration or failure. Most struggling readers are disengaged and unmotivated. Perhaps they exhibit self-handicapping strategies, such as procrastination. Perhaps they feel socially marginalized (Guthrie & Davis, 2003). But this grim portrait can be altered. Finding out about children's attitudes and interests is an important first step in this process.

The best ways to find out about attitudes and interests are to observe children's behaviors in the classroom and ask students to share their ideas in conversation or writing. Questionnaires or surveys can also assist (e.g., Henk & Melnick, 1995; McKenna & Kear, 1990). Although surveys are efficient when dealing with groups of children, teachers cannot rely solely on their results. Children often see through to the purposes behind the questions and may respond with "right" answers rather than those that reflect their true feelings. Observations permit teachers to check survey responses against actual behavior, and interviews allow teachers to extend or clarify children's responses (Rhodes & Shanklin, 1993).

OBSERVATION

Careful observation may be the most effective way to learn about students' attitudes and interests. Observations should be conducted objectively, over time, and in a variety of situations. With regard to attitudes and interests, it is important to focus on both independent and organized reading in the classroom. Observation is easier when the teacher focuses on key questions, such as these, which focus on independent reading:

- How does the child react to independent reading?
- Does the child choose to read?
- Does the child appear to enjoy reading?
- Does the child appear to concentrate?
- Does the child use books as resources?
- What types of reading material does the child select?

Attitudes toward reading instruction may be different from attitudes toward independent reading. Questions like these can frame observation of these attitudes (Padak, 1987):

- Does the child participate willingly?
- Does the child stay actively involved and seem able to concentrate?
- Does the child interact freely with teacher and peers?
- How does the child react when asked to read orally? Silently?

See Chapter 2 for further information about observation, including suggestions for recording information.

INFORMAL DISCUSSION

Informal discussion can yield information about children's attitudes and interests if children feel comfortable sharing their thoughts honestly. If not, discussions can suffer the same "right answer" syndrome that often plagues written surveys. Discussion can also confirm hypotheses generated through observation. Moreover, teachers can learn about interests by talking informally with children about hobbies, leisure-time interests, favorite books or authors, and so forth.

SURVEYS AND CHECKLISTS

Teacher-made surveys or checklists are yet another way to investigate students' attitudes and interests. To explore independent reading, for example, you might ask

- Do you like to read at home? Why or why not?
- Do you like to read at school? Why or why not?
- Do you like to go to the library? Why or why not?

Survey questions can also yield information about students' attitudes toward reading instruction (Padak, 1987):

- What's your favorite thing to do during reading instruction? Why?
- If you could change one thing about our reading class, what would you change? Why?

Checklists and surveys are efficient ways to gather initial information about children's reading interests. A simple approach is to prepare a list of broad topics, such as animals, real people, mysteries, sports, make-believe, or humor. Then ask children to check topics of interest or rank the topics by preference. We can also examine lists of books that children have read to draw some conclusions about their reading interests. Figure 4.1 provides additional questions that teachers frequently use to explore children's interests in reading, what they enjoy reading, and their interest in reading and writing as activities.

FIGURE 4.1   Surveying Reading Interests and an Interest in Reading

Reading Interests

1. What sorts of books do you like to hear others read?
2. What's your favorite school subject?
3. If someone were going to buy a book for you, what would you want it to be about?
4. What kinds of stories do you like to write?
5. What kinds of magazines do you like to read?
6. What are your all-time favorite books?
7. Who are your favorite authors?
8. What section do you head for first in the library or a bookstore?

Interest in Reading

1. If you had a free day from school, what would you do?
2. Do your parents (or someone else at home) read to you? How often? Do you like this?
3. Do you read to your parents or someone else at home? How often? Do you like this?
4. Do you like to go to the library? How often do you go there? Do you usually find some books to take home?
5. Do you like reading by yourself? Do you like reading with others?
6. Where do you like to read at home? Is there a time of day when you like to read? How long do you usually read when you read at home? How often do you read at home?
7. What's the best way to become a better reader?

Barb, introduced at the beginning of this chapter, uses all these tools to find out about her students' attitudes and interests. "I usually give kids a couple of written surveys at the beginning of the year," she says. "It's a good way to start getting to know them and their interests, and I pick up a few clues about their attitudes, too, which are usually pretty negative." Next, Barb observes as children begin adjusting to her classroom. "I look for the good times—instances where children are actively involved as readers and seem happy to be here. I use these to plan instruction. That is, after I have figured out what children enjoy, I try to plan more and more sessions like that." Barb saves conversations about attitudes and interests until she and the children know each other better. "It takes a while for the kids to trust me, and I know that they won't share the real in-depth stuff until then, especially if it's negative."

Helping her students develop and maintain positive attitudes is important to Barb. She also wants to know about their reading interests to better plan instruction, suggest books, and help children form interest groups for inquiry. Barb uses what she knows about attitudes, motivation, and interests and what she learns about her students to develop a classroom environment in which her students can learn to expect success and value reading.

Learning to Expect Success

Most of Barb's students, like others who find reading difficult, expect *not* to succeed as readers. They have developed these expectations based on previous reading experiences in school. Unfortunately, these expectations may take time to change, especially for older students who felt failure for longer periods of time. The good news is that students can and do change their expectations for success. Classroom environments in which this sort of change occurs share some common characteristics.

EXEMPLARY CLASSROOMS

Mike Rose (1995) spent five years searching for exemplary classrooms (preschool through high school) throughout the United States. He spent time with teachers and students in those classrooms, identifying what the classrooms had in common. Rose summarized these critical instructional characteristics eloquently:

> These classrooms, then, were places of expectation and responsibility. Teachers took students seriously as intellectual and social beings. Young people had to work hard, think things through, come to terms with each other—and there were times when such effort took a student to his or her limits. (p. 415)

Rose (1995) found four similarities among these diverse classrooms:

* *Students felt safe, both physically and psychologically.* They knew their ideas were valued, that they wouldn't be insulted, that they could "push beyond what you can comfortably do at present" (p. 413).

- *Teachers demonstrated respect for students, and students demonstrated respect for the teacher and each other.* This attitude of respect fostered feelings of psychological safety.
- *Authority and leadership were distributed in the classrooms.* Students and the teacher shared responsibility for leading classroom activities. When appropriate, students had opportunities to be "experts." In other words, classrooms were characterized by community and cooperation (see Chapter 3).
- *Students believed that classroom learning was vital.* They saw the importance of what they did as learners and believed that instruction was in their best interest.

We can use these four characteristics to develop a literacy learning environment in which students learn to expect success as readers. For example, consider the issue of psychological safety. Most people feel safe psychologically if they believe that their ideas are of value to others—that they will not be ridiculed or put down based on what they say. If others are interested, then people are more likely to share their ideas and share them more successfully. Over time, the accumulation of these successful experiences can alter expectations about the likelihood of future success. In other words, providing a psychologically safe learning environment can reverse the thinking that initially led students to expect failure.

Vital classrooms begin with vital teachers. Students will feel good about what they do when the teacher is excited and enthusiastic about their abilities and the topics studied. Enthusiastic teachers can transmit a love of learning to students as well as help them learn to believe that they can be successful. We have heard that the great anthropologist Margaret Mead was asked why children in some cultures find certain things easy to learn while those in other cultures find the same things difficult. Mead responded that children find it easy to learn things that important adults in their lives value. Teachers (and parents) need to communicate to children that reading is important and useful and that they expect children to learn to read successfully.

CONDITIONS OF LANGUAGE LEARNING

Like Mike Rose, Brian Cambourne has attempted to understand "exemplary learning" and provide instructional suggestions based on his insights. Cambourne has studied the environmental factors and conditions that support children as they learn to speak their native languages. The findings of this research, conducted over 20 years, offer another way to think about creating classroom environments in which students learn to expect success as readers. Cambourne (1995) has identified eight conditions always present when language is learned. He believes that these conditions co-occur and are synergistic—that is, each affects and is affected by the others. The following paragraphs briefly describe each condition.

1. Immersion *Immersion* refers to being immersed in or engulfed by what is to be learned. For example, young children are typically surrounded by conversation and other forms of oral language. In terms of effective environments for literacy learning, immersion refers to the quality, quantity, and availability of reading (and writing) materials. As we noted in Chapter 3, the classroom should be filled with interesting and attractive reading materials. Students should have ample opportunity to browse through materials and read them.

Although reading materials are usually dispersed throughout the classroom, the classroom library should house the majority. Every classroom should have a library stocked with a variety of books, at least 10 per child. To the extent possible, children should be involved in book selection for the classroom library; they should also be responsible for organizing and maintaining the library. Children in the Palmer, Codling, and Gambrell (1994) study overwhelmingly reported selecting "most enjoyable" books from their classroom libraries. This finding points to both the quality of the classroom library and the children's access to books as significant factors in motivating children to read. Dina Feitelson also experimented with factors related to book access and children's "ownership" of classroom libraries (Shimron, 1994). Both factors led to increased engagement with books and reading, which led her to conclude that literacy growth can best be supported in an environment "in which an individual can discover that reading is interesting and fun and in which it is considered a virtue to be a 'reader'" (p. 95).

2. Demonstrations   *Demonstrations* provide the examples and raw data that enable learning. Demonstrations occur naturally as others in the environment use what children are learning. For example, listening to others talk helps young children decide about the functions and forms of language. Cambourne has noted that demonstrations associated with oral language learning always take place in a meaningful context and serve relevant purposes.

Likewise, demonstrations that arise from peer discussions about books and reading help students find success as readers, which ultimately leads to their expecting to be successful readers. Classroom demonstrations of literate behavior are vitally important as well. This is one of many reasons why classroom reading activities should be as authentic as possible: Students need repeated opportunities to engage authentically and successfully as readers to develop expectations for success.

As teachers, the models of literate behavior we provide—whether reading aloud, talking about a favorite book, or participating in an authentic story discussion—are also demonstrations. Teacher-as-model is a common theme throughout this book, but here we wish to underscore the affective nature of modeling. Students cite their teachers' behaviors as motivators for their own behavior (Gambrell, 1996). They can learn to appreciate reading from teachers who genuinely love to read. Teachers who demonstrate their own real, personal affection for reading are much more likely to have students who share that enthusiasm.

3. Engagement   *Engagement* refers to active participation in reading. This is influenced, of course, by attention, perceived need or purpose for reading, and willingness to make attempts. Children learn to talk because they actively try to talk. And they try because they believe they are capable of succeeding, see the value of learning to talk, and feel no anxiety about attempting it.

So it is with learning to read. In fact, Cambourne believes that engagement is the single most important condition of learning. The feelings and attitudes associated with engagement, such as seeing value and being free from anxiety, are remarkably similar to those Mike Rose found in his exemplary classrooms. Thus, activities, strategies, and instructional routines must promote active participation or engagement—real reading.

4. Expectations   *Expectations* about the learner's ability and eventual success are communicated by others, both overtly and subtly. About learning to talk, Cambourne (1995) stated, "Try asking the parents of very young children whether they expect their offspring to learn to talk. Pay attention to the kind of response you get" (p. 185).

Teachers' expectations have an enormous influence on children's learning. This has been a persistent finding from decades of research (e.g., Good, 1987). At the root of this relationship are two facts: (1) teachers are "significant others" in their students' lives and (2) expectations often translate into behaviors, which in turn influence learning. Thinking through the effect of teacher praise or criticism may help us understand how this cycle works.

Consistent verbal encouragement, such as "You can do this, Jeremy. I know you can!" or "Good thinking, Marie!," can lead students to believe that they *can* achieve and *are* good thinkers. Such beliefs may lead to positive learning gains. Unfortunately, the reverse is also true. Excessive criticism, for example, leads to anxiety, and anxious people have divided attention: Part concentrates on doing the task while the other part worries about how well they are doing. Thus, anxiety can actually contribute to attention problems in school. In fact, Cooper (1977) found that children's behaviors changed when their teachers stopped criticizing them. Children began to interact more positively with the teacher and their peers; they were also more actively involved in their academic tasks. Differential praise and criticism—that is, expectations—influence children's motivation to achieve.

5. Responsibility   *Responsibility* refers to decision making and choice. Children learning to talk decide what they will attempt to say and to whom. They also choose to pay attention to some noises and ignore others. Other people provide opportunities to learn, of course, but children decide the nature of the language interaction in which they will participate.

This condition also applies to the literacy learning classroom. Self-selection of reading materials, for example, fosters student responsibility for learning. Likewise, providing choice during instructional sessions (see Chapter 3) and encouraging choice in responses to reading (see Chapters 9 and 10) enable students to develop feelings of control and responsibility for their own reading.

6. Approximations   Children don't wait to talk until they can enunciate fully formed sentences. Instead, they *approximate,* or say whatever they can, and their attempts are received enthusiastically. No one worries about approximations because adults know that immature forms of talk will eventually be replaced by more conventional forms. No parent frets that a child will continue saying "da-da" into adulthood. Like learning to talk, learning to read and write are gradual, developmental processes in which first attempts are approximations of skilled, mature behavior. Beginning readers and writers, too, need support and encouragement for their efforts. Thus, positive attitudes toward and acceptance of approximations (or mistakes) are essential components of the classroom's psychological environment.

7. Employment   *Employment* refers to opportunities to use and practice oral language. Most of these opportunities occur in interaction with others, especially parents or caregivers, but children also practice talking to themselves. Just as oral language opportunities are authentic—real and functional—for the language learner, reading and writing opportunities should be as authentic as possible, and plentiful and consistent, too. Children should have opportunities throughout each day to engage with the written word.

8. Response   *Response* is the final condition of language learning. Children receive feedback and additional information as they attempt to talk, which they use to support further learning. As in the reading classroom, some of this feedback comes from adults in the form of praise or scaffolding to foster further learning. Students also need opportunities to respond in personal ways to their own reading. Response journals, poetry, discussion groups, artistic responses, notes to the teacher, skits, and music are some ways students can respond to their reading. Opportunities to respond to peers are equally important, as are times for quiet reflection so that learners can respond for themselves.

When Tom, a sixth-grade classroom teacher, allowed students to give creative oral book reports on Friday afternoons, enthusiasm for reading swelled in his class. Some students who read books together did book talks that resembled television movie reviews (thumbs up—thumbs down), others shared artwork and skits they had created, and still others brought in artifacts from home that represented special items and events from their stories. "I couldn't believe what they were coming up with, and they were selling the other kids on the books they had read. This was the start of a classroom book club for us," Tom said. By tapping into students' responsibility and choice, employment, and personal response, Tom unwittingly unleashed previously restrained potential for making reading come alive for his students. This led to greater enthusiasm and motivation for reading, which led to even more reading.

EXCELLENT LITERACY EDUCATORS

Recently, several groups of researchers have spent countless hours observing excellent literacy educators at work in order to identify common factors associated with effective instructional environments. In exemplary first-grade and fourth-grade classrooms, for example, Pressley and colleagues (2001) and Allington (2002) found excellent classroom management and a positive, cooperative tone. Skills instruction was explicit; teachers provided support and scaffolded children's learning. Students spent abundant time reading, writing, and working independently in these academically "busy" classrooms. They had access to excellent literature. They had abundant opportunities to talk about what they read.

Instruction in these exemplary classrooms was challenging but not frustrating. Children's work was substantive, challenging, and required more self-regulation than commonly observed in elementary classrooms. Miller (2003) noted that most motivation theories address the benefits of challenging academic tasks. In a two-year study of challenging academic tasks in grade 3, Miller found that the lowest-achieving readers were not at all put off by these challenging tasks; in fact, they thrived as long as they had access to appropriate supports.

Another study of primary-grade classrooms (Taylor et al., 2000) compared effective teachers to less-effective teachers in low-income schools. Compared to their less-effective colleagues, accomplished teachers provided

- More small-group instruction
- More coaching/scaffolding
- More phonics teaching with emphasis on application in real reading
- More higher-order questioning (e.g., inferences, integration, application)
- Greater outreach to parents
- More independent reading
- More engagement (greater amounts of time spent reading and writing).

A SUCCESS-BASED CLASSROOM

Can students who find reading difficult learn to expect success? We believe the answer is a resounding yes! Expectations of success are critical to long-term reading growth and the development of lifelong reading habits. Teachers can create success-based reading classrooms by using researchers' descriptions of effective classrooms as a framework for making instructional decisions.

That's what Barb did, and here's what she says about it:

When I realized how pervasively negative my students' attitudes were, I knew I had to do something. I did some reading, I talked to a few colleagues whose opinions I respect, and I did a lot of thinking and soul-searching. I finally decided that it all boiled down to several key factors. I wanted students to see reading as vital and to be active, frequent readers. For this to happen, I knew I needed to provide lots of good books, to set aside blocks of time for reading, and to encourage kids to try to read what interested them. I also knew that my own attitudes would be critical. I really *did* respect my students as learners and expect them to be successful, but I needed to find ways to communicate these feelings to my students.

Quite a bit of this fell into the "easier said than done" category for me. But I believe the goals are important, so I made a plan. I have separate sections of a small notebook for the goals I want to achieve. In each section, I have made some notes about the kinds of things I think I should do to help achieve the goals. And then every so often I look at the goals and the plans and ask myself, "Have I been doing what I planned to do? What else could I be doing?"

This is the way I work at implementing the goals consistently throughout the school year. Other people will probably have other ways of doing this, but for me it's important to keep the goals in mind and to make and evaluate concrete plans. And I think my plans are working. I have seen a difference in students' attitudes. I believe that they are beginning to believe that they *can* do it.

Learning to Value Reading

Learning to expect success is only one part of the equation for helping struggling readers develop and maintain positive attitudes toward reading. Learning to find value in reading is the other. It's easy to see how these two factors are related. For example, Barb's efforts to help her students begin to believe in themselves as readers have the added benefit of showing children that reading is a worthwhile activity, that it is fun and can help them learn and satisfy their curiosities.

HOW DO WE DECIDE ABOUT THE VALUE OF READING?

People value what they find desirable, useful, or important. Students' attitudes about the value of reading are no doubt influenced by their families and home reading practices. Children who routinely watch their parents and others at home read for enjoyment, learning, and work come to see the value of reading for all these purposes. In this way, parents and others at home become powerful models for both literate behavior and positive attitudes toward reading.

Children's peers may also influence their attitudes about the value of reading. Peers who view reading as a desirable and important activity encourage others to value reading. This is one reason for the powerful influence of social interaction around literacy activity.

Interactions with parents and peers can influence children's reading outside of school. And reading outside of school is important. Research has consistently shown that reading ability is positively related to recreational reading. An analysis of results from the National Assessment of Educational Progress (NAEP), a standardized instrument administered to thousands of 9-, 13-, and 17-year-olds across the United States every few years, showed just how powerful this relationship is. Students who reported reading for fun at least once a week had higher achievement scores than students who reported never or hardly ever reading for fun (U.S. Department of Education, 1996, 2000).

Of course, teachers and classroom activities also influence the value that children perceive in reading. Gambrell (1996) has stated that children value reading in classrooms that feature "choice and voice": choice in what to read, whether to read, and how to respond to reading; and voice in terms of the teacher's and peers' respect for children's ideas. Moreover, she has found that classrooms where children are motivated to read often feature an activity she calls "blessing books" (Gambrell, 1998). Several times a week, teachers select several books they think children will enjoy and do brief book talks about them. Teachers add value to the books by holding them and making brief comments ("blessing"). Books are then displayed, and children quickly check them out to read. This guidance in choosing reading material is especially important for struggling readers who often select books on their own for the wrong reasons (e.g., number of pages, presence of illustrations, size of print).

Guthrie and colleagues (1995) provided another view of developing positive attitudes about the value of reading. They studied how classroom experiences influence children's interest in reading by analyzing NAEP results. They found several aspects of instruction associated with increased amounts of reading (which itself was associated with increased reading achievement) and high interest in reading:

- *Social interaction:* Students who said they read many books also reported spending lots of time talking with others about books, reading in general, and writing, both in and outside the classroom.

- *Cognitive strategies:* Teachers created interest in reading in part by helping students find and understand books that met their needs. They taught reading strategies that helped students read to fulfill their own purposes. Moreover, interested and voracious student readers often reported that their teachers asked them to share their opinions about their reading, to think about how books were alike and different, and to support their ideas with reference to books they had read. Baumann, Hooten, and White (1999) explored this relationship between strategy instruction and increased motivation in a year-long study of teaching comprehension through literature in a fifth-grade classroom. They "sensed a kind of synergy between the reading strategies and literature appreciation. We saw the students becoming more strategic readers, which enhanced their aesthetic understanding, while their growing aesthetic appreciation facilitated their growth in reading ability" (p. 50).
- *Personal significance:* Interested and voracious readers reported that reading was personally significant for them. They said their teachers supported these feelings by giving them freedom of interpretation, choice in reading material, and time to discuss reading with peers.

Guthrie and colleagues (1995) concluded that these factors converge to help students see the value of reading, which in turn sustains long-term motivation for reading. Thus, the factors provide a firm foundation for an instructional program that helps students view reading as valuable.

Special programs to promote positive attitudes can also help students view reading as valuable. In the following section, we describe several programs that appear to work particularly well. Some are schoolwide efforts, and others involve single classrooms.

SCHOOLWIDE PROGRAMS

Reading Millionaires (Baumann, 1995; O'Masta & Wolf, 1991; Shanahan, Wojciechowski, & Rubik, 1998) is a schoolwide program with a single goal: Collectively, students and staff attempt to read independently for a million minutes over a specified period of time. Like other schoolwide programs, Reading Millionaires takes a bit of organizing. Someone, perhaps a group of students, must tally all those minutes; plans for reporting numbers of minutes read must also be developed.

Reading Millionaires can be simple or elaborate. A simple version might involve only advertising the start of the project, periodically announcing total minutes read, and celebrating the achievement of the goal. Baumann (1995) has described some additions that made Reading Millionaires successful in her school. For example, she occasionally held raffles for paperback books, with students' returned reading logs as the "ticket" for the raffle. She also created a "Reading Hall of Fame" bulletin board that spotlighted classes of especially voracious readers. And the parent organization in her school funded the purchase of small mementos for participating students, which were presented at a schoolwide celebration after the goal of 1 million minutes had been met. Shanahan, Wojciechowski, and Rubik (1998) enhanced their program by adding reading posters throughout their school as well as by holding schoolwide gatherings or rallies to encourage the reading habit.

Some schools have annual *read-ins,* somewhat like slumber parties that focus on reading. Larger schools may organize read-ins by grade levels; smaller ones often combine primary grades for one read-in and intermediate grades for another. At some schools only students and staff participate; at others parents may attend.

All read-ins involve children and books. Here is how one might look: Early Friday evening, children (and parents) return to school with books, sleeping bags, and pillows. All assemble in the school gym or multipurpose room with teachers, the principal, and other volunteers. Activities for the evening focus on books and reading. Children and adults read silently. Some might enjoy reading to partners or larger groups. Participants listen to storytellers and reader's theater or watch puppet renditions of stories. Physical activities and snacks round out the night. On Saturday morning, everyone leaves, having spent a night sharing the fun of reading and enjoying the companionship of others.

Schoolwide reading projects can involve the *community,* too (Rasinski, 1992). Some schools form alliances with senior-citizen homes or centers, where children read aloud for their senior buddies or listen to stories the buddies read. Pen-pal relationships may develop. Able seniors sometimes visit the school.

Community connections can also form in more subtle ways. For example, children might create posters advertising the joys of reading and then ask local stores to display them. Some schools organize "Reading Days" at local malls. This usually involves some sort of visual display about reading, a few rocking chairs, and groups of children rocking and reading. Teachers and children can build floats for local parades that focus on books and reading. Some schools even have book parades with children walking through the school neighborhood dressed as book characters or holding posters about their favorite books.

CLASSROOM PROGRAMS

Most teachers are familiar with *Book It!* (www.bookitprogram.com/), a national reading incentive program sponsored by Pizza Hut. The rules for participating classrooms are relatively simple. The teacher specifies the number of books to be read each month, and children who achieve the goal receive coupons for small pizzas. Teachers in some communities have sought similar support from local businesses (e.g., fast-food restaurants, amusement parks, movie theaters, etc.) to reward their students for independent reading. The key here is a connection by which the extrinsic motivator promotes the intrinsic value of reading. Teachers must promote reading for the love of reading, not just for pizzas and prizes.

Classroom Choices is modeled after the annual *Children's Choices* project, which is jointly sponsored by the International Reading Association and the Children's Book Council. Children's Choices involves groups of children from all over the United States reading and rating new books. Their favorites are published each October in *The Reading Teacher*. Some states follow similar procedures to select favorite books among school children residing in the state. (These projects are usually sponsored by state reading or language arts groups. Teachers interested in participating should contact these groups for further information.)

Classroom Choices resembles national and state projects but runs on a much smaller scale: the classroom. For a school year (or a shorter specified period of time), children read and vote on their favorite books. In some classrooms, books are subdivided by genre, such as favorite make-believe book, favorite true story, and so on. Votes are tallied in various ways. For example, children can simply count up yes or no votes about whether or not they liked a book. This can result in some interesting "run-off" discussions at the end of the voting, for many titles may receive unanimous support. Another option is to allow weighted votes, such as a 3-2-1 scale, where 3 is "Terrific! You have to read this book!" and 1 is "I wouldn't bother if I were you." Tallying these weighted votes and determining averages for titles can be an interesting and functional math lesson for older students.

Cheryl has a Classroom Choices project in her second-grade classroom each year. "I started because I noticed that the children were sharing good books with each other naturally," she says. "And so I thought, 'Why not go farther with this?'" Her project begins in early fall each year and ends at the spring recess. "We always write a class letter to the winning author. We tell him or her about the project and explain what we liked so much about the winning book. If we write early enough in the spring, the author usually responds in some way before school is out. Boy, do the kids love that!" Cheryl has found that her Classroom Choices project encourages children to read and share good books with each other. "It *is* a competition, in a way," she says. "But the books are competing and not the kids. I like that aspect of it. I also like the opportunities that arise to talk about what makes good books good, if you know what I mean."

These special programs invite children to engage in authentic reading activities, encourage cooperation rather than competition, and feature celebration of children's abilities as readers. Although each program involves some external motivation, the programs are built on the assumption that internal motivation for reading will naturally develop when a spark for reading is ignited by the externally motivating activity. In other words, special programs alone cannot sustain long-term motivation for reading. Effective teachers also encourage social interaction around reading, provide necessary strategy instruction, and help students view reading as a personally significant and rewarding activity.

Linking Attitudes to Achievement

The relationship between achievement in reading and attitudes, including motivation, is a close one. Instruction to support children who struggle as readers must focus simultaneously on both attitudes and achievement. Oldfather and Wigfield (1996), who looked at the research in both areas, offer concepts that can help teachers plan effective instruction. Students will be motivated for literacy learning when they see themselves as competent readers and writers and when they view literacy skill as personally valuable. These understandings and beliefs are most likely to develop in those instructional environments that allow students to pursue some of their own interests, to find resources (print and people) they need, and to be assured that others will be interested in and respectful of their ideas and their literate actions. These conditions can create and sustain positive attitudes.

Teachers want students to develop and maintain positive attitudes about reading and themselves as readers for at least two critical reasons. First, these attitudes allow students to develop the motivation they need to sustain interest in reading and persist in their efforts to become better readers. Second, knowing how to read is not enough; it's equally important (some would say more important) to value reading. That is, the goal should be to help students become both competent and avid readers, or, as NRRC researchers put it, the "*skill* to read and learn is not sufficient; students must also ultimately acquire the intrinsic *will* to exercise their developing reading proficiencies" (Baumann & Duffy, 1997, pp. 10–11).

Accessibility and availability have major influences on children's choices to read. A classroom environment that nurtures an interest in reading has the following characteristics:

- The teacher is enthusiastic about books and consistently supportive of children as readers.
- Children have easy access to many well-selected books.
- Children have regular time to browse, choose books, and read them.
- Books are the subject of much comment and discussion.
- Appreciation for reading develops through cumulative personal experience and response.

Students who find reading difficult often have negative attitudes about reading and themselves as readers. These negative attitudes can shut down further learning. Teachers, then, must consider sources of attitudes, how they may hamper learning, and what to do about them. In this chapter we have provided a few specific ideas and many more abstract principles that can help teachers think about the relationships among attitudes, motivation, and reading.

DISCUSSION QUESTIONS

Some of the discussion questions for each chapter ask you to think through your own work as a teacher. If you are not currently a practicing teacher, try to respond to these questions from your own school experience (either from when you yourself were a student or from visits to schools that you have made in your teacher education program).

1. Describe a time when you were intrinsically motivated to read as well as a time when you were extrinsically motivated to read. How did you feel about what you accomplished in each of these instances?

2. Attitudes toward reading instruction may be different from attitudes toward independent reading. Have you observed this difference in some students? What causes the difference? What can you do about it?

3. Ask your struggling readers, "If you could change one thing about our reading class, what would you change? Why?" Discuss the results with your study group or a trusted colleague. Ask your best readers what they like best about reading class, and why. Does what the students describe appear in your instruction for your struggling readers? Why or why not? To what extent do you agree with the notion that the kind of instruction given to the best readers should also be afforded to the struggling readers?

4. Describe a "good time"—an instance where your students were actively involved as readers and seemed happy to be in your classroom. How could you use this information to plan instruction?

5. Some teachers avoid reading response journals because of the time involved in responding to them. Brainstorm some ways to alleviate this problem.

Chapter *Five* ❧

Preventing Reading Problems through Early Literacy Experiences

T HREE-YEAR-OLD ELIJAH was playing quietly with his pirate ship when he suddenly turned to his grandma and requested, "Read me a story about pirates." Grandma said, "Oh honey, I'm sorry. I don't have any books about pirates," to which Elijah replied, "No, Grandma, read me a story about pirates *with your mouth.*" Grandma puzzled for a moment and then realized Elijah actually wanted her to *tell a story*, not *read a story*. Although he didn't have the precise language he needed, Elijah's request reflected his developing understanding of literacy—-stories, reading, and talking connected to what was important in his young world.

The best way to overcome a reading problem is to not have one in the first place! And the best way not to have one in the first place is to surround children from the time they are newborns with language, both the formal language of books and the informal language of talk, songs, storytelling, and word play.

Components of Exemplary Early Reading Instruction

How do teachers of young children (and we include parents in this notion of teachers) promote children's successful emergence into reading and writing? In this portion of the chapter we present instructional activities that are most likely to produce successful and engaged readers.

TALK WITH CHILDREN

Reading vocabulary is preceded by listening and speaking vocabulary. We dare not underestimate the importance of talking with children, particularly children from low-income or English-as-second-language families. In a large study of family language use, Hart and

Risley (2003) came to the astonishing conclusion that by age 4, children of professional parents heard 45 million words, whereas children of mothers who were on welfare heard only 13 million words, creating a "30 million word gap." A follow-up study yielded a troubling, but not surprising, conclusion—vocabulary at age 3 was strongly associated with third-grade reading comprehension scores. Young children have a natural curiosity about new words, so we don't need to "talk down" to them. Through ongoing conversations they begin to build a speaking vocabulary that will provide the foundation for reading vocabulary.

READ TO STUDENTS

An enduring research finding is that children who are read to regularly (daily) tend to succeed in literacy learning. In a classic study, Durkin (1966) found that children whose parents read to them regularly at home are more likely to find early success in reading than children who lack such opportunities. More than 40 years later, Durkin's findings still hold true (Mullis et al., 2007; Primivera, 2000; Snow, Burns, & Griffin, 1998). Moreover, the advantage early successful readers have over their nonearly reading classmates remains over the years.

Why is reading to young children so important? First, it communicates that reading is an important part of life, both in the home and in the classroom. Stories are enjoyable, and sharing a story with an important adult makes it even more special. Thus, students who are read to tend to have more positive attitudes toward reading. In addition, the story reading helps students develop comprehension and vocabulary, as well as a sense for the conventions (rules) for stories. These are crucial aspects of becoming fully literate. Being read to by a fluent adult also provides students with a model of what reading aloud should sound like. And finally, if parents and teachers read to students in such a way that the students can see the text, students can naturally develop basic concepts about print (what a word is, directionality in reading, and so on), letter knowledge, and early recognition of words. Need we say more? Reading to students is perhaps the most important literacy activity adults can share with students in preschool, kindergarten, and beyond.

LANGUAGE EXPERIENCE

Dictated texts, sometimes called the language experience approach, are a great bridge from oral to written language, from speech to reading. In language experience activities (see Chapter 6), students dictate a text to the teacher, who then writes the students' words on a piece of chart paper. The text reflects some experience that the children have had, individually or as a group. A walk around the school grounds or a field trip are wonderful experiences to talk about and eventually turn into a text to be read. Because the text reflects children's own experiences and words, comprehension and readability are assured. With the teacher's support, students can read their text chorally and alone, again and again, because they created it.

Language experience (dictated) texts are wonderful vehicles for teaching early reading skills. The teacher can begin to draw students' attention to individual words and letters, helping children make connections between the written text and the pronounced word or sound represented by the writing. Words drawn from several dictated texts can be turned into word banks and can be practiced, sorted, and made into games. The words can also be listed on the classroom word wall (see Chapter 6) to draw children's attention to them throughout the school day. Informed teachers use these easy-to-read and understandable texts to provide sophisticated instruction in vocabulary and word recognition to students.

PREDICTABLE AND ENLARGED TEXTS

As students further immerse themselves into the written word, they need to move on to more conventional texts, texts written by others. Predictable texts work well here. Predictable texts are stories, poems, song lyrics, or other forms of written text that have easy-to-read features such as repetitive words, phrases, sentences, rhyme and/or rhythm. (We have included lists of predictable poetry collections in Appendix A.)

When presented in enlarged formats—big books or on chart paper—predictable texts work much the same as dictated texts. Students read and reread the texts. The predictable nature of the texts may allow students to reach the point at which they can "read the story without even looking at the print." Reading involves paying attention to the written words so teachers who use predictable texts with students need to *decontextualize* the reading— read the text without the pictures; read the text as a set of sentence strips and then reassemble the strips to create the text; read individual words from the text, first in context but later in isolation; and finally explore the letters and letter patterns within words. Words from the predictable text can be added to word banks and word walls for further study and exploration. As with dictated texts, these activities help students develop not only an understanding of whole stories but also an understanding of how texts, words, and letters work in the reading process.

The patterned nature of predictable texts makes it easy for teachers and children to create their own versions. The cumulative story *This Is the House That Jack Built,* for example, can easily transform into *This Is the Trip Our Class Took* as a response to a class field trip. In addition to being an authentic and engaging writing activity, the familiar pattern of the new text makes it easy for students to read, but the new text forces students to closely examine and learn the words.

Stacy, a first-grade teacher took a cue from poet Bruce Lansky's *Poetry Party* (1996) to write several of her own versions of "Yankee Doodle." "All I did was change what 'Yankee Doodle' came to town on and the rest just came." Here's one of her creations:

Yankee Doodle went to town

Riding on a ducky.

Found a dollar on the ground

And called himself real lucky.

Once students read and memorized the original "Yankee Doodle," I introduced the ones I had written, one every other day. I put them on chart paper and we read and reread them throughout the day. Because we had several versions of "Yankee Doodle" hanging from the walls, the children had to look at the words in order to know which one we were reading. Later, we studied the rhyming words for word families and we pulled words out from the poems, put them on our word wall, and practiced them there. What really surprised me was when students began to bring in their own versions of "Yankee Doodle" that they had written at home with their parents. Even some of the students I've been worried about brought in their own poems. We read all the poems the kids brought in. The kids loved it and I did too. What started as reading and reciting one simple text turned into a full-blown words-and-writing activity.

READ TOGETHER—CHORAL READING

A major aim of all schooling is to develop a sense of shared purpose—a classroom community. Community reading, or *choral reading*, can help develop this goal (Rasinski, 2003). In choral reading the entire class or group participates in the reading experience. Younger students chorally read an enlarged predictable text or language experience story. The class reads and rereads the text together as the teacher points to the text. The practice in reading, combined with reading and hearing the words read at the same time, develop students' word recognition and fluency (Kuhn & Stahl, 2000). The added bonus to this activity is that the children have fun reading together.

Moreover, different forms of choral reading add a degree of variety to the choral reading experience (Rasinski, 2003). The teacher can divide students into smaller groups with each group handling a refrain or a portion of the text. In echo reading, the teacher reads a line and the students echo the teacher's reading. A cumulative form of choral reading begins with one student or group reading a line and, with each succeeding line, another student or group joins in. The reading begins softly but ends with gusto! No matter how you do it, choral reading is good reading and good fun.

SHARED BOOK EXPERIENCE

The *Shared Book Experience* (SBE) (Holdaway, 1979, 1981) combines elements of teacher read-aloud, choral reading, and independent reading with an enlarged text. It is a wonderful example of moving from teacher modeling to supported or scaffolded reading, to independent reading.

Children learn best when the task carries meaning. For young children just learning subskills such as phonics or sight words, a *whole-part-whole* model of reading instruction provides the context they need to make sense of the skills. In the Shared Book Experience the class begins with the *whole* story, then works with a designated skill (*part*) within the context of the story, then moves back to the *whole* story or another text illustrating the skill.

Sarah, a kindergarten teacher, regularly uses Shared Book Experience in whole-part-whole literacy lessons. Recently, Sarah introduced and expressively read the big book version of *Mrs. Wishy Washy* (Cowley, 1999) to her students (*whole*). Following a brief discussion and retelling of the story, Sarah reread the text and invited students to join in chorally with the repeating chant, "Wishy Washy, Wishy Washy." The class reread the story over several days. Students began to read fluently and to recognize some words. With this meaningful context in place, Sarah moved into the *part* segment of the whole-part-whole lesson as she and the students began working on the /sh/ sound heard in *Wishy Washy*.

They used sticky note windows to find /sh/ in the story, found things in the room containing the sound, and brought items from home that started with /sh/. Finally, moving back to the *whole*, Sarah led the students in a copy change of the story as they created their own version, "Mr. Splishy Splashy."

ENVIRONMENTAL PRINT

Another bridge between the children's lived-in world and the world of literacy can be built with *environmental print*. Environmental print is simply the print that children see in their daily lives—traffic signs; store, restaurant, and gas station signs; print on grocery bags and cereal boxes; and so on. Informed teachers bring examples into the classroom for their students to read. When that same print is rewritten in a more conventional format, without the context of the sign, teachers focus children's attention on those features that communicate the meaning—the printed letters. These words, taken from children's own environments, can be added to their word banks and examined and played with in the same way as other word-bank words.

DAILY INDEPENDENT READING

Young students need to develop the reading habit. This means giving students time every day to read on their own, even if they are not yet reading conventionally or independently. Students peruse books and the pictures in books or pretend to read during the 10 minutes (or so) of independent reading. They read silently alone or aloud with a partner. The important point is that students are honored with the opportunity to read books of their choosing, for their purposes, and with whomever they wish to read. Teachers need plenty of books and other reading material from which children can choose. In addition, teachers should read during this period so that children see reading as a lifelong avocation.

The amount of reading one does at home and school predicts overall reading achievement. Accordingly, teachers need to nurture this habit early in children's lives.

DAILY WRITING

As with independent reading, many young students cannot write conventionally. Nevertheless, teachers should write every day with students. One approach is for each student to keep a personal journal. During journal time, students write freely. Early writing may be scribbles or drawings, but as students learn more about reading and writing, they begin to apply this knowledge to their writing. Extended line scribbles may begin to resemble individual word scribbles. These scribbles later emerge into conventionally formed words, or words that, although not spelled correctly, can be read as students begin to apply their knowledge of sound-symbol correspondences. We will add to this notion of developmental or phonemic spelling later in this chapter when we discuss phonemic awareness. You may have heard this kind of spelling referred to as "invented spelling," but we prefer the term *developmental spelling* because it truly represents predictable stages of a child's literacy development.

It is absolutely critical that the teacher also write and show students what she or he has written. This provides firsthand proof that those written symbols can be turned into real words that express the writer's thoughts. Students quickly begin to emulate the writing they see their teacher doing.

Terra, a first-grade teacher, makes sure that when her students write, she writes, too.

> And then I show the students what I have written. I read it to them and then they have lots of questions about how I turned my thoughts into writing. I leave my journal open for students to look at it whenever they like. Every day at least one or two students go up to the journal, examine it, read from it, or talk about how they are going to make their writing look like mine. Even though we often do a mini-lesson on some aspect of writing before we write, I think that my modeling is the best lesson I can give my students.

PARENT INVOLVEMENT

Parents of preschool, kindergarten, and first-grade students are most likely to work with their children on reading. Even low-literate parents can help their children read at these grades. The more reading practice children have, the more likely they are to become successful readers. Teachers must urge parents to read to and with their children every day. Parents of children who are already reading conventionally can also listen to their children read and respond with heaps of praise and encouragement. Parents can write with their children, taking dictation, making lists, exchanging notes, or sharing a *dialogue journal* (a journal passed between parent and child in which parent and child converse in writing). Parents can make sure that their home is stocked with literacy materials such as books, magazines, paper, writing tools, and the like.

More formal activities also stimulate learning. See Chapter 13 for a description of *Fast Start*, a parent-involvement program for young students, as well as other approaches for helping parents help their children.

Phonemic Awareness: A Necessity for Reading

The activities and concepts presented so far are absolutely essential to children's early development in literacy. Through conversations, read-alouds, language experience activities, predictable books, environmental print, daily independent reading and writing, and parent involvement, students learn about stories and written texts; they develop their comprehension skills and build their vocabularies; they learn how print works and the basic concepts or conventions related to print; and they begin to examine words to add them to their sight vocabulary and develop understandings of how letters and letter patterns represent language sounds. That's a lot to learn.

But we want to add one more piece to this puzzle—a piece that recent research suggests is a possible reason that many children struggle in reading. It's called *phonemic awareness.*

The issue of phonics instruction has received much attention. Parents, legislators, and the public have been captured by the notion that phonics instruction is the singular key to student reading success. We certainly recognize that proficiency in phonics is necessary for reading. We disagree, however, with the view that phonics is the sole component to effective literacy instruction and the only competency required for proficient reading. This view is much too narrow. Certainly, readers can and do employ other approaches to decode words. Full development in reading and writing requires competencies in language, comprehension, and vocabulary, to name just a few. Moreover, other areas of instructional emphasis are equally important for student success in reading, such as parent involvement in children's reading, time for independent reading during the school day, and opportunities for students to discuss their reading with others. We fear that exclusive attention to phonics will skew the curriculum in such a way that many students lose the opportunity or instruction they need to become full-fledged members of the literacy community. We must recognize the importance of phonics and also its proper place in a comprehensive reading program.

Although we discuss phonics in Chapter 6, we introduce you to it here to place phonemic awareness in proper perspective. *Phonics* involves associating written letters with sounds in order to decode or sound out words in print; it is the knowledge of letter-sound correspondences. Readers use phonics when they visually examine letters or letter combinations in words and produce a sound or sound combination that corresponds to the visual stimulus. Blending the separate sounds in a word should result in pronunciation of the word.

Phonics depends on one's abilities to *visually* examine words and to recognize, segment, and blend sounds of language. Phonemic awareness, on the other hand, depends on one's abilities to *aurally* recognize, segment, and blend the sounds of language apart from print. Phonemic awareness, then, is a necessary precondition to successful phonics learning as well as, for most readers, to successful reading. Obviously, children have to hear the sounds before they can associate them with letters.

Recent research into phonemic awareness suggests that it is an important precondition for learning phonics as well as general progress in reading (Adams, 1990; Ball & Blachman, 1991; Fielding-Barnsley, 1997; Hiebert et al., 1998; Yopp, 1992, 1995a) and writing (Eldredge & Baird, 1996). Students who lack phonemic awareness are among those most likely to experience difficulty in reading (Armbruster, Lehr, & Osborn, 2001; Catts, 1991; Pressley, 2005). So, even before asking students to make connections between oral language sounds and written symbols (phonics), teachers must ensure the children's ability to deal with (recognize, segment, and blend) sounds (phonemic awareness).

HOW STUDENTS DEVELOP PHONEMIC AWARENESS

Fortunately, most students develop phonemic awareness naturally through their everyday early childhood experiences. Young children have many opportunities to play with language sounds. These opportunities range from reciting nursery rhymes and childhood poems with parents, family members, and friends, to chanting and creating jump-rope cadences and chants, to singing childhood songs (e.g., "Old MacDonald"), to simply conversing with family members and friends. As they manipulate the sounds of language, children begin to develop this awareness of sounds and how they work. By the time children enter kindergarten, they have developed enough awareness of language sounds to begin to profit from phonics instruction.

It works this way for most children, but not all. Some children enter school with insufficient awareness of the sounds of language. Researchers do not fully understand how this fails to happen for them. Some children may have had chronic ear infections that inhibited their development of this awareness. Other children may have lacked opportunities to play with language through childhood rhymes and songs. Many of our kindergarten and first-grade teacher colleagues tell us that more children are entering school with less knowledge of common rhymes and songs than children in previous years have had. Other researchers suggest that some children have within them a less-developed ability to perceive, segment, and blend language sounds. Whatever the cause of this problem, children with insufficient phonemic awareness will not profit from phonics instruction to the same extent as children proficient in phonemic awareness. If certain children have difficulty perceiving sounds even when not associated with letters, how can teachers expect them to make the next step into phonics, which involves associating letters and sounds and then blending the sounds into words? For many young children, this will be one of their first frustrations in reading, and if not addressed early on, perhaps the first of many reading frustrations through the school years.

ASSESSING PHONEMIC AWARENESS

Phonemic awareness is important to reading success, and good tools for assessing it are a necessity. Fortunately, a fairly simple assessment instrument can be administered to young children as well as to older students. Our adaptation of the Yopp–Singer Test of Phonemic Segmentation (Yopp, 1995a), in which we have removed difficult-to-perceive *r* sounds, is a set of 22 words that students segment into constituent sounds (see Figure 5.1). For example, the teacher says the word *bat* and the student says the three separate sounds that make up *bat*: /b/-/a/-/t/.

The 22-item test takes only minutes to administer, yet the results can provide some indication of students' later success in reading. Yopp (1992) has followed children to whom she administered the phonemic segmentation test in kindergarten through their later years in school. She found that students' scores are significantly correlated with reading and spelling achievement through grade 6. Clearly, this and similar research results (Stanovich, 1994) suggest that teachers must consider phonemic awareness when assessing young children and students experiencing difficulty in reading and when designing instructional programs for students who appear to lack sufficient awareness of sounds.

Yopp has found that second-semester kindergarten students obtained a mean score of 12 on the test. That suggests to us that kindergartners who fall significantly below this threshold, say a score of 5 or below, should have additional instruction in phonemic awareness. As we shall discuss later in this chapter, many children who appear deficient in the area of phonemic awareness can be taught successfully with methods that fit well within a normal kindergarten classroom.

The Test of Phonemic Segmentation has implications well beyond kindergarten, however. We routinely administer this assessment instrument to many students, ranging from second grade through high school, who are referred to our clinical reading programs. Although not all struggling readers perform poorly on the test, a surprising number do. By the beginning of second grade, students should be able to complete the test with little trouble. We expect all students at second grade or beyond to score 20 or better. And yet, it is not unusual to find fifth- and sixth-grade students, frustrated in reading, who score between 10 and 15.

FIGURE 5.1 Test of Phonemic Segmentation

Student's name _____ Date _____

Student's age _____

Score (number correct) _____ Examiner _____

Directions: I'd like to play a sound game with you. I will say a word and I want you to break the word apart into its sounds. You need to tell me each sound in the word. For example, if I say "ham," you should say "/h/-/a/-/m/." *(Administrator: Be sure to say the sounds in the word distinctly. Do not say the letters.)* Let's try a few practice words.

Practice items: kite, so, fat *(Assist the child in segmenting these items as necessary. You may wish to use blocks to help demonstrate the segmentation of sounds.)*

Test items: *(Circle those items that the student correctly segments: incorrect responses may be recorded on the blank line following the item.)*

1. to	_____	12. knock	_____
2. be	_____	13. lace	_____
3. might	_____	14. mop	_____
4. mow	_____	15. this	_____
5. he	_____	16. jet	_____
6. vain	_____	17. slow	_____
7. is	_____	18. nice	_____
8. am	_____	19. cot	_____
9. my	_____	20. shoe	_____
10. feet	_____	21. bed	_____
11. jack	_____	22. stay	_____

Source: Adapted from H. Yopp, "A Test for Assessing Phonemic Awareness in Young Children," *The Reading Teacher, 49* (1995a): 20–29.

We wonder if these children's struggles in reading might have begun in their early years when they were asked to master phonics, for which they were developmentally unready. Moreover, many of these older students, failing to learn to read through phonics, simply received more phonics, slower phonics, and intensive phonics. Rather than an alternative route to reading, many of these students were pushed down a road that already had too many obstacles to negotiate successfully. It is easy to imagine how they became turned off to reading. While their normally achieving classmates moved on to reading for pleasure and information, these students were stuck reading less and drilling more (Allington, 1977, 1983, 1994).

The Test of Phonemic Segmentation is a tool of enormous value. Identifying students at risk as early as possible may save many children from years of reading frustration. Insight into the problems of older readers allows educators to either help these students overcome their problems in phonemic awareness or design an alternative instructional program that bypasses phonics.

A number of other assessments for phonemic awareness are available commercially, in professional journals, and online. DIBELS (Good & Kaminski, 2001) is a commonly used, though sometimes controversial, assessment. It is not in the scope of this book to go into the controversy. Suffice it to say we believe good teachers are capable of making professional decisions about assessment and do not need to employ a tightly scripted method. We are confident that informed teachers will research possible phonemic awareness assessments, find what works best for them and their students, and proceed to do what is best for the children.

TEACHING AND NURTURING PHONEMIC AWARENESS THROUGH WORD PLAY AND WRITING

One of the most useful strategies for bringing phonemic awareness into kindergarten and preschool classrooms is simply bringing rhymes, chants, and songs that feature and play with language sounds into the classroom or clinic. Younger children may profit most from the reading and rereading of nursery rhymes, jump-rope chants, and children's poetry and songs. Playing with nursery rhyme lines such as

Dickery dickery dare, the pig flew up in the air . . .

Hey diddle diddle, the cat and the fiddle . . .

Diddle diddle dumpling, my son John . . .

helps children grasp the concept of the sound of *d* (/d/). And the tongue-twisting rhyme, "Peter Piper picked a peck of pickled peppers . . ." will help children develop an awareness of /p/.

Jump-rope chants, poems, and songs can serve the same purpose. Griffith and Olson (1992) recommended that teachers read rhyming texts and other texts that play with sounds to students daily and help develop students' sensitivity to sounds. Moreover, these texts can be altered to feature different language sounds (Yopp, 1992). For example, the familiar refrain of "Ee-igh, ee-igh, oh" in "Old MacDonald" can be transformed into "Dee-igh, dee-igh, doh" to emphasize /d/. The "Camptown Races" exclamation can be changed from "dooh dah" to "booh bah" or "sooh sah," depending on the sound being emphasized.

Older students can approach the same task with more sophisticated texts. Rhymed poetry for older children, as well as tongue twisters and lyrics to popular songs and raps, lend themselves to being learned, altered, rewritten, and ultimately performed to emphasize particular language sounds.

Hinky Pinkies are another type of game activity for developing sound awareness in a playful way. Hinky Pinkies are simply riddles for which the answer is two or more rhyming words. To make one, begin with the rhyming answer and then come up with the riddle that describes it. For example, if "sandy candy" is the answer, the question might be *What do you call sweet stuff that you drop on the beach?* Students love making and figuring out Hinky Pinkies.

These textual activities require students to attend to language sounds in order to perform the song or rap, or provide the correct response to the riddle. Inviting students to play with language in this way develops their sensitivity to sounds. In addition to songs and poems, many books deal with sounds. For example, the letter *M* page of *Dr. Seuss's ABC* (1963) states, "Many mumbling mice are making midnight music in the moonlight . . . mighty nice." Another example is Cameron's *"I Can't," Said the Ant* (1961); children can't help but hear the rhyming words on every page. Look for books with rhyme, alliteration, onomatopoeia, and sound repetition—look for books that tickle the tongue! (See Yopp, 1995b, for an extensive list of books.) Although these books are most appropriate for younger children, older students needing help with phonemic awareness can pair with younger students and learn to read such books to their younger buddies. The books also lend themselves to many useful extensions, including having students write their own versions of the stories by changing the sounds emphasized.

Some literacy scholars suggest that reading and sharing alphabet books can help develop phonemic awareness in students (Brabham, Murray, & Hudson, 2001). Many of the letters of the alphabet have their sounds embedded in their names. Moreover, alphabet book texts often contain alliterative sentences and passages aligned with the target letters that focus readers' attention on distinct sounds associated with the letters.

Other scholars (Clay, 1985; Griffith & Klesius, 1990; Morris, 1998) argue that writing—in particular writing in which students are encouraged to use their knowledge of sound-symbol correspondences, also known as developmental (invented) or phonemic spelling—is a powerful way to help students develop their phonemic awareness as well as basic phonics knowledge. When students attempt to write words using their knowledge of language sounds and corresponding letters, they segment sounds in words and order and blend the sounds to make real words. Even if the words are spelled unconventionally, this type of writing provides students with unequaled practice in employing their knowledge of sounds. When a child, for example, spells the word *truck* as *chruk,* that child is making a written and phonological representation of the word that is probably closer to the actual way that most people pronounce *truck* than the correct conventional spelling itself. Thus this child, although not spelling the word correctly, is still making wonderful use of sound and letter knowledge.

The research behind developmental or phonemic spelling, by the way, makes clear that it is simply a developmental stage. Just as children move from babbling and incorrect pronunciation when learning to talk to full and correct pronunciation, children move rapidly toward correct spelling. By the late primary grades little if any difference in spelling proficiency appears between children taught to spell in a highly rigid and disciplined system and other children who receive encouragement and support to play with their knowledge of sounds and letters through invented spelling. In fact, one study of first-graders showed that children encouraged to invent their spellings were more fluent writers and better word recognizers than children who experienced a traditional spelling curriculum (Clarke, 1988). Considering all the sound-symbol thinking that occurs when children invent their spelling, these results are no surprise.

TEACHING AND NURTURING PHONEMIC AWARENESS THROUGH MORE FOCUSED ACTIVITIES

For many children, playful reading, reciting, and performance of sound-oriented texts are enough to develop appropriate sound awareness for reading in kindergarten and primary grades (Ericson & Juliebo, 1998). Other children, younger children at risk, and older students who lack sufficient phonemic awareness skills and have profited little from phonics instruction need more specific instruction. Yopp (1992) has identified several conceptual levels of activity to develop phonemic awareness:

- Sound matching
- Sound isolation
- Sound blending
- Sound substitution
- Sound segmentation

These levels provide a framework for designing instruction that comprehensively treats phonemic awareness instruction in a sequence from easy to more complex and that eventually leads to learning the associations of sounds to written letters and letter combinations (phonics).

Sound Matching   As the name implies, *sound matching* simply requires students to match a word or words to a particular sound. A teacher who asks students to think of words that begin with /p/ challenges students to find words that match that sound. Having students think of the way they form their mouths to articulate individual sounds may help them match to other words and form a more lasting internal concept of the sound. Sound matching can extend to middle (vowel) sounds, ending sounds, and rhyming words.

Another sound-matching activity involves presenting students with three words, two of which have the same beginning sound, for example, *bat, cat, cane*. Students must determine which two words have the same initial sound. Again, this same sort of activity plays with middle and ending sounds as well as with rhyming words.

Sound Isolation   *Sound-isolation* activities challenge students to determine the beginning, middle, or ending sounds in a word or set of words. For example, the teacher may say three words that begin with the same sound (*this, that, them*) and ask students to tell what sound begins the words (Yopp, 1992). The same procedure works for middle and ending sounds as well as for word families or rimes (explained later). As students develop proficiency in determining individual sounds from similar words, they can analyze for individual sounds from single words. For example, the teacher may ask what beginning sound students hear in these words: *bake, swim, dog, pin, that*. Using the same set of words, students can work to determine (isolate) the middle and ending sounds.

Sound Blending   *Sound-blending* activities move students to the kind of synthesis used to decode words using phonics. In a game or sing-song format, the teacher simply presents students with individual sounds and asks them to blend the sounds together to form a word. The teacher might, for example, say to the class, "I am thinking of a kind of bird and here are the sounds in its name /d/, /u/, /k/" (Yopp, 1992). Of course, the children should say *duck* as the correct response. If this sort of task is too difficult, teachers can make it easier by presenting three pictures of birds and asking students to pick the correct one from the presentation of sounds. Students who are more adept at the activity can come up with their own questions and present their own sounds and riddles to classmates.

Sound Substitution   *Sound substitution* requires students to subtract, add, or substitute sounds from existing words. Questions such as "What word do you get when you take the /p/ off of *pin?*" require students to segment sounds from words and then reblend the sounds using the remaining sounds. Similarly, teachers can add sounds to existing words to make up new words: "Add /t/ to the beginning of *win*, and what do you get?"

   If students can add and subtract sounds, they are ready to try substituting one sound for another in words. You might ask students to consider what the names of their classmates might be if all their names began with a particular sound, for example (Yopp, 1992). If /s/ were the new sound, Billy's name would become Silly, and Mary and Gary would have the same name—Sary. Middle and ending sounds can also be substituted as students develop proficiency with initial sound substitution.

Sound Segmentation   As the title implies, *sound-segmentation* activities require students to go beyond isolating one sound in a word to determining all the constituent sounds. This may begin with simply segmenting words into *onsets* (the sounds that precede the vowel in a syllable) and *rimes* (the vowel and consonants beyond the vowel in a syllable; another name for word family). So, *stack* would be segmented into /st/ and /ak/. Later, students can segment words into their specific sounds. This time, *stack* would be segmented into /s/, /t/, /a/, /k/.

   All the generic activities described here can easily turn into a variety of games, performances, and playful activities. Informed teachers make these activities engaging and enjoyable for students and also share them so that parents can participate in their children's development of phonemic awareness.

Making It Concrete for Students   The notion of playing with sounds is somewhat abstract for many students. Think about it—sounds cannot be seen or held. You can't even make them stay, because as soon as you make a sound, it's gone. Children who learn tasks best in concrete ways often find sound awareness difficult. One way to make the task more concrete is to use physical objects to represent sounds—say, colored blocks. The teacher, for example, might have each block of a different color represent a particular sound. A blue block can represent /b/, the red block can be the /t/, the white block can be /a/, and the yellow block can represent /i/. Using these blocks, then, teachers can work with individuals and groups of students in learning to blend, substitute, and segment sounds in words.

In such activities, teachers put, for example, the blue, white, and red blocks in a row and ask students to blend the sounds into the word *bat*. Then, teachers remove the blue block to make the word *at*. If the red block is moved from the end of the word to the beginning, the sound produced becomes /ta/. Four or five blocks, each representing a sound, can provide many opportunities for students to make sense of how sounds work.

Older students already familiar with the alphabet can accomplish the same task with magnetic letters on a cake pan, with the added important feature of having the letters that represent the sounds in words.

Griffith and Olson (1992) also advocate the use of Elkonin boxes, popularized by Reading Recovery, to add a dimension of concreteness in hearing and segmenting sounds. An *Elkonin box* is simply a series of boxes drawn on a sheet of paper (see Figure 5.2). As students listen to words the teacher reads and hear discrete sounds, they push markers into the boxes, one marker for each sound. Later, as children become more familiar with written letters, they can write individual letters or letter combinations that represent individual sounds in the words.

Creating Powerful Instructional Routines

Informed teachers put these and other texts and activities together to support children's early efforts at reading. Brief (5 to 10 minutes and throughout the day) instructional routines (see Chapter 12) that combine several activities provide powerful and effective instruction for students.

We need to emphasize that phonemic awareness, although important for reading, is not the whole package. Teachers and children should develop student literacy skills in many other ways. For example, children need to be read to daily from the best children's literature available. They need to explore word meanings with the teacher daily, and daily language experience stories should be part and parcel of every elementary classroom. Predictable books, big books, poems, and stories should be read in a supportive environment.

FIGURE 5.2   An Elkonin Box

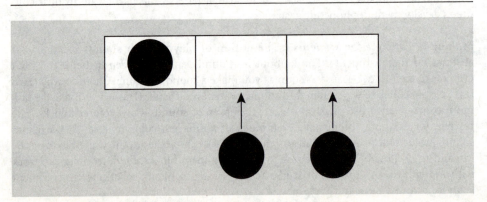

Although phonemic awareness is important for later success in reading, it is only one part of a comprehensive and effective program for young children and many older students who struggle in reading.

As the old saying goes, "An ounce of prevention is worth a pound of cure." In a way, the ideas presented in this chapter are both prevention and cure. That is, we have answered two related questions in this chapter: How can teachers prevent beginning readers from becoming at risk? When beginners struggle, what can classroom teachers or specialists do to help them grow as readers? The answer to both questions is to plan instruction that is developmentally, theoretically, and empirically appropriate.

DISCUSSION QUESTIONS

Some of the discussion questions for each chapter ask you to think through your own work as a teacher. If you are not currently a practicing teacher, try to respond to these questions from your own school experience (either from when you yourself were a student or from visits to schools that you have made in your teacher education program).

1. It is absolutely critical that the teacher also write and show students what she or he has written. Do students see you as a model of writing as often as they see you as a model of reading? What are some ways teachers can share their love of writing with children?

2. Describe a whole-part-whole lesson you have taught or could teach.

3. Do a Google search using the search term *phonemic awareness assessment*. Select an assessment that you believe might be effective. Share the strategy with your colleagues. If you have access to young children, administer the assessment. What did you learn?

4. Fortunately, most students develop phonemic awareness naturally through their everyday early childhood experiences. Does your district have a formal phonemic awareness program? If so, is it taught to all children or only those who need it? If only to those who need it, how is that determined?

5. The term *developmentally appropriate practice* is used so freely in early childhood circles that it is sometimes misused simply to justify what someone wants to do. What does *developmentally appropriate practice* mean to you? How does the National Association for the Education of Young Children define it?

Chapter *Six* ❧

Overcoming Difficulties in Word Recognition

READING INVOLVES CONSTRUCTING MEANING from written text. Clearly, unless readers have some understanding of the text, we can hardly say they are reading. To construct meaning, however, readers must recognize words accurately and effortlessly. By *recognize*, we mean the ability to decode or translate written symbols grouped into words into their oral representation, even if that translation is done within the reader's head, as in silent reading. Word recognition includes phonics—decoding words using the symbol-sound relationships in words. Word recognition also involves using other means to decode words: context, structural cues such as affixes and base words, and the development of students' sight vocabulary (words recognized instantly with minimal analysis).

Research and literacy scholars consistently support the need for instruction in word recognition for students in the elementary grades and those who are not proficient in decoding words (e.g., Armbruster, Lehr, & Osborn, 2001; Bear et al., 2007; Beck, 2006; Ehri, 1994; Fox, 2004; National Reading Panel, 2000; Stahl, Duffy-Hester, & Stahl, 1998). What is less clear is the ideal form or method for delivering word recognition instruction. We believe that optimal instruction in word recognition is not only dependent on the method but also on the critical and dynamic interaction of students and teacher. Certain approaches work best for certain students and certain teachers. Although we do not advocate any specific program or approach, we do know that word recognition instruction needs to be regular, consistent, direct, and systematic. And for students who struggle in learning to recognize words, the intensity of the instruction needs to be higher.

The less efficient readers are at recognizing or decoding written words, the more mental energy they must devote to the task. Thus, they have less mental energy available for making sense of the text as a whole. We want readers to become so efficient at word recognition that they can decode words with minimal effort and focus a maximum amount of their attention on making sense of the author's message. When students encounter familiar words, they should recognize them instantly or automatically—that is, with minimal use of conscious attention. Unfamiliar words (often longer or content-specific words) should be recognized quickly and accurately by using effective word recognition strategies.

In our work with struggling readers, we have noticed many who demonstrate difficulty in word recognition and fluency. When readers misread or mispronounce 10 percent or more of the words in text, they will experience significant difficulty in making sense of their reading. These are readers who labor over too many words, struggle to sound them out, repeating many words several times before pronouncing them, often pronouncing them incorrectly, and hesitating before attempting unfamiliar words. They seem to treat reading as a task of "getting the words right" rather than comprehending the text. We admire students who persevere and make any sense out of what they read when their reading is frustratingly slow and labored. Nevertheless, they find reading much more difficult than it ought to be.

Less proficient readers—the children this book aims to support—are likely to experience even more frequent and debilitating problems with words. Because of the extra effort and time required to decode words, children with word recognition difficulties read fewer words than more proficient readers. As a result, they make smaller gains in word recognition, comprehension, and overall reading proficiency. Without effective intervention they continue to fall behind and associate reading with frustration and failure. Word recognition instruction is appropriate for all students, including ELL students. Many English language learners struggle with word decoding in the same way that native English speakers do; word recognition instruction will certainly benefit these children as well (August & Shanahan, 2006; Goldenberg, 2008)

Word recognition develops as a result of daily and sustained reading experience and through direct and systematic instructional interventions. Word recognition should be so well developed that it becomes an unconscious part of the reading process. Listen to the good readers you know. They recognize words so effortlessly yet precisely that you hardly pay attention to their word recognition. What you do notice is their ability to process the text in a way that makes meaning easily accessible to the reader and listener.

We agree with some literacy scholars who criticize traditional teaching of word recognition. In the past, word recognition instruction was largely divorced from meaningful and engaging reading. More often, word recognition instruction and activities were designed to be completed independently without teacher assistance or interaction. Students passively completed workbooks and worksheets, did incessant and meaningless drills on words or parts of words in isolation, and memorized phonics rules and generalizations. Such approaches are not the most efficient, effective, or meaningful ways to develop proficiency in word recognition.

Word recognition develops best when it is an integral part of meaningful and authentic reading experiences. Children learn to deal with words when they are actively involved in interesting and constructive experiences. The following principles will help you create instructional experiences that keep students' attention focused on reading while allowing them to explore the nature and structure of written words.

- Word recognition instruction should be an inherent part of real reading experiences. It should proceed from a whole text to examination of parts of the text and then back again to the whole. That is, word recognition instruction should begin with authentic reading; move gradually to instruction in particular words and parts of words from that text; and end with a return to the text in the form of rereading, responding, or reading something else. Moreover, after instruction in a skill or strategy, students should have the opportunity to consider its usefulness or applicability to their reading (see an example of whole-to-part-to-whole instruction in Chapter 5).

- Word recognition instruction should allow students some freedom to choose, explore, make, and play with words. This playfulness encourages the risk-taking behavior that leads to insight. By thinking about and acting on words they create for themselves, children develop a thorough understanding of how words work.

- Instruction should include daily and extended times for group and independent reading of authentic texts that offer opportunities for students to put their word recognition competencies to use. Students need many chances to apply their decoding knowledge for the essential purpose of reading: making sense of printed discourse. Only in this way will students master word recognition strategies and, through exposure to a multitude of words in their reading, make their subsequent recognition of words more efficient and effortless.

- Word learning requires students to see and read words repeatedly. In addition to reading words daily on lists or flash cards, students need to see words in a variety of texts. Multiple exposures are the result of seeing and reading the words in many texts that contain the target words. Sandy McCormick (1994, 1995) has called this principle of word recognition instruction *multiple contexts/multiple exposures.* Her own work with struggling readers demonstrates the power of this principle.

- Materials used for word recognition instruction should manifest balance between decodability and predictability. Decodable texts contain numerous words or word parts that students know or can decode, and should be able to read in text. Students can also read predictable texts, with their easy-to-detect patterns of repeated phrases, sentences, or other language units. Because they are so easy to read and memorize, however, repeated readings of such texts should include detailed and focused examination of individual words in the text as part of word recognition instruction. This process of going from a rich authentic text to the study of words and word parts is called *decontextualization.*

- Words are learned most effectively, especially for struggling readers, when students are guided in the manipulation of written letters and sounds. Through thoughtfully planned instruction, teachers guide students in discovering that letters and combinations of letters represent different language sounds; that words are made up of a combination of letters and a combination of sounds; and that when letters are manipulated, the sound of the resulting combination of letters changes. When done well, such guided manipulation of letters and sounds can have the feel of a game for most children.

Any materials that repeat certain words, word parts, or phrases provide a natural context for repeated exposures. Verse poetry, chants, and lyrical songs also provide near-perfect textual environments for word recognition. Often, series books are excellent choices for reading and word recognition; many of the same words and concepts find their way from one book in a series to another. Moreover, familiar characters, plots, and author styles make series books highly predictable (and successful) reads for all readers.

Texts of students' own composition can produce powerful word recognition instruction. Because students express their own words and ideas in the compositions, familiarity is guaranteed. Creative teachers also generate texts—stories or poems—that highlight and use words students are studying. Adding a personal touch by including students' names or familiar settings and events can make such texts even more inviting and predictable. The excitement of knowing the author of a text is added incentive to read it well. A selection with too many unfamiliar words may overwhelm the reader, though, so short texts that contain fairly familiar words are optimal.

- The teacher's role in word recognition instruction is to help students understand and use basic word recognition strategies and then immediately apply them to real reading. Teachers should never treat word recognition development as an end in itself but constantly and vigorously turn students' attention to applying the strategies in real reading. Be cautious about testing students' skills in applying various strategies when their actual reading indicates that they recognize the words they encounter. Never treat word recognition as a set of skills to be taught, mastered, and tested outside actual reading. In fact, word recognition skill is worth little unless it can be applied to the task of reading and making meaning from written words.

Old and New Ways of Word Recognition Instruction

Traditional word recognition instruction features lists of words in isolation, flash cards, learning phonics rules or generalizations (e.g., "When two vowels go walking, the first one does the talking"), and repetitive drills with isolated words. We believe this approach to word recognition has serious problems. The number of children who have difficulty learning to recognize words suggests that they, too, have serious problems with the old way. Theodore Clymer (1996) examined phonics rules often taught to elementary students and found that a significant number apply less often than one might think. The "two vowels go walking" rule, for example, applied to only 45 percent of the words with two adjacent vowels found in elementary reading books.

Many activities in this chapter can extend into flash-card and word-list reading activities, but we are cautious about recommending their extensive and exclusive use. Although some evidence indicates that flash-card work can aid students' word learning (Nicholson, 1998), we suggest it be only a limited part of word-study instruction. Extended and dominant use of flash cards in a reading program tends to communicate the message that reading is simply a matter of sounding the words correctly rather than making sense of the passages. It also implies that word-by-word reading is the way to process text. Even more important, a set of isolated words contains little of inherent interest.

The best complement to word-list or flash-card reading is real contextual reading. In real reading, students practice words and phrases, work to comprehend the author's message, and learn and enjoy the fruits of their efforts in ways that real readers do. It bears repeating that one of the most enduring findings in all reading research is that good readers read a lot and poor readers read little. We must learn to maximize students' contextual reading because it is the best practice for improving their reading.

Jane works with students who have significant difficulty learning words, yet she chooses not to engage in flash-card activities with them:

> I don't use flash-cards for a number of reasons. I know it sends a message to the kids about what's important about reading. It's also a very inefficient activity. As one student is looking at a flash-card, the other students I'm working with are usually thinking about something else. I prefer to encourage my students to read. Through wide reading they will encounter the words on the flash-cards. And they also deal with contextual clues, phrasing, and making sense of the passage. Real reading makes a lot more sense than the humdrum flash-cards.

Other teachers we know use flash cards for quick warm-up activities that foster automatic recognition of high-frequency words.

We advocate word recognition instruction that features a great deal of student choice about and ownership over words. Students will more easily and enduringly learn words meaningful to them and their friends. Word recognition should provide opportunities for students to think, talk about, act on, and use words and elements of words and consider how they work. To become good at recognizing words, students need to know how words work and how elements from known words can inform them about unknown ones. They accomplish this by discussing words with others, thinking about words, playing with and acting on words, and using words in the context of real reading and writing, not by mindless drill and memorization.

In the following sections we describe various effective word recognition strategies. We have used them with success in our classrooms and clinical programs. As with all instructional strategies, however, they should never be given to students in a mechanical or uniform way. Informed teachers design lesson formats that both meet students' needs and match their own styles of teaching.

PHONICS

Phonics refers to the relationships between sound and spelling patterns within written language and the reader's use of this knowledge to decode unknown words. We believe, and research tends to confirm, that phonics knowledge is extremely useful to readers. Some readers develop and use phonics knowledge naturally. Others need direct and systematic guidance from knowledgeable teachers to understand and use phonics generalizations. We do not question whether phonics should be taught but rather to whom and how.

We disagree strenuously with the uninteresting, mindless, mechanical way in which phonics is presented in many classrooms today. Indeed, we are convinced that many children end up in remedial reading classes, permanently turned off from reading, because of the incessant skill-and-drill activities and worksheets foisted on them. In some classrooms first- and second-graders spend more time saying "buh, aah, tuh; baaaat; bat" than they do reading real, interesting books. As a result, we see many unmotivated children in remedial reading classes who think that reading is more about sounding out the letters than trying to make sense of the passage.

Steven Stahl (1992) has identified several principles that may help guide teachers in developing phonics instruction for their classrooms or clinics. These principles include the following:

1. Phonics learning should proceed from what children already know about reading. It should gradually move from an understanding of stories toward an analysis of letter-sound relationships within stories students have read. Phonics, as part of a total word recognition program, should proceed from whole to part. Moreover, phonics and word recognition instruction is only one part of the total reading program, whether in a classroom or a remedial reading setting. Students, first and foremost, need to both read and talk about what they are reading.

2. Phonics instruction should be clear, direct, brief, and focused on real words and text. Activities in which children circle pictures, color, cut and paste, and so on, do not help them learn the essentials of phonics.

3. Phonics instruction should focus on reading words, not learning rules. It should lead directly to students using their new knowledge to read words and stories. When children encounter unknown words, teachers should model or explain how phonics knowledge can help unlock letter patterns and decode the words.

4. Phonics instruction should focus on onsets and rimes within syllables, with the ultimate goal of students noticing letter patterns within words. *Onsets* are the part of a syllable before the vowel, and *rimes* are the part of the word from the vowel to the end of the syllable. Rather than focusing on individual letters, students who deal with onsets and rimes can attend to larger segments of words and syllables more easily recognized and more consistent in pronunciation. Fry (1998) has demonstrated that knowledge of a limited number of rimes can be used to decode a remarkably large number of one-syllable and multisyllabic words.

5. Children need opportunities to experiment with and manipulate letters and sounds in making words. Developmental spelling, for example, helps students develop and apply phonics knowledge. Successful teachers encourage children to experiment with the writing and spelling system. Although unconventional, these spellings allow children to apply their knowledge of sounds, letters, and letter patterns in their writing. Preliminary work in this area suggests that children who are encouraged to invent their spellings are better at decoding than those who learn to spell and read in more traditional programs. Although many reading scholars call this invented spelling, we prefer to call it *developmental spelling*, as it reflects children's ongoing growth or development in learning about words.

Based on our own work with struggling readers and recent research into effective instruction, we would add a few more principles to Stahl's list.

6. Students learn words by comparing and contrasting words and elements in words as they learn. In a review of effective instructional strategies, Marzano and colleagues

(2001) identified a set of teaching and learning strategies demonstrated as effective through instructional research. At the top of their list is analyzing items under study for similarities and differences, which is done through word sorts. In *word sort* activities, students group words according to criteria established by the teacher or class member (e.g., "Put all words that contain the long *o* sound in one pile and those that don't in another"). We describe word sorts in more detail later in this chapter.

7. Teach only those generalizations students must learn. If a child demonstrates mastery over a phonics element, do not teach it. That student's time and effort would be better spent employing those generalizations in real reading. Of course, this requires teachers to be good observers of students' reading behavior—teasing out what they know from what they don't by watching students read, talking with them, and observing them in interactions with others.

Many of the instructional activities described in this section deal with elements of phonics. Children need to learn how to use phonics, but only within an environment of real and purposeful reading. Encourage other activities that guide students in letter and word manipulation and experimentation, too.

LANGUAGE EXPERIENCE APPROACH

The *language experience approach (LEA)* to reading is often associated with beginning reading instruction, but we have found it an excellent format for providing word recognition instruction at a variety of levels. In LEA, students use texts that they themselves have composed; therefore, they have the important benefit of dealing with stories and words with which they are already familiar and understand. Students own the text and words.

In the basic form of LEA, students dictate, either individually or in a group, their own brief text to the teacher. The teacher writes the students' text on a sheet of large chart paper or, for one child, on a sheet of notebook-size paper. After several readings over several days, students become familiar with many of the words and identify them more effectively in other reading settings. In fact, Stauffer (1980), an LEA pioneer, suggests that students have copies of their dictations on which they underline the words they can recognize each time they read the texts.

Once children become adept at reading the whole text, teachers often begin the process of decontextualization: They begin to focus attention on parts of the text (sentences, phrases, words, letters, and letter combinations) as they strip away parts of the context. Students' initial success in reading the story may reflect their use of context (such as pictures or familiar phrases) as well as familiarity with the whole passage. Decontextualization requires students to take a closer look at individual sentences, phrases, words, word parts, and even letters and letter combinations.

One way in which some teachers decontextualize is by using sentence strips and word cards from the passage. Paula, a Title I teacher, has had great success using LEA with students. She tries to do at least two texts each week. For example, on Monday she might discuss an interesting experience from the previous week with her students. After the discussion, the group dictates a story related to the experience, which Paula writes on chart paper. At the end of the session the students and Paula read the dictation several times—chorally, individually, orally, silently, and with Paula reading while the children follow along.

On Tuesday, after a few rereadings of the story (as well as stories from previous lessons), Paula engages her students in decontextualization activities. She creates a second copy of the text on chart paper and begins to cut this copy into sentence strips in front of the students. Together, the group practices reading the sentences and puts them in their original order to remake the story. They also experiment with reordering the sentences. After some work with sentence strips, Paula cuts the strips into phrase strips and word cards that are also practiced, sorted into various categories of the students' choosing, put together to form new sentences, and played with in other ways. Students and teacher experiment with changing word beginnings, middles, and ends to make new words. Paula also makes copies of the story for all students to read on their own in school and at home to their parents.

On Wednesday, Paula may continue reading the story and playing with its words and sentences, depending on how well the students have learned the story and its parts. She also will begin a new LEA story with her class about the interesting speaker who came to school on Tuesday. She will make it a point to return to Monday's story periodically over the next several weeks.

KEY WORDS AND WORD BANKS

Key words and word banks are forms of decontextualization that give students some personal control and investment in the words they learn. This personal ownership of words provides a powerful incentive for students' learning. A *key word* is simply one that the student chooses from a reading. Students choose particular words because they find them interesting—the way they sound, their length, or what they represent. Children will often choose words well beyond those typically found in materials for their age or grade level. Because the words are their own, however, students learn them easily and recognize them quickly in future reading. We have seen kindergartners and beginning first-graders choose and learn words such as *microphone, pondering, carriage,* and *malevolent.*

When key words are written on index cards, they become part of a student's word bank. A *word bank* is a collection of words taken from students' reading and chosen by the students and the teacher. We have found that one or two story words chosen by the student and one chosen by the teacher are sufficient to maintain an active word bank. Students may choose any words they like, but teachers might choose those that can be generalized into other words by substituting letters or adding word parts. (For example, *dog* can be expanded into *doggy* or can be part of a word family that includes *log* and *jog.*) Children should control the size of their word bank as well as the words that go into it.

One idea is for students to keep two word banks: one in which they keep words they are learning, and another in which they keep words they can recognize on sight. Students choose the bank appropriate for each word and decide when a word moves from one bank to another. Words in both word banks can be practiced, sorted, used to make sentences, or used to play word games with other people. Moreover, teachers can use the contents of students' word banks to teach phonic principles. For example, students can sort their *a* words into groups according to the sounds that *a* makes in the words.

This immersion and practice with words develops students' word recognition proficiency. For every LEA story, Paula's students write their key words on cards and share them with the group, telling why they chose their particular words and making up sentences that include the words. Paula also chooses a word that students write on cards and add to their word banks. From the most recent LEA story, Paula chose *table,* which she will use to illustrate the words that can be made from the *-able* word part and discuss the "consonant plus *le*" generalization.

Several times a week Paula's students warm up for reading by reading their word bank words with a partner. Partners also use their word-bank words to make sentences. At least once a week students sort their word-bank words into categories that Paula provides or that students think of. Students also use their word banks for games such as Word Match (duplicate sets of word cards are laid face down and players find matching pairs) and Word War (the word played with the most letters and read correctly wins the war). In addition, Paula uses word banks to practice alphabetizing and other word-related concepts such as word families and phonics generalizations.

COMMUNITY WORD BANK

Most word banks are year-long affairs. Students begin their banks early in the year and add and remove words throughout the year. The sense of continuity and accomplishment garnered as words are mastered and removed from the bank is a positive feature of such banks. However, teachers and students may wish to add a bit of variety to their word-bank activities; moreover, teachers may want banks that contain the same words for all students. This may be accomplished through an alternative we call the *community word bank.*

One major positive of a community word bank is its connection to real literature read by or to students. The weekly word bank begins with the students reading a selection or the teacher reading a selection to them, usually near the end of the week. Students are asked to identify words from the selection they find interesting. Between 10 and 20 words are identified and discussed after the reading. Students explain their reasons for choosing their words. This helps them understand the power that comes from an unusual word, a word that has a peculiar sound, or a word that fits the context of a selection perfectly. Students will become better wordsmiths in their own writing after they think about words chosen by authors whom they read.

The chosen words are displayed on a sheet of chart paper, whiteboard, or smartboard. Students (and teacher) use the words in their writing and conversation throughout the next week. Students also make word cards and store them in individual envelopes. Students may practice the words with a partner, use the words in their writing, play games with the words, put them in alphabetical order, or try to make up sentences using two or more words for each sentence. But the most important part of the weekly word bank is the daily word-sort activities students engage in during the week.

WORD SORTS

Word sorts invite individual and small groups of students to categorize words according to some dimension identified by the teacher or a student. Students use their knowledge and learn from and with each other. Teachers can focus on particular word elements, depending on student need, or the activity can be totally student centered. Moreover, word sorts work particularly well when students in small groups sort the words from their individual word banks. Here are some categories we have seen teachers use in their word-sort activities with students:

- Words sorted into three piles: words with one syllable, words with two syllables, and words with three or more syllables
- Words that contain consonant blends (anywhere in the word) and words that don't
- Words with long vowel sounds, words with short vowel sounds, and words with both
- Words with other words spelled within them
- Words sorted into nouns, verbs, adjectives, and all others
- Words that describe a person's feelings and words that don't
- Words you really like and want to use in your speaking and writing and words you don't particularly like
- Words with more than one meaning and words with only one meaning

As you can see, students may enjoy an almost limitless number of sorts.

Paula uses word sorts with her students several times each week. After a mini-lesson on syllabication, Paula's students work in groups of three to sort their word-bank cards into words containing one, two, three, and more than three syllables. On other occasions, she asks students to sort words by initial consonants, vowels sounds, long and short vowels, prefixes and suffixes, and other word characteristics with which she wants her students to become familiar. She says,

> I think it's important for students to put into practice the strategies we are exploring. Word sorts give students the opportunity to test their knowledge with words they are already familiar with, and the sorts allow me to observe how well students have grasped and can use the strategies. I think it's also important to note that when groups of students use word sorts they actually teach and reinforce each other as they go.

Word sorts work because they are a two-barreled approach to word recognition. On the one hand, several word sorts with a set of words give students repeated exposure or practice with those words. This is a critical element of successful word recognition learning. On the other hand, every word sort requires students to examine each word from a particular perspective. During one sort students may look at a set of words for the number of syllables they contain. A second sort may require students to examine the same words for consonant blends or vowel digraphs. A third sort focuses on word meanings. With each new exposure to the words, students examine them from different perspectives. This helps students develop fully analyzed, in-depth knowledge of words, an essential word recognition skill, especially for those students who struggle in reading (Gaskins et al., 1997). Students can also sort their words into their own creative categories, an approach that Paula sometimes uses with her class. After a few minutes of sorting, groups of students try to guess (infer) the categories created by other groups. Sometimes Paula simply asks each group to explain its way of categorizing. "But they really prefer the guessing," she says. "It's like a game to them, but I'm constantly amazed at the high level of thinking."

WORD FAMILIES (PHONOGRAMS)

Many words that children encounter in their reading are made up of common word parts, or rimes. Recognizing the *an* word part can help students decode words such as *can, pan, ant, pant, fantasy,* and so on. Edward Fry (1998) has identified 38 of the most common *word families.* See Appendix B for a list of common word families and letter patterns. Knowledge of word families can help students figure out unknown words.

Word families, or phonograms, have had wide appeal to teachers for many years. The big question, though, is how they can be taught in a thorough manner that leads students to reading real text. We believe the following routine does just that. This three- or four-day sequence requires about 30 minutes per day, in which students go from brainstorming words belonging to a particular word family to actual reading and writing text that contains the word-family words. The routine goes as follows:

On the first day, the teacher introduces students to a particular word family. Perhaps the word family is *old,* as in *gold* and *fold.* The teacher begins by introducing students to the three-letter *phonogram* along with the distinct sound associated with the combination of the letters. Students examine the phonogram and its sound. Then, with the teacher, they brainstorm words that contain the phonogram, or that rhyme with it. The teacher writes words such as *gold, fold, mold, bold, sold, scold, cold, hold,* and *told* on chart paper as students pronounce them. Relatively rare or unfamiliar words are discussed as presented. In addition, the teacher and students contribute longer words, such as *golden, unfolded,* and *scaffold,* to illustrate that even longer words can be at least partially unlocked with their knowledge of the *old* phonogram. These words are then read a couple of times and discussed further.

The second day of this instructional routine begins with students again chanting and talking about the words they had brainstormed during the earlier session. The teacher introduces the students to short texts that contain several instances of the phonogram in question. In this case, students see the nursery rhyme *Old King Cole* written on another piece of chart paper. They listen to the teacher read it to them once or twice, then try it themselves, chorally, in groups, and individually if they like. Students may then point out words that contain the *old* phonogram. After this rhyme is read and discussed, a second poem is introduced and students read and examine it just as they did the first one.

When teachers cannot find a suitable poem, they can easily concoct their own or rewrite familiar song lyrics to feature the targeted phonogram. For example, *Mary Had a Little Lamb* could be rewritten as "Mary had a little gold" (that she liked to hold). These texts carry an important message to students. Students need to see their teachers as readers and writers if they are going to become readers and writers themselves.

At the end of the second day's session, the teacher asks students to use the phonogram being studied to write their own 4- to 6-line poems. If younger students or others struggle with the task, older more experienced students may act as coaches and aides to the budding poets. Some students may want to write their poem in pairs or groups in order to make the task less daunting. Teachers may also ask parents to assist their children in developing these simple rhymes. Students write their poems down on a piece of paper and practice them in anticipation of the third day's session.

On the third day, students use chart paper to write enlarged versions of their poems. The chart poems are then hung around the room. Reading instruction for this third day, then, consists of a poetry festival in which the entire class, or small groups therein, go around the room and read each poem several times, making sure to focus on words that belong to the targeted word family. If the author of a particular poem is in the group of students, that student author may begin by reading his or her poem aloud and explaining why and how it was produced. Following is the poem made up by one first-grade student, with his parents, after the class had studied the *et* phonogram and were now engaged in work on the *ick* phonogram.

Icky sticky prickly pet

Porcupines for dinner

Have you had yours yet?

This may not be a prize-winning poem, but the child who wrote it was proud of his composition as well as his fluent performance of the poem for classmates.

Students love to perform, and they love to write when they know that their work will be honored and celebrated. Moreover, when students learn about decoding words at the same time, we'd say you were onto big and powerful instruction.

Once students have written several poems, they can be easily published. The teacher simply collects the poems, types them, adds appropriate student artwork, and has students create a cover. Then the typed poetry collection is copied and bound for each student and the classroom. The pride students take in seeing their poetry published will lead them to reading the poems again and again and writing new ones.

LETTER-SOUND MANIPULATIONS

When students are guided by their teacher in manipulating letters to make words, they discover how written words work, how letters represent sounds, and how changing letters and their order within words changes the sounding (and meaning) of words. *Making Words* is a letter-sound manipulation activity to include in a comprehensive reading program (Cunningham & Cunningham, 1992). The activity has several key features. Students make up their own increasingly complex words by concretely manipulating a limited set of letters. Those who find word recognition difficult are often overwhelmed by the seemingly endless number of letters and letter-sound patterns they must encounter. Limiting the number of letters helps students focus on the essential characteristics of a few letters at a time. As with most activities, we recommend that students work in pairs or small groups so that they can learn more thoroughly by talking with and teaching each other.

Making Words begins when the teacher selects a "secret" word of between five and eight letters from students' previous reading and determines a set of words that can be made from the letters of the "magic" word. Anagram websites (e.g., www.wordsmith.org/anagram) are a good source for words.

The teacher hands out 1-inch squares of paper for each letter to each group, and calls out the letters of the "secret" word. Students write one letter on each slip. Then the fun begins.

Mel makes words with several of his primary Title I classes. He begins by asking student pairs to arrange the letters into two-letter words. Next, students call out their constructions and Mel writes a few of the words on the board. Mel also tells students words and observes their efforts to produce them with their letters. Next, students work through three-, four-, five-, and six-letter words. Mel writes many of these on the board as well. The activity ends with Mel challenging his students to determine the "secret" word—the word that uses all the letters from the day's lesson.

Mel and his students explore some of the words on the board, noticing word families and moving from one word to another through letter changes. "What would I have to do to change *part* to *art* to *par*? To change *art* to *arch*? To change *par* to *parka*?" Mel often cuts up a transparency into squares and does the activity with his students on an overhead projector so that students can see the manipulations. He may do the same with large index cards and a pocket chart. Making Words is fast paced. Students learn, in a concrete way, that words and the letters that form them can be manipulated in a variety of ways. Mel's students like the fast pace of the activity and being actively involved throughout the 10- to 15-minute session.

MAKING AND WRITING WORDS

Making Words is a powerful way to help students understand how words are composed of letters. Its use of letter cards or squares can be a bit messy, as cards fall to the floor or become lost during the lesson. *Making and Writing Words (MWW)* (Rasinski, 1999), a variation, involves students making words by writing them rather than manipulating letter cards. The act of writing the words may facilitate, even more, students' memory for the words that they make. Because MWW requires facility in writing, it may be more appropriate for slightly older students, grade 2 and above. The writing component of MWW adds to its teaching–learning potential by making the activity multisensory. In addition to using their eyes, ears, and mouths in making words, students in MWW also use their hands as they write the words they make on the activity sheet.

Just like Making Words, MWW begins with selecting a set of consonants and vowels to use in the lesson. Students write the letters in the appropriate boxes on a blank form. Then, as with Making Words, students are guided through a series of words using the given letters, from short words to longer words. The final word in the set is always a "secret" word that uses all the letters in the vowel and consonant boxes. Following is a scenario for the MWW activity. (See Figure 6.1.)

FIGURE 6.1   Making and Writing Words

Vowels		Consonants
1	6	11
2	7	12
3	8	13
4	9	14
5	10	15
T1	T2	T3
T4	T5	T6

Vowels: *a, o*
Consonants: *d, g, n, r*

- In box 1, write this two-letter word—*or*—as in "I would like either a bicycle *or* a basketball for my birthday."
- In box 2, write a two-letter word that means the opposite of *off. (on)*
- Box 3 needs a two-letter word that means the opposite of *stop. (go)*
- In boxes 4 and 5, write two words that belong to the *on* word family and that are boys' names; remember what special thing you have to do to names of people. (*Ron* and *Don*)
- For box 6, write a three-letter word that is a name of an animal that people like to have for pets. *(dog)*
- In box 7, write the word *rag.* Who can tell the class what a rag is? *(rag)*

- Box 8 is a word that rhymes with *rag* and that describes what a child says a parent does when asking the child several times to do something the child doesn't want to do. *(nag)*
- In box 9, write the word *drag;* it has four letters. *(drag)*
- Okay, in box 10 write the word that describes what you might have done with a bell; four letters. *(rang)*
- Great. Now, box 11 is the mystery word. See if you can figure out what word uses all the letters we have used. *(dragon)*

This secret word then becomes a segue into a story about dragons or a discussion or study of dragons. In addition, MWW forms include boxes marked T1 through T6 for transfer activities. Here, students write new words that rely on some of the patterns or letters found in the first 11 words, but also require application of new letters (all letters, *A* through *Z*, are now eligible for writing in the Transfer boxes). The transfer activities allow students to generalize some of the letters and letter patterns they had been working with to new words. Here are some transfer words students may be asked to write:

- In box T1, write the word *stagger.* Look at some of the words you have written earlier to help you figure this word out.
- In box T2, write a word that rhymes with *stagger* and means a small knife. *(dagger)*
- In box T3, write *drank.* Notice how *drank* and *dragon* begin with the same consonant blend.
- In box T4, use the same consonant blend as in *drank* to make a word that describes when water comes out of faucet one drop at a time. *(drip)*
- In box T5, add four letters to drip to make the word *dripping.* "The dripping faucet in my bathroom kept me awake all night long."
- And in box T6, make a word that rhymes with *dragon* and is a cart or vehicle that is used to carry things. Many children have one of these as a toy. *(wagon)*

In the final part of the MWW activity, students cut out the words they have just made and sort them into structural, pattern, and semantic categories.

Terri, a third-grade teacher, is a firm believer in Making Words. However, she finds that MWW makes the process easier for her and more engaging for all her students:

It's easy to do; all I do is choose the secret word, determine the words and their sequence to be made from the letters of the secret word, make copies of the Making and Writing Words sheet for each student, and we're ready to go. I like the idea that students actually write the words. Sometimes I ask them to write some of the more difficult words two or three times in the appropriate box so that they get a good mental and kinesthetic image for how the word is written. When I do Making and Writing Words, I usually do it with the students. If they have trouble, they only need to look up at what I have written on the smartboard. Of course, sometimes I make purposeful mistakes to make sure they check my work, too. We often take two or three days with one set of letters. I try not to take more than 15 minutes on this activity. I want to do other word and reading activities with my students. So, on the first day, we might do the making and transferring part of the activity. On the second and third days we usually do a quick review, especially of word families, do a few more transfer words, and then do some quick word sorts. Students like the fast pace to the activity. And they also like the fact that they can be successful at it themselves.

WORD LADDERS

Like Making Words and Making and Writing Words, *word ladders* allow students to build and examine words with support throughout the process. In word ladders, each new word students make is based on the previous word. Thus, students gain support from their previously made words.

Word ladders begin with the teacher asking the students to create a numbered list and write the first word of the ladder next to number 1. Then, the teacher guides students in making a new word for each number. The following word ladder demonstrates the process.

1. *trick*
2. *track* Change a letter in *trick* to make a word that describes what trains ride on.
3. *trace* Change a letter in *track* to make a word that describes the process of copying of a picture by placing a transparent sheet of paper atop the picture and drawing the copy.
4. *Grace* Change the first letter to make a girl's name.
5. *grate* Change a letter to make a word that describes what you do to shred a hunk of cheese into smaller pieces.
6. *great* Rearrange the last three letters in *grate* to make a homophone word that means big or wonderful.
7. *treat* Change a letter in *great* to make a word that goes with the word next to number 1.

In word ladders, the last word ideally should be associated with the first word. This simple feature often invites students to develop their own word ladders. Teachers can challenge students to go from *first* to *last* or from *girl* to *boy* by adding, subtracting, or changing one letter at a time, or rearranging the letters already in a word.

WORD WALLS

One goal in word recognition instruction is to create a physical classroom environment that encourages word exploration and play. One step toward creating such an environment is through *word walls*. Pat Cunningham describes word walls as one aspect of a four-part instructional strategy in reading (Cunningham & Cunningham, 1992; Cunningham, Hall, & Defee, 1998). We like to think of word walls as part community word bank and part graffiti wall—a place where students feel free to write their own words and commentaries.

A teacher may choose from several types of word walls and may have more than one word wall in her class. One might focus on words belonging to particular word families and be organized by word families. You might add selected words built during Making Words or Making and Writing Words activities to your word wall. Another word wall may direct students' attention to high-frequency sight words, such as those found in Appendix C. These words may be introduced at a rate of 3 to 5 per week (over the course of grades 1 through 3) and arranged alphabetically on this second word wall. A third wall, which we like to call the *graffiti wall*, contains words that teachers and students find interesting and provocative in their own reading. These may be placed alphabetically on the word wall, or randomly, as graffiti is often arranged. Finally, words that students encounter in other content areas may become the content of a fourth word wall. Of course, some teachers may want to integrate different types of words onto one word wall, but distinguish them by color or code (e.g., all words that have an asterisk next to them belong to a particular word family).

One of the great appeals of word walls is the implicit message they send to students and any other visitors to the room. Just imagine walking into a classroom in which you are greeted with words, words, and more words. Word walls tell students that words matter, that words are interesting, and that words are worth exploring and knowing. We can think of no other way to make this powerful message more apparent than through classroom word walls.

A word wall begins when the teacher places a large piece of butcher or chart paper on a classroom wall. Every day the class adds a word or two to the wall. Teacher and students explore other words related to the chosen words for the day and write them on the wall, often connecting them with lines like an idea web. Teacher and students also look for letter patterns in the chosen words and brainstorm other words that contain the pattern. Students practice and refer to the words on the wall often. In some classrooms, students may use the word wall to jot down their own words or ideas to be read by all students and to spur lively oral and written discussion.

Sherrie is a fifth-grade teacher. A visitor to her class can't miss the word wall; it takes up an entire bulletin board. One day the word *portage* was selected for the wall because a student encountered it in his reading. (The school, incidentally, is located in Portage County.) After talking about the meaning of the word, Sherrie and her students added and discussed other related words (either by meaning or structure). Among them were *canoe, river, port, porter, portable, sort, porous,* and *sage.* Sherrie reports that each word wall fills up in less than two weeks. She leaves it up for a few days after it is filled because her students often refer to the words in their own writing or discussion and continue to add words that connect to the ones on the wall. Even though the wall may look a bit messy after several days of student contributions, Sherrie notes that it is important to the class as a whole because the words are meaningful for students, and the wall itself is a joint venture to which all students want to contribute.

CONTEXTUAL ANALYSIS

In addition to analyzing letters and letter combinations to decode or recognize words, proficient readers use *context*. In other words, readers use passage and sentence meaning as well as their own knowledge about the world to predict unknown words. For example, consider the following sentence:

The mail carrier was bitten by a _____.

Readers figure out the unknown word by combining sentence information with what they know about the stereotypical predicament of postal carriers on their rounds. Combining this information leads to the prediction or inference that the missing word is most likely *dog*. Thus, a reasonable prediction can be made without using any letter or phonic information from the word itself.

You can help readers use context by asking them to think about what an unknown word might be, based on the meaning of the passage, rather than always advising them to "sound it out." Similarly, teachers occasionally explain to their students how they figure out unknown words in their own reading. Some experts call this explanation of one's problem-solving process "think-alouds." Teaching is about making such subtleties clear and apparent to students.

Another activity that helps develop readers' use of context is the *cloze procedure*. Cloze may seem like an odd name, but it is based on the psychological understanding that human beings attempt to provide closure or completeness to incomplete illustrations or objects. In the cloze procedure the reader attempts to impose closure on incomplete linguistic data by using the available contextual information. The teacher deletes certain words from a passage by marking over them with a marker or retyping the passage with blanks for the deleted words. Cloze texts for younger readers may be big books or chart stories in which the teacher simply covers selected words or word parts with sticky notes. Here is an example of a cloze activity taken from *Strega Nona's Magic Lesson* by Tomie dePaola (1982):

Bambolona, the baker's daughter, was angry. Every day, summer, fall, _____, and _____, she had to get up before the sun to bake the _____. Then, piling the _____ on her head, she went to deliver them.

When creating a cloze passage, it is a good idea to leave the first sentence intact so that readers can establish a mental framework for the text.

The reader's job is to use the context before and after the deleted words to identify the deletions. After completing a passage with 20 to 30 deletions, students share their guesses with one another and discuss the clues they used to make their predictions. The teacher may also provide the author's actual words. Cloze activities work well in groups as students verbalize their own strategies for predicting words with their partners.

The cloze procedure has several variations. Students unfamiliar with the procedure or who are dealing with a difficult text may be overwhelmed by a passage containing many deleted words. The task can be made easier by placing possible answers next to each blank or listing all the deleted words at the end of the passage. The activity is then called a *maze* or a *multiple-choice cloze*.

One day Bambolona said, "Papa, there is too much _____ (work, noise, money) to do. I need some _____ (fun, work, help)."

"Get up earlier," her father said.

"But I get up now before the _____!" said _____. "And I'm the last one in town to _____ to bed."

"That's the way things are," _____ father said as he went out the _____ on his way to the _____.

(Bambolona, square, her, go, door, sun)

Good readers simultaneously employ both context and letter information to decode difficult words. Cloze activities can be designed so that students integrate both sources of information about words. Here's an example from Gary Paulsen's *Hatchet* (1999):

Somehow the plane was still flying. Seconds had passed, nearly a m_____, and the plane f_____ on as if nothing had happened, and he had to do something, had to do something but did n_____ know what. . . .

He st_____ one h_____ toward the p_____, saw that his fingers were trembling, and touched the pilot on the chest. . . .

The pl_____ lurched again, hit more t_____, and Brian felt the nose dr_____. It did not d_____, but the n_____ went down slightly and the down-angle i_____ the speed, and he knew that at this angle, this slight angle d_____, he would ultimately f_____ into the tr_____.

In this passage readers employ both context and the beginning letter or letter combination, which are the most salient graphic cues for trying to recognize missing words.

Key elements in succeeding with the cloze procedure include choosing texts that challenge but do not overwhelm, giving students time and assistance in predicting the missing words, and encouraging students to share strategies and clues in identifying the unknown words. Karen, a Title I teacher who works with primary-grade children, finds that many students become so hung up on sounding out words that they fail to attend to the meaning of the passage. Karen designs cloze passages for these children. She chooses stories that students have read a few days previously and found interesting. "This ensures that the students have a familiarity with the content and that they have a motivation for reading," she says. As students become more adept at using context she may choose unfamiliar passages from a sequel or written by a familiar author.

She may also add challenge by increasing the number of blanks within a given passage but always ensuring that enough context remains for making good predictions. As a rule of thumb, Karen provides at least four words of text for every word she deletes when developing her most challenging cloze passages.

Karen believes that student talk really counts in cloze activities. "I think that the most important part of the cloze activity is when we talk after the groups have had a chance to fill in the blanks. Students talk about the various strategies they used to figure out the blanks. This is where you see the lights go on in students' heads as they say to themselves, 'Oh yeah! I didn't think about doing it that way.'"

DEALING WITH LONGER WORDS

Long words can daunt young and struggling readers, and initially these unfamiliar words are often difficult to handle as whole units. When proficient readers come to longer words, they tend to break the word into manageable chunks and apply basic word recognition strategies to the chunks until they become familiar with the word. Struggling readers should be guided to use the same type of approach. Readers can choose among several strategies to break down longer words into more manageable units.

Syllabication Rules   Longer words can often be broken into vowel-dominated sound units called *syllables*. Two basic syllabication rules can be quite helpful for students.

1. VCCV   When two vowels are separated by two consonants (each representing a consonant sound), try separating the word into syllables between the two consonants (e.g., *center, bottom, winter, cancel, mentor, chapter*).
2. VCV   When two vowels are separated by one consonant, try separating the word into syllables before the consonant (e.g., *open, basic, pilot, laser, final*).

Compound Words   *Compound words* are combinations of two whole words. For example, *everybody* divides into *every* and *body*, and either can be identified as a whole word or analyzed in smaller units.

Meaningful Word Patterns   Earlier in this chapter we mentioned the importance of recognizing patterns of letters within words in decoding words. Those patterns—called phonograms, word families, or rimes—are sound-based patterns. The combination of vowel and consonant produces a consistent sound that is helpful when attempting to decode an unknown word.

These are just a few kinds of patterns students should learn. Many worthwhile meaning-bearing patterns are found in prefixes, suffixes, and word parts derived from Greek and Latin. These are often called *morphemes*. Longer words are often divided into smaller parts by morphemes (prefixes, suffixes, base words) (e.g., *microscope, uniform, interplanetary, bicycle, submarine*).

Because these patterns bear meaning, knowledge of morphemes helps students decode and determine the meaning of words. For example, knowing that the following word patterns are derived from Greek and are meaningful—*acro* meaning high place, *polis* meaning city, and *phobia* meaning fear—will help readers decode and understand the words *acrophobia* and *Acropolis*. Indeed, creative minds can even invent new words, such as *poliphobia* (fear of cities), and challenge classmates to determine the meaning of the new words. Appendix E and Chapter 8 have more information about the use of Latin and Greek derivations to develop vocabulary.

Teaching these meaningful word patterns may resemble the routine used with phonograms. Day 1 might be a mini-lesson to introduce one or two patterns and invite students to identify words that contain them. Subsequent days could be spent writing, reading, and having fun with texts that contain the targeted patterns. With regular use, students will begin to make good use of their knowledge of meaningful patterns in their reading.

READING AND GAMES

The best way for students to put their word recognition strategies to use is through plenty of contextual reading. Through actual reading, readers become adept at using helpful word recognition strategies. Moreover, through repeated exposure to many words, they add to their sight vocabularies—words that can be recognized instantly at sight without having to rely on any recognition strategy. Thus, reading actually reduces the number of words readers must decode.

Many families take great enjoyment in playing games. Many of the games that our families play are word games. Games such as Scrabble, Boggle, Balderdash, Wheel of Fortune, Password, Buzzword, Taboo, and others are great ways for families and friends to spend an evening. More than that, these games involve words. We contend that people who engage in word games such as those mentioned above, as well as crosswords, word jumbles, and other paper-and-pencil games learn much about words through the playing of these games. Interestingly, we have observed that in many classrooms, students who struggle in reading and word decoding don't often get to play word games. They are the ones who usually have not finished their work, so they don't get the opportunity to play games. We think that a good classroom word recognition program should include opportunities for all students, especially those experiencing difficulty in word recognition, to play games that involve words.

Occasional games can add a different dimension to reading instruction while giving students enjoyable practice at recognizing words. Most are simple, and many are variations of popular television game shows. Here are a few of our favorites.

Scrabble   This classic board game challenges players to construct words from a limited set of letters that fit within an array of letters already on the board.

Hangman and Wheel of Fortune   Players guess unknown words and phrases by calling out possible letters within the words and having the letters entered into the word frame. Players have limited opportunities to call out letters that might fit into the unknown word or phrase.

Wordo   This game is a variation of Bingo. In Wordo, blank bingo cards are randomly filled with words that students have been practicing (see Figure 6.2). Using no particular order, the teacher or game leader calls out the words, their definitions, or sentences containing the words in which the target word is left blank. Players find and cover up their word squares as the words are called or identified. (Dried lima beans are excellent inexpensive markers for covering words.) The first player with a complete line of words running across, down, or diagonally is the winner.

The traditional 5×5 Wordo matrix works well with upper elementary grades. Teachers may wish to give younger students a 4×4 or 3×3 matrix so as not to overwhelm them

FIGURE 6.2 A Blank Wordo Card

W	O	R	D	O
		Free Space ☺		

with too many words. Wordo is a good game for practicing and reviewing words under instruction, words that need extra practice to develop automaticity, and key words from other subject areas such as science and social studies.

An alternative form of Wordo does not require a Wordo card. Rather, students use a selected number of words on word cards (these could be words from the students' or community word bank). Students choose 9 or 16 word cards and place them face up in a 3 × 3 or 4 × 4 matrix. This then becomes their Wordo card. As the teacher calls out a word or a word clue, students flip over the appropriate words in their matrix. When a row, column, or diagonal is turned over, the student calls out "Wordo" and is declared the winner.

Match   Match is a variation of Concentration, a memory game popular with young children. Match is played with 15 or 20 matching pairs of word cards. The cards are randomly laid in a grid on a flat surface. Players uncover two cards at a time, saying each word as it is turned over. If the two word cards contain the same word, the player keeps the cards and is allowed to uncover two more cards. Play continues until all cards have been matched and removed from the playing grid. The player with the most cards is declared the winner.

Word War   In Word War, a variation of the popular card game War, each player has a deck of cards. (One child can use the word-bank deck and deal it out evenly to all players.)

Each player plays one card at a time by uncovering the card at the top of his or her deck, saying the word, and laying it on the table. The child who plays the word with the most letters and says the word correctly wins the round and takes the other players' cards. In a tie, each player involved uncovers a second card and says the word. In this tie-breaking round, the player with the most letters wins all the cards played in the entire round. Another tie results in another tie-breaking round.

Gary teaches remedial math and reading to intermediate-grade students. He reserves one day every two weeks for word games and uses quick games whenever a few extra minutes remain at the end of class. "Students respond well to the games and the games make our word study more like playing around with words, which is how I want them to think of it."

Although many commercially prepared reading games exist, we think games that teachers and students make or adapt are best. Teachers and students have ownership of these games, and students' own words integrate better into the game.

MULTISENSORY APPROACHES TO WORD RECOGNITION

Some children still struggle with word recognition even with effective and varied instruction. They seem unable to perceive common familiar words and have tremendous difficulty seeing patterns in longer unfamiliar words. One approach for helping these children involves the use of several sensory modalities. This is often referred to as the *visual-auditory-kinesthetic-tactile approach (VAKT)*. *Kinesthetic* refers to the position and movement of body parts, hand, and mouth in recognizing words. *Tactile* refers to touch. An early version of this approach was described by Fernald (1943), who developed a multisensory approach that she used successfully with children having extreme difficulty in learning to recognize words.

In VAKT approaches, students initially learn words of their own choosing by seeing, saying, tracing, and touching printed versions of the word until they can trace or write the words without looking at them. Thus, students perceive words visually and aurally as they say and see them. Kinesthetic perception develops through the body movement involved in saying and tracing the word, and tactile perception happens when the student touches the written word as she says or traces it. The learned words become a word bank used in language experience stories created by the student and teacher.

Often children with severe reading difficulties need two or more months of instruction before beginning to recognize words without having to trace them. As students become more adept at perceiving words and word patterns, the teacher begins to reduce some of the modality support. Students might trace the words in the air while looking at a printed copy or move to the point of recognizing and writing words just from seeing and saying them. Students also move from reading their own stories to reading books, beginning with easy texts and progressing to more challenging ones. Eventually, students should learn to recognize new words by recognizing familiar patterns in them, as most proficient readers do.

The VAKT approach is labor intensive. It usually requires considerable time and is most effective in individual instruction. Thus, we consider it a method of last resort for children experiencing severe difficulty in word recognition. Nevertheless, teachers do use variations and portions of multimodal approaches within their regular classroom or clinical instruction.

Kim, a Title I teacher, had one group of second-graders facing considerable difficulty recognizing and remembering the words they encountered in their reading. When these children added words to their word banks by writing the words on blank cards, Kim had them trace each word several times while slowly saying the word. Then she asked them to turn over the word card and write the word on a piece of scratch paper. Similarly, she encouraged students to trace with their fingers words added to the group's word wall when they were at the wall practicing the words or making an entry. "I really find that for these students the added practice of touching and tracing the words makes them easier to remember. And I found that I only had to do this for about eight weeks. Students quickly began to pick up key patterns in words. When they hit unfamiliar words, they began to trace them on their own. They saw the value of the tracing and touching without my even having to tell them."

FLUENCY BUILDING AND WIDE READING

Learning how to decode words accurately is only part of how proficient readers deal with text. They also read with fluency. That is, they read effortlessly and expressively in phrases and other large chunks of text, not word by word.

In Chapter 7 we discuss instructional strategies that help students become more fluent in their reading. Fortunately, these strategies for building fluency also help students with word recognition. Studies have found that students who engage in fluency-building activities such as repeated readings or paired reading also make substantial improvement in their ability to recognize words accurately and quickly. As you read Chapter 7, keep in mind that these strategies can also help children who experience difficulty in decoding written text.

Once again, we repeat this critical point: Wide and authentic reading must be at the heart of all successful reading and word recognition instruction. All readers, whether proficient or struggling, need to read real texts of their own choosing. Through wide, in-depth reading, children practice their word recognition strategies. Moreover, by encountering new words and becoming exposed to words and word parts that appear frequently, students begin to recognize many words automatically.

Reading programs that successfully help children learn to read, overcome difficulties in learning to read, and develop a genuine love of reading seem to have one thing in common: Students read plenty of connected discourse. They read daily in their regular classrooms; for a large portion of their corrective or remedial reading time; and at home, encouraged and supported by parents. The more children read, the better they become in all aspects of reading—word recognition, fluency, attitude, vocabulary, and comprehension. As Gary has told us, "You can't expect children to *learn* to read if they don't get the *chance* to read. . . . You have to read!"

Making It Work through Instructional Routines

Knowledge of instructional strategies is only one part of developmental, corrective, or remedial reading instruction. The other part is designing coherent instructional packages or routines that use selected strategies in informed ways. Sensible instructional routines begin and end with students who are reading real texts. Word recognition should be a significant and consistent part of instruction for all students (Tier 1 instruction). For students who are experiencing difficulty in learning to recognize words more intensive, Tier 2 instruction is called for.

There is no one approach to word recognition instruction that works for all students. We believe that teachers should be empowered to design word recognition instruction that meets the needs and interests of their students and matches their own style of teaching. In the earlier portion of this chapter we provided you with a menu of approaches to word recognition instruction that have the potential for helping students learn to recognize words in text. Informed teachers need to design powerful instructional routines using the instructional approaches as the building blocks for the routines.

Don't try to use every instructional activity presented here. Rather, choose a few that make sense in light of your students' needs and apply them consistently and rigorously from one day to the next. In this way, instruction becomes predictable for students, and teaching time is used most efficiently in actual instruction rather than in explaining new activities or managing off-task behavior.

That's how Mary designs instruction for her primary-grade students with word recognition difficulties. Her students receive regular phonics and word-study instruction for approximately 20 minutes per day from their regular classroom teacher. That instruction is very traditional—short lessons are followed by students completing worksheets that are supposed to reinforce the instruction.

Mary works with groups of five to six students for 30 minutes a day, five days a week. The first 15 minutes of the instructional period begins with Mary reading a short text selection (100 to 200 words) or poem to the students while they follow along. Next, the group chorally reads and rereads the same text but the text is presented in an enlarged format (perhaps on chart paper). Then students choose several words from the text to add to a community word bank that is listed on chart paper and copied by students on word cards. For 5 or 10 minutes students work in pairs on various word-bank activities, including word sorts and games.

Two days a week, Mary works with students on word-family exploration. She introduces a rime to students and then changes the initial letters so that students read a variety of words. Later she adds various endings to the words and also changes the word families so that students focus their attention on various features of the words that Mary is presenting. Here is a sequence of words that she presented to students.

-at	*paddy*
cat	*daddy*
pat	*dad*
hat	*lad*
sat	*clad*
sad	*bad*
saddle	*bat*
paddle	*battle*

This quick-paced presentation of words is accompanied by Mary's explanations and elaborations of what is happening to the sound of the words when the letters are changed. She is helping students see inside the words. Sometimes the words are presented on a written chart, sometimes on word cards, and sometimes typed and projected on the classroom wall. Mary wants her students to see words in a variety of contexts. Students will often be asked to write the words in their own journal. Mary sees students' writing as a way to add one more sensory modality (physical movement of the fingers, hand, and arm) to reinforce the words in students' heads. Once read, Mary will have the students read, chant, sing, and shout them several more times, often in a different order from the initial reading.

On two days each week, Mary's groups work through cloze texts taken from passages the students have recently read in Mary's class or their regular classroom. Students work in pairs and attempt to determine words that have been deleted from a contextual passage. Once done, Mary asks students to explain the strategy they employed to figure out the unknown words.

On Fridays, Mary's groups of students engage in Making Words or Making and Writing Words. The secret word is often one that is related to a current event or holiday. Mary says that her students enjoy these word-building activities. Little do they know that through such play they are learning how letters work to make words and how words are made up of letters.

Each day's lesson ends with a 2-minute word ladder. Mary guides students through a process of starting with *planet*, and going to *plane*, to *plan*, to *pan*, to *par*, to *ear*, to *hear*, to *heart*, to *hearth*, and finally to *earth*. Students take great delight in discovering how the last word is usually connected somehow to the first. She challenges students to make a sentence that contains the first and last words, and as many from the middle as possible. She writes the sentence as students dictate. They read it as they leave and once again as they enter her room the following morning.

Mary's instructional periods are all business. Because students are familiar with the routine, they are highly engaged in reading throughout the lesson and benefit well from instruction. Progress in word recognition accelerates for most students, as does the students' enjoyment of words.

Mary recognizes that her routine may not work for all teachers, nor for all students. However, she feels very comfortable with this instructional framework and can easily plan lessons that students enjoy and need. We have found many other colleagues who have designed instructional routines that are much different from Mary's but that are based on the building blocks presented in this chapter and are equally effective in moving students forward.

Word recognition is only one part of learning to read proficiently. It is an important and necessary part, however, and many struggling readers cannot recognize words accurately and quickly. Word recognition instruction should have two major aims: to help children learn to decode unknown words, and to help them recognize familiar words quickly or automatically. The best way to accomplish both goals is to provide a little direct instruction in word recognition and a lot of guided authentic reading experiences. Thus, children can apply the instruction immediately and repeatedly in real reading situations. Games can provide enjoyable practice in word recognition.

DISCUSSION QUESTIONS

Some of the discussion questions for each chapter ask you to think through your own work as a teacher. If you are not currently a practicing teacher, try to respond to these questions from your own school experience (either from when you yourself were a student or from visits to schools that you have made in your teacher education program).

1. Certain approaches of instruction in word recognition work best for certain students and certain teachers. Discuss a word recognition strategy you have used effectively with one student that didn't work as well with another student. What do you think caused the difference in their responses?

2. Some struggling readers treat reading as a task of "getting the words right" rather than comprehending the text. What do you do if a reader substitutes a word that does not interfere with comprehension (for example, she might read *house* instead of *home*)? Why?

3. Share one word recognition strategy you have found especially effective in working with ELL students or students who struggle in reading.

4. Locate Clymer's article that lists the utility of phonics rules. (See References.) Did any of his findings surprise you? What are the implications of his findings for working with struggling readers?

5. Frequently parents are asked to help their children practice sight words, often using flash cards. How might you tailor some of the word recognition strategies in this chapter for home use so that parents understand the importance of reading for meaning as well as for accurate word recognition?

Chapter *Seven* ❧

Developing Fluent Reading in Struggling Readers

ACCURACY IN WORD RECOGNITION does not ensure proficient reading. On the surface, students often exhibit good word recognition skills, reading with few noticeable errors. A slightly deeper analysis, however, may show that they read with excessive slowness and choppiness; their oral reading seems dull and expressionless, almost labored, as if they gain no satisfaction or enjoyment from reading. Most likely, these readers have significant trouble in achieving fluency.

Most people can tell when they are listening to a fluent reader or speaker. Words and phrases such as "quick," "with expression," "good phrasing," or "reads in a meaningful way" indicate fluent reading. We agree that these terms, and others, are valid indicators of reading fluency.

Rasinski (2006) stated that reading fluency involves three critical aspects of negotiating printed language. First, fluent readers read the words in text accurately. This suggests the need for instruction in word recognition (we dealt with this issue in the previous chapter). Second, fluent readers read the words in text not only accurately but automatically, or effortlessly, so that they can use their limited amount of cognitive resources for constructing meaning, not decoding words. Third, when reading orally, fluent readers read the words in text with prosody, or expression. Expression in oral reading (and we also would argue silent reading) gives evidence that readers are making meaning and that they are parsing or phrasing the text into meaningful units.

One of the best ways to think about fluency is to consider that fluency deals with larger, multiple-word units of texts. Disfluent readers read so slowly that they appear to deal individually with each word they encounter. Fluent readers, on the other hand, read quickly enough and with appropriate phrasing and expression to make clear that they are working with larger units of text. Phrases, clauses, and sentences are more important units of text and meaning for fluent readers. Moreover, they appear to breeze through the written text with such ease, it is clear that they are not using all their mental energy to deal with the words, but also to make meaning.

Why is the ability to read quickly and in appropriate textual units so important? We like to use the analogy of fluent and disfluent speaking when discussing the importance of reading fluency. Fluent speakers actually help listeners understand their message. They speak fast enough that the listener can quickly process the message. They speak in meaningful phrases and embed expression and pauses into their speech to help the listener make sense of the speech as easily as possible. Disfluent speakers, on the other hand, speak in a slow, labored, word-by-word fashion that makes it difficult for the listener to discern the intended message.

In the same way, a fluent reader efficiently processes the text's surface-level information to make it as easy as possible to comprehend. Word-by-word, expressionless, slow reading diminishes the reader's ability to understand the text. Those listening to disfluent oral reading often have similar comprehension problems. Problems in fluency are a major contributor to reading difficulties among elementary and middle-school students.

The National Assessment of Educational Progress (NAEP) (Pinnell et al., 1995) study of students' reading fluency development showed that 45 percent of all U.S. fourth-graders read below minimally acceptable levels of fluency. Indeed, only 13 percent of fourth-graders were found to be reading at the highest level of fluency. According to NAEP, then, nearly one out of every two elementary readers fails to read with acceptable fluency. Similar findings were reported in a more recent replication of this study (Daane et al., 2005). Fluency was a concern in 1995. More than decade later, students continue to struggle in acquiring fluency. In our own work, we studied elementary-grade children from a large urban school district who were referred for special tutoring in reading in the Title I program (Rasinski & Padak, 1998). As part of their initial diagnostic assessment, children read and answered questions about two passages that were near their grade placement. From this reading we could measure students' word recognition, reading fluency, and comprehension. Fluency was measured by rate of reading. We found that students' performance tended to be below grade level in all three areas. Word recognition and comprehension, however, were not drastically below grade level, but fluency was. These students' reading performance was dramatically and consistently marked by excessively slow and labored oral reading. Anyone listening to these children read knew that they were struggling.

We believe that reading fluency is a significant obstacle to proficient reading for elementary students and many older struggling readers. Indeed, a large majority of the students referred to our university reading center for corrective reading tutoring manifest significant problems in achieving fluency. Duke, Pressley, and Hilden (2004) suggest that close to 20 percent of poor comprehenders are not sufficiently fluent. The NAEP studies mentioned earlier suggest that upward of 40 percent of elementary readers are not fluent, and that these students also tend to perform poorly in reading comprehension.

Fluency is an equally important issue for ELL students. Recent reports on best instruction in reading for ELL students indicates that the very same research-based factors identified for English-speaking students apply as well for ELL students learning to read (August & Shanahan, 2006; Goldenberg, 2008). Fluency was one of the factors identified.

Although important, fluency has been an ignored instructional goal for reading. In 1983, Richard Allington called reading fluency the neglected goal of the reading program. Fluency suggestions were largely absent from reading instructional materials. Rasinski and Zutell (1996) examined published instructional materials for reading and found little mention of fluency as an instructional goal More recently, an evaluation of Reading First schools—schools that are mandated to include fluency instruction in their reading curriculum—found that approximately 4 minutes per day were devoted to fluency instruction (Gamse et al., 2008). More than 25 years after Allington's claims about fluency, researchers still find that fluency is largely neglected in reading classrooms around the country. The students who suffer most from this lack of instructional focus, we believe, are those who struggle in reading. It is imperative, then, that informed and dedicated teachers see that students receive adequate and appropriate instruction in this absolutely essential aspect of reading.

Despite its relative neglect, recent reviews of research on reading fluency (Kuhn & Stahl, 2000; National Reading Panel, 2000; Rasinski & Hoffman, 2003; Rasinski et al., in press) have determined that fluency is an important and necessary component of successful reading instruction. Moreover, our own work with struggling readers indicates that it is an area of concern. Fortunately, the research also indicates that reading fluency can be effectively taught. In the following sections we address how teachers assess and provide effective instruction in this critical area.

Assessing Reading Fluency

Readers' levels of fluency may be assessed in several ways. When teachers desire a quantifiable method for assessing fluency, reading rate offers a relatively simple and direct approach. An easy way to calculate rate is to ask a reader to read a text orally in his or her normal manner. The chosen text should be at the reader's grade level in difficulty. At the end of 60 seconds tell the reader to stop or mark the point in the text where he or she has reached in 60 seconds. Then count the number of words read correctly (or corrected if they were initially read incorrectly). This is the reader's rate in words correct per minute (wcpm). Do this procedure a few times and determine an average rate. Compare the student's oral reading rate against the following norms for grade level and time of year (see Hasbrouck & Tindal, 1992, 2006; and Howe & Shinn, 2001):

Grade	Fall	Winter	Spring
1		25 wcpm	55 wcpm
2	50 wcpm	70	90
3	70	90	110
4	95	110	120
5	110	125	140
6	115	130	145
7	150	160	170
8	155	165	175

If the reader's rate is consistently and substantially below the appropriate grade-level rate, you can assume the student has fluency difficulties.

Another approach to assessing fluency is simply to listen to students read orally. By paying attention to students' expression, phrasing, and pace, teachers build a good idea of each student's reading fluency. Choose a text at or below each student's instructional level. Usually a text one or two grade levels below grade placement will ensure this. Allow the child to read through the passage silently and answer any questions about the pronunciation or meaning of specific words in the passage. After this preview, ask the student to read the same passage orally for you. Record the passage and simply observe the student during the reading. Look for signs of frustration or strain during the student's oral reading.

Later, when you are alone, listen to the student's recorded reading. Without looking for word recognition errors, rate the reading in terms of expression and volume, phrasing, smoothness, and pace. The multidimensional fluency scale (Rasinski & Padak, 2005a, 2005b) in Figure 7.1 can guide you in assessing this aspect of fluency. Students rated in the lower half of the scale for any of the dimensions may be at risk for fluency and overall reading proficiency. Information from this scale, combined with the reading rate, provides a solid assessment of fluency.

Teaching Fluency

Although fluency may be an elusive goal for many students, it is not necessarily difficult to teach. Several authentic, engaging, and effective approaches for improving reading fluency exist (Rasinski, 1989; 2003; Rasinski & Hoffman, 2003; Rasinski et al., in press); moreover, these approaches also boost students' proficiency in word recognition proficiency and students' feelings of success as readers. Before sharing effective strategies for teaching fluency, let's deal with a common misconception about reading fluency.

ROUND-ROBIN READING IS *NOT* FLUENCY INSTRUCTION

Fluency is often associated with oral reading. We agree. The evidence suggests that what is learned in oral reading transfers into silent reading. Because fluency and oral reading are associated, some teachers may think that round-robin reading (sometimes called popcorn reading) is an appropriate form of fluency instruction. Round-robin reading is the form of oral reading in which the teacher randomly chooses students in a reading group to read aloud without the benefit of rehearsal, often correcting errors as students read.

There is no evidence to support the use of round-robin reading, or any of its variations, in any classroom for any reason (Opitz & Rasinski, 1998; Rasinski et al., in press). Students should never be asked to read something aloud in instructional settings that they have not been given the opportunity to practice in advance. Moreover, students should never be asked to read text if the purpose is something other than to make meaning. Round-robin reading violates both of these principles. Round robin is a poor choice not only for its lack of instructional effectiveness but also because it has many negative consequences that are a particular concern for struggling readers. The embarrassment that many struggling readers feel when forced to read aloud and display their lack of fluency can severely damage a child's sense of adequacy and self-efficacy. There are much better ways to teach reading fluency.

FIGURE 7.1 Multidimensional Fluency Scale

Score	Expression & Volume	Phrasing	Smoothness	Pace
1	Reads words as if simply to get them out. Little sense of trying to make text sound like natural language. Tends to read in a quiet voice.	Reads in monotone with little sense of phrase boundaries; frequently reads word-by-word.	Makes frequent extended pauses, hesitations, false starts, sound-outs, repetitions, and/or multiple attempts.	Reads slowly and laboriously.
2	Begins to use voice to make text sound like natural language in some areas but not in others. Focus remains largely on pronouncing the words. Still reads in a quiet voice.	Frequently reads in two- and three-word phrases, giving the impression of choppy reading; improper stress and intonation fail to mark ends of sentences and clauses.	Experiences several "rough spots" in text where extended pauses or hesitations are more frequent and disruptive.	Reads moderately slowly.
3	Makes text sound like natural language throughout the better part of the passage. Occasionally slips into expressionless reading. Voice volume is generally appropriate throughout the text.	Reads with a mixture of run-ons, midsentence pauses for breath, and some choppiness; reasonable stress and intonation.	Occasionally breaks smooth rhythm because of difficulties with specific words and/or structures.	Reads with an uneven mixture of fast and slow pace.
4	Reads with good expression and enthusiasm throughout the text. Varies expression and volume to match his or her interpretation of the passage.	Generally reads with good phrasing, mostly in clause and sentence units, with adequate attention to expression.	Generally reads smoothly with some breaks, but resolves word and structure difficulties quickly, usually through self-correction.	Consistently reads at conversational pace; appropriate rate throughout reading.

MODEL FLUENT READING

Struggling readers often do not know what fluent reading should sound like. They lack good self-awareness of fluent reading. They are often segregated into groups of children with similar difficulties. The readers they hear are usually like them—disfluent and frustrated. Most educators would agree that learning something is difficult if one doesn't understand what it should look or sound like. That is why modeling fluent reading, commonly called reading aloud to and with children, is especially important for less able readers.

When these children learn what fluent reading sounds like, they can develop their own models of what fluent reading is. Reading to children helps accomplish this goal, which can be further reinforced by talking with children about fluency after read-aloud sessions. Before the read-aloud begins, the teacher might ask students to listen for variations in voice, phrasing, rate, expression, or volume. After reading, the teacher might ask students, "How did I communicate love or hate or fear or excitement with my voice during the reading?" Asking students to listen for various aspects of fluent reading and talk about them is a first step toward helping students read fluently on their own.

Another appropriate practice is for the teacher to read a text aloud to students before asking them to read it on their own. This preview reading helps students develop a sense of how the text should sound; it also conveniently and unobtrusively introduces students to words they may not have encountered before in print.

Terri knows about modeling fluent reading for her third-grade class. She recognized early in the school year that several of her lower-achieving students were disfluent readers. She has developed a program that involves her students in paired and repeated reading, which we describe later in the chapter. But an equally important part of her fluency instruction involves reading to her class every day:

> About once or twice a week I try to talk with the class about fluency after my reading. At first I had to ask them specific questions about my reading. After a few weeks I only had to ask, "What did you think about my reading?" They began talking about my voicing, phrasing, rate, emphasis on words, and how I used these elements to help convey meaning. Now, when I ask my students to read orally, I remind them to think about fluency. Not only do they think about it, they read with greater ease and expression. Even the lower kids have gotten into this. I think I've noticed them more because they've made the greatest gains of all.

Terri frequently reads a passage to students and then asks them to read the passage to themselves or aloud to a partner. She believes that preview reading is a good alternative to asking students to read the text silently or introducing the text through a discussion or other activity not directly related to the text reading. "This way students get a good introduction to the passage itself because they hear and understand it before they actually read it."

REPEATED READINGS

Repeated readings is a simple instructional procedure in which students are asked to practice reading one passage several times until they achieve a predetermined degree of fluency, usually defined in terms of rate or word recognition accuracy. Like musicians or athletes, readers must practice to achieve fluency. Although the activity itself may be simple, the effects of repeated reading are quite powerful. In an early study of this method, Samuels (1979) asked students diagnosed as learning disabled in reading to practice reading short texts until they could read a passage fluently (85 wpm). Samuels found that his students exhibited progress on the passages they were practicing and on new passages. In other words, the benefits of repeated readings were internalized and transferred. Other studies (Dowhower, 1987, 1994; Herman, 1985; Kuhn & Stahl, 2000) have validated Samuels's original finding that repeated readings can help improve students' fluency, word recognition, and comprehension.

Teachers often ask, "How can we persuade students to read a passage more than once?" The best answer to this dilemma is to create situations in which students have a real reason to do so.

In writing classrooms, the desired outcome for most writing is some form of publication. In a similar fashion, the natural outcome for practiced reading should be some form of performance. Teachers must think of ways and reasons for students to read for others. Poems are meant to be shared orally, as are play scripts. Informed teachers use poetry, scripts, and dramatic reading as vehicles for repeated reading. Students also practice reading short stories to share with reading buddies in another class or grade. Some students are motivated by the opportunity to work with a friend. Koskinen and Blum (1984, 1986) found that repeated reading is successful in group situations called *paired repeated reading,* in which students read a passage to a partner several times. The partner provides positive feedback and assistance. After several readings, the roles are reversed. Koskinen and Blum found that students enjoyed the alternative format and demonstrated strong gains in fluency, word recognition, and reading for meaning in as little as 15 minutes a day, three times a week, for five weeks.

When fluency difficulties are so severe that performance is not a reasonable option, easier texts may serve. After all, everyone can become disfluent when reading material is difficult. After students develop the fluency habit by practicing with easy, predictable texts, they can return to more challenging material.

Some children in our university tutoring program enjoy reading their texts into recording equipment. They then listen to their oral reading and, with the tutor, decide how to make the next reading more fluent. This process may be repeated several times until the children are satisfied with the sound of their reading. At that point a more public performance may be planned. Recording and analyzing repeated readings helps children develop fluency and an awareness of their own progress in becoming fluent readers. Another suggestion is to track students' performance as they practice reading texts. Then, using a simple graph of reading performance, teachers can show students their progress in increasing their reading rate or decreasing the number of word recognition miscues over several readings of the same text.

Sheila noticed that several of her sixth-graders exhibited fluency difficulties—their oral reading was excessively slow with little attention to meaningful phrasing and expression. Sheila believed that these students had developed negative attitudes about reading and themselves. They balked at any opportunity to read aloud and began to cause disruptions during any type of in-class reading. Sheila decided that these students needed opportunities to engage in repeated readings with relatively easy texts so they could experience success in reading. She made arrangements with Tim, a first-grade teacher in her building, to pair each of her sixth-grade students with a first-grader. The reading buddies met once a week, and during each visit the buddies read a book to one another. The sixth-graders were encouraged to choose books appropriate for first-graders. (These were also ideal for the disfluent sixth-grade readers.) Sixth-graders practiced these books diligently throughout the week. By Friday they had them down pat, and when they shared them with their buddies, they glowed about their reading success and the awe they inspired in the first-graders.

After a few months, Sheila was delighted with her students' progress. "These students have begun to believe in themselves again as readers. They see that they can read fluently and that their reading can have an impact on other children. When I provide instruction for these students they can relate it to their work as tutors and buddies."

Her students have thrived on their weekly sessions. Nonetheless, Sheila has begun to think of other ways for her students to have authentic purposes for reading to others. These include reading at home to parents and developing partnerships with residents of a nearby retirement center. "It really doesn't take a lot for something like this to work," Sheila says, "just someone willing to honestly listen to these children read and give them encouragement. After experiencing so much failure in reading, these kids need to practice to get good, and they need people to tell them that they are good."

Performance   Students will eagerly practice a passage several times if they know that somewhere down the road they will be asked to perform it. Think of times in your own life when you may have been asked to read a passage or a prayer orally at a friend's wedding or family function. Chances are you practiced that text several times through so that you could read it without error and with good and meaningful expression. We have found that the same is absolutely true for elementary students. The key questions in this notion of performance address just what kinds of performances and texts teachers want students to engage in. Actually, several types of wonderful performance opportunities work well in elementary classrooms and clinics.

Poetry is almost perfect for performance. By its very nature, poetry is meant to be read aloud. The meaning of a poem comes not only from the words but also from the way in which the words are spoken—fluency! Poems feature rhyme, a sense of rhythm, and repetition, which make them highly predictable, easy, and enjoyable to learn to read. Finally, poems are generally short, and students can practice a poem several times through in a short period of time.

Poems should not be a sort of practice text. Rather, we think that poetry study, performance, composition, and appreciation should be a natural part of any elementary classroom. Students and teachers should learn to love poems. Poetry can add unique and valuable benefits to the classroom community. Just one great byproduct of poetry study and performance is the opportunity to foster fluency.

We recommend strongly that teachers develop a space in their professional bookshelves for poetry anthologies. (See Appendix A for a list of poetry resources.) Find poems that match a mood, a time of year, or a special event and share those poems with students. Read and reread poems to students regularly and encourage them to do the same. If you make books of poetry available to students, if you read poetry to your students and enjoy it and invite your students to do the same, you will find your students choosing their own poems, practicing them, and performing them for their classmates. The result is a love affair with poetry and a natural way to nurture fluency in students.

One of our colleagues, Maureen, loves to share poetry with her third-grade students. Indeed, she has taken her love of poetry to new heights. About once or twice a month, students will walk into her classroom and find books of poetry as well as individual poems scattered throughout the room. Students know that this is the signal that they will be having "poetry club" that Friday.

After a brief browsing period, students choose a poem. Some students work in pairs, trios, or quartets for their poems. Other students decide to write and perform their own original poems. Then, throughout the week, when students have an opportunity, they practice their selected poems, making sure that they will be ready to read them during "poetry club."

When Friday afternoon rolls around, the last hour or so of the day is given over to poetry performance. The room is rearranged to resemble a coffeehouse atmosphere. A stage area is created in the front of the room with a stool and microphone (a karaoki machine can fill this purpose nicely). Overhead lights are dimmed, a few desk lamps are lit, and appropriate music plays in the background to create just the right ambience. Maureen usually brings in popcorn and makes hot cider or hot chocolate to complete the coffeehouse. Of course, parents, the school principal, and other school staff are invited to the poetry club.

After everyone has their refreshments, the poetry begins! Students come to the stage and perform their poems. Usually, students will talk about why they chose a particular poem or share information they discovered about the poet. Initially, each performance was greeted with applause until a grandparent attending the poetry club, a child of the 1950s, suggested that audience members snap their fingers as a way of demonstrating their approval of a poem while not making so much noise that other classrooms were disturbed. Students thought this was really cool.

Maureen thinks her poetry club is cool, too. "My students love it. They ask for it all the time. It just goes to show that when we create real-life environments for students, and when we trust students to do their best, they will. Maybe I can't give all the credit to the poetry club, but I have seen some really significant gains in several students' reading since we started the club. And, I have even seen some student writing that has bowled me over!"

Another type of performance activity to consider is *reader's theater,* in which a group of students performs a script. However, the performance has no costumes, props, movement, scenery, or memorization of lines. Performers simply stand in front of the audience in their normal attire and read the script to the audience. Of course, for the script to have any effect on the audience it needs to be read with expression—hence reader's theater is a superb fluency activity. Performers must practice their lines to eventually perform for their audience in a convincing and entertaining way.

Scripts are found in many places. Collections of short plays are available for elementary readers. Occasionally, the basal reading series or the weekly news magazine for students will have a topical script for performance. Make sure each script can be successfully performed in a reader's theater format. Some books for children are written in a reader's theater format. Books such as Angela Johnson's *Tell Me a Story, Mama,* Donald Hall and Barry Moser's *I Am the Dog; I Am the Cat,* Mary Ann Hoberman and Michael Emberley's

You Read to Me; I'll Read to You series, and several books by Paul Fleischman (e.g., *Bull Run, I am Phoenix: Poems for Two Voices, Joyful Noise: Poems for Two Voices, Big Talk: Poems for Four Voices,* and *Seedfolks*) have delineated parts that make them a natural for reader's theater performance.

Of course, the best reader's theater scripts are those written by students themselves. This often means simply recasting a picture book or a segment or chapter from a longer book into script form. If you want to try this with your students, direct them at first to short books with a clear plot and lots of dialogue. This is a highly scaffolded experience for students, as they have the original text to support their writing. Students choose the main characters and number of narrators, making sure that all students in a group have a part. They can simply rewrite the original text as a script without any changes, or they can make additions to the script and delete characters and portions of the text from the original to make it more their own. In all cases, the original text supports, guides, and models their own writing. (If you're thinking this may be an unauthentic writing activity, simply cast your eyes to Hollywood, where an entire industry is devoted to taking books and rewriting them into screenplays!)

Once the script is found or written, a group of students chooses parts within the script and practices the text. The text's interactive nature helps students develop a sense for creating meaning through a shared text. When students feel comfortable with the text and believe they can read it and convey the appropriate meaning, a performance should follow. Usually the performance is for one's own classmates. However, really well-done scripts often "go on the road" to other classes or groups such as PTAs, school boards, retirement centers, and so on.

Fourth-grade teacher Lorraine Griffith has been using reader's theater for several years (Griffith & Rasinski, 2004; Prescott, 2003). She had read an account of reader's theater in a second-grade classroom where students experienced a year's growth in reading in just 10 weeks (Martinez, Roser, & Strecker, 1999) and decided to try it in her own classroom. Students were assigned scripts each Monday, practiced throughout the week, and performed their scripts for the class on Fridays in a reader's theater festival. During the years in which reader's theater has been an integral part of Lorraine's reading program, her Title I students have averaged approximately three years' growth in reading per year.

A final type of performance is through great speeches (and documents) from history. You may be thinking, "Memorize and perform speeches? Yuck!" Yet, great oratory from U.S. history is a superb way to integrate reading and fluency into the social studies curriculum. Many great events from history are marked by speeches. The study of the Civil War is not complete without a rendition of Lincoln's "Gettysburg Address." The history of the women's rights movement needs students to hear Sojourner Truth's "Ain't I a Woman" speech. How can the American Revolution be studied without a performance of Patrick Henry's "Give Me Liberty or Give Me Death" oration? And wouldn't an exploration of the Great Depression miss something important if at least a portion of Franklin Delano Roosevelt's first inaugural speech, "We Have Nothing to Fear," were not presented by someone in the class taking on the role of FDR?

Memorizing and presenting speeches in a monotone voice is deadly. However, when students know some background for the speech and are asked to go back in history and become part of the audience for the speech, and when the speaker presents the speech with verve and expression, a classroom study of the Civil War or women's rights can come alive. Again, for students to perform the speech with appropriate meaning and expression, they must practice and, for even a few minutes, take on the role of the person who originally delivered it. Interestingly, speeches and documents of U.S. and world history are easy to find. Many printed versions of famous speeches are readily available on the Internet.

David teaches fifth-grade social studies and reading. He has found that exploring U.S. history by combining textbooks, trade books, and students' performance of speeches is an unbeatable combination.

> I start by reading the "Gettysburg Address" to them, usually in November near the anniversary of the speech. But beforehand, I tell them some of the background to the speech: The Battle of Gettysburg that occurred in the middle of the previous summer, the invasion of the North by Lee's Confederate army, the unbelievable number of deaths in such a small town, the need to create a cemetery and bury all these dead soldiers, the dedication of the cemetery and the three-hour speech given by the featured speaker. And then I tell them to place themselves in Gettysburg, as citizens who have seen the tragedy of war over the past several months. "You have listened to a man speak for hours at this dedication, and now you see President Lincoln heading to the podium. What are you thinking? How do you feel about all that has happened? Now listen to President Lincoln's words." I read the speech with all the expression I can muster. And you know, the students listen with such intensity that you can hear a pin drop. After they see what I can do with a speech, they want to do the same. That's when I give them their own speeches to study and perform.

ASSISTED READING—READING WHILE LISTENING

Paired Reading   In the 1960s, the professional literature began describing a new approach to corrective reading (Heckelman, 1969), the *neurological impress method (NIM),* which is much simpler than its name implies. Basically, NIM involves pairing good and poor readers. The readers sit side by side and read one text aloud and together.

Early research about the approach was impressive. Pairs read together for relatively short periods of time, usually no more than 15 minutes per session. Heckelman (1969) found that poor readers made substantial progress relatively quickly. One student, for example, made gains of 5.9 grade levels after doing NIM for a total of 7.25 hours over 6 weeks. The average gain was 1.9 grade levels for 24 students over the same time period.

For whatever reason, NIM never fully caught on in the United States. Few teachers seemed to use it with their less able readers. But this was not the case in England, where researchers developed an activity similar to NIM, called *paired reading*. Perhaps the more easily understood name has helped its popularity.

Paired reading was originally intended as an at-home supplement to children's reading at school. The approach calls for parent and child to read one text aloud and together. Normally, the parent reads in a moderately loud voice at a pace that tends to pull the child along. When the child wants to read alone, he or she signals the parent who then stops reading aloud or reads in a whisper at a rate that slightly trails the child's voice. As soon as the child begins to experience difficulty, the parent returns to his or her original role as leader.

Keith Topping (1987), who has led the paired reading movement in England, reports that students can make remarkable progress in a short period of time. With sessions of only 5 minutes per night, he reported struggling readers made three to five times their normal progress in word recognition and comprehension. Because children and parents read connected texts together fluently, it is easy to expect that fluency would improve as well. Paired reading also works well if peers or other adults take on the role of parent (Topping, 1989).

Katherine has been a Title I reading teacher for 15 years in an inner-city school. She takes seriously the Title I mandate to involve parents in her programs to improve her students' reading. Until a few years ago, however, she had difficulty with parental involvement. "We had all kinds of problems," Katherine says. "Either the parents didn't show up for the training program, or they didn't follow through and I didn't have the time to follow up with every child, or the program was more fun and games and really didn't involve sustained reading on the part of the child."

After hearing about paired reading at an in-service workshop, she decided to try it out with her students and their parents. She arranged for one-hour training sessions at various times throughout the day and advertised it furiously. Most parents came and were enthusiastic about paired reading. "This was something they could do with their children pretty much on their own," Katherine recalled.

On Fridays, students bring in record sheets that document the previous week's paired reading. Children select a book to read for the upcoming week and receive a new record sheet. Parents have stayed with the program. Katherine notes, "They see that it works, and I do, too. Children who do paired reading with a parent make significantly more progress during the year than those who don't. Paired reading is one of the best strategies for helping our less able readers that I have ever seen or tried."

Recorded Passages   Paired reading may be impossible for some students. They may not have anybody at home who can read with them. One alternative is to provide students with a recording of the reading text that they can listen to while reading the written version. Marie Carbo (1978) calls this approach "talking books." Carbo studied this approach for readers with learning disabilities. After only a few weeks, Carbo reported that students made reading gains significantly beyond expectations. They learned to read fluently what they were previously unable to read at all. In another study, students listening to high-interest recorded stories at their instructional levels for 15 to 25 minutes daily for about 27 weeks made average gains of 2.2 years in their reading achievement (Smith & Elley, 1997).

Although a variety of commercially prepared recorded texts is available for purchase, we believe that recorded passages prepared by the teacher or someone else in the school may be more effective. The commercial recordings often have distracting sound effects. They also may not provide a word-for-word rendition of the passage, may be read at an inappropriate rate for students, or have unconventional or inadequate signals for page turns. These potential difficulties disappear if the teacher, aide, student, or parent helper prepares the recording. In addition, students may find the voice of the teacher or some other familiar person comforting and encouraging.

Ted uses recorded books in his elementary Title I reading program. Students who struggle with reading fluency choose a book and recording from the extensive library he has collected and made over the years. Students read the book over several days on their own and come to class on a designated day and read the book (or a portion of it) to him.

Ted believes this activity gives students some control over and responsibility for their own learning; at the same time, they learn to read and enjoy a good book. "Most of my students really like learning to read these books on their own," he says. "It's an accomplishment they can feel proud of." Once students have become familiar with Ted's format for the recorded versions of the books and developed some degree of fluency, he invites them to make their own recorded books to add to his library. Students like listening to books recorded by their classmates.

Recorded books also work well with students who are English-language learners. Koskinen and colleagues (1999) found that having ELL students use books and recordings for reading practice resulted in increased reading achievement and interest as well as greater self-confidence. Students, parents, and teachers noted significant improvements in students' reading. Least proficient readers reported practicing their reading more often than more proficient classmates. In their use of recorded books, Koskinen and colleagues recorded two readings per story. The first reading was a slower, more deliberate presentation, and the second was a faster, more fluent rendition. This allowed students to move from an initial focus on individual words and phrases to a more fluent reading of the stories.

Choral Reading   Choral reading—reading orally in groups—is similar to paired reading in that less able readers receive simultaneous support while reading. Choral reading has become something of a lost art in elementary schools. In past generations, students learned and chorally recited poems, songs, famous speeches, interesting passages from stories, and other selections. Even the least able readers could join in without risk of failure or ridicule. After several readings they were able to read the passage on their own with considerable fluency. Today, however, with so much emphasis on silent reading, children have few opportunities to engage in this community form of reading.

Choral reading captures readers' interest through antiphonal reading and other variations. In *antiphonal reading* the class is divided into groups (girls and boys, January to June birthdays and July to December birthdays, etc.). Different parts of the text are assigned to each group. The entire group may read some parts, and individuals may read others. Thus, the choral reading becomes a complex and orchestrated arrangement. Students enjoy deciding on parts for antiphonal reading. To do so, of course, they must read the text several times, which is good fluency practice, and think about how different groups of voices can convey meaning. In addition, assigning parts and directing practice with the texts help students develop ownership of their reading and foster a sense of a reading community. Choral reading activities let less able readers benefit from group support, the camaraderie and joy of participating in a group activity with peers who have a variety of abilities, and the valuable practice of reading one text in a variety of ways.

Choral reading is a way of life in Elizabeth's second-grade classroom. Each morning she uses choral reading to warm up the class to reading and language. She usually finds a short, suitable poem for the class to read together. She either writes the poem on chart paper or puts it on an overhead transparency so that all the children can see it. Her routine is to read the poem to the class first, talk about it with the children, then invite them to read it chorally several times and respond to it through discussion.

I really like doing this at the beginning of each day because it helps create a sense of togetherness and community in the class. After reading it a couple of times I might ask four or five individual students of varying reading ability to read it to the class. Choral reading really lets those less able readers shine with their peers! Later in the day, when I'm working with those struggling readers, we will usually go back and practice the poem together some more and do some word-analysis activities with it. Really, you can create a whole lesson that's fun and interesting from this initial group choral reading.

Not every day means a new poem. Sometimes Elizabeth reintroduces students to an old favorite, and about halfway through the school year, students begin to read the poem to the class each morning. The day before, she gives a selected student a copy of the poem for the next day. She asks the child to practice reading it at home and to lead the class in reading it the next day. For some less fluent readers, she will supply a recorded version of the poem to aid their practice.

MARKING PHRASE BOUNDARIES

Phrasing is important to fluency because meaning is embedded in multiple-word chunks of text or phrases, not in individual words. Peter Schreiber (1980, 1991) has theorized that many readers characterized as disfluent suffer from a poor ability to phrase text appropriately while reading. This may reflect lack of sensitivity to semantic and syntactic cues that mark phrase boundaries in the text, or disfluent readers may have routinized their word-by-word reading and not have automatic recognition of most words. Regardless of the cause, the result is continued difficulty in fully understanding the text.

Consider the following sentence:

The young man the playground equipment.

At first reading, the sentence may sound like nonsense. That is because you probably chunked or phrased the text as most readers would: after the noun *man*. However, in this contrived sentence, if you chunked the text this way, your comprehension suffered—the text has no verb phrase. Rephrase the text (hint: *young* can be a noun and *man* a verb). Rephrased, the sentence is easily understood. When readers have difficulty determining appropriate text boundaries, many sentences can give them similar comprehension problems.

Repeated reading, where the focus is reading with expression and appropriate phrasing as opposed to reading for speed, can help students overcome this difficulty. Schreiber has noted that repeated reading activities give the reader practice in discovering text cues that mark phrase boundaries. Another approach is to mark or highlight phrase boundaries in the text itself, using a pencil slash or vertical line to specify the boundary (see Figure 7.2). A review of research shows that marking phrase boundaries has considerable potential for improving reading performance and comprehension, especially with less able readers (Rasinski, 1990, 1994).

Ted has found that marking phrase boundaries for them helps his less fluent Title I students:

If we are studying a short passage or poem that I want students to read orally, I will lightly mark phrase boundaries in the passage with a pencil and run enough copies of

FIGURE 7.2   Phrased Text

Grant was not a military genius/who took brilliant gambles/and made flashing strikes.// His position/as one of America's premier field commanders/was the result/of more solid qualities:/ a wide vision of the war/and what had to be done to win,/balanced judgment,/dogged courage,/common sense,/and good luck/at the right time.//[1]

Today/Kevin and I turned out/for track. //Mr. Kurtz,/the coach,/gave us a pep talk/about the importance/of taking part/and doing the best we can.// He said/it's not the winning,/it's the competing that's important.// He stressed/looking for improvement/within ourselves.//[2]

Sources: [1] J. I. Robertson, *Civil War! America Becomes One Nation* (New York: Knopf, 1992), p. 79.
[2] B. Cleary, *Strider* (New York: Morrow, 1991), p. 126.

the text for each student. I use single slash marks for within-sentence phrase boundaries and double slashes for the ends of sentences. After talking about the role of the marks, we might read the passage chorally and attend to the phrase and sentence breaks.

Later, as students become fluent and phrase-sensitive to the text, Ted gives them the same text without the slash marks. He believes this is a good way for students to transfer their newly learned sensitivity to phrase boundaries to passages in a conventional format. He occasionally gives students new passages as well and asks them to mark their own phrase boundaries. This is followed by a discussion of the marks and the need to read in chunks or phrases. Ted notes that his students appear to make real progress in their ability and desire to read in appropriate phrases when reading both orally and silently.

CHOICE OF TEXTS AND THE ISSUE OF TEXT DIFFICULTY

The texts chosen for reading can aggravate or ameliorate fluency problems. More often than not, aggravation is the result. Students with fluency difficulties often face texts too difficult for their current reading level. Such texts ensure disfluent reading and perpetuate students' evaluations of themselves as poor readers. In dealing with fluency problems, choose texts relatively easy in terms of word recognition and syntactic complexity. If the text is challenging, provide students with sufficient support before and during reading to ensure success. Reading relatively easy texts helps students develop power and self-confidence in their reading.

Easier texts that ensure fluency are usually a sound choice for independent reading. Allington (2002) found that highly effective teachers were more likely to guide their students into easier materials than less effective teachers. Predictable or patterned texts are particularly well suited to helping students develop fluency when reading independently. These texts are written in a distinct and easily detected pattern that makes them not only easy to read but also require readers to attend to the pattern through phrasing and expression.

Patterned texts can also be found in poetry and song lyrics for children. These are particularly well-suited for struggling readers as poems and songs are relatively short in length and can be mastered easily through repeated readings (Biggs et al., 2008; Padak & Rasinski, 2005; Rasinski & Stevenson, 2005). Moreover, the melodic aspects of poems and songs lend themselves to reading with appropriate expression. Children's verse poetry is also written in rhyme, which makes the poems even more appealing and predictable. (Poetry collections that we have found useful are listed in Appendix A.) For example, Shel Silverstein's *Where the Sidewalk Ends* and *A Light in the Attic* contain poems sure to delight children of all ages. Brod Bagert's poetry is written in the voice of the child. Students find his material well suited for reading with expression and performance. Many poets write verse for children, and several published poetry collections can be read for both sheer enjoyment and to build fluency. Teachers and children can also compose their own original verse or verse modeled after favorite poems and put them together into class collections for reading.

Jean's students are in transitional second grade because they did not successfully complete the first-grade curriculum during the previous year. They have particular trouble emerging into conventional forms of reading. Jean has found that predictable books and poems are great ways to capture the reading interest of students who previously spent most of their reading time doing worksheets and unsuccessfully manipulating letters and sounds. Each day she introduces one or two new predictable stories written in the form of big books or poems written on chart paper. She explains, "The large texts allow the reading to be a community and choral reading experience."

As the lesson begins, students read several patterned stories and poems from previous lessons—perhaps Joy Cowley's *Mrs. Wishy Washy* or Sue Williams's *I Went Walking*. Jean points to the words and lines in many of the stories. After reading them several times as a group and asking individuals and pairs of students to read them, Jean helps students detect individual letters, word parts, and words. She makes word and letter cards, which students match with words and letters in the stories. Children work in groups to find words from the stories that begin or end with particular sounds, letters, or letter combinations.

After several minutes spent looking at various aspects of the familiar texts, Jean introduces her students to a new book. Her routine includes showing students the cover or telling them the title and asking what the story may be about. She asks students to brainstorm various possible plots and select the most plausible. After this discussion, she reads the text to her students, pointing to individual words as she reads. Students then talk about the story. Were their predictions correct? What did they like about the story? Were any words particularly interesting? After a brief discussion Jean rereads and points to the words again. Then she invites the class to join her in a third reading. After a few more choral readings she moves on to other activities. But she makes sure that the text is available for her students so they can read and explore it on their own during free time. In upcoming days, the class continues to read the patterned story and explores in more detail the sentences, words, letters, and sounds in the text.

After sufficient practice and performance with easier texts, students may be ready for more challenging texts. Steven Stahl and colleagues (Kuhn & Stahl, 2000; Stahl & Heubach, 2005) found that students who engage in fluency instruction with more challenging texts are likely to achieve the greatest gains in reading. Although such texts may be challenging for students, the opportunity to read and reread them with teacher support or with other fluent readers will eventually lead the reader to read them as well as similar texts with fluency and comprehension. The sense of accomplishment for struggling readers that comes from reading and performing a challenging passage cannot be understated. A fine example of this notion comes from Esquith (2004, 2007), a Los Angeles teacher who works with fifth- and sixth-graders, many of whom are ELL students. Esquith's students routinely perform Shakespeare for thrilled audiences. The supported practice and rehearsal that precedes the performances are the kinds of instruction that all students, but especially struggling readers, need.

Although we do not recommend routinely giving students frustration-level texts to read, occasional challenges are appropriate, especially if the students are given appropriate support and scaffolding, opportunities to rehearse, and the chance to perform for an audience (which give legitimacy to the repeated readings). More often than not, students will rise to the occasion and amaze you with what they can accomplish.

Instructional Routines

FLUENCY DEVELOPMENT LESSON

So far we have been discussing individual aspects of successful fluency instruction. When fluency instruction includes these aspects, such as choral reading and reader's theater, students are very likely to improve in fluency and overall reading proficiency. As a form of Tier 1 instruction, these approaches are superb.

However, some students, especially those who struggle, need deeper and more intense instruction (Tiers 2 and 3). Instructional routines that employ more than one aspect in a synergistic manner will increase the effectiveness of the instruction. In essence, when you are able to design fluency instruction that includes modeling, repeated readings, and other elements mentioned earlier, the impact of combining elements will be greater than the sum of the elements alone.

One example of this principle is the *fluency development lesson (FDL)* (Rasinski et al., 1994). We devised the FDL for teachers who work with students experiencing difficulty in achieving even initial stages of fluent reading. The FDL combines several principles of effective fluency instruction in a way that maximizes students' engagement in authentic reading in a relatively short period of time and requires cooperation between two or more students. The FDL has been used as a supplement to the regular reading curriculum. Implemented at the beginning of each day, it takes 10 to 15 minutes to complete. Teachers make copies of brief passages (50 to 150 words) for each child. Often the passages are in verse form.

A typical fluency development lesson looks like this:

1. The teacher distributes copies of the text to each student.
2. The teacher reads the text to the class while the students follow along silently with their own copies. This step can be repeated several times.

3. The teacher discusses the text content as well as the quality of her or his reading of it with the class.

4. The entire class, along with the teacher, reads the text chorally several times. The teacher creates variety by having students read in antiphonal and echo styles.

5. The class divides into pairs. Each pair finds a quiet spot, and one student practices reading the text to his or her partner three times. The partner's job is to follow along in the text, provide help when needed, and give positive feedback to the reader. After the first three readings, the roles are switched. The partner becomes the reader and reads the text three times as well.

6. Students regroup, and the teacher asks for volunteers to perform the text. Individuals, pairs, and groups of up to four perform the reading for the class. Sometimes students perform the text for the school principal, secretary, custodian, and other teachers and classes. The performing students are lavished with praise.

7. Students take the passage home and read it to their parents and other relatives. Parents are asked to listen to their child read as many times as they would like and to praise their child's efforts.

During our work with the FDL, teachers implemented this technique three to four times a week from October to June. We found that nearly all children benefited from the lesson: They experienced greater improvement in their overall reading achievement, word recognition, and fluency than did a comparable group of children who received more traditional supplemental instruction using the same passages. The poorest readers made the greatest gains. Teachers and students who used the FDL liked reading and talking about the enjoyable passages, the opportunity to read chorally and with friends, and the noticeable improvement the approach offered students.

Maria has used the FDL in her class for more than two years. As a result, several of her second-graders have made extraordinary progress. "The main thing about this lesson is that it allows children to be successful in reading. Even though this is second grade, several of my students essentially begin the school year not reading. These kids need intensive help in word recognition and developing fluent reading habits. I honestly think that FDL is one answer to helping these youngsters."

At the beginning of the year Maria asks parents to purchase a particular collection of poems for children. Each day, whenever possible, Maria and her students explore one or more poems from the collection using the FDL format. She has made one significant modification that she believes (and we agree) helps reinforce students' word recognition learning. After each FDL, she asks students to choose a favorite or interesting word (or two) from the poem, write it on an index card, and add it to their personal word banks. These banks are then used in word practice and word-sort activities. (See Chapter 6 for a complete description of these activities.) Students like the opportunity to work with others when practicing their reading and enjoy performing their readings for others. Indeed, Jean (whom you met earlier in this chapter) has recently worked with a first-grade teacher to develop a program where second- and first-grade readers are paired for reading practice in much the same way as in the FDL.

SUPPORT-READING STRATEGY

Morris (2008; Morris & Nelson, 1992) developed the *support-reading strategy (SRS)* in response to the needs of low-achieving second-grade students. This strategy contains several fluency instruction elements and is meant to integrate into a traditional class using basal materials. It follows an instructional cycle that lasts 20 to 25 minutes at a time.

- *Day 1:* The teacher reads a story to a small group of students in a fluent, expressive voice. Throughout the reading, the teacher asks students to clarify text information and predict upcoming events. The teacher and students then echo-read the story, with the students reading from their own books. The teacher monitors individuals' reading and provides assistance, support, and encouragement as necessary.
- *Day 2:* Students are divided into pairs that include a good reader and a less proficient one. The pairs reread the story, alternating pages as they go. The children are then assigned a short segment (100 words) from the story. In pairs, the students read to their partners, who provide help as needed. Finally, if enough time remains, the pairs reread the entire story, alternating pages so that each child reads the text read by the partner in the initial partner reading.
- *Day 3:* During a seatwork period, individual children read their assigned parts to the teacher, and the teacher checks the reading for word recognition accuracy.

Many students in this program had made virtually no progress in reading during the 11 months preceding it and were still at the initial stages of reading development when they began SRS. After 6 months of SRS, their reading ability had increased substantially (Morris & Nelson, 1992).

FLUENCY-ORIENTED READING INSTRUCTION

Fluency-oriented reading instruction (FORI) integrates fluency instruction into the regular basal reading program (Stahl, Heubach, & Cramond, 1997). The lesson begins with the teacher reading the assigned story to the students and engaging students in a discussion of the story and other comprehension activities. The teacher also leads the students in rereading or echo reading portions of the story. The story then goes home with the students for additional practice with parents. (Children who are struggling in reading take the story home over several days.) The next day, students orally read the assigned story with a partner, alternating pages as they work through the text, while the silent partner monitors the reading.

Testing FORI over two years in primary-grade classrooms, Stahl and Heubach (2005) found that students made an average gain of approximately two years in reading in one year of instruction. Moreover, they found that only 2 of a total of 105 students were reading below grade level at the end of the school year.

The fluency development lesson, support-reading strategy, and fluency-oriented reading instruction are offered only as examples of how teachers can design powerful Tier

FIGURE 7.3 Procedures for Fluency Routines

Repeated Reading

- Students practice reading texts until they achieve fluency.
- Students perform texts for interested audiences—peers, younger students, family members, and so on.

Paired Reading

- Student selects book.
- Student and parent (or other good reader) read book aloud together.
- Parent's reading slightly leads or follows, depending on student's need and desire.
- Student logs paired-reading activities.

Choral Reading

- Teacher or students select text and determine or assign parts (if it is antiphonal reading).
- Teacher reads text aloud; students listen and read along silently. Discussion may follow.
- Teacher and students read text together.
- Choral or antiphonal choral reading is performed.

Recorded Passages

- Teacher or other competent reader prepares recordings of texts.
- Student selects book and recording. Student reads and simultaneously listens to book several times.
- Student performs book or a portion of book for an audience.

Fluency Development Lesson

- Teacher selects short text and prepares copies for students.

- Teacher reads text; students listen and critique reading. Discussion may follow.
- Teacher and students read text together.
- Student pairs take turns reading the text to each other. Listeners provide assistance and positive feedback.
- Students perform the text for interested audiences.
- Students add words from text to their word banks.
- Students read text at home for parents.

Support-Reading Strategy

- Teacher reads story; students predict upcoming events.
- Teacher and students echo-read story.
- Student pairs reread story, alternating pages once or twice.
- Students practice 100-word segments with partners.
- Students read assigned segments to the teacher, who checks reading accuracy.

Fluency-Oriented Reading Instruction

- Teacher reads story to students.
- Teacher and students discuss story and do comprehension activities.
- Teacher and students reread portions of the story.
- Students reread story at home.
- Next day, students orally reread the story with a partner.

2 instruction for their students who find reading most difficult by combining those elements of fluency instruction that we know work—modeling, assisted reading, repeated readings, and phrasing—in creative and engaging ways for students. We challenge you to design equally powerful instruction for your students who struggle with fluency. Your students are sure to benefit from your efforts.

Do Not Neglect Reading Fluency

The activities we have described in this chapter share a common purpose: to help students develop the ability to read fluently and with comprehension. This goal is important because fluent readers can better identify unknown words and comprehend text. For example, the repeated readings embedded in fluency activities allow readers to develop their sight vocabularies naturally and without special emphasis or instruction. Moreover, knowing that one's reading sounds good boosts self-esteem. Students enjoy these activities, and their successes engender positive attitudes toward reading and about themselves as readers. Finally, these fluency activities frequently involve joint decision making and cooperative activity and performance, all of which develop a sense of community among students.

Each of the fluency activities highlighted in this chapter has been proved and endorsed by teacher practice and professional research. They all work with many types of texts, but they may be most appropriate with short, predictable pieces such as poetry or patterned books. Figure 7.3 summarizes the steps involved in each of the activities we described in this chapter.

Allington (1983) argued long ago that fluency is a neglected goal of the reading curriculum. Subsequent research has found that fluency is indeed important, especially for struggling readers. The source of difficulty for many readers who struggle lies in fluency. We are certain that focused, intensive, engaging, and authentic activity in this essential area of reading will help turn many struggling readers into succeeding students.

DISCUSSION QUESTIONS

Some of the discussion questions for each chapter ask you to think through your own work as a teacher. If you are not currently a practicing teacher, try to respond to these questions from your own school experience (either from when you yourself were a student or from visits to schools that you have made in your teacher education program).

1. Think of someone you would consider a fluent speaker (e.g., John F. Kennedy or Martin Luther King Jr.). What are the characteristics that define this person as fluent?

2. Look up the term *prosody* in the dictionary or online. How does this definition help you better understand reading fluency?

3. Is fluency instruction included in your district-adopted reading materials? Does it include all components of fluency—prosody, automatic word recognition, accurate word recognition? Is rate/speed emphasized more than other aspects of fluency or is there balance? If it is unbalanced, what could you do to reach balance?

4. Talk to secondary teachers in your district. To what extent do they see disfluent readers in their courses? Is fluency taught in their curriculum? How do they feel about including it?

5. Students should never be asked to read text if the purpose is something other than to make meaning. Have you observed instances of students reading for a reason other than making meaning? What was the teacher's purpose in giving those assignments? Could that purpose have been achieved in another way?

6. With your colleagues generate a list of ways you could have students read orally other than round robin (e.g., read your favorite part; read what the character said the way you think he would have said it; read the part that describes the setting).

zebra
panda
cheetah
tiger/eagle
lion/ostrich
gorilla
~~see~~ ox
bull

Building Deep and Wide Vocabularies in Struggling Readers

I T WAS THE WEEK BEFORE VALENTINE'S DAY and Mrs. Henshaw was reading children's trade books to her students that had a "love" theme. Today's book was William Steig's *Caleb and Kate*, a tale about the relationship between Kate the weaver and Caleb the carpenter who had been transformed into a dog by a local witch. After having read the first few pages of the picture book to her third-grade class, she asked students to "harvest" or call out words they thought were interesting and noteworthy. Mrs. Henshaw wrote the words on a sheet of chart paper posted on the wall as the students called them out. In less than five minutes, students called out the following words, which she transcribed on the chart: *fierce, fragrant, odious, cantankerous, wheezed, crowed, green sleep, hoddy doddy, brogans, breeches,* and *shuffling*. As she wrote the words, Mrs. Henshaw expounded on them—their meanings, what they imply, how they are used. She also invited students to add their own comments to the list of words.

Later we asked Mrs. Henshaw about her word list, which she calls her "literacy word wall." Here is what she had to say:

I think the best place to find words to teach students is in the very books and stories that I read to students and that they read on their own. We try to harvest from five to ten words every day. We talk about the words, but most importantly we use the words in our speech and writing through the next several days and beyond. I try to use the words myself in my own language with children. I can't wait to call out the students who may be misbehaving and tell them about the odious consequences of their actions should they continue. (Mrs. H. chuckles.) To be honest, I think this is one of the best ways to teach children about those academic and literary words that are essential to their growth in reading and in the various subject areas. I know they are learning these words when I hear my students using them spontaneously in the cafeteria, playground, and hallways. My colleagues have noticed this as well. That's why you will find literacy word walls in nearly all the classrooms in my school.

Clearly, Mrs. Henshaw is a wise teacher whose students not only are growing in their knowledge of words; they are also growing in the love of and appreciation for well-chosen words and in their reading comprehension!

An early finding that has remained consistent in more recent research has been the remarkably strong association between vocabulary knowledge and reading proficiency (Davis, 1944; RAND Reading Study Group, 2002). Good readers tend to know many words and understand many concepts, and people who know many words tend to be good readers. That finding makes sense to us. To comprehend, you must understand the words that make up the text. Moreover, as you read, you encounter new ideas, concepts, and words, and you see existing ideas, concepts, and words in new ways. As a result, your knowledge of words grows. Indeed, vocabulary and direct instruction in vocabulary are among the most potent predictors of reading comprehension and overall proficiency in reading (Anderson & Freebody, 1981; Bromley, 2007; National Reading Panel, 2000; Van-DeWeghe, 2007).

That's the good news, but here is also some bad news: If reading frustrates you or gives you little enjoyment, you may choose to read less or to avoid reading altogether. This decision leads to fewer encounters with new and interesting words; and as a result your vocabulary plateaus, your growth in reading slows, and reading becomes even more difficult and frustrating. The cycle is the same as the one described in the previous paragraph—but in the wrong direction.

Many struggling readers have limited word knowledge. Particularly when they read instructional texts, they may be overloaded with the vocabulary and overwhelmed by the conceptual load of the text. Reading is slow, laborious, and frustrating; learning is impeded (Rupley & Nichols, 2005). In fact, when any reader confronts text that contains many unfamiliar words, comprehension suffers. Thus all teachers must engage students in regular vocabulary exploration, particularly teachers in specialized subject areas and those who work with struggling readers.

We like to think of vocabulary exploration as word play, word exploration, or simply having fun with words, but this does not characterize traditional forms of vocabulary instruction. Before we present instructional suggestions, let's take a look at how vocabulary is very often taught.

Traditional Vocabulary Instruction

Nearly every person who has attended school in the United States can remember being regularly assigned lists of words to learn. More often than not, the words had little or no connection to curricular areas; they might even have been words that students had never encountered. The weekly assignment usually went something like this: "Find and write a definition for each word," or "Use each word in a sentence." At the end of the week came a test, and by the following Monday the words were forgotten and never thought of again!

When Mike (son of author Tim Rasinski) was in seventh grade, he received a list of 75 words to define for an upcoming vocabulary test (see Figure 8.1). Reluctantly and with great frustration, Mike spent the better part of a weekend completing the task. He looked

FIGURE 8.1   Traditional Vocabulary List and Assignment

Part of Speech & Definition
Due Next Fri

Mike Rasinski
Read per 1
March 1

② Antonyms Sent

VOCABULARY LIST

Do First 5

1. adroit - adj skillful & clever
2. apprise - v. to notify
3. aromatic - adj having an aroma
4. ascetic - adj self denying, austere n. one who leads a life of self denial
5. bayou - n. in Southern U.S. A marshy inlet or outlet of lake, river, etc.
6. bellicose - adj. quarrelsome, warlike
7. choleric - adj. easily angered
8. cloister - n. a monestary or convent
9. conjecture - n. guess, inferring without complete evidence
10. copious - adj copious abundant
11. coquetry - n. a girl or woman flirt
12. cornice - n. a horizontal molding projecting along the top of a wall, etc.
13. courageous - n. brave
14. debris - n. bits & pieces of stone, rubbish, etc.
15. decorum - n. whatever is suitable or proper
16. diadem - n. - crown, ornamental headband
17. docile - adj. easy to discipline
18. dogmatic - adj. asserted w/o proof, positive or arrogant in stating opinion *not on test*
19. doleful - adj. sad, mournful
20. efface - v. keep from being noticed, blot out

21. garrulous - adj. talking too much about inconsequential things
22. grapple - n. hand to hand struggle, a grip
23. guidon -
24. impose - v. to place a burden on to force onto others
25. interpose - v. to intervine, interrupt
26. knell - v. to ring slowly, ominously - ommen of death
27. languor - n. lack of vigor, weakness
28. ludicrous - adj. causing laughter because absurd or ridiculus
29. malevolence -
30. maudlin - adj. foolishly, often tearfully sentimental
31. melee - n. confused general hand to hand fight
32. molten - adj melted by heat
33. myriad - n. adj very many persons or things
34. orb - n. globe or sphere
35. ostracism - n. practicing banishing one
36. pantaloons - n. trousers
37. pariah - n. any outcast person formly in India any oppressed class
38. pathos - n. quality of something arousing pity
39. perilous - adj dangerous, involving peril
40. plaintive - adj expressing sorrow

41. restive - adj restless, uneasy hard to manage refusing to go ahead
42. reverie - n. dreamy thinking of pleasant things
43. roseate - adj. rosate color, cheerful optimistic
44. rueful - adj sorrowful unhappy causing sorrow
45. sallow - adj. having a sickly yellow complexion
46. sardonic - adj bitterly sarcastic, scornful or mocking
47. savant - n. a learned person
48. sententious - adj saying much in few words
49. sexton - n. person who takes care of a church, rings bells, arranges burials
50. sinuous - adj having many curves or turns ② indirect, untrustworthy
51. suffuse - v. overspread (with liquid, dye, etc.)
52. surmount - adj. rise above ② overcome
53. surplice - n. broad sleeved white gown worn by members of clergy or choir
54. sylvan - adj. characteristic of woods. wooded.
55. tableau - n. presentation of a scene by costumed person or group
56. tedious - adj tiresome boring hackneyed
57. travail - n. hard work or severe pain
58. undulate - v. to cause to move by waves
59. vanquish - v. to defeat
60. venerable - adj worthy of respect because of one's dignity etc.

the words up in a dictionary, and he did reasonably well on the examination. However, it had a cost: Mike found the assignment "stupid." This was his way of saying that the words had little or no connection to his world or any content he was studying. The words were too difficult for a middle school student. He saw simply too many words to learn, for no real purpose, and no connection to what he was studying or his own life. He was over-whelmed and unmotivated.

Tim recently asked Mike, now an adult, if he remembered any of the words from the list and, if so, what they meant. His memory of the assignment was burned painfully into his memory. However, his memory of the words or their meanings was vague at best! Indeed, we recently asked a group of graduate students to define a set of words from this list. Most were unable to define more than half of the words.

Unfortunately, this type of vocabulary instruction continues in too many classrooms. Yet most teachers, not to mention students, would agree that rote memorization of words and their definitions rarely improves vocabulary. It only adds to many students' frustration with words and reading, magnifies their negative attitudes toward reading, and contributes to lack of growth in reading. Moreover, students may come to believe that words and concepts are not important, at least not beyond the test on Friday.

Such approaches are exercises in futility for at least three reasons. First, the words have little connection to students' existing knowledge or what they are studying in other subjects. Learning new ideas, concepts, and words involves connecting or integrating the new information into what learners already know. If students have little background knowledge about the new words and concepts or cannot see the connections, then the process of integration drags. Learning will occur neither efficiently nor effectively.

Second, finding definitions or using words in sentences does not ensure understanding. Official definitions can be just as confusing as the words they are supposed to clarify, and sentences that students compose often demonstrate a remarkable lack of understanding. Take, for example, the following sentences from student compositions, compiled by Lederer (1987) in his book *Anguished English:*

Socrates died from an overdose of wedlock.

Solomon, one of David's sons, had 500 wives and 500 porcupines.

The inhabitants of ancient Egypt were called mummies.

What command do the students who wrote these sentences have over the major concepts in the sentences? How well do they understand the content to which these sentences are connected?

Finally, this age-old method of vocabulary instruction is no fun at all. It is drudgery, and students treat it as such. The unfortunate consequence is that students may learn that any type of word exploration is boring and to be avoided.

Vocabulary instruction need not be boring. Indeed, it can be a delightful, engaging, and insightful learning experience for most students, especially those whose vocabularies are limited, who speak English as a second language, and whose reading growth is slow for a variety of other reasons. To be truly effective, word play must be based on words that students need to know or have some interest in. Therefore, teachers must help them see connections between unknown words and familiar words and concepts. Teachers must also make sure that vocabulary activities are interesting and playful. When students become interested in and knowledgeable about words, reading comprehension and writing proficiency will inevitably improve.

Two Important Dimensions of Vocabulary

When thinking of vocabulary learning, one usually thinks of adding new words, ideas, or concepts to one's mental dictionary or lexicon. Although this is certainly an important aspect of vocabulary learning, there is another.

If adding new words can be thought of as increasing the breadth of one's vocabulary, the flip side of vocabulary learning involves adding depth to students' knowledge of words that already exist in their lexicon. Words can have connotative as well as denotative meanings. *Denotative* meanings are explicit. For example, the word *right* denotes something correct or acceptable. However, *right* also has a *connotative* or implied meaning of skepticism. When a person utters, "Right," after hearing a friend argue a point, that *right* can either denote that the person agrees with the argument or it can connote that the person is skeptical of it. Additionally, words can have several denotative meanings. *Right* can also mean good or a particular side or direction (as opposed to *left*), among other meanings.

Exemplary vocabulary instruction, then, is multidimensional. Just as it focuses on developing students' breadth of word knowledge, it also works to increase students' depth of word knowledge as well. A student may understand a word one way or in one context and yet lack a full understanding of the word. Good vocabulary instruction both develops the richness of already known words and also introduces new words.

Best Ways to Learn New Words

Before we share specific instructional activities, we want to describe two of the best ways for students (and all of us, for that matter) to learn new words and concepts. Learning words and concepts is not exclusively a school activity. Children learn thousands of words and word meanings before they ever set foot in a school. How? They learn most words and concepts through life experiences that they later discuss with their parents and other important people in their lives. A child going to McDonald's will learn about hamburgers, cheeseburgers, french fries, and McNuggets. A visit to the dentist can help someone learn about dentists, X-rays, cavities, and novocaine. A person's life experiences, no matter the age, provide wonderful opportunities for learning new words and concepts, especially if the person discusses her or his experiences with others. A summer vacation to Europe or the Black Hills of South Dakota will lead a child or an adult to discover new words in a rich and concrete context. All experiences are important. Successful teachers remember the great opportunities available to expand student vocabularies through direct experience—everything from school field trips to investigations within and around the school itself. The conversations that surround these experiences can provide fertile ground for vocabulary development.

People also learn words through secondhand or vicarious experience. Movies, television shows, and reading are examples of ways in which individuals share experiences they do not actually have. Reading, in particular, is a superb way to increase vocabulary. We mentioned previously that reading is associated with vocabulary growth. The reason should be clear. When reading, readers encounter words unfamiliar or only partly familiar. The story context (its meaning, synonymous words, and illustrations) helps readers understand more about these words.

We believe that reading is far superior to other forms of vicarious experience for learning vocabulary. Movies and television often deal with familiar situations and incorporate known words. Such events are often directed toward a lowest common denominator—those viewers with the smallest conceptual and vocabulary backgrounds—so that everyone can understand the story. In reading, however, authors often take readers to new experiences, even within familiar situations. And authors choose vocabulary that is rich and interesting, that creates a particular mood, feel, or texture. In other words, reading gives readers many opportunities to learn new words, literary words—words that are used in written language more than oral language, words that are most likely to improve students' reading and writing (Cunningham & Stanovich, 1998).

This is another reason to encourage reading in and out of school: Reading expands readers' vocabularies, which makes further reading easier. The effect of reading can be expanded, especially for struggling readers and ELL students, when the teacher explains the meanings to certain words (Biemiller & Boote, 2006; Coyne et al., 2004; Hui-Tzu, 2008). Listening to stories can have much the same effect. Indeed, because elementary-grade students have limited word recognition abilities, they usually comprehend stories at a higher level of sophistication when they listen than when they read. Reading to students can have an even more powerful effect on students' vocabulary development than their own reading, and its facilitative effect is well established in the research (Beck & McKeown, 2007; Blachowicz & Fisher, 2005; Cohen, 1968). Now you have one more reason to read every day to your students, no matter their grade or age. To expand this effect, take a few minutes after a read-aloud and talk with students about the interesting words they heard as well as their meanings and use in much the same way that Mrs. Henshaw described at the opening to this chapter.

Principles of Effective Vocabulary Instruction

Students can also learn and explore words through direct instruction or word-play activities. Students must learn many words for success in school—it has been estimated that from elementary through high school, students learn 7 words per day, or 2,700 to 3,000 per year (Snow, Burns, & Griffin, 1998). Teachers must do everything possible to expand and enrich students' vocabulary. Recent research and research reviews have demonstrated that direct instruction in vocabulary, in a variety of forms, leads to improvements in vocabulary and reading comprehension for students (e.g., Boulware-Gooden et al., 2007; Kamil, 2004; Nelson & Stage, 2007), including those who struggle in reading (e.g., Ebbers & Denton, 2008; Lubliner & Smetana, 2005) and ELL students (e.g., Schmitt, 2008).

We recommend regular direct instruction and focused activity on vocabulary, especially for struggling readers. A daily 10 to 20 minutes of word play or word exploration can go a long way toward expanding vocabulary and improving comprehension. As we have already explained, traditional vocabulary instruction can be deadly to students' interest and growth and is largely ineffective. Nevertheless, alternatives exist to word lists and memorization. Vocabulary researchers Nagy (1988) and Stahl (1986) offer several principles for effective vocabulary instruction; to this list we add one final and, we believe, essential principle.

1. *Vocabulary instruction should be integrative* (Nagy, 1988). Vocabulary instruction should help students connect new words with their existing knowledge of words. Students must learn, for example, that *bullpen* is a word connected to baseball in general and pitchers in particular. That sort of connection makes words memorable. A dry, abstract, or out-of-context definition may not stick with the student. Vocabulary instruction, like all instruction, should move from what students already know to what is new. Their existing knowledge serves as an anchor for their learning.

2. *Vocabulary should be learned deeply through active processing and discussion* (Beck, McKeown, & Kucan, 2002). Stahl (1986) calls the process of making connections between new and known information and between contexts *deep processing*. Making such connections involves active and deep thinking; the result is a better understood concept. Class or group discussion is one of the best ways to encourage deep processing—so are making associations, categorizing, and semantic analysis. As students talk about and manipulate new words and concepts, they make connections to other knowledge domains and share these connections with classmates. Stahl suggests that deep processing consists of three levels:

- The first level is *associative*. This occurs when students make a simple connection between a word and another word or a specific context. For example, providing a synonym for an unknown word is a form of association.

- The second level is called *comprehension*. This happens when students demonstrate understanding of the word through application, such as categorizing a set of words, or filling in a word deleted from a sentence.

- The final and deepest level of word learning is *generational,* or using a word in new ways. Examples are defining a word using one's own words, using the word in authentic writing or conversation, or using the word in new ways (Stahl, 1986).

3. *Vocabulary instruction needs to include repetition* (Nagy, 1988; Stahl, 1986). Students must see, hear, and use words many times in many contexts to learn them. Few people can see a word once and know it. Most people require multiple exposures to cement a new word and its meaning in their memories. The repetition needs to be within meaningful contexts and not simple or drill-like repetition with word lists or flash-cards.

4. *Words and concepts are best learned when presented in meaningful ways* (Nagy, 1988), *through multiple encounters* (Flynt & Brozo, 2008), *with attention to definitional knowledge* (Stahl, 1986). Meaningful repetition can simply involve connecting a read-aloud, student reading, and a direct experience concerning the same topic. Meaningful and multiple encounters should involve reading, writing, listening, and speaking (Pearson, Hiebert, & Kamil, 2007) and may also involve technology (Kamil, 2004). These meaningful contexts provide the repetition that helps to ensure thorough word learning. Meaningful repetition makes thematic units of study inviting. Such units expose students to words

and concepts numerous times and in several meaningful contexts over the course of the unit study. Meaningful use entails not only seeing the words in meaningful contexts but also thinking about and using them in meaningful ways. When students use new words meaningfully, their understanding is enhanced, and they develop more flexible control over their use.

Stahl (1986) adds, however, that contextual presentation along with definition may be the most powerful way to learn new words. Effective vocabulary instruction combines definitions and various contextual presentations or examples of how the words are actually used.

5. *Word learning can be made generative when students learn that certain common word units (roots and affixes) have meaning that can help readers unlock the meaning of new words on their own.* A growing body of research is pointing to the strategic importance of morphemes (word meaning units), especially those derived from Latin and Greek, to build English vocabulary, especially for students with reading difficulties (Baumann et al., 2003; Ebbers & Denton, 2008; Harmon, Hedrick, & Wood, 2005; Padak et al., 2008) and younger students (Mountain, 2005). Since well over half of English words and a large portion of the low-frequency academic words in English (Bear et al., 2007; Padak et al., 2008) are derived from Latin and Greek, it makes good sense to help students capitalize on the meaningful Latin and Greek roots that are embedded in so many of these words.

6. *The teacher's own attitude toward words and word learning plays a critical role in vocabulary instruction* (Bromley, 2007). Words can be a fascinating area of study. However, students' attitudes depend on teachers' attitudes. If teachers find word study fascinating, many of their students may also become interested in words. This means escaping the vocabulary workbooks and developing a playful attitude toward words (Blachowicz & Fisher, 2004).

Many words have interesting stories behind them. Words and word combinations can make uninteresting sentences and paragraphs come to life, and words can be the fodder for enjoyable classroom activities. Students and teachers can even invent words. Word learning is most effective when teachers have a playful, inquisitive, and inventive attitude toward words. Attitude can be highly contagious! Figure 8.2 provides a list of some of our favorite books that contain interesting and engaging stories about words.

FIGURE 8.2   Books That Tell the Stories of Words

John Ayto. *Dictionary of Word Origins*. New York: Arcade Publishing, 1993.

Charles Funk. *Thereby Hangs a Tale: Stories of Curious Word Origins*. New York: Harper & Row, 2002.

Paul M. Levitt & Elissa Guralnick. *The Weighty Word Book*. Boulder, CO: Court Wayne Press, 1999.

The Merriam-Webster New Book of Word Histories. Springfield, MA: Merriam-Webster, 1991.

Marvin Terban. *Guppies in Tuxedos: Funny Eponyms*. New York: Houghton Mifflin, 1988. (one of a series of books on words by the author)

In the remainder of this chapter we present specific instructional strategies that share these characteristics. We recommend that you be flexible in your use of them. Apply them before reading to acquaint students with specific words they will encounter. Integrate them into a regular and consistent classroom instructional routine of word exploration or word play. Whether you broaden students' vocabulary for a specific topic or the more general purpose of fascination with words, their overall reading will improve as well.

Instructional Strategies for Teaching Vocabulary

LIST GROUP LABEL

List Group Label (LGL) fits within almost any curriculum area and can be used at any age level. The instructional heart of the activity involves drawing out students' own knowledge of a topic and inviting them to organize that information (Marzano, Pickering, & Pollock, 2001). Because the students supply most of the material for the activity, they control its difficulty. Here's how LGL works:

1. The teacher or students choose a topic for study. It may come from a subject area, an upcoming reading, a theme to be explored by the class, a holiday, or other possibilities.

2. Groups of students brainstorm all the words they can think of related to the topic. Words are listed on the chalkboard or a sheet of paper that everyone can see. The teacher may also participate in this activity and call out a word or two to be entered into the mix. After brainstorming, students may be asked to explain unfamiliar words.

3. When students exhaust their store of words, they organize their list by choosing two or more words that share a common characteristic, listing them together, and supplying a title or label that describes the category. This new organization is also recorded on the chalkboard if the whole group is working together, or on sheets of paper if the students are working in small groups. Students categorize and label the categories until the list is exhausted.

4. Next, students add words to the categories on their organized lists. When a meaningful organization is imposed on a list of concepts, students usually find they can more easily recall related concepts from memory. Students might discuss the reason: meaningful organization assists memory.

5. If students are working in groups, each group shares with the entire class its method of categorization and the added words. Lively discussion takes place as students analyze words and concepts for shared and defining features.

6. Students can extend the activity by transforming their list of organized concepts into a semantic web (see Figure 8.3) or prototypical informational outline. The final product as well as the related discussion introduce students to new concepts and can act as a guide and background for further study.

FIGURE 8.3 Semantic Web for "Baseball"

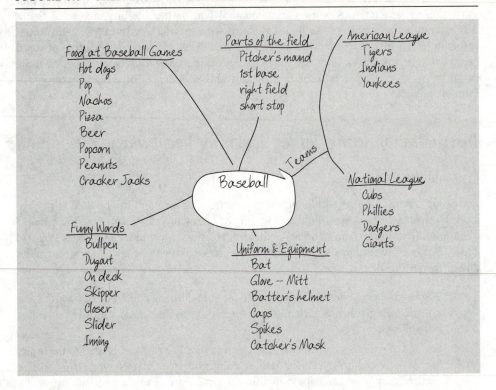

Karen, a Title I teacher, likes to use List Group Label when she introduces students to a new set of readings. She finds that students like to brainstorm their own words and mention and explain words unfamiliar to others. "The part I like best about this activity," she explains, "is the student control. They're not working with words I chose or the text provided. My students love to do this, and all students, even the brightest, learn new words or new ways for thinking about words they already know. If you think about it, LGL requires kids to do some pretty sophisticated and creative analysis of words and concepts."

OTHER CATEGORIZATION ACTIVITIES

As students put similar concepts together, the process of categorization helps make their world more manageable. It also gives students the chance to meet new words and think about familiar words in new ways. Similar to List Group Label, word sorts, which we have mentioned in several chapters in this book, also challenge students to categorize words. If your students maintain a word bank in the form of a deck of word cards, you can ask them to sort their words into categories that you name. For example, when teaching word recognition skills, we ask students to sort their word bank words by number of syllables, sounds, affixes, and so on (see Chapter 6) to give them practice and to focus their attention on certain aspects of words. Later, we might ask students to sort their cards into more semantic categories such as words mostly used at home and words mostly used at school, indoor words and outdoor words, words related to fun and words related to work, and so on.

Word sorts can also be related to a topic under study. For example, if the class is studying animal life, the teacher might present words such as *bear, dog, elephant, mouse, horse, tiger, giraffe, wolf, rabbit,* and *coyote.* Word-sort categories could include North American and non–North American animals, predatory and nonpredatory animals, domestic and wild animals, and so on. Sorting the same set of words in a variety of ways helps students think about word features. In the animal-life sorts, for example, students can think about bears as North American *and* predatory *and* wild.

If the teacher provides the categories, the activity is called a *closed sort. Open sorts,* on the other hand, encourage divergent thinking among students. The teacher presents words, often derived from past or current readings, and asks students to work in pairs or small groups to arrange the words into meaningful groups. When they have finished, students share their reasoning with the rest of the class.

Another categorization activity we call *Pair 'Em Up* requires students to justify their thinking as they pair up words. The teacher (or a student) presents three words to the group. Students determine which two go together and provide a justification for the pairing. Recently, we observed a second-grade class that had a few extra minutes before heading off to lunch. After introducing the activity, the teacher called out, "Trees, sky, and dirt."

One student said, "Trees and dirt go together because they both are on the ground."

"Okay," said the teacher. "Anyone else have other ideas?"

Another child responded, "Sky and dirt because they're not alive."

A third child answered, "I think it's trees and the sky because trees grow into the sky."

Then, a fourth said, "Hey, how about this? Trees and sky go together because they have long vowel sounds."

After a brief discussion on the merits of each response, students continued the activity in pairs. The idea behind Pair 'Em Up is not so much to elicit the correct answer as to challenge students to think about the many ways that words can be connected to one another. This flexible categorizing helps students create depth and breadth in their vocabulary.

CONCEPT MAP

When a List Group Label activity is converted into a semantic map, students see the connection between words and higher-order or categorical concepts. The visual display helps many students develop the notion that words connect to one another through meaning.

A refinement of this notion is a concept map, sometimes known as a concept-of-definition map (Schwartz & Raphael, 1985). A *concept map* is a visual representation of the definition of a concept or word. Besides defining particular words, concept maps help students understand the variety of ways to define words and concepts. One can define words by contrasting words or concepts (using opposites) or identifying the hierarchical category to which they belong. Subordinate categories or examples can also help clarify the meaning. Finally, words or concepts can be defined by their essential characteristics or properties. Figure 8.4 is an example of a completed concept map.

The teacher usually begins a concept map lesson by presenting only the word to be defined, which is written in the center of the map. As a class or in several smaller groups,

FIGURE 8.4 Concept Map for "Dog"

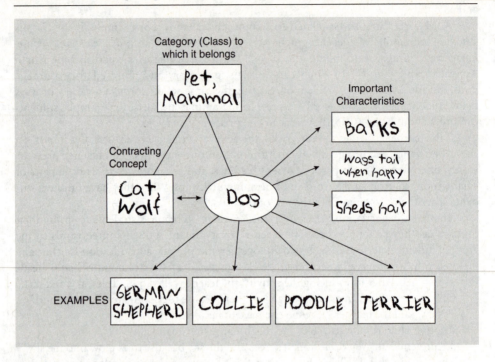

students define the word by filling in the various elements of the map. Small-group work can demonstrate divergent thinking: Some groups are conventional in their definitions, whereas others are more creative. All maps are acceptable, however, as long as students can defend their decisions.

Wayne, a fifth-grade teacher, has used concept maps for several years.

> We do a word a day—I choose from current events or what we are studying in a thematic unit, or I'll ask a student to think of a word to share with the class. You need to choose words for which higher-order concepts as well as examples or subordinate concepts exist. We usually do it at the beginning of each day as a sort of warm-up for the class. Most of the time the students work in small groups or pairs and then share their work with the class. What I really like about concept maps is that they help students understand how words are defined and that they don't need to rely totally on a dictionary to provide meaning for a word.
>
> Once the maps are done I'll put them on display in the hallway or we'll create our own classroom dictionary that consists of a set of maps put in alphabetical order and bound into a book or three-ring binder. It's interesting to see how students will look over the maps on display or actually leaf through the class concept-map dictionary. I know I'm touching some of the kids' interest in words through this and some of the other word activities we do.

SEMANTIC FEATURE ANALYSIS

Concept maps provide students with a visual way of representing the various dimensions of meaning to one key word at a time. *Semantic feature analysis (SFA)* provides a visual way of examining the various dimensions of meaning to a group of words that are related in some way.

The visual used in SFA is a grid (see Figure 8.5). In the left vertical column, list the words that are to be analyzed. Across the top row, list meaningful features that distinguish at least one of the words from the others. The features should be written in such a way that they can be answered with a yes/no or +/– response. Students can brainstorm the words and the semantic features, or the teacher can determine them in advance. Once the words and features are in place, students then engage in analyzing the list of words by determining the characteristics manifested by each word on the list. Although this may be thought of as a word-list definition activity, the fact that students engage in making the list, determining the features, and analyzing the words according to the features makes it an activity in which students have ownership and are active participants (as opposed to the passive action of looking up definitions in the dictionary).

The words used in an SFA activity can come from any content area. Animals, trees, types of clouds, simple machines, presidents, authors, book titles, months of year, and parts of a car are examples of the general categories from which we have chosen words for SFA with students.

Students can complete an SFA grid on their own or with partners. If they are unsure of an answer, students can do some research. Not all features can easily be answered in a yes/no, all or nothing, fashion. For example, in the American Cities SFA (Figure 8.5), heavy industry may have been a feature that students were asked to consider. All large cities have some industry, but some are known more for their industry and manufacturing than others. A yes/no response choice is not sufficient for students to make finer distinctions in features. Here is where a numerical scale (1 = definitely no, 3 = somewhat, 5 = definitely yes) may be more appropriate. Using a scale, Cleveland and Houston may rate 5s, whereas 3s and 4s would be more appropriate for the other cities.

Semantic feature analysis provides students with a tool for creatively analyzing a number of words or concepts that are in some way similar. We have found that students enjoy the activity and love taking on greater responsibility for the creation of the SFA grid as well as the subsequent analysis. The discussion that coincides with the SFA often produces lively arguments that force students to dig even deeper into the meanings of the words they are analyzing.

VOCABULARY TIMELINES

A vocabulary timeline is another visual display of words. In this case the words have shared meanings. They differ in terms of the degree to which they share a critical feature. Teachers we know have found vocabulary timelines to be an excellent way to interest students in using a resource that is often underused in the classroom—the thesaurus.

A vocabulary timeline begins with a horizontal line that is drawn across a large chart or sheet of butcher paper hung on a classroom wall. The teacher selects a major concept or word for which there are many synonyms. Fourth-grade teacher, Rosa, loves using

FIGURE 8.5 Semantic Feature Analysis for American Cities

Topic: _____

Columns = features or attributes

Rows = word or exemplars

Topic: *American Cities*	Played a role in the American Revolution	Located on an ocean or part of an ocean	Capital city	City population is over a million	Cold winters		
New York City	Yes	Yes	No	Yes	Yes		
Chicago	No	No	No	Yes	Yes		
Los Angeles	No	Yes	No	Yes	No		
Houston	No	Yes	No	Yes	No		
New Orleans	No	Yes	No	No	No		
San Francisco	No	Yes	No	?	No		
Philadelphia	Yes	No	No	?	Yes		
Boston	Yes	Yes	Yes	?	Yes		
Cleveland	No	No	No	No	Yes		
Washington	No	No	Yes	?	Yes		

FIGURE 8.6 Vocabulary Timeline for *say/said/tell/told*

Soft				Loud
whisper	murmur	declare	shout	scream

uninteresting words that her students tend to overuse in their talk or writing. A good example is *say/said/tell/told* (see Figure 8.6). Once the major concept is identified, the teacher and/or students determine the critical feature against which the various synonyms for *say/said/tell/told* will be analyzed or plotted. In the current case, volume is likely critical feature, and so the far left side of the timeline will be identified as "soft" and the far right side identified as "loud."

Once the timeline is set up, students are asked to think of words that have the same or similar meanings of *say/said/tell/told* and plot them on the timeline. When Rosa did this activity with her students, they chose the following words: *shout, scream, whisper, murmur, state, declare, announce, blab, inform,* and *mention*. Rosa has her students write the words on sticky notes and place them where they think they should go on the timelime. *Whisper* and *murmur* found their way to the soft side, and *shout* and *scream* were plotted on the loud side of the timeline. Somewhere near the middle was *declare*.

For the next several days, Rosa informs her students that they are to try to avoid using *say/said/tell/told* in their oral or written language. She notes that the words on the wall in front of them and encourages them to use the wall to choose those other more interesting words. Students add words to the vocabulary timeline throughout the week as well. Rosa finds that words are most often added immediately after sustained silent reading or teacher read aloud. That is when students notice the choices authors make to use words other than *tell* or *say* in order to make their writing more interesting for readers. From *Caleb and Kate* (Steig, 1986) students chose *wheezed* and *crowed* as interesting words from the story. Where would you plot them on a vocabulary timeline for *say/said/tell/told*?

POSSIBLE SENTENCES

Predicting is a metacognitive strategy that is often used as a method for improving students' reading comprehension (Palinscar & Brown, 1984). Predicting can also be used to explore vocabulary and text meaning simultaneously. *Possible Sentences* is a simple predicting method for exploring vocabulary in content area reading (Moore & Moore, 1986). In this activity, the teacher previews an upcoming reading and selects six to eight challenging words from the text. These are usually key concepts for the reading. Then, the teacher chooses an additional four to six words that are a bit more familiar.

The teacher displays the words for students and provides brief definitions as needed. Students are then challenged to devise sentences that contain two or more list words they think they may encounter in the reading. The sentences students come up with, both accurate and inaccurate (but all possible), are listed and discussed. After students talk about the possible veracity of the sentences, they read the passage.

Following the reading, the teacher and students return to the possible sentences and discuss whether each sentence could be true based on the passage. If a sentence could not be true, students talk about how it could be modified to make it true.

Possible Sentences and similar activities generate considerable discussion. Stahl and colleagues (Stahl & Vancil, 1986; Stahl & Clark, 1987) have found that talk is an important aspect of vocabulary learning. Stahl and Kapinus (1991) found that the Possible Sentences strategy was more effective than semantic mapping in helping intermediate-grade students learn the targeted words and comprehend the texts. Thus, Possible Sentences not only enhances vocabulary but it is also is an effective comprehension strategy. Stahl and Kapinus note that "the group discussion appears to improve learning by having students more actively process the information about the to-be-learned words. . . . Students think more deeply about the relations between the new words and the words they already know. These links lead to learning" (p. 43).

ANALOGIES

Analogies are formal statements of the relationship between several words or concepts. Research by Marzano and colleagues (Marzano, 2004; Marzano, Pickering, & Pollock, 2001) indicates that solving analogies is a powerful learning and teaching tool that promotes vocabulary learning and complex thinking. Analogies are usually in the form *A is to B as C is to D* (sometimes written as *A : B :: C : D*). Here's an example of an analogy problem that fifth-grade teacher Wayne has used with his students:

Abraham Lincoln is to the Civil War as William McKinley is to what?

To solve the problem, one must determine the relationship between the first pair of words or concepts (i.e., "president" to "war during his term") and then apply that relationship to the next pair. When one determines that McKinley was president during the Spanish-American War, then one knows the answer.

As you see, analogies easily apply to nearly any topic or subject area. Moreover, students engage in sophisticated reasoning as they determine or infer the relationship between word pairs and extend the relationship to a second pair. Again, this activity focuses on helping students make connections between words and concepts to create greater depth of understanding.

Wayne's students enjoy doing analogies, but he adds the following:

I always present them as a type of play or as riddles to solve. I think kids get a kick out of trying to figure these out and then explain their reasoning to the rest of the class. What's really neat is asking students to create a few analogies as a response to their reading, using words or ideas they encountered. Once they get the idea, the best analogies come from the students. We have a ball playing around with them. I find that through analogy play my students are more able to think flexibly about words and think about various ways that words might be related.

Because the analogies are developed from students' own interests and areas of study, difficulty level is self-controlled. Analogies work well with both primary-grade children and older students.

Examples of Analogy Problems

Steering wheel is to car as handlebar is to _____. (part to whole)

Night is to day as win is to _____. (opposites)

Storm is to rain as blizzard is to _____. (cause and effect)

Mt. Everest is to the Himalayas as the Matterhorn is to _____. (geography)

Boat is to ship as firearm is to _____. (synonym)

WORD STORIES AND MORPHEMIC ROOTS

Words often have interesting histories. Exploring word origins with students helps them develop indelible memories as they link specific words to stories of their origins. In addition, they learn to appreciate the historical context of certain words and concepts. For example, a teacher might mention that *tank,* a heavily armored military vehicle, was originally used as a code word among the Allied powers to help conceal the vehicle's development and existence from the Axis powers during World War I. That interesting story not only describes the word and concept but it also helps students understand an aspect of world history.

Learning the origin of place names, particularly those within their own community, is a great way for students to link history with vocabulary play and development. In a local elementary school, Jeanine, an intermediate-grade teacher of students with learning disabilities, interests children in words by relating the stories and rationales for place names in nearby communities. Jeanine works in Summit County, where Akron, Ohio, is located. She invites students to speculate on the origin of the county's name. A few students know that *summit* refers to a high place and suggest that Summit County contains the highest point in the state. Jeanine compliments her students for a good guess and then shares the real story of Summit County: It was the highest point on the Ohio and Erie Canal, which ran from Lake Erie to the Ohio River. Her story leads to a discussion about the numerous canal locks in the county, their purpose, how they worked, and their relation to the type of land where that part of the canal was built.

Jeanine notes that the origin of the name *Akron* is also related to summits. She points out that the city's name is derived from the Greek word *akros,* which means "topmost." Then she challenges her students to find other words that include the *akro* or *acro* word part and determine how they relate to a high place. Within minutes, students find *acrobat, Acropolis,* and *acrophobia.* After everyone discusses the meanings of these words, Jeanine ends her mini-lesson with "akros = summit or high place" written on the chalkboard. Students have a clear idea of what these words mean and how they fit into the texture of their own communities. Familiar place names such as Pittsburgh, Pennsylvania, Florida, Baton

Rouge, Vermont, Montana, Los Angeles, Palo Alto, and many others have interesting and important word histories.

Many English words are derived from other languages such as Greek, Latin, French, and Spanish. Indeed, it has been estimated that nearly 75 percent of the words in English are derived from Greek or Latin. Gaining insight into words and word parts from other languages will give students strategies for understanding many new words (Baumann et al., 2003; Mountain, 2005). Appendix E (Padak et al., 2008) lists some common word parts derived from Greek and Latin that will help students unlock the meanings of many other words they encounter.

Teaching one derivation per week can go a long way to developing students' vocabulary. Knowing that the Greek root *duc* means "lead" can help you learn the meaning of these words: *educate, educator, duct, conduct, conductor, induce, induct, induction, deduce, deduction, reduce, reduction, irreducible, duke, duchess*, and many more.

Tanya introduces her fourth-graders to a new derivation every Tuesday. She spells the word on the chalkboard, circles it, describes the meaning of the root, and asks students to find English words related to it. After introducing *terra* (meaning "land" or "earth") she was surprised to find that students came to class the next day with *terrace, territory, terra cotta, terra nova, extraterrestrial, terrarium, inter, internment, lumbricus terrestris* (earth worm), and *Terra Haute* ready to connect to the root word on the board. But even so, Tanya dazzled her students with a few additional words for the chart: *Mediterranean, terrapin*, and *terrier*. She invited students to speculate on how each new word had the concept of land or earth locked within it.

According to Tanya, her students love the opportunity to expand their vocabulary in this way. It makes them feel smarter. Learning one Latin or Greek root can expand students' knowledge of many English words. According to Tanya, "They may not learn every word on our Root List, but they do learn many, and they now have a tool for closing in on meaning when they encounter those roots in other words in the future."

Exploring word histories with students is fun, but when we share these ideas with teachers, the first question they ask is often, "But how do we find out about words and where they come from? We can't be expected to have all these words and their histories at our fingertips." The solution to this problem is as close as the public library. Just ask the librarian where you might find a few of the many books written about word histories. For a start, look over our list of favorite books on Latin and Greek derivations in Figure 8.7. Then design your own captivating entrée into the world of word origins for your own students.

FIGURE 8.7   Source Books for Classical (Latin and Greek) Vocabulary Study

Edward Fry, Jacqueline Kress, & Dona Lee Fountoukidis. *The New Reading Teacher's Book of Lists* (4th ed.). San Francisco: Jossey-Bass, 2000.

Ida Ehrlich. *Instant Vocabulary.* New York: Pocket Books, 1988.

John Kennedy. *Word Stems.* New York: Soho Publishing, 1996.

Timothy Rasinski, Nancy Padak, Evangeline Newton, & Rick Newton. *Greek & Latin Roots: Keys to Building Vocabulary.* Huntington Beach, CA: Shell Publishing, 2008.

IDIOMS

Some of the most challenging words for any student, but especially for ELL students, are figurative language, especially idioms. Idioms are figures of speech, peculiar to certain groups of people or regions, that are metaphorical in nature. The meaning of an idiom is not embedded in the literal meaning of the words themselves but in an inference they suggest. The meaning is outside the words in the idiom. When you say it's "raining cats and dogs" you don't mean that pets are falling out of the sky; you mean that it is raining hard. Idiomatic language is prevalent in daily speech and in many reading materials, yet it is such a part of the language environment that most people often are not even aware of its usage. That is why we think the study of idioms is often neglected in our literacy classrooms.

Idiomatic language can be difficult for most students. But for struggling readers and ELL students, idioms can be particularly challenging. Struggling readers who often have not had wide exposure to language and students for whom English is not their first language often tend to take idioms literally or largely misunderstand them. When idioms are understood incorrectly, reading comprehension falters.

Janice has found a wonderful way to play with idioms with her fifth-grade students. Once a week she chooses a theme or concept and invites students to think of idioms that contain the theme or concept. For example, for the first week of school, she chose the concept of *baseball* as her theme with her students since baseball season was still in full swing and many of her students were passionate fans of the game.

She asked students to come up with idioms or expressions that make reference to something in baseball but have meaning that may extend outside of baseball. Students huddled together and after a few minutes came up with the following expressions that Janice wrote on a chart that hung on a wall in the classroom

Three strikes and you're out!

Give me a ballpark figure

Throw me a curve

Playing hardball

Take a swing

Who's on deck?

Batting a thousand

Rounding third and heading home

Caught stealing

After students had exhausted their list, Janice added a few of her own ("All I have to do is google 'baseball idioms' on the Internet and I come to several websites that have them listed, as well as their definitions"). These included *cleanup hitter, play ball, extra innings,* and *rhubarb.*

Janice then led her class in a quick discussion of the meanings of each of the idiomatic expressions. Then, throughout the week, Janice and her students found ways to use these expressions in their own language—written and oral. Later that day two arguments erupted among her students in the hallway. That gave Janice the opportunity to note to her class that "one more strike and certain members of the class will be called out. Any future rhubarbs today will result in some extra innings after school for the offenders." The students immediately picked up on the meaning of her message.

In following weeks, Janice will spend 20 minutes one day exploring other idioms that are connected to a theme. Future themes will include dogs, cats, ducks, football, birds, food, numbers, color, and more. Janice feels that figurative language is one the most neglected areas of vocabulary instruction. "It's unfortunate that we don't spend more time having fun with figurative language. The passages students read on the state reading exam are filled with idiomatic language. And so many students do not know what these expressions mean or how to use them in their own language. I really like the weekly lesson I have developed, and I know my students like it too— even those children who are having a hard time with reading and writing."

Figure 8.8 lists resources that will help you explore idioms with your own students.

WONDERFUL WORDS FOR THE DAY

Students learn on average seven words every day (Snow et al., 1998)—that is a lot of words. One way to keep students thinking about words is to begin each day with "Wonderful Words for the Day." As students (and teacher) come across new, interesting, or important words from the news or their own reading and interests, they take note and

FIGURE 8.8   Resources for Exploring Idioms with Students

Websites

www.readwritethink.org/materials/idioms

www.idiomconnection.com

www.idiomsite.com

Tradebooks

Fred Gwynne. *The King Who Rained. A Chocolate Moose for Dinner. A Little Pigeon-Toed.*

Peggy Parish. The entire *Amelia Bedelia* series of books.

Terban, Marvin. *In a Pickle and Other Funny Idioms.*

Arnold, Tedd. *Parts. More Parts. Even More Parts.*

Curriculum Materials

Timothy Rasinski. *Understanding Idioms and other English Expressions: Grades 1–3.* Huntington Beach, CA: Shell Publishing.

Timothy Rasinski. *Understanding Idioms and other English Expressions: Grades 4–6.* Huntington Beach, CA: Shell Publishing.

contribute them to the class's daily word list. Because students choose most of the words, they are more likely to know and use them in their own language.

List the words on the chalkboard or a sheet of chart paper. Students tell why they chose the word, how they found it, and what they think it means. Notes are made on the chart, and students (and teacher) make efforts to use the words throughout the day in their speech and writing. Most students take it a step further by looking for the words in their own reading.

Jane, a sixth-grade teacher, makes a list of 5 to 10 words every day with her students. "Sometimes I have them make concept maps with the words. Mostly, though, we just encourage each other to use the words throughout the day. It's a challenge for all of us, and we take note when one of us uses a particularly unusual word, like *recession,* which has been in the news lately. I can't believe how sensitive students become to interesting words in their world after a few weeks of doing this simple activity." At the end of the day, Jane posts the list of words on her word wall so that students continue to see the words from previous days. "When they are writing, I often see them gazing at the word wall to find interesting words."

GAMES AND PUZZLES

Vocabulary learning should be fun, and one way to accomplish this is through games and similar activities. It is easy to create variations of well-known games that students find engaging and entertaining. Here are just a few that we have found to be student pleasers.

Wordo   This form of Bingo uses *Wordo* cards almost identical to bingo cards. (See Chapter 6 for an example of a Wordo card.) Choose 24 words to review and play with. Students randomly write one word in each square, leaving the center square as a free spot. The teacher then randomly selects one word at a time and presents the definition, an antonym, a sentence with the target word missing, or some other clue to the meaning of the word. Players must determine the word from the meaning clues, and cover it with a marker. As in Bingo, a player wins when a vertical, horizontal, or diagonal line is covered. Then a new game starts. Individual games can last 5 to 10 minutes.

John has used Wordo with his Title I students as well as his fifth-graders:

> At the beginning of the year, I run off a hundred or so of the Wordo sheets. ... Then we're ready to play whenever we have the time, and the students and I want to play. They really like it. I think they'd play it every day if they could. Sometimes I give out cheap prizes to the winners. I have three empty coffee cans, two with prizes and one with a slip of paper that says "Zonk." The kids think this is fun.
>
> I've found that after a while, rather than my saying the clues or giving the antonyms, a student can do that job, too. It gives them extra practice in playing with word meanings. Of course, a student will want to play emcee for only one or two games. Then, they'll want to get back and play the game!

Concentration (or Match)   In *Concentration,* two decks of cards are laid out in a grid. One set of cards contains words to be learned and practiced; and the other set contains definitions, synonyms, or antonyms or some other way of matching the first set. As in the television version of the game, players (or teams of players) uncover pairs of cards seeking matches. When a match is made, the player takes the cards and keeps playing. If no match is produced, then the cards are turned back over, and the next player takes a turn. Players who find the most matches win the game.

Scattergories *Scattergories* can be played with the commercial version or one adapted for instructional use. In the adapted version, a set of 5 to 10 letters or blends is determined and listed vertically on each player's paper. Then categories are determined—for example, vegetables, countries, presidents' last names, or rivers. (See Figure 8.9 for an example of an

FIGURE 8.9   Adapted Scattergories Sheet

Initial Consonants & Blends ↓	CATEGORIES				

adapted playing sheet.) The categories can also be developed from themes and content areas. For example, a unit on state geography can include categories of cities, manufacturing products, agricultural products, rivers, boundary states, and so on. Working with a time limit of several minutes, individuals or groups of players think of words that begin with the given letters and fit the category. Players with the greatest number of unique words (words chosen by only one individual or team) win that round.

Balderdash　This game also is available in both commercial and adapted forms. An adapted version of *Balderdash* goes like this: Each player chooses an uncommon word from the dictionary. One player presents a word and a definition—either the real definition or a made-up one. The other players individually guess whether the definition is correct. Presenting players earn a point each time they fool another player.

Hinky Pinkies　*Hinky Pinkies* are word riddles. Students love to apply their word knowledge to solve them and make their own. The answer to a Hinky Pinky is two or more rhyming words. For example, a cold place of learning is a *cool school;* an obese feline is a *fat cat.* A variation of Hinky Pinkies uses alliterative combinations of words instead of rhymes. Thus, a sleepy flower might be a *lazy lily,* and a 4,000-pound farm vehicle would be a *two-ton tractor.*

Hinky Pinkies are fun, easy, and quick. Many teachers save them for when they have a few extra minutes in the school day. Other teachers use them as alternative assignments in various content areas. After studying the states, students in one class were asked to describe states using Hinky Pinkies. California was described as *west, warm, and wild,* whereas Florida was *fun in the sun.*

Regular use of games and puzzles adds another dimension to vocabulary learning. Students appreciate the variety that these games can bring to the study of words and concepts. Sometimes, they exercise their creative talents by developing their own vocabulary games and puzzles.

Integrating Vocabulary Routines throughout the Curriculum

The strategies and activities we have outlined in this chapter have the potential to increase students' interest in and knowledge of words, which in turn will have a positive effect on their reading. Informed teachers modify and use these approaches to fit their own curricula, teaching situations, and styles of teaching to meet their students' needs and learning characteristics. These teachers integrate and mass their approaches in planned and purposeful ways. They do not use them hit-or-miss once or twice a week for a few minutes or during a lull in the instructional day. Instead, they incorporate these strategies into their own framework of teaching. The key is to get students to regularly (daily) think deeply about words in a variety of ways.

Most teachers, especially at the elementary level, teach a variety of subject areas. Even those who specialize in one area teach a variety of topics within the subject. Each topic or subject area brings new words and concepts for students to understand, use, and learn successfully and efficiently. Selected strategies and activities from this chapter should become an essential, integral, and regular element of subject-area reading and learning. Key words and concepts can be explored with students using the strategies and activities in this chapter before and after lessons and readings so that students develop solid understandings of the vocabulary essential to the subject area.

However, just as we think of science or social studies as specific and separate areas of the curriculum, word play and word study need "spotlighted" time during the school day. Teachers promote vocabulary learning by massing the activities, by putting together 10- to 20-minute vocabulary lessons three to five times per week for students to explore and play with words. They may tie the words to a particular subject, or not. They may extract words from interests, hobbies, current or upcoming events, anniversaries, holidays—almost anywhere. Then, they play with them. Thus, students develop an interest in, improved knowledge of, and greater flexibility in learning and using words they encounter in their lives.

In addition to content area integration and word play, teachers can dedicate specific times of the day to instructional routines devoted to vocabulary development. Rich, a third-grade teacher, does "Wordshop" three times a week:

> I like to play with and learn new words, and I try to share my enjoyment with my students.... For about 15 minutes on Mondays, Wednesdays, and Fridays right before lunch, we play with words. We might do three or four activities during this time such as a couple of analogy problems, introduce the origins of two or three words, or learn about some Latin or Greek roots, and play a game like word Concentration or Wordo. It's really fast-paced, and the kids like it. Best of all, I see many of them playing with words on their own!

Janice, whom you met earlier in this chapter, has a five-day routine for her fifth-graders that is somewhat different than Rich's. Each day is devoted to a different type of word and word activity. Mondays are devoted to a vocabulary timeline and the use of a thesaurus. Tuesdays are devoted to idioms. On Wednesdays, Janice takes her students into an exploration of a Latin or Greek root. Thursdays are reserved for a semantic feature analysis activity; and every Friday is game day where students and teacher play one of the many word games that Janice has found and created. "The weekly routine makes it very predictable for me and my students. And, since each day is different, there is a lot of variety also for students." Students keep a word journal for their new words, and about every four weeks Janice gives her students a quiz over the preceding month's words.

Word knowledge or vocabulary is an important part of reading, one that challenges many struggling readers. Many students think of word learning as drudgery; as a result, they avoid it or make inefficient use of their time and efforts for learning words. Word learning need not be that way. Tapping into students' own interests and knowledge; employing interesting, effective, and challenging learning activities; allowing students to collaborate with others in shared learning experiences; and creating a playful environment in which words are played with, played on, manipulated, and used in a variety of ways can make the difference between vocabulary instruction that hinders reading and vocabulary instruction that nurtures reading.

DISCUSSION QUESTIONS

Some of the discussion questions for each chapter ask you to think through your own work as a teacher. If you are not currently a practicing teacher, try to respond to these questions from your own school experience (either from when you yourself were a student or from visits to schools that you have made in your teacher education program).

1. In order to help students enjoy learning new words, teachers must be word-lovers. During the next week jot down some "wonderful words" you hear or read. Share the words with your colleagues. Define your words, tell where you encountered them, and talk about what makes them "wonderful words."

2. Good vocabulary instruction both develops the richness of already known words and also introduces new words. Give a specific example of a time when your vocabulary instruction developed the richness of an already known word.

3. This chapter began with an illustration of rich vocabulary in the children's book *Caleb and Kate*. Bring three children's books containing rich vocabulary to your next class or staff development session. Share your books and make a list of some your colleagues shared that you want to use.

4. Give specific examples of the three levels of deep processing of words: associative, comprehension, generational.

5. Try one of the instructional strategies from this chapter that you have not tried before. Tell your colleagues about the lesson. Would you use the strategy again? Why or why not?

Chapter **Nine** ❧

❧ *Developing Comprehension with Narrative Text*

COMPREHENSION IS WHAT READING IS ALL ABOUT. Reading is the "process of constructing meaning from written texts . . . a holistic act" that depends on "the background of the reader, the purpose for reading, and the context in which reading occurs" (Anderson et al., 1985, p. 7). Whether you're reading a novel, a technical manual, or a number from the telephone directory, comprehension is involved. Thus, a primary goal for literacy instruction, regardless of age, grade level, or achievement level, is to help students become purposeful, independent comprehenders.

Yet, most struggling readers are neither purposeful nor independent. Instead they try, usually in vain, to guess at desired responses. Or, even sadder, they simply choose not to participate at all. Effective comprehension instruction can make all the difference for these children.

Effective Comprehension Instruction

What kinds of discussions or activities help students learn strategies for constructing meaning from print? How can educators foster students' thoughtful interaction with text? These are critical questions that effective teachers consider as they plan instruction. In the mid-1980s, the Commission on Reading (Anderson et al., 1985) suggested that comprehension instruction should help students focus on relevant information, synthesize the information, and integrate it with what they already know. Discussions should provoke thought and motivate higher-level thinking.

More recently, research reviewed by the National Reading Panel (2000; Armbruster, Lehr, & Osborn, 2001), the RAND Commission on Comprehension (Snow, 2002), and others (e.g., Dymock, 2007) has underscored the same issues:

- Comprehension is purposeful and active.
- Students' comprehension is enhanced through strategy instruction.

- Strategy instruction should be explicit; it works best when one strategy is the focus at one time.
- Students need to learn self-regulating strategies.
- Instruction must ensure children's immediate success.

Unfortunately, teachers might not be spending enough time teaching students comprehension strategies. An observational study in 43 third-grade classrooms (Connor, Morrison, & Petrella, 2004), for example, found that, on average, teachers spent only about a minute each day in comprehension strategy instruction. Obviously, that's not enough time. So time may be the place to begin thinking about comprehension instruction. Teachers should ask themselves how they currently teach comprehension strategies and how much emphasis this instruction receives.

Some struggling readers may be unable to read materials worth discussion, which may add a wrinkle to your instructional plans. If this is the case, teacher read-aloud can be used to teach comprehension strategies because research has shown that children will transfer what they learned to their own reading (Garner & Bochna, 2004).

Struggling readers may also need scaffolds or models for using strategies. Three general instructional moves seem most successful in this regard:

- *Invite self-reflection through conversation.* You might ask, "Who made a prediction that was confirmed? That needed to be changed? How did you know? What did you do?" Alternatively, a simple checklist could prove useful. Items might say "I made predictions" or "I used information in the text," and students might respond "not at all," "a little," or "a lot" (Walker, 2005).
- *Begin simply.* To teach narrative structure, for example, you can begin with "beginning, middle, and end" and then shift to setting, characters, plot, and theme ("What does this story teach us?"). Eventually more complex literary elements can be introduced, but children will be building on the early foundation (Dymock, 2007).
- *Provide scaffolds.* A character comparison chart might list names and age, physical appearance, personality—whatever is pertinent. Or students may brainstorm using a web with the title of a story in the center and spokes radiating to story parts (Dymock, 2007). Likewise, children's ability to retell can be scaffolded in three steps: guided oral retellings, retellings supported with graphic organizers, and written retellings (Flynt & Cooter, 2005).

What kinds of strategies are worth teaching? Flynt and Cooter (2005) suggest selecting key strategies from state standards and then spending at least three weeks teaching mini-lessons about them, a process they call "marinating." Another way to determine focus for strategy instruction is to rely on research conducted by Marzano, Pickering, and Pollock (2001), researchers at Mid-Continent Regional Educational Laboratory. They gathered research studies of instructional strategies, grouped the studies by type of strategy, and applied a research technique called meta-analysis to determine the relative power of the particular strategies. Categories of strategies that made a significant difference in student learning included those that focused on

- Identifying similarities and differences
- Summarizing and note taking
- Nonlinguistic representation (nonword responses)
- Cooperative learning
- Generating and testing hypotheses

In both this chapter and the next we discuss many instructional activities that encompass one or more of these characteristics.

To help struggling readers become purposeful, active, and strategic comprehenders, several other guidelines are worth noting:

- *Comprehension instruction must involve students in real reading situations.* Instruction must keep the process whole and real rather than focus on artificial bits and pieces that draw attention away from authentic purposes for reading. In other words, completing exercises about specific skills enhances comprehension less effectively than reading interesting material and talking about it with others.

- *Strategy instruction should help students focus on meaning as thoughtful readers.* Children must learn to develop their own understanding of what was read, not try to guess the teacher's interpretation. Thinking is at the center of all reading. Readers actively construct meaning, and this process depends at least in part on their own knowledge, experiences, and purposes for reading. In terms of effective instruction, this means that teachers must acknowledge that two readers may comprehend the same piece of material in different ways without one being right and the other wrong. Comprehension is relative, not absolute. Moreover, some students, particularly English language learners (ELLs) who come from different cultures, may need help dealing with authors' assumptions about what readers already know. Literature is culture bound (Haynes, 2007).

- *The instructional environment must promote risk taking.* Proficient readers are active and strategic; they speculate. Making predictions, or educated guesses, and evaluating them are essential aspects of reading. Making a guess means taking a chance, and readers are unlikely to take chances in an environment that stresses being "right" or that exposes their ideas to ridicule or dismissal. Rather, teachers must show that they care about their students' reactions to what they read, that their thoughts are important. Relatedly, some ELLs may need teacher support to learn how to brainstorm or express opinions, again depending on the way children learned to "do school" in their native lands (Haynes, 2007).

- *Students must interact with text and each other to enhance their abilities as comprehenders.* Because learning is a social process, interacting with others can help develop comprehension abilities. The instructional environment should foster group inquiry and problem solving by giving students opportunities to clarify their thinking and to understand the thinking of others. Instructionally, two or three heads working together are almost always better than one.

- *Readers need opportunities to respond to what they have read.* Moreover, children need a choice of options for responding to reading. Students may wish to talk with others, write down their thoughts or feelings, develop written or oral narratives that explore or extend various aspects of their reading, engage in creative drama or art activities, or participate in reader's theater. The list can go on and on. By making time for responses, sharing a variety of response activities with children, and encouraging students to respond to reading in personally meaningful ways, teachers show students that "reading/thinking continues after the book is closed" (Goodman & Watson, 1977, p. 869). Equally important, children learn that their personal responses to reading are important and that others value their thinking.

All these instructional priorities reflect our current understanding of the reading process and effective comprehension instruction. Each activity described in this chapter and Chapter 10 reflects these instructional priorities. This chapter focuses on activities that work especially well with literary materials, especially narratives. By *narrative*, we mean story, whether imaginary, such as fiction, fables or tales, and many poems, or true, such as biographies, autobiographies, and memoirs.

Supporting Comprehension before Reading

To understand what they read, readers need some knowledge of the topic. This can be as true for narrative as it is for informational material. Knowledge of concepts in the reading and familiarity with the author and his or her writing style as well as characters, settings, and problems presented in the text can help any reader make meaning while reading. Many struggling readers have limited knowledge of the topics they encounter in their reading. A few minutes spent to develop interest and background before reading can greatly benefit students' understanding of the text.

Of course, one way to ensure that students have some background about a topic is for them to choose their own reading materials, but free choice is not always possible or desirable. Brief before-reading activities can generate interest and help students develop some initial understanding of the topic. Here are several easy ways to support comprehension before reading.

JACKDAWS

Jackdaws are collections of artifacts built around a particular book topic or theme. By bringing in real or facsimile artifacts connected to a book and talking about them with students, teachers help create background knowledge and interest about a story. Figure 9.1 lists the types of items that may go into a jackdaw.

As students become familiar with the concept, they can add to the teacher's jackdaw, which is then displayed in a mini-museum for all students to see, touch, and ponder. Students can also create and share their own jackdaws as an after-reading response activity. What a creative and interesting way for students to demonstrate understanding of a text!

FIGURE 9.1 Jackdaws

A *jackdaw* is a collection of interesting artifacts that provides information about a particular subject, period, or idea. The term comes from the British name for a bird, similar to the American grackle, that picks up brightly colored, interesting, and attractive objects and carries them off to its nest.

The number and types of items in a jackdaw are limited only by imagination and creativity. They might include the following:

1. Clothes of the type worn by particular characters in a book—catalog pictures, paper dolls, collages, old photos, and so on

2. Songs or music from a period or event depicted in a book—sheet music, recordings, demonstrations, titles, or musical instruments

3. A news article from the period, real or a facsimile

4. Photographs from the time period or geographical area depicted in the book

5. Household items from the period depicted in the book

6. A timeline depicting the occurrence of events in a book (may also include real-world events not mentioned in the book)

7. A map showing any journey that the main characters make

8. Recipes and food dishes typical of the time period in the book

9. Selected poems that reflect the theme of the book

10. A glossary of interesting or peculiar words in the book

11. Dioramas that illustrate particular scenes from the story

12. A biographical sketch of the book's author

13. A list of other related books (by story, theme, characters, and so on) that students can read to extend their literacy experience

Note: The term *jackdaw*, when used for a collection of artifacts assembled for educational purposes, is copyrighted by Jackdaw Publications of Amawalk, New York.

For the past several years, Tim's sixth-grade class has explored the Great Depression in the United States. One of the core books is Irene Hunt's *No Promises in the Wind*. Tim says:

> This can be a difficult book for many students, as they don't have a very good understanding of what it was like to live through such desperate times. Several years ago, my mother-in-law was going through some of her old things. I noticed she had many items from the Depression—an old camera, some clothing made from sackcloth, old records, an iron that was heated by sitting on the stove, some letters from her broth-

ers who had to leave home to look for work, and many other things. I thought to myself, "What a wonderful way to introduce my students to the Depression!"

With her permission I took the items in and shared them with my students prior to reading the book. I was amazed at how just touching and talking about these items created instant interest and gave students enough background to read the book successfully. Even our discussions of the book seemed livelier as a result of the jackdaw.

Tim has used jackdaws with various books and themes concerning U.S. history, and he frequently uses them with stories that take place in unfamiliar settings. "I guess Show and Tell has a place in the upper grades," he says.

RELATED READINGS

Just reading one story or text about a topic can often create sufficient interest and background for further reading, even texts that are more complex and sophisticated. This is why thematic readings and units of study are such a powerful approach to learning.

When selecting texts for theme study, the issue of what "counts" as text is worth initial thought. Douglas and Jeannette Hartman (1993) advise teachers to foster student exploration of selected themes by selecting both linguistic texts—stories, chapters, articles, and poems—and nonlinguistic ones—art, music, video or film, and speakers. Access to as many different types of texts as possible promotes understanding of the concepts or themes under study and also helps students realize that many "ways of knowing" are valuable resources for their learning.

Themes can develop around topics, authors, or series. Author study is a great way to familiarize students with a writer's style. Books by William Steig, for example, contain many common elements, such as magic, animals that assume human roles, rich vocabulary, a subtle sense of humor, and much alliteration. Developing these understandings about Steig can help any reader tackle his next book. In addition, series books provide effective focus for themes because they combine one author's style with common characters, settings, and similar story lines. Students can read the texts themselves, or the teacher can read aloud to establish background for further reading.

Kathy, a primary-grade teacher of struggling readers, teaches students about Cinderella stories from various cultures. She says that one story sets the stage for the next. She begins the thematic exploration with Judith Viorst's poem "And then the prince knelt down and tried to put the glass slipper on Cinderella's foot" (from *If I Were in Charge of the World and Other Worries*). "This really gets the talk started," she says. Talk leads to thought, and Kathy and her students are on their way.

PREVOKE

Prevoke is an instructional activity based on words children will encounter in their reading. (Variations of this activity, which is a type of word sort, are also called Prereading Predictions, Probable Passages, and Predict-o-Gram; see Billmeyer & Barton, 1998.) To prepare a Prevoke activity, the teacher selects 12 to 20 words or short phrases from a text that students will read. The words may be written on the chalkboard or chart paper; some teachers have students write the words on small slips of scrap paper.

The teacher also prepares a two- or three-column chart that students will use for sorting the words. Good sorts for younger children may be "People," "Places," and "Things that happen." Older students may work with columns called "Characters," "Setting," "Plot," "Problem," "Solution," "Theme," and so forth. Prevoke involves pairs or small groups of students deciding which words might fit into which columns and (of course) why they think so. Students often share their ideas with others before reading, and the teacher sometimes asks students to speculate about the story based on the ways they have sorted the words. After they read, they may return to the chart to reorganize the words and phrases.

Charlie, a school librarian who sponsors a book club, selected these words and phrases from the first two chapters of Christopher Paul Curtis's *Bud, Not Buddy: case workers, Bud, blue flyer, Herman E. Calloway, suitcase, Rules and Things, Toddy, home, street urchin, depression, Momma died, Flint, giant fiddle, best liar, Mrs. Amos, beastly little brute,* and *padlock.* "Eavesdropping on students' conversations was fascinating," she says. "Most groups thought *depression* and *Momma died* would be related—that the kid would be depressed because his mother died. I heard a few gasps when students encountered *depression* in the text—that's one of the things I really like about Prevoke. Students are so engaged in their reading!"

STORY MAPPING

A map is helpful when driving in an unfamiliar city—becoming familiar with important intersections, street names, and landmarks can help you find your way. Similarly, introducing students to a story by sharing a map of the text can help familiarize them with the major characters and events they will encounter in their reading. A *story map* (or story board) is simply a visual display of the major characters, settings, and events arranged in story order (see Figure 9.2). It can depict the complete story or provide only enough information to start readers into a text. Students can also create their own maps or complete partial maps as a postreading activity. Some teachers ask students to make notes on maps as they read, as well.

Bob, a teacher who works with upper-elementary students who have difficulty reading, puts it this way:

> Sometimes I ask students to read stories that are quite complex. I know that the story can be confusing for them. For these times I will often sketch out a map for them to show them how the story develops and point out some of the diversions that may get them off track. I think many of my kids are helped a lot by the maps. Often, they go up to the map that's on a wall chart and study it as they read. It helps them make sense out of the story.

OTHER MEDIA AND ACTIVITIES

Another way to build background and interest is to role-play some aspect of a story before reading it. This often allows students inside the issues and characters that form the story. Before Jane read *Say It* by Charlotte Zolotow to her students, her second-graders went out to the playground. She asked students to walk in pairs pretending to be mother and

FIGURE 9.2   Story Map for Bernard Waber's *Ira Sleeps Over*

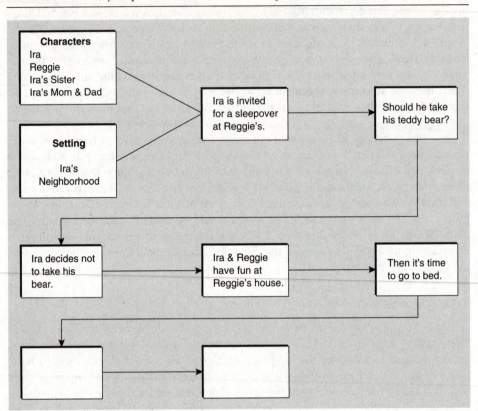

daughter or father and son. Then she challenged them to think of ways to say that they loved or were angry with the other person without using the words *love, angry, mad,* or other words that directly expressed those feelings. Later, the students talked about how they did. Jane recalls, "It was a challenging task, and many students had difficulty with it. But it got all of us thinking about the subtle ways we can communicate with each other, it made our reading of *Say It* that much more personal and meaningful, and it led to an excellent discussion when I finished reading the story."

Guest speakers from the local community (perhaps parents who are experts in particular areas) can excite students about a topic that they will later explore in reading. Before his students read Jane Yolen's *The Devil's Arithmetic,* James, a fifth-grade teacher, invited a Holocaust survivor to speak with the class. Her moving story created an interest that sped many students through the book and into several other books about the Holocaust.

Field trips and movies or portions of television programs can develop interest and background for reading. In his class's study of slavery and the Civil War, Tim arranged for a field trip to a preserved station on the Underground Railroad. Before reading Paul Fleischman's *Bull Run* and performing it later as a reader's theater, Tim showed the class selected segments from the PBS television series *The Civil War.* He says, "I think sometimes we assume that students have a good background on a topic when they really don't.

Then we're disappointed when they have a poor understanding and don't enjoy a story we thought would knock their socks off. I really think that a key to successful reading experiences . . . is making sure that students have a solid background in the topic they are to encounter."

Even illustrations can generate conversation about and interest in a story. Many primary teachers invite children on "picture walks" before they read or listen to a new book. By showing several illustrations and asking children what they see and what they think might be happening in the story, teachers help students discover much that will aid their comprehension.

All of these activities aid comprehension. Whether students learn something new or are reminded of what they already know, whether they make predictions or simply become curious, their minds are engaged and they're ready to read.

Supporting Comprehension During Reading

Meaning construction (comprehension) depends on several types of prior knowledge as well as on active thought. To read, one must understand the features of written language—*graphophonology* (sound-symbol relationships), *syntax* (word order), and *semantics* (vocabulary and meaning). Reading also involves thinking and predicting, which are based on experiential and conceptual background. In other words, both the text and the reader's thoughts, language, and experiences are important to comprehension.

Situational pragmatics, or the context in which a person reads, also influences comprehension. External contextual influences such as lighting or distractions can affect comprehension, as can other, more subtle contextual factors. One of these is *purpose,* which one uses to determine if one has comprehended adequately. Students' perceptions of the instructional environment, including the kinds of interactions encouraged, are equally important. To support meaning construction, communication should be open during text discussions. Free and voluntary exchange of ideas allows students to try out their ideas and modify them after they hear what others have to say. As Lehman and Scharer (1996) noted, "Children's primary personal responses are valuable and form the basis for literary conversations. However, left unexamined they can also be limiting" (p. 33). Teachers can expand children's personal understanding through activities that encourage them to express their thoughts, explore new possibilities, and even challenge others' opinions.

DIRECTED READING–THINKING ACTIVITY

The Directed Reading–Thinking Activity (DR–TA) (Stauffer, 1980) is a problem-solving discussion strategy designed to support comprehension. Lessons evolve through cycles in which students generate hypotheses and subsequently validate, reject, or modify them.

First, students make predictions about story content based on the selection title (and, if appropriate, initial illustrations) and prior knowledge. Students read silently to predetermined stopping points. Discussions follow, which the teacher facilitates by asking students to indicate whether or not their predictions were confirmed and encouraging them to support their ideas. Next, students refine their original predictions and/or make new ones. This cycle of predicting; reading to confirm, modify, or reject; providing support from the text; and making further predictions continues until the entire selection has been read.

To prepare for a DR–TA, the teacher decides where students will stop for discussion. Divisions between episodes in a story often work well. Preparation may also involve becoming comfortable with typical DR–TA questions, such as, "What do you think this will be about?" The teacher then may ask for elaboration or clarification, asking, "Why?" or "What makes you say that?" "Did anything surprise you?" or "Did things happen like you thought they would?" "What will happen next? Why?"

Bonnie conducted a DR–TA with a group of eighth-graders, and we reproduce several excerpts here. The students were reading and discussing the short story "All the Years of Her Life" (Callaghan, 1935), which tells what happens when a mother learns that her son has been caught shoplifting.

Bonnie: What do you think this story's going to be about?

Lucy: Somebody's life. . . .

Joseph: A diary. It'll be a diary about her life. . . .

Lucy: She's going to be older.

Bonnie: Why do you say that?

Lucy: Well it's a story about her life.

Heather: It says, "All the Years." . . .

Lucy: So, that means she's going to be, like, older. . . .

Bonnie: Some other predictions? . . .

Joseph: Someone's problems.

Bonnie: Why do you say that?

Joseph: I don't know. You can just tell by her life. And usually people have problems.

[Students read. Later in the lesson the conversation continues.]

Bonnie: Well, what do you think will happen next?

Joseph: I don't think they're going to go get a cop.

Bonnie: No? Why not?

Joseph: Why not? I just don't think that. Uh, with the mother's attitude, the way she came in, I think that it might have changed the owner's mind.

Lucy: Yeah, you know, with a mother like this maybe the kid'll turn out okay.

Bonnie: Is there any sign of that in the story?

Lucy: Yeah. Well, he couldn't believe the attitude that his mom came in with. Maybe that might change his opinion about her. . ..

Andrew: Yeah, because he thinks that she's probably not going to do anything to him, or punish him for what he did. . . .

Bonnie: What do the rest of you think?

Joseph: Well, maybe the store manager let him off the hook because he'll probably punish himself enough. . . .

Bonnie: Tell some more about that.

Joseph: Guilt.

Heather: Yeah, the way he'll feel about himself from now on.

Lucy: And he probably won't do it again.

Did you notice how little Bonnie said? In a DR–TA, students do most of the talking. Did you notice that she did not provide important ideas or generalizations for students? Her goals were to encourage thinking and facilitate group interaction rather than manipulate students' thinking or test their recall. The instructional context signaled that students' ideas were valued—that they should explain their ideas so others could understand their reasoning and listen to and talk with each other.

The DR–TA is a staple in Bonnie's classroom. She says:

> We probably do DR–TAs more often than any other "while-they-read" strategy. The kids love it. They enjoy telling us all what they think, and they seem to find others' ideas fascinating. These discussions really support kids' reading, especially when we have different hypotheses going as they read. Maybe it's because we stop to talk while they read, maybe it's the personal commitment they make or the curiosity that develops so naturally, or maybe it's because kids know we'll want to know where their ideas are coming from—for whatever reason, the DR–TA is really a powerful reading strategy!

THINK-PAIR-SHARE

Think-Pair-Share also provides students with opportunities to talk about a story as they read it. To prepare for the activity, students find partners. The teacher identifies stopping points for discussion and shares these with students, who can make light pencil marks in their texts to remember where to stop.

Students read to the first stopping point and then pause to think about the reading. They might consider what they found interesting, important, or puzzling; they often make brief notes about their thoughts. After each partner has completed this thinking, the pairs talk with one another using their notes to remind them of the points they wish to make. Finally, the larger group shares, focusing on interesting issues that arose during the partner discussions. Depending on students' interests and needs, these discussions may be brief or lengthy. When the first Think-Pair-Share cycle is complete, students read the next portion of the story and begin the cycle again.

Think-Pair-Share is an extremely adaptable organizational structure for conducting classroom discussions. For example, it can also be used as an after-reading activity and works well with expository text. Harold, who uses the strategy frequently in his work with students with disabilities, sees two major benefits:

> My students often need support as they are reading a story. If we use Think-Pair-Share a couple of times while they read, the thinking and talking allows everyone to be successful. I also like the fact that individuals think things through for themselves (and often write their ideas down) before discussing them with partners. They don't "shoot from the hip." This activity encourages individual response to reading, which I believe is important to helping kids learn, and the writing beforehand makes the partner discussions more lively.

CHARACTER SKETCHES

In *Character Sketches,* students use the Think-Pair-Share structure to focus their attention on character development. At the first stopping point in their reading (or listening), students jot down words and phrases to describe one or two major characters. This becomes information that they share, first with their partners and then with the larger group. At each successive stop, students return to their notes about the characters, modifying them based on the new insights they have developed through reading. A character who initially seemed selfish or unfeeling, for example, may be revealed as shy or grieving. After modifying their lists, students again talk with partners and the entire group. The Think-Pair-Share cycle continues until students have completed the story.

At this point, students have notes that reflect their descriptions of major characters. These can be used for a discussion of how authors develop characters or a variety of other follow-up activities. Students also have an increased understanding of the story because characters typically reveal their personalities through what they say and do.

LINGUISTIC ROULETTE

This small-group discussion technique was developed by Jerry Harste. After reading a portion of a story, each student skims through it again looking for a single sentence that is interesting, important, or special in some other way.

Discussion begins when all members of the group have read and selected their sentences. Each student reads a sentence aloud and invites group response. Students often explain why they selected their sentences, which can give rise to interesting comprehension discussions. After all group members have shared, students read the next portion of the story, and the cycle is repeated.

Linguistic Roulette fosters comprehension in several ways. First, stopping periodically to talk with peers supports comprehension. Moreover, students must think again about the story to select their sentences for discussion. Hearing others' sentences and participating in the small-group discussions sometimes encourages consideration of alternate perspectives.

Karen provides resource-room support for intermediate-grade children with learning disabilities. "To tell the truth," she says, "I was pretty suspicious about Linguistic Roulette at first. I wondered how anything that *easy* could really work." But Karen was curious, so she tried it.

> And, let me tell you, I eavesdropped on those first discussions. What a surprise! I found that my students were perfectly capable of discussing a story independently and that they were really proud that they could do so without me. In fact, the Linguistic Roulette discussions are usually freer and more wide-ranging than they are when I'm part of the group. I like the way it provides a framework for kids—because they know what they need to do, they can manage the discussion on their own.

IMAGERY

Narratives lend themselves to rich images that readers create as they read. The images that individuals create reflect their own interpretations, which may explain why people usually like the book version of a story better than the movie version in which a director imposes images on the audience.

Good readers may take for granted this ability to create internal images as they read. It seems so easy and natural. But many struggling readers fail to spontaneously create text-related images. To nurture this ability in most children, teachers simply remind them to form images as they read and invite them to talk about their images after reading. For example, a teacher might say "Can you picture this? What do you see?" Quick sketches can be effective as well. (See Sketch to Stretch in the next section.) Title I teacher Janet told us that many of her students seem to have difficulty creating images of texts:

> I found it helpful to begin with stories and poems that lend themselves to images. We always talk about students' "mind pictures," too. This seems to help their retention of the stories. Also, after reading a story I'll sometimes bring a videotaped version and we'll watch part of it. Then we'll talk about how our own images compare with the tape. It makes for a lively discussion.

Text discussions during reading encourage students to read actively and thoughtfully. The instructional environment fosters sharing, group inquiry, and problem solving. Over time, such instruction helps struggling readers learn that they can (indeed, must) construct meaning as they read.

Extending Comprehension after Reading

After-reading activities should encourage continued interaction with text content. We want students to continue thinking widely and deeply about what they have read and to integrate the text information into their own cognitive structures. The teacher's role in all these activities is to promote sharing, encourage and model critical thought, and moderate discussions. The students' roles require reading, thinking, solving problems, making decisions, and interacting with the text and each other.

GROUP MAPPING ACTIVITY

The *Group Mapping Activity* (Davidson, 1982) promotes individual response to reading and provides a framework for discussion. After reading, students create maps, which they share with and explain to others. Classmates may ask questions or make comments, which generally prompts continued discussion.

A map is a diagram or symbolic representation of the reader's personal response to text. Young readers often make pictures when asked to map; older readers tend to use lines, arrows, or other symbols to represent their responses. Students may use a few words to label portions of a map, but mapping is primarily a nonverbal activity. The first time students map, the teacher can help them understand the concept by offering directions: "Put your ideas about the story in a diagram. You can sketch if you want to, or use circles, boxes, or arrows. Try to show your ideas without using too many words. Don't worry about a 'right' way to map; there isn't one." This detailed explanation is necessary only for students' initial encounter with mapping. When they see the variety of responses, their concern about being right quickly diminishes.

Students' maps need not be detailed; in fact, making one should take only a few minutes. Mapping allows readers to synthesize their responses to the text. Its real purpose, however, is to provide a framework for the discussion that follows, which typically allows students to develop further insights about the text. The Group Mapping Activity helps readers recall and retain text information while providing them with a means to respond personally to what they have read.

SKETCH TO STRETCH

Sketch to Stretch, another nonverbal response activity, is an interesting elaboration of imaging. Individual students draw a quick sketch of a favorite or memorable event or scene from a story they have read and show it to a small group. Rather than describing and explaining the picture, however, each student invites classmates to provide their own interpretation of the drawing: "What is this a picture of?" and "What did the illustrator think was important about the story? Why?" After others give their interpretations, the illustrator is free to explain the drawing. Students' sketches become the basis for interpretive discussion of the story.

Anna began using both the Group Mapping Activity and Sketch to Stretch some time ago. When she learned about them, she said, "I knew they were *made* for my second-graders. They love to draw, and many are still beginning writers, so they often have more to say than they have patience to write." Anna has been pleased with children's responses: "The diversity of responses is truly amazing! Children show genuine interest in each other's maps and sketches, and the discussions that accompany sharing are fascinating. I feel certain that the kids' understanding is enhanced."

TABLEAU(X)

A third type of nonlinguistic representation involves "illustrations" that students create with their bodies instead of pencil and paper. We learned about *tableaux* from our colleague Mary, who used them in her high school English and drama classes. The activity, every bit as effective with younger students, begins with a text students have read or listened to. Next, groups of students select some aspect of the text to represent by means of a tableau, which is a "living picture" or a depiction of a scene by silent and motionless people. Students prepare and share their tableaux with the rest of the class, who then attempt to determine what is being portrayed and what roles individual members of the tableau play. To manage this aspect, we ordinarily encourage the audience to whisper their ideas with others and then to raise their hands when they think they know what the tableau is. If the audience cannot decide what they're looking at, we tap the shoulder of one person in the tableau, who then provides a clue.

"The energy and excitement is amazing," says Jocelyn, who works with intermediate-level struggling readers. "At least once or twice a week, kids request tableaux, and I usually relent because I quickly noticed how much learning goes into this activity. The kids like it because it seems like a game, but I like it because the groups dig deeply into meaning as they decide on their tableaux and then the audience does the same—it's like two or three comprehension activities all rolled up into one!" Jocelyn has expanded her use of tableaux into content areas. Children may, for example, depict events from history. She has used tableaux in science as well: "You should have seen their simple machines in science. Amazing!"

(WRITE AND SHARE)[2]

Responses to literature may vary among readers, and comprehension is enhanced by considering others' ideas as well as developing one's own. *(Write and Share)*[2] fosters response by incorporating both these opportunities (Davidson, 1987). Students write twice and share twice (thus the name) in response to text they have read.

In small groups, children first read the same text. Then students write, quickly jotting down words and phrases that represent their responses to the text. Teachers often tell students not to worry about putting their ideas into sentences but rather to make quick notes. This helps students attend to their ideas rather than the mechanics of writing. The first small-group discussion follows, with each student sharing notes and all students reacting to the ideas presented.

Next, students again write, this time developing their thoughts into prose, using the text, their own initial notes, and the shared responses as "raw material." Then, they share this writing with each other and discuss both the text and their reactions to it. Time permitting, volunteers may read their final pieces to the whole group, or each small group may select one piece to be shared with the larger group.

As in Think-Pair-Share, the initial note taking allows students to capture their thinking before sharing it with others. With the first discussion, the note taking serves as a kind of prewriting activity as students generate and organize their ideas. Both sharing sessions often help students see and appreciate different ideas about the same text as well as deepen their own understanding. In short, this easy-to-implement activity has a variety of powerful effects on students as comprehenders.

AGREE OR DISAGREE? WHY?

In this small-group discussion activity, students talk about statements related to what they have read or heard. To prepare for the activity, the teacher writes several statements that reflect issues and may yield differences of opinion. For example, the following statements might accompany the first chapter of E. B. White's *Charlotte's Web:*

- Fern's parents showed that they loved her.
- Animals should be treated like people.
- Sometimes adults have to do cruel things.
- Mr. Arable should have killed the runt.

Small groups assemble after students have read or listened to the story or a chapter. Group members discuss each statement to decide if they agree or disagree with it and make notes about their reasons. When the small groups have completed their discussions, the teacher may wish to convene the larger group to facilitate further discussion of the story.

Carol frequently uses Agree or Disagree? Why?—especially when she reads aloud to her primary Title I students. "Sometimes the books kids read independently are rather straightforward," she says, "but those I read aloud hardly ever are. I tend to select read-alouds that encourage children to think about life's complexities. Agree or Disagree? Why? provides a framework for them to share their thinking about some of these ideas. It's also a perfect way to extend the read-aloud experience for kids."

BLEICH'S HEURISTIC

David Bleich (1978) has long argued that individual, subjective responses to literature have worth and power. His heuristic, or framework, provides a structure within which students develop individual responses and see how they may connect to both the text and their own knowledge and experiences.

Bleich's Heuristic asks students to think about their response in two ways—affectively and associatively. Affective response is prompted by questions such as, "How did you feel about this story?" and "What's your reaction/response to this reading?" Questions can also promote associative thinking, in which students consider connections among their responses, their own experiences, and the text: "How did you come up with this reaction?" "What did the author do to create your response?" "Why did you respond like that?" "Have you ever had an experience like the one the author describes?" and "What's the most important word in this piece? Why?" As students ponder these questions, they often make the kinds of connections that are critical to comprehension: text-to-self, text-to-text, and text-to-world (Keene & Zimmerman, 2007).

Students respond to these questions by talking or writing; both writing and talking, as in Think-Pair-Share, also works well. Wayne, who has tried all these variations, advises flexibility but cautions that sharing is essential.

> I first learned about this as a writing activity, so that's the way I introduced it to the kids. It was okay, I guess, but I noticed that students were naturally talking with each other about what they had written. So then I tried just tossing the questions out as discussion starters. We all talked about our responses, even me. And that was okay, too, but it seemed like some of my more hesitant students got kind of bowled over by others who had firm ideas. So, I have also asked kids to write their answers to the questions or at least jot some ideas down before the group convenes to share. That, too, is okay. I guess my advice to others would be to try it all three ways and evaluate students' responses. For me, and my students, the sharing is really important. It's a powerful activity, though, so it's hard to go wrong.

COMPARE-AND-CONTRAST CHARTS

An important aspect of comprehension is the ability to make thoughtful comparisons across texts, between events within stories, and across other aspects of stories that students read. For many students, making comparisons can be daunting, and neither textbooks nor teachers always explain the process sufficiently. *Compare-and-Contrast Charts (CCC)* help students make good comparisons. The foundation for this activity is rather generic. We've

FIGURE 9.3   Compare-and-Contrast Chart: Tomie dePaola Books

Books	Country or Setting	Main Characters: How Are They Special?	Our Feelings
Fin M'Coul	Ireland	Fin—he's a giant	It's a funny story. Fin acts like a baby.
Strega Nona	Italy	Strega Nona— Grandma witch. She has magic powers.	Funny. Big Anthony makes a mess with Strega Nona's magic.
Now One Foot, Now the Other	U.S.?	Bob—his grandfather	Kind of happy. The boy has to help his grandpa.
Nana Upstairs and Nana Downstairs	U.S.?	Nanas—they are grandmothers	It's sad. Nana Upstairs dies.

seen versions of it before in many other activities, including distinctive-features activities or charts (described in Chapter 10).

To prepare, teachers create a grid either on chart paper to be displayed for the entire class or on individual sheets of paper. Along one axis of the chart are listed the items to be compared (e.g., books by Tomie dePaola, Cinderella stories, biographies, or characters in William Steig stories). On the other axis students brainstorm key characteristics that distinguish at least one item from another (see Figure 9.3). Students then work in pairs or groups to fill out the remainder of the chart. Students use the completed charts to compare and contrast the items listed.

"These really do work," says Toni, an elementary reading specialist.

I use this with children from first through sixth grade. With the younger ones we make the charts simpler—fewer things to be compared and fewer characteristics against which to compare them. And in some cases students dictate their thoughts to me and I write them in the appropriate boxes. But over time I see really noticeable gains in my students' ability to analyze and compare two or more stories or other items.

READER'S THEATER

Reader's theater, which we describe in Chapter 7 as a fluency development activity, is also an enjoyable and beneficial way for students to respond to their reading. Because performers in reader's theater use only their voices and facial expressions to convey meaning, the audience must imagine the action. Thus, reader's theater can be a powerful comprehension activity for the performers, who must comprehend to convey meaning to others, and the audience, who must comprehend to understand the script. We agree with Worthy and Prater (2002) that reader's theater is an "instructional activity that not only combines several effective research-based practices but also leads to increased comprehension even in very resistant readers" (p. 294).

RESPONSE JOURNALS

The reading–writing combination is powerful. In fact, opportunities to respond to reading in writing are associated with higher comprehension scores on standardized tests (e.g., NAEP, 2000). Response journals provide a special place for capturing reactions and thoughts related to reading. Journal entries can be either open or closed. An *open entry* is just that: Students can write whatever they want about what they have read. A *closed entry* focuses students' thinking in a particular way. A teacher who wants to encourage summarization, for example, might ask students to write brief plot summaries. Similarly, a prompt such as "Write about your favorite part of the book so far. Tell us why you like that part so much" encourages evaluative response. Both open and closed entries support students' efforts to construct meaning as they read.

Kate's fourth-graders are active journal writers. "Children's ideas provide us with an unending supply of topics for small-group or whole-class instruction," she says. Kate also uses response journals as a way to link reading and writing. "If we're working on great details or ways to 'show, not tell,' I frequently ask children to use their response journals to jot down snippets of language that grab them from the books they are reading. We collect all of these, put them on the board, and talk about what makes them so special so that we can use them in our own writing."

Response journal entries have several uses. That's what makes them so powerful. The teacher may read and respond to entries, or students may trade journals among themselves to read and respond to a peer who is reading (or has read) the same book. Sometimes students may read entries aloud so that classmates can talk further about the issues or ideas raised. Closed journal entries can become that basis for mini-lessons on particular areas of focus. For example, students can share their summaries and talk about what makes a good summary. Students can also keep response journals as a record of their thinking during reading.

Readers' Workshop and Literature Circles

Readers' workshop and *literature circles* are student-centered instructional routines that support individual comprehension development within the collaborative context of classrooms. Although more teacher-centered versions of these routines exist, they are most effective when students control decisions about what to read and how and when to share their responses with others (Heald-Taylor, 1996).

Readers' workshop was originally designed for middle school students (Atwell, 1987), but its effectiveness has led to widespread use in elementary and high schools as well. To initiate readers' workshop, teachers need a block of time—daily or several times each week—and lots of books. Teachers often begin each workshop session by asking students to plan their activities for the session. Brief mini-lessons are often part of readers' workshop as well. Early in the school year, these may focus on book selection or response options; later, mini-lessons may address comprehension fix-up strategies, literary features such as character development, or authors' stylistic features. The mini-lessons are focused, brief, and related to children's current needs as readers.

The biggest chunk of readers' workshop time belongs to students. They read; share with peers; respond individually; and occasionally prepare more public responses, perhaps using art, drama, or writing. The teacher circulates to ensure that students are engaged but may also confer with individuals, conduct small-group response discussions, or even facilitate book selection. The teacher may also set expectations for activity completion by requiring a certain number of response log entries or interpretive activities over the course of a week or month.

Literature circles (Daniels, 2002; McMahon & Raphael, 1997; Noe & Johnson, 1999) may be part of readers' workshop or conducted as a separate instructional routine. In either event, small groups of readers discuss their books. Students can self-select groups (the teacher may want to "book talk" the titles or provide time for students to peruse books), or the teacher can assign them. Possible models for organizing texts and readers are as follows (adapted from Fountas & Pinnell, 2001):

- *Whole group, same text:* Students read or listen to the same text. The whole group formulates questions for discussion. Small groups meet to discuss, make notes, and report back to the whole group.
- *Small group, same text:* Teacher "book talks" several titles. Students select titles of interest, and groups are formed. Groups may plan a culminating activity (reader's theater, drama, technology) to share with the whole group.
- *Small group, different texts:* Students choose from a variety of different texts that have something in common (e.g., strong characters; genre, such as biography; same author; issues, such as coming-of-age or race relations; content area study, such as Civil War books or books about hurricanes; etc.). Groups may be formed somewhat randomly. Students read their individual titles. Group discussions focus on the common element (e.g., characterization, qualities of a biography, etc.). A culminating activity summarizes and synthesizes all group discussions.

Group discussions should be held at least two to three times per week. The students read or listen to text before the discussion group assembles. They might want to prepare for the discussions by making notes, writing in response journals, using sticky notes to mark places in the text for discussion, and such. As they become accustomed to literature circle discussions, which are largely student directed, it's often helpful for the students to select roles before reading or listening to the text. Many teachers have found assigned roles unnecessary as students become more comfortable with literature circle discussions. Possible roles include:

- *Group leader:* Leads discussion, encourages participation, keeps track of time.
- *Summarizer:* Begins discussion with summary of text.
- *Comparer:* Compares text to other text(s).
- *Connector:* Compares text to other nontext people and events.

- *Sentence finder/Word finder:* Finds and shares interesting sentences or words.
- *Questioner:* Finds and shares unresolved issues.
- *Predictor:* Leads discussion about upcoming portions of the text.

With appropriate preparation and support, even primary-level students can participate in effective discussions (Jewell & Pratt, 1999). Literature circle discussions aim to be entirely student led, although teachers may want to lead occasional mini-lessons about the qualities of effective discussions or remind students of response options. Activities such as Linguistic Roulette, Group Mapping, or Sketch to Stretch, all described earlier in this chapter, provide excellent preparation for literature circle discussions.

Particularly if children are unaccustomed to working independently, it may take a while for them to learn how to work together productively. It's important not to abandon either readers' workshop or literature circles prematurely. Instead, you may need to diagnose dysfunctional behaviors. For example, excessive absences or high student turnover can affect either routine. If this is the case, perhaps new students can sit in a literature circle group without initially participating, and excessively absent students can be provided time to catch up on their reading before rejoining their groups.

Social interaction and conversational skills may also cause problems. Videotaping a couple of discussions and then analyzing children's interactions may help to pinpoint problem areas. That's what Clarke and Holwadel (2007) did in a sixth-grade class where groups appeared to be malfunctioning. They discovered: "One of the main difficulties was the tension in the classroom. There was a pervasive feeling of hostility between the students, and many of their everyday interactions seemed to be punctuated by verbal assaults such as 'stupid' or 'ugly,' as if these words were to be routinely attached to the end of a sentence" (p. 22). The solution to this problem with literature circles was found in addressing the larger hostility issue.

Students also need to learn conversational skills. In analyzing videos of conversations, teachers might make note of off-task behavior, if someone is dominating conversation, and so forth. "Sharing the Airtime" (Daniels & Steineke, 2004) can help with these problems. Each student in a literature circle gets a stack of poker chips, dried beans, or similar marker. Each time a child speaks, he or she must relinquish one of the chips. When the chips are gone, so are the student's chances to participate in discussion. Daniels and Steineke note that this procedure encourages "group members to think before they spoke and engage in less off-track arguing and side conversations" (p. 25).

Readers' workshop and literature circles provide frameworks within which students have time to read and opportunities to respond. Although each routine may require some adjustment on students' parts, both promote reflection, interpretation, and inquiry, all of which support comprehension growth.

Balance Strategy Instruction and Independent Reading

Comprehension is like model building. Readers construct text interpretation or their own models of the text by relying on many raw materials: content and linguistic information provided by the author, their own knowledge and experiences, and their understanding of how written language works. All this happens in a social, environmental, and instructional context that is critical in determining both what and how students comprehend. Moffett and Wagner (1992) synthesized these factors and influences quite well: "People read for diverse reasons and in diverse ways—casually to sift, studiedly to recall, raptly to become spellbound. The more schools open up the repertory of authentic discourse, the more apparent this becomes. Thus reader response is a factor of reader purpose and the kind of discourse. But response and purpose go back to choice" (p. 142).

Response and reflection (Rosenblatt, 1938, 1978) are hallmarks of literary comprehension and therefore worthy instructional goals. Within this overall framework, teachers can focus students' attention on *literacy* development, basic learning-to-read issues such as constructing main ideas or developing vocabulary knowledge. But too heavy an emphasis in this domain may not serve students well: "Unfortunately . . . literature [may be] treated more like information to be memorized and tested than an experience to be enjoyed and appreciated" (Dugan, 1997, p. 87). Providing opportunities for *literary* development can help avoid this situation. Barbara Lehman and Pat Scharer (1996) urge teachers to plan instruction that also focuses on the "understanding of literature and how it acts as a work of art to generate readers' responses" (p. 26). Fortunately, strategy instruction and the development of appreciation for literature can coexist in classrooms. A combination of strategy teaching and plentiful opportunities for students to read independently appears to provide the balance that makes this possible (Baumann, Hooten, & White, 1999).

DISCUSSION QUESTIONS

Some of the discussion questions for each chapter ask you to think through your own work as a teacher. If you are not currently a practicing teacher, try to respond to these questions from your own school experience (either from when you yourself were a student or from visits to schools that you have made in your teacher education program).

1. Define comprehension in your own words (try not to use the word *understand*). How do you know when you comprehended something you have read? What do you do to enhance your comprehension of what you have read?

2. *Situational pragmatics*, or the context in which we read, also influences comprehension. What are some implications of situational pragmatics for instruction with struggling readers?

3. Choose one of the instructional strategies in this chapter that you have never used and try it with struggling readers. Share the experience with your colleagues.

4. In a seminal research study on comprehension, Dolores Durkin (1979) found that teachers were *checking* comprehension rather than *teaching* comprehension. Do you think that is true today? What is your evidence? Describe the difference; give specific examples.

5. The chapter cited one research study that found that teachers, on average, spent only about a minute each day in comprehension strategy instruction. Keep a log for one week on how much time you spend teaching comprehension strategies with your struggling readers. Reflect on what you learned.

6. Literature is culture bound. Give an example of what this quote means using an ELL, ethnic, or minority student in your classroom.

Chapter Ten

Developing Comprehension with Informational Text

O UR FOCUS IN THIS CHAPTER is on informational text. Why "informational text" rather than "nonfiction"? Here's why. In explaining his book, *Black and White Airmen: Their True Story* (2007), author John Fleischman says,

> I need to declare what I mean by a "true story." . . . True books like this one are usually called "nonfiction," which is a funny word. All it guarantees is that this book is "not fiction," that is, that I didn't make it up entirely. Imagine if food were labeled that way; imagine that the ingredients listed on an ice cream wrapper said only "Not stones." (pp. 10–11)

Not stones??!! Well, then, how can we define informational text? This chapter, which is about developing students' comprehension for informational texts, is framed on the following expository text types (definitions from Harris & Hodges, 1995):

- *Description:* Gives verbal picture
- *Sequence:* Ordered (chronological, easy-to-difficult, part-to-whole, etc.)
- *Causation:* Stated or implied association between outcome and conditions that brought it about
- *Problem–solution:* Gives problem and its solution(s)
- *Compare/contrast:* Places like characters, ideas, and so on, together to show common and contrasting features

Certainly an informational text can contain more than one of these types. Moreover, there's the issue of online texts, many of which are also informational in nature. As you read this chapter, then, we encourage you to keep this broad definition of *informational text* in mind.

When is it appropriate to use the various strategies described in this chapter? That choice has more to do with purpose than with classroom schedules. Teaching strategies for informational text are appropriate when students' and teachers' main interest is in learning something new or more thoroughly or acquiring information. Although instruction designed to help students learn new information has always been a major goal of schooling, the information explosion sparked by technological advances makes it even more critical. To be lifelong learners, students must learn how to learn. This demands more of them than acquiring facts. Students will need "to recognize when information is needed and have the ability to locate, evaluate, and use effectively the needed information" (American Library Association Presidential Committee on Information Literacy, 1989, p. 1). Well-crafted instruction can help students develop these skills.

Principles for Comprehension Instruction of Informational Text

Instructional strategies for ensuring students' comprehension of informational text must incorporate understandings about readers' interactions with text and students' interactions with the teacher and each other. Toward that end, we offer several principles for developing effective instruction:

- *Activating and engaging readers' background knowledge about a topic enhances learning.* Students need opportunities to become aware of what they already know about text content and to think about it before they begin reading. They also need opportunities to consider what they don't know but want to learn about a topic. Activating background knowledge allows students to make rapid connections between what they already know and what they are to learn. This both eases and deepens comprehension (Hirsh, 2003).

- *Predictions about text content must be encouraged.* Good readers think backward and forward when reading; they draw conclusions about what they have read and make predictions about what they are likely to encounter. Like scientists, proficient readers constantly entertain and test hypotheses about the content in the text.

- *The instructional environment should help students learn to comprehend actively and purposefully and evaluate their own efforts as readers and learners.* This critical stance is particularly significant as students learn how to read the Internet: "Even more than with traditional texts, then, we need to help students develop the skills that they need to determine the accuracy, authenticity, and point of view of Internet materials" (Burke, 2002, p. 38). Teachers support this learning by providing frameworks for sharing, discussion, and exploration and modeling literate, inquiring, and learned behavior themselves.

  Thinking about what expert readers do can help teachers decide how to support children's efforts with informational text. Teachers can model how to look through a text before reading or how to fix comprehension difficulties that inevitably occur. Peers can think aloud as they read a text together. All this can help children learn to read strategically (Block & Israel, 2004).

- *Activities that foster cooperative involvement and joint problem solving enhance learning.* The instructional environment features lots of talk. Students' collaboration is genuine and substantive. They learn to take risks and share ideas; they also learn that their thinking is valued.

  This instructional environment is critical for all students but is especially important for children learning English. Immigrant Latino/a students are accustomed to working together for the good of the group, a process they learn from their families (Rothstein-Fisch & Trumbull, 2008). Moreover, academic texts are challenging for English language learners (Vacca & Vacca, 2008), so activity-based supplements and genuine, rich conversation can support their learning.

Instruction based on these criteria helps readers grow in their ability to comprehend and learn from informational text. In this chapter we describe several teaching strategies, appropriate for readers of all ages and abilities, that work especially well with informational text. Over time, these strategies help students learn to read strategically and successfully. We then consider how teachers can support students' reading on the Web.

Prereading Activities

Just as athletes warm up before a game to prepare their bodies for success, a few minutes spent on prereading activities can help students read and learn successfully. Effective prereading activities, such as those described here, should invite students to:

- Consider what they already know about the reading and share these ideas with others.
- Anticipate and make predictions about what they are likely to encounter as they read.
- Develop their own purposes for reading.
- Build curiosity and motivation for reading.

WORD SORTS

Open word sorts (see Chapters 6 and 8) can be an effective prereading activity to prime students for comprehending a text (Bear, Invernizzi, Templeton, & Johnston, 2007; Gillet & Kita, 1979). The teacher selects about 20 words or phrases from the text students will read. For example, Becky, an intermediate-grade Title I teacher, selected these words and phrases from an article about spiders:

liquid silk	orb weaver	tarantula
four pairs of legs	tiny claws	egg sac
spinnerets	poison fangs	mandibles
wolf	water	trap door

After Becky prepared and distributed sets of word cards to pairs of students, she directed the children to "put these into groups that make sense to you. Be ready to explain your reasons." Students examined the words, looking for relationships between and among them. To establish and agree on categories, students discussed the chosen concepts, shared knowledge with each other, and engaged in hypothesis testing.

When the small groups completed sorting the words, Becky invited groups to share both the categories and their reasoning. Here's how one group of fourth-graders sorted the words:

Things Spiders Have	*Where Spiders Live*
liquid silk	trap door
tiny claws	water
four pairs of legs	egg sac
poison fangs	

Kinds of Spiders	*We Don't Know*
tarantula	mandibles
wolf	spinnerets
	balloon
	orb weaver

These students know something about spiders, but they also recognize what they can learn from the article. Whole-group sharing encouraged further exploration of key concepts. Finally, Becky asked them what they expected to be reading about and why. This summarized the conversation about words and encouraged students to make and share predictions. Then, the students read, armed with their own relevant knowledge.

Possible Sentences, described in Chapter 8, another variety of word sort, is an excellent prereading activity, particularly with challenging text. Research has shown that it fosters both word and concept learning and text information recall (Stahl & Kapinus, 1991). Whatever their format, word sorts help students activate and share their prior knowledge about concepts and predict text content. They enhance curiosity and provide natural, meaningful purposes for reading: Students are eager to see if their ideas are accurate.

BRAINSTORMING

Brainstorming activities are identical to word sorts except that students, rather than the teacher, generate the words and phrases. The brainstorming we describe here is similar to the List Group Label vocabulary activity presented in Chapter 8. Students can brainstorm in small groups with one student serving as the recorder, or the teacher can serve as recorder for the entire group. In either case, the teacher provides a key word or phrase and asks students for any words that come to mind when they think about the key word. Students should generate words quickly rather than stop for analysis or evaluation. Another group of Becky's students produced this list of words in response to the key word *spider*: *black widow, web, flies, bees, insects, ants, silk, haunted house, gross, neat, plants, basement, desert, round, furry, tarantula, jumping spider,* and *eight legs.*

FIGURE 10.1 "Spiders" Web

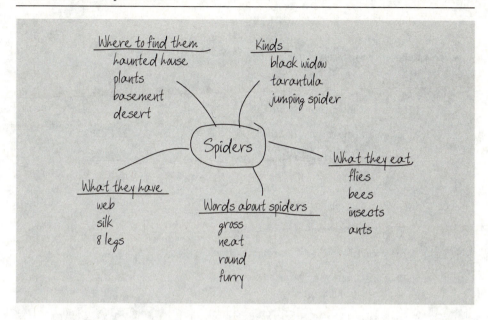

After 2 or 3 minutes of brainstorming, small groups categorize the words and provide titles for the categories, much like an open word sort. Students use chart paper and markers or an overhead transparency to record their categories so that others can easily see their decisions during the discussion and sharing that follows. Figure 10.1 shows a web that one group of children made with the words they had brainstormed. After discussion and sharing, students read.

Brainstorming is a cooperative activity; students learn from and with each other. Such cooperation fosters successful, purposeful reading among all students, but may be particularly helpful for struggling readers, including those who are learning English.

ANTICIPATION GUIDES

A third prereading activity that activates prior knowledge and promotes purposeful reading is the *anticipation guide* (Herber, 1978; Vacca & Vacca, 2008). The teacher prepares written statements for students to think about and discuss before (and often after) they read. The statements are intended to activate prior knowledge and arouse curiosity. A sample anticipation guide, developed for a science article about spiders, appears in Figure 10.2. Note that the directions ask students to indicate those statements with which they agree and to be ready to explain their thinking. This process of justifying or explaining their thinking allows students to sharpen and organize what they know about a topic and become aware of what they don't know.

After individuals make decisions about the statements, the teacher leads a discussion in which students share their ideas and knowledge with each other. The anticipation guide shown in Figure 10.2 directs students to return to the statements after reading the article,

FIGURE 10.2 "Spiders" Anticipation Guide

Directions: Read each statement about spiders. In the "Before" column, check the ones you agree with. Be ready to explain your thinking.

Before		After	Page(s)
_____	1. Spiders are insects.	_____	_____
_____	2. Spiders can move in any direction.	_____	_____
_____	3. Spiders have eight eyes and eight legs.	_____	_____
_____	4. Spiders are helpful.	_____	_____
_____	5. Some spiders can float through the air.	_____	_____
_____	6. Spiders use the same webs over and over.	_____	_____
_____	7. The silk in spider webs is stronger than iron.	_____	_____
_____	8. The silk in spider webs has been used in microscopes and telescopes.	_____	_____
_____	9. Spiders won't bite unless they are disturbed.	_____	_____

Directions: Now that you've read about spiders, read the statements again. This time check the statements you agree with in the "After" column. In the "Pages" column, write down the page or pages in the book that helped you decide. Again, be ready to explain your thinking.

again indicating the statements they agree with but now supporting their ideas by referring to pages from the text.

Don provides resource assistance for intermediate-grade students with learning disabilities. He relies frequently on anticipation guides because, he says, "the kids really enjoy them, and I think they help kids' learning. It reassures them to know that they already know something about what they will be reading. Talking about specific issues seems to help them develop a purpose for reading, too." Although Don varies the way he uses anticipation guides, he typically asks pairs of students to complete the guides together. Before the group reads the text selection, he asks students to indicate whether they agreed or disagreed with each statement and give reasons for their decisions. Sometimes, this discussion proceeds quickly because students arrive at the same decisions for the same reasons. At other times, more lengthy discussions ensue because students' opinions differ or they raise complex issues. After reading, Don generally directs discussion to focus on those areas where students have changed their minds or have additional information to share based on their reading. He says that this postreading discussion allows students to share what they have learned and raise issues for further exploration.

K-W-L

Students complete two portions of a *K-W-L* chart before reading (Ogle, 1986). This activity derives its name from the column labels on the chart: "What we *know* about the topic," "What we *want* to know from reading about the topic," and "What we *learned* from reading." Pairs or small groups of students can work independently to complete the K-W-L activity, or the group can work together as a whole, with the teacher serving as recorder.

As with a brainstorming activity, the teacher begins a K-W-L discussion by providing a topic, key word, or phrase related to what students are about to read. They share what they already know about the topic and pose questions they want answered or issues they hope to learn more about. Notes are made in the *K* and *W* columns of the chart. After students read the text, they complete the third column by recording what they have learned. This may include answers to questions, information related to issues, or other information students find important or interesting. Students can use information from their K-W-L charts for writing, such as writing a summary, or to guide additional inquiry.

Betsy frequently uses K-W-L charts with her Title I students who are beginning readers. She says these discussions often offer her some effective incidental teaching opportunities: "Sometimes the ideas really come pouring out! After everyone has shared, we need to decide how to record children's ideas on the chart. So I say, 'Okay, how should I write this down?' and the students have to think back through the discussion and summarize and synthesize it so that we can decide what to record." Betsy also notes that sometimes children's questions about the topic (from the *W* column) aren't answered by the text selection. "This is good, in a way," she says. "If the kids are really curious, we find other resource books—a great reason for a trip to the computer or the library!"

BUILDING BACKGROUND KNOWLEDGE

Word sorts, Possible Sentences, brainstorming, anticipation guides, and K-W-L charts all invite students to activate their background knowledge by thinking about general topics related to their reading and recalling and organizing what they already know about those topics. In many cases, these prereading activities provide plenty of support for subsequent reading.

Sometimes, however, students need additional support. In cases where content is new, important, abstract in nature, or loaded with unfamiliar terms, the teacher may wish to help students *build* background knowledge—that is, learn new things about the topic before they read—rather than simply *activate* what they already know.

Activities to build background knowledge can involve reading or listening to additional texts—trade books, newspaper or magazine articles, speeches, or webpages. Two characteristics of these texts make them especially effective for helping students build background knowledge: They tend to offer more elaboration or detail than textbook selections and are often storylike. These features can heighten interest and make information easy to remember, thus allowing students to learn new information that can, in turn, support their textbook reading.

Sometimes discussion can serve to activate and build background knowledge. For example, consider how two fifth-grade teachers introduced *No Promises in the Wind* about the Great Depression. In one class, the teacher passed out the paperbacks and said, "We are going to be reading this book. It's about the Great Depression. Read Chapter 1 tonight and be ready to discuss it tomorrow. Now take out your spelling books." In another class, after distributing the books, the teacher said, "We are going to be reading this book. It's about the Great Depression. What do you know about the Great Depression?" (blank stares) "What do you know about being poor?" Although these were students in an affluent district, they had seen things on TV, read stories about poverty, and so on, so they had some discussion. "What do you know about wanting something you can't have?" the teacher asked. Lots of discussion. The teacher added, "That's what it was like in the Great Depression. It was a hard time financially for our country. There were many poor people, including people who had been accustomed to having what they wanted. Please read Chapter 1 tonight, and we'll discuss it tomorrow." These few minutes of discussion provided children in the second classroom with an overview of issues related to the novel.

Informational text is a great source for read-alouds (see Figure 2.4 for assistance in finding books). Former teacher and librarian Ray Doiron (1994) offers this guidance for selecting and using books:

- Choose texts that ignite the imagination rather than stuff in facts. Begin with books you enjoy. As with any other read-aloud, practice beforehand.
- Look for authors who write with clarity, authority, and in a vivid style. Talk with students about the author, illustrator, publication date, and authority with which the text was written. Encourage them to think about the author's language and point of view.

Reading for information can be fun. Children are naturally curious, with a great thirst to know about the world around them. This "need to know" is a powerful motivator for reading or listening to informational texts (Moss & Hendershot, 2002). Indeed, Smolkin and Donovan (2003) argue convincingly that it's a mistake to wait to address informational texts until students can read them independently. Rather, they urge teachers to begin strategy instruction in kindergarten and first grade through teacher read-alouds. They point out, for example, how young and struggling readers can learn to ask good questions when they listen to informational text because these texts typically feature things that children are interested in but don't know about.

Nonreading activities are equally effective ways to build background knowledge. Jackdaws, described in Chapter 9, can provide vehicles for exploring background and learning. As students examine and talk about the items included in the jackdaws, teachers have natural opportunities to share relevant information. Experiments and demonstrations also work well, as do media or audiovisual presentations, whether viewed on the Web or through more traditional means. Increasingly, teachers use Internet resources to build students' background knowledge. They search for relevant information on the Web, evaluate the content of websites, and bookmark a few especially good ones for students to explore.

Activities to build background knowledge take time—a precious commodity in most classrooms. Although we have no magic rule for deciding when such time is well spent, when information is important or abstract, or when students need extra support to read successfully, it probably makes sense to include some background-building activities.

These prereading activities share common elements that make them successful. Each provides a framework and reason for students to consider what they already know (and don't know) about text content and to hypothesize about the upcoming reading. Each also promotes sharing so that students learn from and with each other. These factors combine to create readers ready to read actively, purposefully, and enthusiastically.

Supporting Students During Reading

Text discussions during and after reading have long been recognized as effective means of enhancing students' comprehension and learning. Good questions are key to effective discussions. What makes a question good? First, it's authentic; it is asked because the asker doesn't know and wants to know the answer. Here are some "authentic" question starters, all of which have been found to have significant effects on children's academic gains (Heyman, 1983; Hiebert & Wearne, 1993; Wolf, Crosson, & Resnick, 2005):

- What do you think about . . . ?
- Tell how you . . . .
- Why do you think so?
- What do you mean?

Notice that these questions do not focus on literal information, but students are apt to provide literal information in their responses. This use of literal or factual information—to provide support for one's ideas—enhances text discussions and learning more than questions intended to test what students remember.

Authentic questions often motivate higher-level reasoning, another characteristic of good discussions. Discussions differ from conversations because they are planned, but in many respects a good discussion should be like a conversation: a social exchange of ideas, information, and opinions. A good environment for discussions should invite (but not demand) verbal participation; in other words, students should feel free to speak or not, as they choose. Furthermore, students should be encouraged to talk with each other rather than filter everything through the teacher. The result of effective text discussions is more than a collection of students' individual meanings and verbal reports; new meaning is constructed as students listen to and talk with each other and make new connections between ideas.

Effective discussions provide a framework for thinking and sharing about text. The strategies described next provide this sort of framework, as do several introduced in Chapter 9 (e.g., Linguistic Roulette, Think-Pair-Share).

DIRECTED READING–THINKING ACTIVITY

The *Directed Reading–Thinking Activity (DR–TA)*, described in Chapter 9, is also effective with informational text (Stauffer, 1980). As with fiction DR–TAs, discussions evolve through cycles in which students generate hypotheses and subsequently validate, reject, or modify them. Preparation involves selecting readings for students and deciding where they will stop for discussion. Subheads in articles or textbooks provide natural stopping points.

In this excerpt Jane's eighth-grade students are reading a chapter in their history books that describes social reforms of the nineteenth century.

Jane: What do you think this passage is going to be about from just looking at the heading?

Katy: What's a reformer?

Karen: Yeah.

Jane: Who can tell us?

Matt: A person who likes to reshape or something.

Jane: What would a person be doing if he were trying to reshape?

Matt: Change it.

Katy: Make it better.

Mike: Try to make it better for people.

Jane: Can you give us an example of what you think they wanted to change back at that point?

Matt: Slavery.

Mike: Government.

Jane: All right. What else?

Tony: Laws.

Jane: Read the first two paragraphs only.

[Students read.]

Jane: Were you right about anything?

Tony: Yeah.

Matt: Slavery.

Jane: Anything else?

Karen: Trying to help people defend themselves and that.

Katy: What *reformers* meant.

Jane: What do you think it means now?

Katy: The same thing. Helping people . . .

Karen: A person who makes change.

Matt: Try to do something better.

Mike: Try to improve something.

As you can see from the excerpt, the questioning cycle resembles the cycle for narrative. Jane encouraged prediction, reflection, and integrating text and prior knowledge. Good prediction questions for a DR–TA with informational text include "What do you think this will be about?" "What issues will the author address?" and "What will we read about next?"

After students have read a portion of the text, the teacher can ask questions such as "Were your predictions on target?" "Did anything surprise you?" "Have you changed your mind about anything based on what you've read?" and "Now what do you think?" Either before or after reading, questions and comments can invite elaboration or clarification: "Why?" "What makes you say that?" "Tell us some more about that," and "Anything else?"

The teacher's talk activates student thought, encourages the use of prior knowledge, and facilitates group interaction. Students learn that their ideas are valued, that they should justify their opinions so that others can understand their reasoning, that they should listen to and talk with each other, and that the responsibility for learning is theirs.

IMPORTANT IDEAS AND WORDS

If texts contain a great deal of new information, students may struggle to decide what is important enough to remember. The dialectic journal and the important words strategies offer students support as they learn to make these decisions.

The *dialectic journal* (Watson, 1987), a during-reading strategy, helps students identify important information from informational text, share these ideas with others, and develop their own opinions about what they have read. The strategy involves several stages:

- *Stage 1:* As students read a portion of an informational text, they make notes about what they think is important. Notes can be made on separate paper or in a journal, as the title for the strategy suggests; or students can write on sticky notes or use pencils to write on the text itself.

- *Stage 2:* Small groups share what they have identified as important. As students listen to others' ideas, they may revise their own notes, add or erase underlines, and so on. Stages 1 and 2 continue as students complete the text.

- *Stage 3:* Having decided on important information from the text, students now make notes on their own opinions about what they have read. They consider issues such as what they agree or disagree with, how the information might be useful, and how new information fits in with what they already knew.

- *Stage 4:* Students share their individual opinions with others in their small groups. Groups discuss individual opinions, synthesize discussion, and may prepare written or oral summaries or lists to share with the entire class.

Important words is similar to the dialectic journal, except that students identify words rather than ideas as they read. Then, in small groups, they share their individual choices, create a master set of important words, and categorize or organize the words in some way that shows the relationships among the words and the text. Carly, who teaches third grade, has found the important words strategy an effective way to introduce her students to note taking. "I recycle office paper by making little word cards for the children," she says. "This makes it easier for them to combine their words and move them around so they can test out possible organizations." Carly even uses the activity to provide a framework for units of instruction. "We began our simple machines unit with columns on the chalkboard labeled with types of simple machines. The children brainstormed important words related to each type. Then, they read from the science text and added more important words that they had found in their reading. Finally, pairs of children did copy change [see Chapter 11] writing using *The Important Book* [Brown, 1949/1999]. I was amazed at how much more the children remembered!"

SAVE THE LAST WORD FOR ME

This activity, developed by Carolyn Burke, is also designed to provide support for students as they read challenging material (Watson, 1987). As with the dialectic journal, students first read a portion of a text and write individually. Then, they discuss the reading in small groups.

To begin the activity, students make notes on separate paper, in their journals, or on sticky notes as they read. They might note important information, copy a critical sentence, record what they don't understand, or jot down unfamiliar vocabulary; each student decides what to write. Discussion begins after all small-group members have completed reading one portion of the text. One by one, students introduce an idea from their notes for group discussion. Others in the group may respond to the idea, answer the question, or provide their own definitions for vocabulary words. Conversations take many directions. After all others have offered their thoughts, the student who introduced the topic has the "last word" and may offer an opinion or summarize the discussion. The next student in the group offers another topic, and the discussion begins again. After each group member has started a discussion, students read and make notes about the next portion of the text.

Ted teaches middle school students who find reading difficult. He relies on all of these during-reading strategies because "the kids need the support that the strategies can provide." Ted uses several criteria to decide which activity to use.

> Probably the most important factor in my planning is the difficulty of the text. I think the DR–TA is the most supportive strategy, so that's the one we use if I think the reading might be tough for the kids. I also think about variety, though. It's more fun for all of us if we vary the routine. And after we've done these things a few times, I sometimes ask students which strategy they want to use. I really don't worry about students' choices because I know each strategy helps them understand what they read.

Ted finds that his students "read for their own purposes or for purposes that arise as part of the discussions. Either way, they care about what they read, and that's half the battle, as far as I'm concerned. Besides that, the discussions themselves foster learning." Students must think carefully while they read and listen carefully during discussions. As a result, according to Ted, "they learn content information. But they also learn that reading is an active, problem-solving process."

Postreading Activities

Good postreading activities give students continued opportunities for dynamic interaction with the text and among themselves. Sometimes students revisit prereading activities after they read. For example, open word sorts work well for refining and extending concepts after reading. Students can reorganize the words and phrases based on their reading and discuss the changes they made. Brainstorming, too, can follow reading, this time as a means of integrating new information with prior knowledge. And students can record what they learned as a result of reading and discussion in the *L* (what we learned) column of their K-W-L charts. Several other postreading activities foster continued interaction with text.

DISTINCTIVE FEATURES

Reading informational text often helps students think about similarities and differences between and among related concepts. In such instances, *distinctive-features* activities make effective postreading lessons. Figure 10.3 shows a distinctive features chart that Becky and her students developed for their science lesson about spiders.

After students read, Becky asked, "What kinds of spiders did we read about?" The children's answers, recorded on the chalkboard, ultimately became one dimension of the chart. Becky asked for the features of spiders described in the text: "What were some things that we learned about all of these spiders?" This information became the other dimension of the chart. Students returned to the text to verify their recollections and make any necessary changes before the final version of the chart was constructed.

Students then worked in pairs to complete the chart. They talked with their partners, reread if necessary, and decided what to write in each cell of the chart. After pairs had completed their charts, Becky reconvened the whole group and asked some questions to focus on similarities and differences, a very powerful learning focus (Marzano, Pickering, & Pollock, 2001). Distinctive-features activities provide frameworks for organizing, categorizing, synthesizing, and making notes about what students have read. In addition, the completed charts are useful for later review and study.

FIGURE 10.3   "Spiders" Distinctive Features Chart

	SPIDERS			
FEATURES	Tarantulas	Trap-door Spiders	Wolf Spiders	Water Spiders
Size				
General areas where found				
Habitat				
Prey				
How prey is captured				

FIGURE 10.4   Herringbone Chart

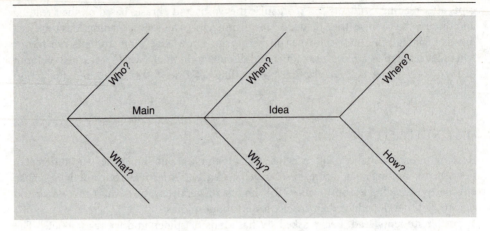

HERRINGBONE

The *herringbone* activity also uses a chart to help students summarize and synthesize what they have read (see Figure 10.4). Students read and then work with partners to complete the chart. Together, they must decide on answers to each detail question on the chart. This frequently involves rereading but always involves discussion as students identify a variety of potential answers to each question and settle on the most important. Finally, they combine these details to develop a main-idea summary statement for the entire passage. The herringbone chart is a supportive framework for students to make their own decisions about what is important and to think about the main idea, significant details, and the relationships among them.

DISCUSSION WEB

This activity, developed by Donna Alvermann (1991), is especially useful when students read about a complex problem, issue, or situation—one that generates controversy or has no simple solution. After students read (or listen), they work in pairs to complete a *discussion web* (see Figure 10.5) that contains a question developed by the teacher. Pairs generate as many reasons as possible for answering "yes" to the question; they do the same for "no." Next, each pair joins with another; the group of four considers all the "yes" and "no" responses and tries to agree on a conclusion. During this discussion, students make notes on the discussion web. Finally, groups share their conclusions with the entire class.

Belinda teaches in a multiage primary classroom in a community where a controversy arose over cats. At issue was whether the current situation, allowing cats to run free, should be changed.

> I wasn't planning to address this issue, but the children were eager to discuss it. Predictably, kids who had "free-range" cats thought the status quo was just fine, and those who had others' cats in their yards didn't. I thought the discussion web might provide a way for the children to see both sides of the issue. So, I put this question on a large piece of chart paper: Should cats be allowed to run free in [city]? I tried to

FIGURE 10.5 Discussion Web

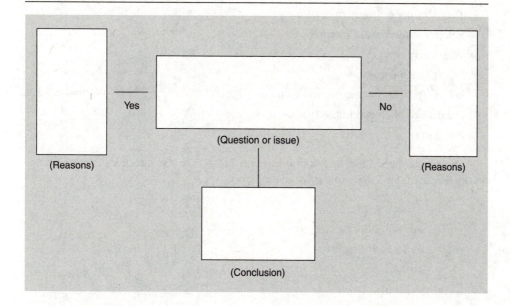

pair older students with younger ones, and I asked the older students to be the note takers. The children recorded their own thinking, but I also read newspaper articles and letters to the editor to them, after which they added more "yes" or "no" reasons based on what they heard. We never reached consensus, and I don't think too many children changed their minds. But I could tell that the children thought deeply about how others might think. And when the city resolved the situation by requiring people to register their cats and put ID tags on their collars, we had the chance to talk about compromise. What a civics lesson!

RESPONSE ACTIVITIES

Response activities (see Chapter 9) are effective ways for students to summarize, synthesize, and react to informational texts. For example, writing helps students extend their thinking about text concepts (see Chapter 11). Writing an alphabet book to capture new learning offers a way to summarize and synthesize. Both brief, informal writing, such as writing a learning log entry, and extended, formal writing, such as writing an inquiry paper or preparing a class newspaper or magazine, have value.

Poetry writing is often an effective response activity. In addition to "name" poems or acrostics (see Chapter 11), biopoems, diamantes, and other form poems work well. A *biopoem* (Gere, 1985) offers a framework for synthesizing what students have learned about a person, group, event, concept—almost anything they study. The lines for the biopoem can include name; location in time or place; relatives (or related concepts); and lists of needs, wants, fears, hopes, important contributions—whatever the teacher or students decide would provide a useful framework. Here, for example, is a biopoem based on *Bud, Not Buddy* (Curtis, 1999):

Bud

Thoughtful, persistent, funny, lonely

Relative of Mama and Herman

Who feels alone

Who needs a family

Who fears foster homes, the dark, and monsters

Resident of Michigan in the 1930s

Not Buddy

Diamantes, named for their diamond-shaped form, are also effective response frameworks. The form for a diamante is based on parts of speech:

noun

adj. adj. adj.

-ing verb -ing verb -ing verb

adj. adj. adj.

noun

Artistic representations such as murals, pictures, sculpture, or dioramas may be appropriate response activities in some instances. Skits, reader's theater, or role-playing activities can also be useful. Amber and Dana, who use integrated thematic units in their classes, frequently encourage this sort of response as a culminating activity. "It's always an option," Dana says. "Some students are naturally drawn to these more creative ways of responding, and others have the opportunity to look at things somewhat differently. Trying to role-play characters or situations from history, for example, really gives you a different slant on what you've learned."

Reader's theater has a place in their classrooms as well. "It really solved a problem for us," Amber notes. "We study Ohio history and have struggled for years with the section about the Amish, Quakers, Mormons, and Zoarites. The text is very dry, and library books are too hard for the children to read independently. Reader's theater to the rescue! We found information in the library and on the Web. The children were delighted with the four scripts we wrote, and we were delighted with their learning."

Amber, Dana, and their students occasionally enjoy a day of celebration after they have spent some time exploring a theme or issue: "We take part of a day to sit back and reflect on what we've learned. We invite parents and grandparents to join us. The kids present their skits, explain their newspapers, or whatever. The children enjoy these days, and they're a great way to involve families in what we do in school. There's value to the sort of summary-thinking that leads students to their culminating projects."

Supporting Web-Based Learning

"We live in a society that is experiencing an explosion of alternative texts" (RAND Study Group, 2002, p. xiv). Online reading is quite different from more conventional reading.

Think of it: If you're looking at a single site, you may have access to hyperlinked information, audio and/or video clips, graphics, and more. Images, sounds, and text combine to create new ways of conveying meaning (Coiro, 2003). Moreover, using the Web as a research tool requires knowledge of effective search procedures and how to consider issues related to trustworthiness. As Tapscott (1998) noted, "Never before has it been more necessary that children learn to read, write, and think critically. It's not just point and click. It's point, read, think, and click" (p. 63).

To be sure, this explosion of alternative texts or new media has instructional implications related to the topic of this chapter: reading informational text. Struggling readers may be even more befuddled in the complex online environment. Children who live in poverty may have limited access to computers outside of school. Teachers can help children read successfully on the Web by providing questions that can serve as a framework for online exploration and by modeling how to use strategies flexibly.

Asking questions and then thinking about responses, especially in the company of others, can help students learn to navigate the Web. With regard to the purpose for working in a particular Web-based environment, for example, students may need to consider such questions as (Baildon & Baildon, 2008; Coiro, 2003):

- Is this website easy for me to read and understand by myself?
- How can I be sure that this information is accurate and current? Can I find one more source that includes the same information?
- Will this website help me answer my questions?
- How should I navigate this information?

Baildon and Baildon (2008) taught fourth-graders how to answer questions like these in a study of ways to support children's independent research capabilities on the Web. They taught children to use an R–T–U framework: Readable, Trustworthy, Useful. Children learned to apply the framework in small-group discussions about a variety of websites about a topic of interest. Some sites were authentic and potentially helpful for children; others were too difficult or did not contain useful information; still others included "overexaggerated and silly" information (p. 639). At the end of the study, students' attitudes about and independence in Web researching had significantly improved. This study provides evidence that students can learn to ask pertinent questions to evaluate Web resources.

To successfully read informational texts on the Web involves flexible strategy use, so helping students become comfortable with approaching tasks in a variety of ways is important. A three-step process that is based on gradual release of responsibility is useful for this purpose (Palmer & Stewart, 2005):

- *Step 1:* The teacher directs a small whole-group research project, from searching through site selection and evaluation. The teacher can think aloud about the steps of research, thus showing students how to think and learn in an online environment.
- *Step 2:* The teacher selects a broad topic for scaffolded student investigation (e.g., animals, countries). Next, the whole class brainstorms generic questions related to

the topic and selects specific questions for focus (e.g., for animals: "Where does this animal live?" "What does this animal eat?"). Pairs of students then select an instance of the topic to research (e.g., orangutans, if animals; Brazil, if countries). Struggling readers could be paired with classmates who are better readers. Together the students search the Web looking for good answers to their questions. An inquiry chart (see Chapter 11) might be useful for making notes. Whole-group sharing, perhaps using a comparison-contrast chart (see Chapter 9), concludes this step.

- *Step 3:* After the teacher can see some student expertise in research with partners, students can do Web research independently. Occasional whole-group discussions can be used to share effective research strategies or to identify and solve problems.

Technology is advancing and changing so rapidly that planning comprehension instruction in Web-based environments can be tricky. Yet, as Malloy and Gambrell (2006) point out, such instruction is critical: "As educators, we need to commit to preparing students for their technological journey to the future. It is a journey toward literacies that grow and change more quickly than we can keep up with them. But by learning together, teachers and students can become fully literate in every sense of the word" (p. 484).

Purposeful Comprehension Instruction

The strategies described in this chapter share assumptions about how teachers create effective comprehension instruction in which students read, think, solve problems, make decisions, and interact with the text and with each other. Teachers purposefully facilitate the process of comprehension attainment rather than direct it or test whether students can remember what they've read.

This instructional framework, the *Teacher–Student Generated Lesson* (Davidson, 1986), takes "into account the social nature of reading and its relationship to comprehension, thinking, and learning" (p. 89). Teacher–student generated lessons are based on four premises:

- Learning is a social process.
- Students need maximum opportunities to use the language associated with the content area.
- Learners need to be actively involved.
- Students and the teacher construct meaning through interaction with each other and the text.

Lessons based on these principles benefit all students, of course, but they are especially helpful for struggling readers. These students need support, but they also need to maintain control over the thinking and learning processes. Teacher–student generated lessons provide both.

Comprehension is the goal of reading. Before reading, readers must activate their prior knowledge, make predictions, and formulate purposes for reading. Discussions during reading should provoke thoughtful consideration of ideas in the text and promote individual and group efforts at understanding and learning. Finally, postreading instruction should encourage continued interaction with text content and among students. The teacher's role in all these activities is to promote sharing, encourage critical thought, and moderate discussions. The students' roles, on the other hand, require reading, thinking, solving problems, making decisions, interacting with the text and each other, and learning.

DISCUSSION QUESTIONS

Some of the discussion questions for each chapter ask you to think through your own work as a teacher. If you are not currently a practicing teacher, try to respond to these questions from your own school experience (either from when you yourself were a student or from visits to schools that you have made in your teacher education program).

1. Look at several informational books in your classroom library and identify the primary text type: expository, sequence, causation, problem solution, compare-contrast.

2. Richard Allington suggests that teachers can actually spend *too* much time building background knowledge. What could be his reasoning? Do you agree or disagree? What would a "just right" background knowledge lesson look like?

3. Many of the strategies in this chapter and throughout the book are cooperative, designed to help students learn with and from one another. How would you respond to a parent who challenged the notion of cooperative learning, saying she wants her child to learn from the teacher, not from other children?

4. What are some ways to help struggling students understand what "establishing a purpose for reading" means?

5. When using a K-W-L, how do you respond if a student provides incorrect information for the K column? What message might the student assume from your response?

Chapter Eleven

✎ *Writing Development*

*J*ASON AND AMY WERE PLAYING HOUSE. Amy, the mom, was getting ready for work and leaving instructions for Jason, the dad, who was going to watch the baby. She scribbled on a tablet, then tore up the page and began again. When asked what she was doing, she replied, "I have to put more down. I forgot that Jason doesn't know how to make eggs." Both Amy and Jason were 3 years old.

What does Amy know about written language? Quite a bit, actually. She knows that writing serves a purpose, in this case to communicate information about caring for the baby. She also knows that one writes for an audience, that writing is meant to be read. Like many other children, 3-year-old Amy has learned a great deal about written language. Yet she has had no instruction, and she is neither a reader nor a writer in the conventional sense. As with other aspects of language learning, some children learn about concepts of print earlier or more easily than others. Youngsters who have not yet developed notions about the form of written language need opportunities to do so. Until they do, they will find reading and writing instruction frustrating and confusing. In short, they will struggle.

We have written this book to help teachers help these children. In other chapters we describe instructional strategies for reading that focus children's attention on important aspects of written language. Although critical, reading instruction is not enough. Frequent opportunities to write are also essential to support the development of understandings about written language.

Writers learn about both writing and reading. Young writers learn about the conventions of print. Writers of all ages learn how to think like authors, which helps them as they read what other authors have written. Moreover, writers learn the importance of using just the right word or sentence to communicate their intended meaning. This way of thinking about words and sentences also applies to reading. Writing is also a powerful means of response to reading. Indeed, the National Assessment of Educational Progress (2000) reports that high achievers in reading are more likely to write in response to their reading than low achievers in reading. Thus, a strong focus on writing is an important component in programs for struggling readers. In this chapter, we address why and how writing can inform reading as well as provide suggestions about supporting writers and describe classroom activities that seem to enhance the reading–writing connection.

Learning about Written Language

As young children learn to read and write, they begin to think about written language as a system and hypothesize about how it works. They learn how to use books, for example, and they learn that lines of print run from left to right and lines on a page run from top to bottom.

Children also develop concepts about units of written language. One critical understanding is that print carries meaning. An eager toddler may grab for a book being read to him, cover up the print, and look puzzled when the reader has to stop. Within a year or two, the same child may ask, "What does it say on this page?" or "Where does it say that?" Such comments demonstrate that the child has discovered that reading involves print. Related to this is the understanding that the print stays the same from one reading to the next.

In addition, children learn about the conventions of print—how written language represents meaning. Developing a concept of *word* as a unit of written language is particularly important, and this is no small task. First, children must be able to think about language as a system, to separate the form of language from its function. Then, they must be able to impose psychological segmentation on a steady stream of oral speech. In other words, children must learn to separate, think about, and become aware of individual words within spoken language. Finally, they must use their knowledge of oral speech to discover that words are also units of written language. In addition to the basic concept of the written word, children must learn about the convention of unmarked space before and after words and that the beginning of the word is on the left and the end is on the right. Further, they must develop similar understandings of concepts such as *sentence, line,* and other features related to written language.

As children write (not copy), they reinforce their own understandings about how letters and letter combinations represent sounds in language. Thus, writing supports students' phonics and word recognition development. Learning about written language continues as students age. They may explore the common characteristics of a particular form of writing, such as mysteries or newspaper articles, or become interested in different types of poems, perhaps haiku or sonnets. Students of all ages may become fascinated by the way in which authors use language to communicate with others. In fact, readers and writers continue learning about written language throughout their lives.

Children learn about written language, as with other aspects of language learning, gradually and informally through many opportunities to hear, think about, and talk about written language. All children, especially those who find reading and writing difficult, need time and exposure to writing to develop these understandings. The learning process for developing concepts about written language is the same as for any other language learning: hypothesis generation and testing. For example, simply telling a child that words have spaces around them cannot guarantee understanding of the concept. In essence, children must invent their own understandings about written language and then test them as they interact with print and other readers and writers.

Certainly, children can learn a great deal about written language conventions through reading instruction. Accordingly, most teachers focus some instruction for beginning readers on the physical aspects of print. Much of this instruction is informal. When children watch something being read, such as a language-experience text or a big book, they gain knowledge about print conventions. Likewise, saying words while writing them during dictation is helpful. Some teachers even provide running commentary about the conventions of print as they take dictation. For instance, while they write, they might say, "That's the end of the sentence, so I'll put a period here. This new sentence will need a capital letter." Over time, such informal and incidental learning pays dividends in terms of children's understandings.

As children become readers, they must learn how written language works. To mature as readers, they need opportunities to explore the complexities of written language. Much of this learning can occur through reading instruction described elsewhere in this book, but a strong writing component can and should complement reading instruction.

WHY SHOULD READERS WRITE?

Children learn a great deal through writing that applies to their reading. Children who write frequently learn how writing works and come to understand what authors do and why. Through their own writing, children learn about the writing cycle (what writers do) and the writing process (how writers think). These understandings help children "see" the authors behind what they read and perhaps understand their purposes and processes. In two studies, teachers noticed connections between reading and writing (Menon & Mirabito, 1999; Silvers, 1986). Children read more and differently as they grew to believe in themselves as writers. The amount of free reading increased, and children's comments about books were more frequent and more critical. In other words, they read as authors to see how other authors had written. Graves and Stuart (1985) said it well: "Just as children who grew up on a farm know where milk comes from, children who write know where writing comes from" (p. 119).

As children write, they learn about the physical and mechanical aspects of written language; this, too, applies to their reading. Writing can help children crystallize their concepts of *word* and *sentence.* In addition, temporary or phonemic spelling provides valuable practice with the sound-to-letter system. Moreover, young writers learn that the beginning-to-ending sequences of sounds in words relate, although not exactly, to the left-to-right sequences of letters in words. Writers must attend to other aspects of directionality as well, such as words in a line and lines on a page. Children must solve all these problems to develop as literate persons, and they solve them most easily and naturally when they read and write often and purposefully.

A final answer to the question "Why should readers write?" is more practical: Lots of writing yields lots of reading and reading material. Like all authors, young authors read and reread drafts in progress. They also read their finished products, both for their own pleasure and to share with others. And, of course, children like to read what their classmates have written. An active writing program, then, complements a reading program by providing a wealth of reading material in addition to helping children develop concepts about authorship and writing that form a foundation for reading development.

DISCOVERING WHAT CHILDREN KNOW ABOUT WRITING

Planning an effective writing program is easier if you know a bit about children's current understandings of how writing works. In this section we describe several ways to gain these insights. You can learn about children's concepts of print and current hypotheses

FIGURE 11.1   Entry from Mary's September Journal

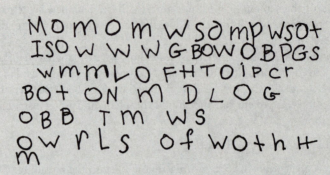

MOMOM WSOMPWSOt
ISOWWWGBOWOBPGS
WMMLOFHTOIPCr
BOTON M DLOG
OBB TM WS
OWRLS OFWOtHH
m

Me and my mom were sitting on the couch talking about birthday presents because my brother is going to have a birthday in two more weeks.

about the writing system, including their graphophonic knowledge (what they know about sound-symbol relationships), by examining their unaided writing. Look at Figures 11.1, 11.2, and 11.3, for example—pages from Mary's first-grade journal. Mary struggled with reading during much of that year. Examine how her concepts of print are revealed in her writing, what she knows about the sound-symbol system, and how these understandings changed during the year.

Figure 11.1 accompanied a picture of two people sitting on a couch. Mary wrote to explain and elaborate on this picture, showing that she knows the difference between drawing and writing. She knows that writing can communicate meaning, and she knows how lines of print are arranged on the page. Mary's teacher watched as she wrote and noticed that she wrote in left-to-right and top-to-bottom fashion. Although some concepts about print are evident in her writing, Mary's writing also reveals concepts still developing. She knows how to make letters, but not how to make them work for her. Fur-

FIGURE 11.2   Entry from Mary's January Journal

my mom sad Totobr
I am gom get my
onrm at Totobr

My mom said October. I am gonna get my own room at October.

FIGURE 11.3   Entry from Mary's May Journal

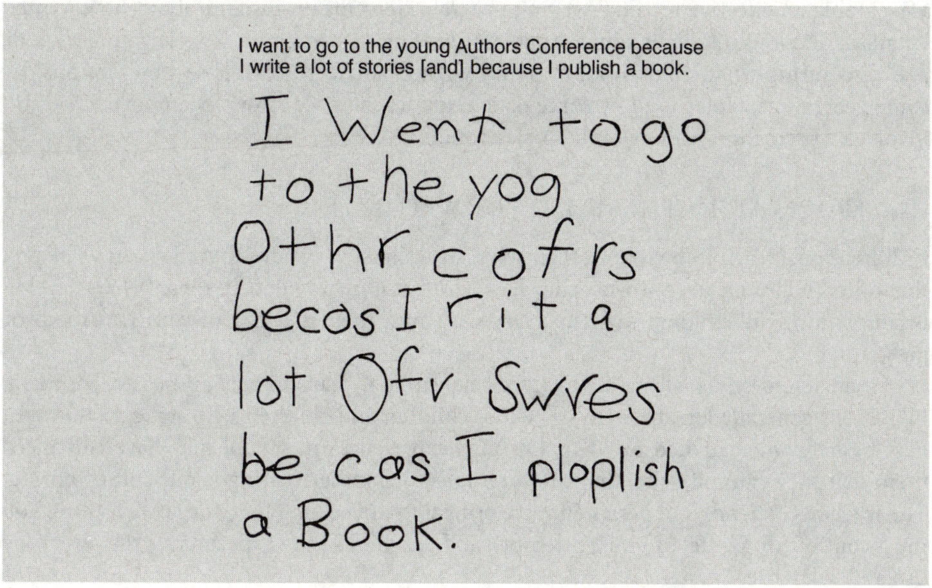

I want to go to the young Authors Conference because I write a lot of stories [and] because I publish a book.

I Went to go
to the yog
Othr c of rs
becos I r i t a
lot Ofr Swres
be cas I ploplish
a Book.

ther, her writing lacks word boundaries, which suggests that her concept of word is still developing.

Mary's January journal entry (Figure 11.2) demonstrates growth in her understanding of print concepts. Her writing is fairly easy to read, and she has begun to leave spaces between words. By May (Figure 11.3), this concept of *word* is even stronger; space boundaries around words are clearly evident. Thus, we can see that Mary has developed important concepts about print during her first-grade year. What she knows is visible in her writing.

Examining Mary's journal entries from a graphophonic perspective reveals her growing understanding of sound-symbol relationships. She has invented the spellings of many words, but these inventions are not random. They are governed by her current hypotheses about how oral language and written language relate, which demonstrates her ability to use phonics as an aid to identifying words.

Scholars have been exploring the characteristics of young children's spelling since the early 1970s, when Charles Read's (1971; Bear et al., 2007) landmark work established the predictability of young children's spelling errors and the developmental progression of growth in spelling. In brief, this research has helped teachers understand how spelling develops: from random, incomprehensible strings of letters (and sometimes other symbols) to spellings that exhibit some understanding of sound-symbol relationships to conventional spelling. Thus, important word knowledge is revealed through invented spellings.

Supporting Writers and Readers: General Principles

Developing an effective reading–writing program depends on insights about how written language develops, understanding the role of writing in a program for struggling readers, and discovering what children know about written language. In this section we consider some general principles used by some of the best teachers we know to support active and involved writers (and readers) in their classrooms.

CLASSROOM ATMOSPHERE: LOTS OF WRITING

Children must learn to believe in themselves as writers, to believe that they can write and that others will want to read what they have written. One way to help these beliefs develop is simply to invite children to write every day, from their first day in your classroom or program.

Young children usually come to school expecting to learn to read and write. For them, invitations generally lead them to try. Older children and children who struggle, however, may hesitate when invited to write. Previous experiences in school may have convinced them that they cannot write, that they are not writers, that writing is difficult or boring. The teacher's patience and persistence are critical to unlearning these negative lessons. You must continue to invite, to praise attempts, and to establish the expectations that everyone can and will write.

Tina, a Title I teacher who works with intermediate students, knows the power of teacher expectations from experience. Her students write in their personal journals several times each week. Because she knows the power of teacher-as-model, Tina writes during this time as well. This choice has led to student independence and to students understanding the expectation that they will write. "I've noticed a dramatic drop in requests for assistance since I started writing with the children," Tina says. "It's almost as if they don't want to interrupt me. So, what happens is that the children become more independent, more willing to guess and try. That surprised me, but I'm delighted because so many of my students *need* to learn to try."

TALK ABOUT WRITING

Opportunities to talk and listen are another important feature of the reading–writing classroom. Children talk for several reasons when they write (Graves, 1983). They sometimes plan their writing by talking to themselves or others. They may also read parts of drafts to themselves, as if to take a running start at what should come next. Some children compose aloud and translate their speech into writing rather than use the thought-to-writing process most adult writers employ. Others play with *prosodics* such as rhythm or intonation. Children may also talk themselves through writing by making procedural comments such as "There! Now I need to write 'The End.'"

Of course, children read drafts of their work to others, either to help solve problems or for more general feedback. This use of oral language may be particularly important for struggling readers and writers. Reading drafts aloud to an interested audience shows children that their writing has value and demonstrates the communicative power of writing and the link between reading and writing. Talking about revision possibilities also helps children understand and examine their options, which aids them in critically analyzing their own writing (Hanser, 1986). Those who respond to children's writing learn to listen carefully and ask pertinent questions. Of course, all this learning relates to reading as well. In fact, the concepts and procedures used in writing conferences with students easily apply to discussions about books written by authors outside the classroom.

SUPPORT, ENCOURAGEMENT, AND ACCEPTANCE

Children need teacher support to develop as writers. Some of this support is mundane, such as having necessary supplies readily available. But other aspects of support, such as encouraging spelling efforts, may require a bit more thought. Accepting invented or temporary spelling allows children to be true to their own meanings and precise in their language because they can write what they want to say, not just what they know how to spell. In addition, children need opportunities to manipulate words and discover spelling principles so that phonological relationships become clear to them. In essence, children test their hypotheses about the way the alphabet works by contrasting the words they spell with the same words used in others' books (Templeton & Morris, 1999).

Teachers can foster growth in spelling by encouraging independence and accepting the inventions that independence produces. Rather than directly answering a child's question about how to spell a word, the teacher can encourage the child to say the word and then ask, "What sound do you hear at the beginning? What letter would that be? Good. Write it down. Now, say the word again. What sound do you hear at the end?" and so on. This strategy encourages children to develop independence as spellers. Listening for sounds and representing them with letters supports children's efforts at phonemic segmentation, or separating words into their component sounds. Children also learn phonics as they think about how to write the sounds in the words they want to use. In fact, one year-long study of phonics instruction in eight exemplary first-grade classrooms showed that nearly half of the phonics instruction occurred in the writing program. Researchers Karen Dahl and Pat Scharer (2000) note,

> Although discussions of phonics often center on reading, an important finding of this research was the linkage between reading and writing in these classrooms and the contribution that the linkage with writing made to the children's understanding of letter–sound relationships. As children used their reading experiences in their own writing, their need for knowledge about letters, sounds, and words became both immediate and purposeful. (p. 593)

Children's first recognizable efforts at spelling will bear strong resemblance to the sounds they hear as they articulate words. Later, as children become readers, visual memory also plays a role in spelling; that is, children may inspect their efforts to see if they "look right." This is when standard spelling becomes an issue, particularly if the child's written work will be read by others. Like our colleague Jane Davidson, we suggest that teachers reply to students' queries of "Is it right?" with a statement like this: "It's good enough for now. You can read it, and I can read it. We both know what you're saying here. Later, we can make a few changes, if you'd like, to make your words look like they do in other books." This sort of discussion helps lessen concern about spelling at the idea-generation stage, yet assures writers that their efforts will receive the polish they deserve.

MODELING AND CORRECTIONS

Two other general principles are important to consider as writing programs are planned: teacher as model and opportunities to connect reading and writing. In a way, these two principles are related, for both provide children with opportunities to learn from more sophisticated writers. Teachers who write when their students do, keep journals, and share their writing with students demonstrate why writing is important and how writers work. Likewise, writers benefit from opportunities to make the reading–writing connection—to use others' writing as a model (see the copy-change activity later in this chapter) or conclude a read-aloud session with a discussion of how the author used language.

The atmosphere and attitude that best foster writing (and reading) development are characterized by support and encouragement. We can support children's writing efforts by nurturing their beliefs in themselves as writers. Belief leads to feelings of control and ownership, which in turn allow children to make their own decisions about the content and form of their writing. Having made these decisions, children are in a better position to understand the decisions other authors make.

Reading–Writing Activities

Most children are eager to express themselves in writing, particularly if they believe that others will read and enjoy their writing. Children should have daily opportunities for individual and shared writing. Although classroom writing activities should allow them to explore all the ways in which writing can be used, our focus in this section is on ways to foster the reading–writing relationship.

In the activity descriptions that follow, we describe both formal and informal writing activities. These differ in terms of purpose, audience, and what constitutes "acceptable" form. Consider the differences between writing a grocery list and writing a research paper, for example:

	Purpose	*Audience*	*"Acceptable" Form*
Grocery list	To remember what to purchase	Self	Any—no sentences; it's OK to misspell broccoli
Research paper	To synthesize new knowledge	Professor, other students	Eventually, formal perfection

This is a rather silly (and simplistic—sometimes rough writing is a precursor to formal writing) example, but we hope you see that as adult writers, we use why we are writing (purpose) and for whom we are writing (audience) to make decisions about the amount of effort to put into the written piece and about what level of perfection is acceptable.

Students need to understand this framework to write effectively. You may find it useful to use the three descriptions that follow to help students make good choices about the level of formality to strive for in their writing:

- *For your eyes only:* No one else will see this, so use whatever form works for you. *Examples:* lists, notes to yourself
- *"Sloppy copy":* Someone else may see this, but they won't care about form. The writing just needs to be readable. *Examples:* journal entries, rough drafts
- *Good copy:* This will be displayed/read by others, so you want to polish the writing as much as possible. *Examples:* final drafts, letters

Figures 11.4 and 11.5 summarize the writing activities described in Chapters 9 and 10. Use with fiction or informational text is noted as is the level of formality. In the next section we describe several additional reading–writing activities. All these activities help students develop as writers in addition to fostering their understanding of what they have read.

FIGURE 11.4   Writing Activities from Chapter 9

Activity	Page Reference	Fiction, Informational Text, or Both	Informal, Formal, or Both
Think-Pair-Share	175	Both	Informal
Character Sketches	176	Fiction	Informal
Group Mapping Activity	177	Fiction	Informal
(Write and Share)^2	179	Both	Both
Agree or Disagree? Why?	179	Both	Informal
Bleich's Heuristic	180	Fiction	Informal
Compare-and-Contrast Charts	180	Both	Informal
Readers' Theater (student-written scripts)	181	Both	Formal
Response Journals	182	Both	Informal

FIGURE 11.5   Writing Activities from Chapter 10

Activity	Page Reference	Fiction, Informational Text, or Both	Informal, Formal, or Both
Possible Sentences	190	Informational	Informal
Brainstorming	190	Both	Informal
Anticipation Guides	191	Informational	Informal
K-W-L	193	Informational	Informal
Dialectic Journal	197	Both	Informal
Important Ideas and Words	197	Both	Informal
Save the Last Word for Me	198	Both	Informal
Distinctive Features	199	Both	Informal
Herringbone	200	Both	Informal
Discussion Web	200	Informational	Informal
Alphabet Books	201	Both	Formal
Poems (biopoem, diamante)	201	Both	Formal

Informal Writing–Reading Activities

DIALOGUE JOURNALS

Sometimes people write to share information with a reader. *Dialogue journals,* essentially notes written back and forth between two writers, let children sustain written conversation with others. Most teachers initiate dialogue journals by responding themselves to children's journal entries. This is a good way to get to know children at the beginning of the year, help them understand how dialogue journals work, and encourage fluent written expression without undue concern for mechanical perfection. Moreover, dialogue journals offer important vehicles for encouraging children to write in response to the books they read. Teachers can ask about characters or plot, for example, in their responses to children. In some classrooms, children use dialogue journals to write notes to friends. Many teachers we know encourage students to write weekly letters to their parents in which they recount the week's learning. Parents respond to the letters in writing.

E-mail dialogue journals, either for general correspondence or for sharing responses to reading (e.g., McKeon, 1999; Sullivan, 1998), are becoming common in classrooms. Blogs are another fruitful venue for writing. No knowledge of programming is necessary to create a blog; Google has a free and easy way to establish a blog at www.blogger.com. Kajder and Bull (2003) describe six characteristics of blogs that are relevant to instruction:

- *Economy:* Blog entries must be precise and concise.
- *Archiving:* Posted entries are dated and remain at the website. This allows students to follow the progression of ideas over time
- *Feedback:* Student writers can receive immediate response from their peers.
- *Multimedia:* Students can add images and sound to their blog entries.
- *Immediacy:* Students' entries are posted immediately.
- *Active participation:* Although not all children can speak at once, they can all blog at once. So everyone can be actively involved in the learning community.

Students are generally eager to keep dialogue journals, whether in paper-and-pencil or online. Jeff provides resource assistance to middle school students with learning disabilities. He and his students rely heavily on dialogue journals. Jeff has noticed that students frequently want feedback from him, especially early in the school year. He likes this because through journals he comes to know his students and establish a trusting relationship with them. "I have a tendency to ask questions in my written responses to students, and that sometimes encourages them to do the same." As a new group of students becomes comfortable with one another, "they start writing for people besides me. It's kind of funny, in a way. I think it's like teacher-authorized note writing to some of them. And I guess that's exactly what it is! They're so eager to read what someone else has written to them and then to write back."

LEARNING LOGS OR CONTENT-AREA JOURNALS

Sometimes people write to remember—to record thoughts, ideas, or facts for later use. Effective teachers encourage this purpose for writing. Gloria, who teaches first grade, introduces new units of study in science or social studies by asking small groups of children to talk about what they would like to learn. One child in each group serves as a secretary to record group members' ideas. Figure 11.6 shows one group's report from a discussion that preceded a new science unit about space.

As each group read the report of its conversation about space to the rest of the class, Gloria prepared a large chart, titled "What We Want to Learn about Space," with enough room beneath each child's contribution to record information discovered during the course of the science unit. Every few days, Gloria and the children reread the chart, discussed what children had learned, and recorded new information where possible.

Children also write individual accounts of content area lessons, record results of science observations or experiments, or write their own definitions of new concepts or

FIGURE 11.6   Group Report about Space

Mia said "she wants t to larn abut earth
Karey Said "I want larn abut spass.
Regina Said " I want to larn How the earth
Moves.
Tommy Said "I said How you fly a spass ship
Sarah Said " I want to larn abut spass
Shotles.

descriptions of new procedures. This sort of writing resembles response journals (see Chapter 9). *Learning logs,* or *content area journals,* can be helpful for storing and organizing these writing efforts.

Learning log entries may be open or closed (Davidson, 1987). Open entries encourage personal response or reaction because students decide what to write for themselves. Closed entries provide for more structured response, such as note taking, outlining, charting, synthesizing, or comparing. For example, students may summarize a class demonstration or movie, record their observations about something they are studying, or make notes or a graphic, such as a Venn diagram, to remind themselves about what they have learned. In Potenza-Radis's (2008) study, third-graders recorded "book thoughts" in their journals in preparation for literature circle discussions.

Fifth-grade teacher Christine Evans (1984) asked her students to make three types of log entries during two units of math instruction: definitions of new math concepts; explanations of new procedures, such as how to multiply decimals or draw a geometric figure; and troubleshooting, where students analyzed their errors and wrote about how and why they had made mistakes. Another fifth-grade teacher taught the two math units in the traditional manner. Both classes took publisher-prepared tests before and after each unit. Test results indicated that Evans's students began each unit with less math knowledge. After instruction, however, her students' test scores matched the other group's for one unit and exceeded them by 10 percent for the other. Evans attributes this growth to writing: Learning logs "get students to 'own' knowledge rather than just 'rent' it" (p. 835).

All learning log entries should be dated so that students can easily refer back to them. Children who forget how to perform particular tasks, such as subtracting three-digit numbers, for example, can simply look them up in their learning logs. Keeping logs also introduces children to note taking in a natural and functional way. In fact, Vacca and

Vacca (2008) have suggested that students annotate their entries with the title of the book they're responding to and the page number that prompted the response. In this way, the logs become valuable learning resources for students as the school year progresses and thus enhance learning.

Informal writing is a powerful complement to reading. Keep track of the ways in which you write informally over the next few days and you'll see what we mean. Then work to share these informal writing options with your students.

Formal Writing–Reading Activities

GENRE STUDY

Students can experiment with different discourse forms as they write about what they have read or about their content area learning. For example, they might write newspaper accounts of historical happenings and scientific discoveries or letters to the editor about past and current events. They might write first-person accounts of life in other places or at other times. If children read or hear tall tales or fairy tales, discussion and subsequent dictation and a class text can focus on key elements or characteristics. Then, using the dictation as a guide, children can write their own tall tales or fairy tales.

Students might also write poetry as a means of reacting to or summarizing what they have read and learned. "Name poems," or acrostics, which use letters of a name or word to begin lines of a poem, can easily suit content area concepts or response to fiction, as can "I used to think . . . but now I know" form poems (Koch, 2000). Here, for example, is a class poem that Deb's students developed after their inquiry into sources of heat (described in Chapter 3):

> We used to think the sun makes heat;
>
> Now we know that it does—the sun's energy makes light, which makes heat.
>
> We used to think our bodies make heat;
>
> Now we know they do—muscles make energy, which makes heat.
>
> We used to think our hats and scarves make heat,
>
> But now we know they don't—they trap the heat our bodies make.
>
> Now we know that energy can make heat.

Skilled readers can comprehend texts representing various genre successfully. Skilled writers understand the characteristics of the genre—what are the common features of a newspaper article, for example—and can use them as a framework for their own writing.

COPY CHANGE

Children often create their own stories based on actual or fanciful happenings. Children's literature can be an effective springboard and scaffold for this type of writing. Individuals or groups can write their own versions of books, too. This activity is sometimes called *copy change* because children use the author's copy as a framework for writing but change it to reflect their own ideas. Hesitant writers often need extra support or scaffolding to compose on their own, and the framework or ideas supplied by an exemplary author can provide this support.

Simple poetry works well as the impetus for copy-change activities. Children often find success with short poems in particular, which tend to be less overwhelming than longer pieces or stories. But predictable pattern books also work well for introducing children to copy change. For example, the pattern that Bill Martin Jr. used to develop *Brown Bear, Brown Bear* is easy to discern and use to dictate or write new versions:

Mr. Jones, Mr. Jones, what do you see?
I see some first-graders looking at me.

Copy changes can also be more complex. Figure 11.7 presents an example written by a group of fifth-graders who applied the pattern in *If You Give a Mouse a Cookie* to their learning in social studies. Alphabet books also offer wonderful possibilities for copy change. One teacher we know assigns a letter of the alphabet to each child who attends a field trip, for example. During the trip, the child notes all the words that begin with his or her letter. When the class returns, children make an ABC book to record and remember what they learned.

FIGURE 11.7 Example of a Copy-Change Activity

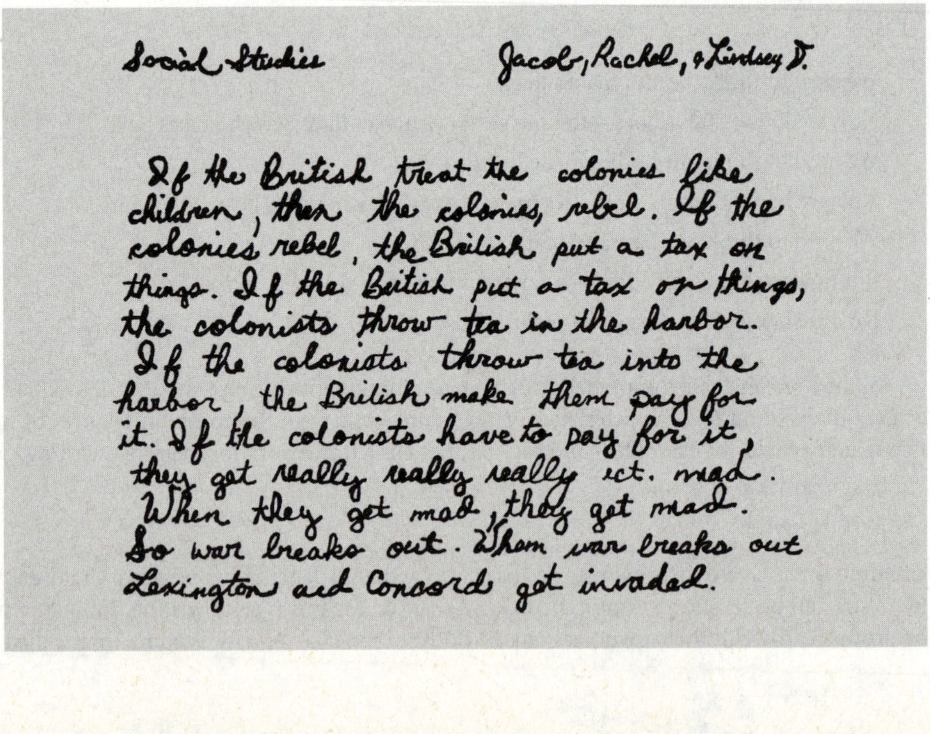
Social Studies Jacob, Rachel, & Lindsey D.

If the British treat the colonies like children, then the colonies, rebel. If the colonies' rebel, the British put a tax on things. If the British put a tax on things, the colonists throw tea in the harbor. If the colonists throw tea into the harbor, the British make them pay for it. If the colonists have to pay for it, they get really really really ect. mad. When they get mad, they get mad. So war breaks out. When war breaks out Lexington and Concord get invaded.

Our favorite copy change book is Margaret Wise Brown's (1949/1999) *The Important Book*. This book offers observations about simple objects such as a spoon, an apple, shoes, the wind, and so forth. Each description follows a pattern: The important thing about _____ is _____. [Other details follow.] But the important thing about _____ is _____. Children quickly learn this pattern and use it to write *Important Book* pages about themselves, their classmates or family members, a character in a book they are reading, or what they are learning in science or social studies. The students in Alicia's Title I classes use *The Important Book* as a frame for writing reports in science and social studies. Figure 11.8 shows what Hannah learned about crayfish. "The children are so proud of their reports,"

FIGURE 11.8   Hannah's Copy Change of *The Important Book*

The Important Thing About Crayfish

By Hannah

The important thing about crayfish is that it is a living thing.

A crayfish is short, and active, and smart, and harmful.

But the important thing about a crayfish is that it is a living thing.

The exciting thing about a crayfish is that it can do many things.

It can crawl, pinch, and walk.

But the exciting thing about a crayfish is that it can do many things.

The regrettable fact about a crayfish is that it pinches.

It will hurt and sting.

But the regrettable fact about a crayfish is that it pinches.

The incredible news about a crayfish is that it can grow back body parts.

It is called molting, and it is unbelievable.

But the incredible news about a crayfish is that it can grow back body parts.

The terrible truth about a crayfish is that they can kill each other.

It is scary, and incredible, and gross.

But the terrible truth about a crayfish is that they can kill each other.

Alicia says. "This book has helped children see alternatives to copying information from a website or the CD encyclopedia. It saves me from reading all that, too. I much prefer the creativity of these *Important Book* pages!"

Students can recast a story as a script to perform as reader's theater (see Chapter 7). This, too, is a form of copy change because students rewrite a favorite story in a different form.

Copy change, or what second-grade teacher Peter Lancia (1997) calls "literary borrowing," appears to come naturally in classrooms where lots of reading and writing is encouraged. Peter noticed that some of his students "wrote new stories about familiar characters, such as George and Martha, Frog and Toad, Lyle Crocodile, Arthur, and Miss Frizzle. Others retold the original plot in their own words or modified the same events to fit a new setting. And occasionally some attempted to imitate the writing style of a particular author, book, or genre" (p. 470). One year, Peter decided to look more carefully at this natural copy change. He found it pervasive—all but one student "borrowed," and more than half (57 percent) of students completed pieces of writing showed evidence of borrowing. Peter believes that if students "have the opportunity to interact with books and authors every day and to practice writing in an environment built on support and encouragement, authorship becomes real as they imitate their role models and write their own stories" (p. 475). We agree!

Whether they're simple or complex, copy-change activities encourage careful reading or listening so that students can discover and use the author's pattern. Thus, the pattern itself may provide a supportive framework for young authors, in much the same way as a poet might use a haiku or sonnet framework. Indeed, copy change and creating scripts from stories are authentic types of writing. Hollywood is filled with professional screenplay and script writers.

INQUIRY

Even graduate students we know complain about the challenges involved in writing inquiry or research papers. We have a hunch about this. We think that experience and support, beginning from an early age, can help all students learn to combine reading and writing in this way that's so critical to academic success. A copy-change format is one useful framework for reporting on results of student inquiry (see Figure 11.8). Jim Hoffman's (1992) I-chart framework is another. Figure 11.9 shows the chart that students use to make notes. Some teachers we know put the chart online so that students can keep their notes in a computer file.

Teachers can use the three-step process described in Chapter 10 (Palmer & Stewart, 2005) to support students as they learn to conduct inquiries independently. To begin, the whole class can select a topic and generate questions about the topic that they would like to answer. Next, the teacher can guide students through the process of selecting several resources (paper and online) that seem useful for finding answers to the questions. Each resource is then read, and the teacher models the note-taking process for students. When notes are complete, a class discussion about each question can lead to dictation of a summary. After students develop comfort with this inquiry process, pairs of students can com-

FIGURE 11.9   Inquiry Chart

Topic:	Question 1:	Question 2:	Question 3:	Question 4:	Other Info/ New Questions
What we know					
Source 1: [bibliographic info]					
Source 2:					
Source 3:					
Source 4:					
Summary					

Source: Adapted from Hoffman (1992).

plete the inquiry process together. Finally, students should be able to conduct independent inquiries.

STUDENT PUBLISHING COMPANIES

Some schools sponsor student publishing companies to encourage authorship. (See Appendix F for bookmaking ideas.) One such effort, at Central Elementary School in Morgantown, West Virginia, was a collaboration among several classroom teachers and the Title I reading teacher (Barksdale-Ladd & Nedeff, 1997). All children were invited to write books, either singly, in pairs, or in author–illustrator teams. The Title I teacher, older students, and parent volunteers helped when needed. The upper-grade children even handled the business end of the publishing company by pricing materials, contacting vendors, recording sales, and so on. The student publishing company had a positive influence on children's self-esteem and attitudes about reading and writing. "In the library we hear statements like, 'Oh, I've read that book. It's an adventure story. We read adventure stories last year, and I wrote one'" (p. 573).

FIGURE 11.10   Motivating Students to Share Writing

- Have students make individual books for the classroom library or the school library. Children's books from one classroom can be loaned for children in another classroom to read.

- Encourage students to make class magazines, newspapers, or books. These can be collaborations, where children work together on one cohesive product, or collections, where children contribute their favorite story or poem to a class book. Children can also make class books related to content area study.

- Provide support for students' to create bulletin boards or corridor displays of their writing. These should be displayed at children's eye level.

- Create students' interest in making posters of poetry, jokes, riddles, and so on.

- Share photocopies of students' writing with families and friends.

- Have students present their writing through drama, puppetry, and so on.

- Provide time and encouragement for students to read their writing aloud to classmates during writing conferences, to classmates during daily sharing time, to students in other classrooms, or to the school community via the intercom.

SHARING WRITING

Children need to write both for their own purposes and for others in and beyond the classroom. In fact, sharing writing can be one of the most gratifying aspects of the writing cycle. Figure 11.10 offers several ways for students to share their writing with others. All these activities make the connection between reading and writing strong and explicit for students.

Writing and Reading; Reading and Writing

From informal notes or lists to published inquiry projects or books, writing is meant to be read. This, of course, is a strong motivation for writing and a solid rationale for including writing activities in a program designed to strengthen children's reading. Through writing, children learn how written language works; they develop and deepen understandings about the conventions of print, the ways in which stories and other text forms work, and graphophonic knowledge. Moreover, by becoming authors, students learn to think like authors. They learn to think about purpose and audience and to analyze the author's craft. They discover that authors have options. All of this helps students understand that both reading and writing involve the manipulation of language and the construction of meaning.

DISCUSSION QUESTIONS

Some of the discussion questions for each chapter ask you to think through your own work as a teacher. If you are not currently a practicing teacher, try to respond to these questions from your own school experience (either from when you yourself were a student or from visits to schools that you have made in your teacher education program).

1. How would you explain your acceptance of developmental spelling to a parent who wants his child to spell every word correctly?

2. Sometimes the task of responding to students' journals can become overwhelming. With your colleagues, brainstorm some ways of making this task manageable yet effective.

3. Who is your favorite children's author and favorite adult author? What writing techniques do they use that make them your favorites?

4. Compare your perceptions of students' writing in your classroom with their perceptions. Complete the first column of the chart below with no input from students. Next, ask your students the same questions and complete the second column. What did you learn? How can you use what you learned in writing and reading instruction?

5. What is your biggest challenge in helping English language learners with writing? With your colleagues, brainstorm possible instructional strategies to meet that challenge.

	Teacher's Perception	*Students' Perception*
How many students would describe themselves as good writers?		
How many students would say they hate to write?		
What writing assignments do students like best (i.e., journals, research papers, poetry, etc.)?		
What writing assignments do students like least?		
Do students think the teacher is a writer?		

Chapter Twelve

Putting It All Together

DEVELOPING INSTRUCTIONAL SYSTEMS AND ROUTINES THAT WORK FOR STUDENTS WHO STRUGGLE IN READING

W E SAT DOWN RECENTLY WITH KRISTEN, a third-grade teacher who had just completed her first year of teaching. Our first question was a simple one: "How did the year go for you?" Kristen's response was a bit more complex. She indicated to us that overall the year went very well. She thoroughly enjoyed her students, her colleagues, the principal, and her students' parents. Her biggest challenge, and one we suspect that many teachers share, was how to put it all together.

Kristen indicated that she left her preservice training with a superb set of skills and strategies for teaching reading. However, she was overwhelmed by the diversity of her students, knowing what sort of instruction worked best for certain students, how to know her students were progressing in a satisfactory manner, and what to do when some students seemed not to be making the progress she had hoped.

Fortunately, Kristen found a lifesaver in the reading coach assigned to her building. Once a week she would meet with the reading coach to go over her emerging questions and concerns, and to receive assistance in putting it all together—designing instruction and instructional routines that worked best for the full range of students in her classroom. "Without my reading coach I am not sure I could have survived the year," Kristen declared. "I am sure I would have muddled through, but I am not at all certain that the instruction I would have given my students was what they needed. This past year was a great learning experience and I know that, from this experience, I will be even more ready to work with my new class when the school year begins."

In the preceding chapters we presented sets of instructional strategies aimed at overcoming difficulties that children often encounter in their reading development. These strategies assist students just beginning to experience difficulty and children whose reading development has been significantly disrupted.

Authentic, engaging, and effective corrective or remedial instruction, however, is more than just the sum of these various strategies. It is not enough to use them as separate instructional activities. Effective teachers develop an instructional synergy in which the thoughtful combination and regular implementation of a set of logically sequenced instructional activities results in an effect that is larger than the sum effect of the activities implemented in a willy-nilly manner. Teachers must consider how the instructional pieces fit together to form a coherent and effective instructional package or routine. Effective corrective instruction means looking at the big picture and designing complete programs that make the best use of students' time in helping them achieve the goal of proficient reading.

By now you know that we believe firmly that teachers are in the best position to make instructional decisions for students who find reading difficult. Many reasons exist for this belief, but perhaps one is most important: Teachers must teach in ways that reflect their beliefs about literacy learning. Students should also be actively involved in setting the direction of instruction. Packaged curricula, teacher's manuals, and other instructional resources can be good for finding ideas or provoking thought (indeed, that's why we wrote this book), but teachers, reading coaches, and students together create curriculum and instruction in classrooms.

Teachers' instructional styles differ, as do students' needs and preferences. Moreover, aspects of the instructional environment vary from classroom to classroom. Imagine, for example, 10 Title I teachers teaching the same lesson to 10 groups of children in 10 different classrooms in 10 different schools in 10 different communities. What do you think would be the same about all these lessons? Beyond the general instructional focus, probably not much. Such pragmatic realities also support teachers in developing their own curricula: No one knows you, your students, and the specifics of your teaching situation as well as you.

In this chapter we deal with a critical but too often ignored issue: developing instructional systems that work. In essence, we discuss putting the strategies in this book into systems designed for children's specific needs and teachers' styles of instruction. We suggest principles or guidelines for designing corrective instruction and provide examples of existing instructional packages based on these principles. We also discuss how individual teachers design such systems for themselves and their students.

Guidelines for Program Development

This section offers several guidelines for developing a program that will successfully meet the needs of struggling readers. We recommend that you think about these guidelines (and others that may be important to you) within an overall, four-step framework for developing curriculum and planning instruction:

1. *Formulate an instructional philosophy.* All educators have philosophies or sets of beliefs about literacy learning. Sometimes, however, teachers fail to articulate them or consider the relationship between their beliefs and their instructional practices. The first step in the curriculum-development framework is to decide what you believe about the reading process, children as language learners, the role of the teacher, the classroom atmosphere, and appropriate materials and activities. We recommend that you write down these statements because you will need them in all other steps of planning and reading

instruction. Also, you may want to consider the extent to which your beliefs are based on research or theory.

2. *Develop a few broad instructional goals.* The goals serve as a foundation for planning instruction. As such, they should reflect your philosophy, describe the general areas within which literacy instruction will occur, and be based on broad notions of children's needs. We have found that too many goals are hard to manage and tend to fragment instruction, so limit the number—perhaps no more than five. The National Reading Panel (2000) has identified phonemic awareness, phonics (decoding), fluency, vocabulary, and comprehension as essential elements of effective reading instruction. This framework developed by the panel, along with the addition of writing, provides you with a solid set of goals or foci for your instruction and instructional planning.

3. *Based on your instructional goals, plan instructional routines that consist of effective instructional practices.* Routines (described in Chapter 3) offer children consistent opportunities to achieve the goals you establish. Moreover, because routines are predictable, they foster children's security and independence in the classroom. When you have made preliminary decisions about routines, look again at your goals. Make sure that the routines, as a whole, will help children achieve the goals.

4. *Develop a plan to evaluate the curriculum and students.* You might ask questions such as "How can I determine the extent to which instruction reflects my philosophy?" "How will I know that instruction really is having the desired impact on students' achievement in and motivation for reading?" "How can I find areas that need fine-tuning?" Many of the ideas in Chapter 2 can be use for evaluating both curriculum and children.

Instructional planning is part of teachers' professional responsibility. Many teachers with whom we have worked find the four-step framework helpful for thinking about the planning process and ensuring that what happens in the classroom reflects their best thinking about children and literacy learning. The framework is rather general; it is even useful for planning "regular" classroom instruction. Now let us consider several guidelines for program development that apply more specifically to the issue of helping struggling readers.

FOCUSING THE PROGRAM

Reading programs for struggling readers should aim to help them overcome difficulties in specific areas of reading. They thereby improve their overall reading performance and become lifelong, engaged readers. Thus, to be truly effective, programs should address readers' specific problems and promote purposeful, authentic, engaging, and satisfying reading experiences.

If a child has difficulty in reading fluency, providing experiences in vocabulary development will not solve the problem at hand. Indeed, the student may have a superior vocabulary, in which case providing supplemental instruction in vocabulary may have minimal positive results. If fluency is the problem, you must design activities aimed at strengthening that essential aspect of reading.

The same is true for every difficulty—attitude toward reading, comprehension, vocabulary, word recognition. Please note that we define the area of difficulty rather broadly. We do not mean specific skill areas such as "fluency in multiple-phrase sentences" or "recognition of the -*ed* ending in words." Difficulties in specific skills generalize to difficulties throughout that particular aspect of reading. Thus, corrective instruction should be aimed at the more generalized area of concern.

Developing a focused program also requires some attention to what students do as readers, observing behaviors and attitudes that can facilitate their literacy growth and those likely to impede progress. In other words, teachers must determine what strategies nonproductive readers use so that they can plan instruction to meet their needs. Here are three suggestions to guide this process:

1. *Watch for patterns of behavior across situations and times.* During any day, children read lots of materials for lots of reasons in lots of instructional situations. Drawing conclusions based on one type of reading situation ignores the complexity and diversity of reading demands.

2. *Rely on information from informal assessments, observations, and conversations as well as formal assessments.* To develop an instructional plan to support children, you must understand how the children operate within instructional settings. Therefore, standardized test results are only partially helpful in this type of instructional planning. For example, children who score poorly on the comprehension subtest of a standardized reading test may indeed have difficulties. To help them, however, you need to understand how they approach typical reading tasks and situations. You may know that some of your students have problems in reading, but you also need to understand the *whys* and *hows* of those problems.

3. *Focus on the total reader.* Especially with struggling readers, you might tend to look for problems. These are important, to be sure, but you must look equally carefully at what your students *can* do as readers. This focus on strengths is important psychologically for both you and your students. Moreover, instruction can frequently be planned to use strengths as a platform or scaffold for addressing weaknesses.

Children's attitudes about reading and perceptions about reading and their roles as readers also deserve attention. We know that people who enjoy reading usually read more and consequently have many opportunities to grow as readers. Moreover, children use their perceptions of the reading process to guide their actions while reading and evaluate the success of their efforts.

MASSED AND SPACED PRACTICE OR ACTIVITY

Whatever the reader's difficulty, overcoming it usually requires practice within that area, and plenty of it. Significant chunks of time devoted to the area of difficulty will help achieve meaningful and lasting progress. The teacher must direct the reader's attention to the difficulty using a variety of activities, texts, and contexts. If, for example, a student is having difficulty with word recognition, an effective instructional routine will provide the reader with a variety of activities, strategies, and practice in learning to recognize or decode words quickly and efficiently; the reader also needs opportunities to apply that knowledge in real reading situations.

A more traditional and limited approach might isolate specific areas of difficulty or skills needed for word recognition, such as the *pl* consonant blend or the *ou* vowel diphthong or the *-ing* word ending. Such instruction would focus almost entirely on these skill areas and be in the form of worksheets or skill lessons that isolate the skill at the expense of applying it in real reading situations. These limited approaches fail to give the reader broad enough experience to practice the full range of skills and strategies needed to recognize all words efficiently. Moreover, they provide insufficient breadth to allow the reader to apply the practiced skill or strategy in the larger context of authentic reading.

This leads us to a related issue: the nature of material used for instruction and practice. Throughout this book, we have pointed to the value of using authentic reading material that children find interesting. Additionally, the reading material should be rather easy (independent to instructional level, meaning that students can read at least 92 percent of the words in a passage correctly with good understanding [Rasinski & Padak, 2005a, 2005b]) for children, especially as you begin to focus their attention on an aspect of the reading process that is new or difficult for them. Allington (2002) has reported that highly effective teachers find ways to maximize the amount of easy reading their students do throughout the school day. We advise selecting material carefully to increase the likelihood of success and decrease the possibility of frustration. Think also about what makes reading material easy or hard for students and how you can help make challenging material easier for students to read.

If teachers are locked into using material that challenges students, they must find and implement ways to make that reading easier. This can be done through the teacher reading orally while the students point and follow along in their textbooks silently, echo reading and paired reading with reading buddies, providing prereading background knowledge and postreading summaries for students, and other strategies presented throughout this book.

CONSISTENCY OVER TIME

Readers need consistent instruction over the long term. Massed instruction spaced over the long term, combined with authentic reading practice, are the best assurance that the reader will permanently overcome the difficulty. Moreover, developing a consistent instructional routine that includes authentic reading experiences as well as instructional activity in the area of difficulty makes lessons predictable for students and the teacher. This results in a degree of student independence, more efficient use of time, and greater on-task behavior.

Developing a consistent routine need not result in lessons that students find uninteresting. Within the general lesson framework that includes work on the specific area of difficulty and authentic reading experiences, teachers have the freedom to vary the instructional activities (several activities can be devoted to any one difficulty area, as preceding chapters show), texts to be read and who makes the choices, how the text reading might occur (silent, oral, choral, paired), and the surrounding context for the instruction (such as where the instructional activity takes place: individually, in pairs, or with a group). So many variables ensure that all lessons can be fresh, engaging, and interesting.

PROFICIENT, PROFESSIONAL INSTRUCTORS

We firmly believe that highly qualified instructors provide the best instruction, especially with students who have difficulty reading. Indeed, studies show that excellent reading instruction and high student reading achievement are positively associated with the level of teacher training (Elley, 1992; Fitzharris, Jones, & Crawford, 2008; National Reading Panel, 2000; Postlethwaite & Ross, 1992).

Staying professionally current is every teacher's responsibility, but it is particularly critical for those who work with struggling readers. Professionals learn more about readers and reading each year, and much of this new knowledge has direct instructional application. By maintaining memberships in professional organizations, reading and discussing literacy-related journals, attending professional meetings, and interacting informally with colleagues, teachers can plan instruction based on best practice and state-of-the-art knowledge.

Moreover, those who select a particular program for reading instruction, such as the ones described in the next section of this chapter, must understand the philosophy, purposes, and procedures of the program and be proficient in its implementation. This may involve initial professional development through reading or in-service education, frequent opportunities to talk with colleagues who also use the program, and ongoing in-service education on the program.

Effective Instructional Programs

READING RECOVERY

One of the best-known corrective reading instructional programs is *Reading Recovery (RR)* (Clay, 1993; Pinnell, 1989; Pinnell, Fried, & Estice, 1990; Schwartz, 2005). Reading Recovery is a formal tutoring program in which a highly trained teacher supplements regular classroom reading instruction with a daily 30-minute individualized instructional routine with a first-grade child experiencing difficulty in reading.

Reading Recovery operates under the assumption that the best way to correct reading problems is to treat them early and intensively. Each RR lesson uses a series of brief activities aimed primarily at improving word recognition and reading fluency. The activities that make up the instructional routine are consistent from day to day. Students know what they will do in every session. With such consistency the tutoring sessions are intensive and involve little wasted time.

In the first part of a RR lesson, students read familiar stories they have read previously. The teacher performs a diagnostic check by keeping a running record of the child's oral reading of a newer text, one introduced in the previous day's lesson. Next, the child and teacher engage in letter recognition and manipulation activities. The child dictates a sentence that the teacher records and rereads aloud, after which the child is guided in writing it. After practicing reading and writing the sentence, the teacher rewrites the sentence on a strip of paper, cuts it into individual words, and asks the child to reconstruct the message. The words are taken home for further practice and play. Finally, the teacher introduces a new book that the child will learn to read successfully in subsequent lessons.

After a brief introduction, the child attempts the book with the teacher guiding appropriate strategy use when the text becomes difficult.

Reading Recovery is a formal program that is usually adopted at the school or school district level. Teachers and reading specialists on their own rarely have the opportunity to implement Reading Recovery in their classrooms or schools. However, the essential elements of RR—authentic reading, intensive instruction, consistency of instruction, the whole (passage) to part (letters and word parts) to whole (passage) progression of each lesson—can be used as a model for individual teachers to create their own instructional routine.

LITERACY LESSON FRAMEWORK

Based on her work as a classroom teacher, a Reading Recovery teacher, and a supervisor of a university reading clinic, Susan Tancock (1994) has developed a straightforward *literacy lesson framework* (or routine) for struggling readers that is rooted in literature-based reading instruction. She has noted that students who come to her clinic can be characterized by five areas of difficulty: (1) overreliance on the sound–symbol system (labored sounding out of unknown words); (2) a perception that reading is chiefly accurate word recognition, not meaning making; (3) lack of fluency in reading; (4) minimal self-monitoring; and (5) few writing strategies. Tancock's framework has worked well to address these concerns and move students to more successful reading. The five-step framework is:

1. Reading of familiar material (5 to 10 minutes)
2. Guided reading of authentic literature (30 minutes)
3. Writing (5 to 10 minutes)
4. Word sorting (5 to 10 minutes)
5. Book sharing (5 to 10 minutes)

In the *familiar reading component*, students read easy materials they have read previously, either silently or with a partner, using a fluency technique such as repeated, echo, or paired reading.

In the *guided reading section*, the heart of the framework, the student reads a slightly more challenging and authentic text with the tutor's guidance. Before reading, the student and the tutor focus on relevant background knowledge and entertain predictions or questions about the text. During the actual reading, the tutor supports and monitors the student's reading and encourages the student to monitor her or his own reading. In particular, the tutor encourages the student to employ syntactic and semantic strategies ("Does what you just read make sense?") as well as phonics strategies in decoding unknown words. The actual reading is followed by the student returning to and addressing his or her prereading questions or predictions, and clarifying, refining, and extending his or her thinking about the text.

Writing activities range from students writing a sentence, cutting it up into words, and reassembling it to more extended story, journal, or other authentic writing. During *word sorting*, students analyze words for a variety of common features from structural (e.g., number of syllables, spelling patterns) to semantic (e.g., living things, nonliving things). In the final portion of the lesson, *book sharing*, the tutor reads an engaging and interesting story to the student. Reading to students is more than entertaining; it develops positive attitudes for reading, comprehension, and vocabulary, and it provides students with a model for fluent reading.

THE FOUR BLOCKS

The *Four Blocks* (Cunningham, 2006; Cunningham, Hall, & Defee, 1991, 1998), a primary-grade program, adapts easily to a variety of instructional settings. Students engage in daily literacy instruction through four 30-minute time blocks, each featuring a distinct aspect of literacy.

The *writing* block consists of a 5-minute mini-lesson in which the teacher demonstrates and talks about a piece of her own writing with the students. Writing conventions and strategies are modeled and discussed daily. Next, the child writes independently, receiving assistance and feedback from others and eventually publishing the work. At the end of the block, the group discusses its progress and shares completed work.

In the *guided-reading* block, the teacher engages students in comprehension-focused instruction. During part of this period students read the stories from the text with a partner.

In the *independent-reading* block, the teacher reads a book to students. Students read self-selected books on their own (including books published by fellow students in the writing block). Students also talk about their reading with other students.

The final time block, *working with words,* includes word wall and word-building and letter-manipulation activities. This period develops students' word recognition or decoding abilities. Students and the teacher add about five words each week to the word wall. These common words are written on cards so that they can be arranged in alphabetical order. Students practice the words each day. Making Words is a word-building activity in which students manipulate a limited set of letters to make a variety of words. Both activities are described in detail in Chapter 6.

The Four Blocks helps develop students' facility with word recognition while allowing them to apply their newfound knowledge to real reading and writing situations. Cunningham, Hall, and Defee (1998) reported that with this approach, nearly 90 percent of first-grade students made exceptional or acceptable progress during a year's instruction.

Although we do not advocate a simple copied application of this or any approach for students encountering problems in reading, we appreciate the general sense of balance engendered by this approach. Several aspects of Four Blocks are worthy of notice and adaptation by teachers who face similar circumstances. First, children receive specific and extended instruction in the area requiring attention. Second, they immediately apply the learning to real and guided reading and writing situations. Third, the consistent and predictable daily blocks of instruction enable students to know what they will be doing. They do not waste instructional time learning new routines. We also like the active engagement of readers in choosing books, writing on their own, and making their own words.

A program like this works because students are engaged in real reading, real writing, and real problem solving through effective word recognition activities. Moreover, this good instruction is massed in a significant time period and is consistently applied on a daily basis.

Beth Ann, a fourth-grade teacher, has adapted the Four Blocks approach for her own class. She believes the framework has guided her to develop a reading curriculum that meets the needs of her students, especially those who struggle in reading.

> During the working-with-words block, I have incorporated more fluency activities—paired reading, repeated readings, and vocabulary activities in addition to the word-decoding activities. My students need to move beyond decoding. Their problems are not so much with sounding out words, but in reading efficiently, putting those words together into meaningful chunks, and having a fuller understanding of what the words mean.

LITERACY TEACHING FRAMEWORK

Taking a cue from Cunningham, Hall, and Defee's Four Blocks approach, Timothy Shanahan (2000, 2006) developed his own version of the Four Blocks that he calls the *literacy teaching framework* (also called the *Chicago reading framework* [Shanahan, 2006]). Shanahan keeps the word study, writing, and comprehension (guided reading) components from Cunningham, Hall, and Defee's approach. However, recognizing the importance of reading fluency, especially among struggling readers, he substitutes reading fluency instruction for the self-selected reading block of time. Implementing his approach in the Chicago area, Shanahan (2000) reported strong improvements in reading achievement where previously achievement was poor. In the Chicago Public Schools, where Shanahan led the implementation of his framework, 75 percent of the schools—schools that serve 85 percent low-income students in a minority-majority district—improved in reading, and the lowest performing schools in the district "improved as much as the higher performing schools for the first time in history" (Shanahan, 2006, p. 22).

SUCCESS FOR ALL

The original manifestation of *Success for All* was aimed at children in prekindergarten through grade 3. It has been implemented in a variety of school settings with notable success, bringing students up to grade-level achievement in reading and other basic academic skills (Borman et al., 2005; Slavin & Madden, 2001; Slavin et al., 1992). Tutors work individually with students for 20-minute sessions each day. Instruction focuses on what the students encounter in their regular reading curriculum.

During a 90-minute regular reading period, the tutors work within the classroom and serve as additional reading teachers. Thus, tutors provide additional online support to regular reading instruction and learn about the regular curriculum content in order to coordinate and reinforce their individual tutoring with the regular classroom instruction.

In regular instruction, students are regrouped according to reading achievement across grades so that each class has about 15 students, all reading at the same level. This arrangement allows teachers to teach the whole class; increases time available for direct instruction; and largely eliminates the need for workbooks, photocopies, and other independent, "make-work," follow-up activities.

The reading instruction for beginning readers includes time for sharing and discussing children's literature to develop comprehension and vocabulary, oral reading of big books, letter and sound instruction, repeated oral reading of phonetically regular mini-books, composing, and instruction in specific comprehension skills, including story structure. Older children (grades 2 and 3) also hear and discuss literature and engage in cooperative learning of story structure through prediction, summarization, vocabulary, decoding, and story-related writing using a basal textbook series. Students are expected to read material of their own choosing for 20 minutes each night at home. This reading is discussed in regular "book club" sessions in school. Every eight weeks, students' reading progress is assessed. The results determine which students will receive tutoring in the upcoming weeks. A family-support team made up of social workers and a parental liaison provides parenting education services and encourages home support of children's school learning.

Several aspects of Success for All seem worthy of mention. Professional development and training in Success for All is a priority for the entire school staff. Tutors provide consistent and massed instruction as well as ongoing assessment for those students most in need of corrective instruction. Coordination with the regular reading curriculum is emphasized to ensure consistency and maximize practice within a particular content or skill area. Teacher–student contact is maximized through the efficient use of tutors and regrouping, connection between home and school, and attempts to increase students' voluntary reading. Together, these elements ensure intensive and meaningful instruction that leads to strong gains in reading achievement.

Although Success for All, like Reading Recovery, is normally adopted at the school level, we believe that individual teachers and reading specialists can use the critical elements of the program to develop their own instructional routines for students who struggle.

FLUENCY DEVELOPMENT LESSON/FAST START

Although we detailed the *fluency development lesson (FDL)* and its adaptation for home use, *Fast Start (FS)* (Padak & Rasinski, 2005; Rasinski & Stevenson, 2005), in Chapters 7 and 13, we mention it again as an example of a lesson format that meets students' needs systematically and consistently. Rasinski and colleagues (1994) created the FDL to address the needs of primary-grade students who lack the fluency skills to read texts easily, effectively, and efficiently. The authors combined important aspects of fluency instruction in an instructional package that teachers quickly and easily implemented and students quickly accomplished. The FDL relies on highly predictable texts; the notions of modeling, support, and assistance during initial readings of the passage; multiple readings of the text; a focus on individual words of choice and word patterns; and opportunities for students to respond meaningfully to the passage and perform it for a wider audience.

First, teachers read a short, predictable text to students. Second, students read and reread the text, with initially high levels of support that gradually diminish as children become more familiar and fluent with the passage. At the end of each lesson students read the passage to the class or other groups of children or adults in the school.

The FDL and FS were developed as daily instructional routines that supplemented students' regular instruction. Over the course of 3 to 9 months, students receiving the FDL or FS instruction made significant gains in reading, compared with groups of students who also received comparable supplemental instruction in a more traditional manner (Rasinski et al., 1994; Rasinski & Stevenson, 2005).

Reponse to Intervention

In recent years a new concept called *Response to Intervention (RTI)* has captured the interest of educators and educational policymakers (Fuchs, Fuchs, & Vaughn, 2008). Actually, RTI is not new at all; it is what good teachers have always done with students—make decisions about instruction that are based on students' needs. Essentially, RTI is an overarching more formalized instructional routine that aims to ensure that the instructional needs of all students are being met.

There are several foundational characteristics of RTI in relation to reading. First, there must be a reliable and valid way to assess students' levels of reading proficiency and to identify any significant concerns they may have in reading in order to place them in the appropriate type and level of instruction. Second, the assessment system must also be able to monitor students' progress in reading as a result of the instruction they receive. Third, RTI assumes that within the school and classroom there are various levels or tiers of instruction available to students that meet their instructional needs. Fourth, RTI assumes a data-driven decision-making process in which students' levels of reading development and instructional needs are identified, that they are placed in the appropriate level of instruction based on their determined level and needs, and that their progress is monitored to ensure that the instruction they are given is effective.

Response to Intervention assumes various levels and types of instruction to meet students' needs. Usually this is identified as three tiers of instruction. Tier 1 instruction is the common core curriculum provided to all students. In any given classroom most students (e.g., 80 percent) should make good progress as a result of Tier 1 instruction. Regular assessments of students allow teachers to determine the students who are progressing normally and those who are not. Students who are not progressing move to Tier 2 instruction. Tier 2 is additional instruction (that supplements but does not supplant Tier 1) targeted to meet the needs of students who are not making adequate progress in Tier 1 alone. Tier 3 adds another layer of instruction and instructional intensity for those students who, as a result of regular assessment, have not made sufficient progress in Tier 2.

In theory, RTI makes good sense, and it is something that teachers should be striving for in their schools. However, we must note that RTI makes assumptions that are not necessarily currently in place or easily accessed. For example, RTI assumes that valid and efficient systems of assessment and diagnosis exist for students and teachers. Although one does have the ability to assess reading achievement and diagnose students' reading concerns, the methods are not necessarily time efficient. Suppose that it takes 20 minutes to assess one student; multiply that by 25 students in a classroom and then by nine assessments throughout the year (some RTI models have some students being assessed weekly—35 times a year) and you are looking at 75 hours of instructional time given over to assessment. In a classroom that devotes 2 hours per day to reading instruction, approximately 20 percent of the school year is given over to testing. Time given to assessment is time taken away from instruction.

Also, RTI assumes that the time and resources are available to provide various tiers of instruction to students. Again, given the diversity of students and student needs, creating the various tiers of instruction that meet the specific needs of students may be a challenge that, given the limited time and financial resources available to schools, might not be completely achievable. Creative teachers and schools need to explore how to expand the instructional school day and to find ways to increase effective instruction provided to students.

Despite the concerns we have just mentioned, can RTI work? The body of research that suggests that RTI can work is growing (Brown-Chidsey & Steege, 2005; Haager, Klingner, & Vaughn, 2007; Jimerson, Burns, & VanDerHeyden, 2007). Most RTI scholars would agree that it takes teachers, specialists, and school administrators to think outside the box to make RTI work. One third-grade teacher who has made it work for her is Rachel.

Rachel works in a school where a significant number of students find learning to read a struggle. She notes that most of her students are of average to above-average intelligence. They are able to understand material that is read to them. However, about half of her third-graders still struggle in the area of word recognition and reading fluency.

All her students begin the year in various levels of the core reading program (Tier 1), a commercially developed program adopted for grades K–5 by the school system. Knowing that fluency is a schoolwide concern, Rachel supplements the core program by having students chorally and repeatedly read a daily poem or song that is displayed in large print for the class to see as they read; she also has each student (or pairs or trios of students) select a poem that they rehearse throughout the week and perform at a weekly poetry slam every Friday afternoon.

Very early in the school year Rachel assesses her students by having them read several grade-level passages. Approximately half of her students do poorly in word recognition and reading fluency—they exhibit word recognition below 90 percent, reading rate at 50 words correct per minute or below, or oral reading that lacks appropriate expression and phrasing (see Chapters 2 and 7). These students are placed in Tier 2 intervention in addition to Tier 1. Tier 2 instruction is an additional 15 minutes of instruction daily, usually at the beginning of each school day in which she has created an instructional routine that involves reading high-frequency words in phrases daily and doing a word-building activity (e.g., Making Words, Making and Writing Words) that also involves sorting the words as well. Rachel has also developed a home involvement program that asks parents to engage in a form of paired and repeated reading with students (Fast Start) nightly for 15 minutes.

For most of the Tier 2 students, this additional work is enough for them to begin to make good progress in reading. However, this past year, despite the additional Tier 2 instruction, four of Rachel's students still were not demonstrating the kind of progress she had hoped for in her monthly assessments and close observations of Tier 2 students. These students went on to Tier 3 intervention by early October.

Tier 3 intervention occurred in mid-afternoon and was provided by a specially trained instructional tutor who supported Rachel's classroom. This tutor used the fluency development lesson (see Chapter 7) with the Tier 3 students daily. The fluency development lesson is an intense instructional routine that involves repeated and assisted reading of short texts (fluency) and word recognition instruction and practice (word recognition).

This third level of instruction was an immense help to these students. Although several still were behind in terms of grade-level achievement, all had made substantial progress in reading, some nearly doubling their performance on measures of word recognition and fluency from the beginning of the year.

Rachel is the first to admit that RTI is not the answer for all problems in reading or education. However, it does give her a framework for thinking about providing instruction in reading that meets her students' needs. "Until RTI came along, I wasn't sure if I was giving my students the help they needed. RTI allows me to get my head around this issue. For the first time in years, I can say with some assurance that all my students are making progress."

Make It Work for You

The programs and models we have described in this chapter are only a few of the many effective programs available. Although these programs have proven effective, however, you should refrain from following them blindly. We describe them to demonstrate the wide variety of routines that exist and point out their many common characteristics, such as focus and consistency.

In a review of programs for first-graders who experience difficulty in learning to read, Pikulski (1994) identified several critical instructional elements:

- Instruction should focus where children need help.
- Extra or supplemental reading instruction should coordinate closely with regular classroom instruction.
- Students benefit from additional instructional time.
- Simple, easy-to-read texts, especially those employing predictable and natural language patterns, ensure success.
- Meaningful opportunities to reread passages foster reading development.
- Writing activities foster reading growth.
- Close cooperation between school and home is beneficial.
- Careful monitoring of students' progress is essential.
- Teachers working with struggling readers require professional support and development.

To this list we would add one more:

- There should be high levels of student engagement in authentic literacy. Effective instruction is characterized by students busily engaged in reading and writing. Pressley and colleagues (2001) observed that in the classrooms of effective first-grade teachers 90 percent of students were engaged in reading and writing 90 percent of the time.

We believe that these suggestions apply to reading instruction for students of any age. By employing these guidelines and the principles we have outlined in this chapter and incorporating many of the instructional strategies described throughout this book, teachers can develop effective programs that respond to their own situations.

If you are a new teacher, you may find yourself overwhelmed by all the demands on your time. In addition to organizing your classroom, you must decide the instructional approach you will use with your students, what kinds of parent involvement activities you intend to employ, what materials you will need for your lessons, and so on. We advise you to take it slowly when designing instructional routines. Learn about yourself as a teacher and your students as learners. Acquaint yourself with new ideas about teaching through professional reading, graduate coursework and workshops, and conversations with your professional colleagues, especially the reading coach assigned to your school. Slowly and deliberately develop an instructional system that works for you and your students. Think of the various levels of support that students need in order to move forward in their reading. Begin with a core set of activities or lessons and expand from there. Be willing to make changes if certain initiatives you take are unsuccessful. But never stop working to design instruction that will improve your students' learning. Authentic and engaged teaching demands constant monitoring and work for improvement.

Ownership is one of the concepts that characterizes effective literacy instruction. Student achievement increases when students have ownership over their own learning, as when they choose what they need and want to read, how they respond to their reading, and with whom they read. The same notion applies to instructional design. When teachers have ownership over their instruction, when they determine their own methods and procedures, they invest more of themselves and their ideas in the program and see greater reason to make instruction work. Thus, we urge you to identify for yourself the principles of instruction key to successful intervention, develop a realistic and workable program, and make it work for you and your students.

DISCUSSION QUESTIONS

Some of the discussion questions for each chapter ask you to think through your own work as a teacher. If you are not currently a practicing teacher, try to respond to these questions from your own school experience (either from when you yourself were a student or from visits to schools that you have made in your teacher education program).

1. At the beginning of this chapter you met Kristen, a third-grade teacher who had just finished her first year of teaching. Kristen expressed the difficulty of "putting it all together." If you are a veteran teacher, what advice would you give a first-year teacher for developing a thoughtful combination and regular implementation of a set of logically

sequenced instructional activities. If you are a first-year teacher or teacher-in-training, what questions do you have about developing such a program?

2. We must teach in ways that reflect our beliefs about literacy learning. Write five concise, jargon-free, and specific statements that reflect what you believe about literacy learning. Some things to think about include the reading process, children as language learners, the role of the teacher, the classroom atmosphere, and appropriate materials and activities. Share your beliefs with your colleagues. Discuss the similarities and differences in beliefs among the members of your discussion group.

3. Many teachers and administrators define *curriculum* as the state standards or instruc-

tional materials adopted by the school board. Yet in this chapter, we state, "Teachers, reading coaches, and students together create curriculum and instruction in classrooms." Discuss this statement and how it compares to a traditional view of curriculum.

4. Discuss what makes reading material easy or hard for students and share ideas on how teachers can make challenging material easier for students to read.

5. Staying professionally current is every teacher's responsibility, but we think it is particularly critical for those who work with struggling readers. Share with your colleagues a professional article you have read recently that addresses helping struggling readers.

Chapter **Thirteen** ～

Involving Parents in Children's Reading

RICHARD ALLINGTON WENT RIGHT TO THE HEART of the matter when he asked, "If they don't read much, how they ever gonna get good?" (Allington, 1977). We have emphasized the strong association between students' progress in reading and the amount of real reading they do. Yet, the unfortunate truth is most students read little either in or out of school. The *Scholastic 2008 Kids and Family Reading Report*, a follow-up to a similar 2006 study, found only one in four children ages 5 to 17 say they read books for fun every day. Most likely, your struggling readers make up a large portion of the other 75 percent.

Given the relative absence of children's authentic reading experiences, we wonder why more children don't have difficulty reading. We also wonder just how much better all readers, especially those less proficient, might become if their volume of contextual reading could be increased. Because students currently engage in so little real reading, even a small increase would double or perhaps triple the amount of time they devote to reading. Elementary students spend most of their time at home, yet they do little reading there. Thus, home and parental involvement in reading are truly untapped sources for increasing the sheer amount that students read, which in turn will increase their proficiency in reading.

Several extensive reviews of research suggest that parent involvement has a positive effect on children's academic achievement in general and reading achievement in particular (Epstein et al., 2002; Fan & Chen, 2001; NMSA, 2003; Van Voorhis, 2003). Results from nearly every National Assessment of Educational Progress have indicated that students who regularly participate in literacy-related activities with their families have higher levels of reading achievement than students whose parents are not actively involved in their reading. Similarly, an international study of reading instruction found that the "degree of parental cooperation" was the most potent of 56 significant characteristics of schools most successful in teaching reading (Postlethwaite & Ross, 1992).

Unfortunately, parental involvement is often doomed by lack of understanding on the part of both teachers and parents. On the one hand, there are teachers who seem unaware of issues that might hinder parental involvement such as language barriers, single parents who struggle to make ends meet, or parents who are intimidated by school because of their own negative experiences as a student. On the other hand, there are parents who don't seem to understand the importance of reading to their child, don't know how to help their child, or actually go to the other extreme and ask too much of their child. Still, when parental involvement receives active support from teachers and schools, takes place over the long term, promotes simple yet enjoyable activity, and offers parents ongoing communication and support from teachers, significant and positive results are possible. In fact, parent involvement can become a superb complement to school reading instruction.

In this chapter we discuss several important characteristics of successful parent involvement in reading programs. Using these characteristics as guidelines, teachers and schools can design their own parent-involvement programs that meet their specific needs. The characteristics can also be used to design assessment instruments to evaluate existing programs.

Use Proven and Effective Strategies

Too often, teachers ask parents and children to do educational activities of questionable value for improving academic performance. Drawing and coloring pictures or cutting out photographs from magazines may not be poor activity choices, but they may not be the best use of parents' and children's time together at home. The amount of time that parents can devote to working with their children is often limited. Therefore, teachers and schools should ensure that suggested at-home activities are based on proven and appropriate methods for achieving academic success in reading. Many of the methods and strategies we described in earlier chapters can be readily adapted for home use.

Provide Training and Support

Most parents lack teachers' instructional expertise. They need focused training that includes demonstrations and opportunities for practice, discussion, and questions. Someone who is enthusiastic about and committed to parent involvement should provide the training. Teachers need to understand the realities of busy family life and be sensitive to educational barriers that may impede parent–child reading activity. Some parents may feel uncomfortable reading aloud to their children because of their own real or perceived lack of reading ability. Parents of English-language learners may not themselves be fluent readers of English. Yet, these parents want to help their children succeed. Making books on tape available or suggesting that parents and children "read" wordless books are two ways to promote all families' involvement. With some thought, resourceful teachers can find many more.

Teachers can provide ongoing support by sending home articles from professional journals that might interest parents or by encouraging and taking phone calls from parents. Some schools create a parent lounge/library in the school where parents and teachers can chat and find professional resources. Ongoing support builds bonds between home and school and demonstrates to parents that school personnel care.

Focus on Real Reading

If this book has one theme, it is that *authentic reading leads to reading growth*. The research on real reading is quite clear. One of the best helps parents can give children of any age is to read to them. Research shows that parents and teachers who read to their children regularly tend to have children with larger vocabularies and better comprehension. However, the 2008 *Scholastic Kids and Family Reading Report* found that only about half of all parents begin reading to their children before their first birthday. Every year teachers request that parents read to their children, yet the report also found that the percent of children who are read to every day drops from 38 percent among 5- to 8-year-olds to 23 percent among 9- to 11-year olds. Interestingly, this is the same time that children's daily reading for fun starts to decline.

Why is it difficult for parents to comply with this simple request? Again, it may be the lack of understanding on the part of both teachers and parents. One research study examined parents' and teachers' thoughts about storybook reading at home (Edwards, 1995). When asked how parents respond to requests to read to their children many teachers replied as the following teachers did:

> "As I said before, every year since I have been at Donaldson Elementary School, I have told parents to read to their children. However, I don't think they ever have."

> "I think we have a group of parents who think it is not their job to read to their children. . . . They simply don't get it!"

> "Perhaps some of the parents don't have time and think their children will learn to read in school without them having to help them at home."

On the other hand, when parents were asked, "What does reading to your child mean?" their responses reflected a lack of understanding of the request.

> "I think it means helping your children sound out words."

> "I wish someone would tell me what to do, because I'm fed up with teachers saying, 'Read to your child.'"

> "I don't know what to do when I open the book. I mean I don't know what to do first, second, third, and so on."

If teachers are to elicit parent cooperation, they must clearly specify what is expected and guard against assumptions regarding parents' lack of response.

Make Activities Easy and Consistent

Parents tell us that parent-involvement activities fail if they are too complex, take inordinate amounts of time, or change from day to day or week to week. They have trouble developing a routine of working with their children under these conditions. Even in the best of situations, parents' time is limited. With all their other obligations, they must carefully ration their home time and energy.

Therefore, the instructional activities that teachers send home for parents need to be easy and quick to implement. Because parents are usually unfamiliar with elaborate instructional schemes, it is best to focus on simple, successful activities with some variation to keep interest high. Such activities make it easier for parents and children to develop predictable, time-efficient routines. These, in turn, increase the likelihood that the at-home activities will be conducted regularly and successfully. Simple activities where parents read to, read with, and listen to their child read are powerful ways to promote student growth in reading.

Make Reading Enjoyable

For parents and children to persist in academic tasks over the long term, the instructional activities must be enjoyable for everyone. First, have parents and children read authentic and exemplary reading material. Second, ensure that activities can be successfully implemented and completed. Third, infuse a sense of informality and playfulness into the activities. Parents and children need to have fun as they play with written language. Fourth, encourage parents to be enthusiastic, provide positive encouragement, and support their children's attempts to read. Fifth, the texts children read should be easy; or, if the texts are challenging, design sufficient support for parents to offer their children while reading so that the children will be successful. Practiced or repeated readings, having the children hear their parents read a text before they are asked to do so, and having children and parents read a text together and aloud are just a few ways to make a more challenging text easier for children to read. Finally, allow children some control over the activity. For example, parents can allow children to choose the material to be read in an activity. If the reading is followed by some word games, children can choose the games as well as the words to include. The best type of parent involvement activities are those in which parents and children share ownership.

Provide Parents with Texts and Other Instructional Materials

Some parent-involvement plans fail because parents lack adequate materials, the time or resources to acquire them, or knowledge of where to acquire appropriate materials. Even with explicit directions about materials acquisition, many parents will fail to have the right materials at the right time. The easiest solution is to provide parents and children with the materials. When the materials are present—whether they are books, poems, diaries, or games—parents are more likely to do the activities with their children. The materials themselves act as reminders to parents to do the job.

Provide Ways to Document Home Activities

Documenting at-home activity permits teachers and schools to monitor parent–child involvement and evaluate the program's success in achieving its goal. More important, perhaps, documentation gives parents tacit encouragement and reminds them to continue reading with their children.

Usually, documentation can be accomplished with a log sheet on which parents record their work with their children over a specified period of time. Parents tell us they post the sheet in a prominent place to remind them to do the activity. At the end of the time period the log sheets are returned to the school (see Figure 13.1).

Be Consistent over the Long Term

In Chapter 12 we discussed the importance of teachers developing instructional routines that consist of a set of effective teaching activities implemented regularly and consistently over an extended period of time. This same notion applies to at-home programs. Once an effective instructional routine is introduced, it is best to avoid major changes or disruptions in the parent–child routine. Rather, allow families to develop a level of comfort with activities you know are effective. Create variety by changing the texts and the ways in which parents and children respond to what they read.

With these guidelines in mind, teachers and school administrators can design programs for parent involvement in reading that effectively supplement the instruction students receive in school. When home and school collaborate to provide enjoyable and

FIGURE 13.1   Home Reading Log

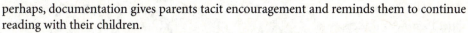

Fast-Start Reading Log

Name _____   Month ___September___

School _____

Please return this log to your child's teacher at the end of the month.

Date	Time Spent on Lesson	Name of New Passage Introduced	Other Reading Activities
9-28			
9-29			
9-30			
Etc.			

authentic reading experiences, students benefit because they have multiple daily opportunities to grow as readers.

Successful Parent Involvement Programs

COMMUNICATION

Communication is key to any successful educational program, including at-home reading programs. Effective teachers keep parents apprised of children's growth in reading, describe classroom activities, and suggest at-home literacy activities. Although communication between classroom and home can occur in several ways, we think that written communication, particularly in the form of a regular newsletter, is especially effective. By its nature, written communication is permanent. Parents can read and reread newsletters and post them in a place that allows easy access and referral.

We know many Title I and classroom reading teachers who send monthly or semi-monthly newsletters home to parents. The better letters share what the children have done in school and what they will be encountering shortly. Teachers also include articles that describe ways in which parents can help their children, lists or brief reviews of appropriate and exemplary books for children, and descriptions of specific literacy-related games and activities that parents can share with their children.

Some newsletters include articles that children write and photographs of children at work. These offer added incentives for parents and children to read the newsletters, and preparing the articles gives children added practice in reading and writing. For example, the Title I program in a school near us publishes a newsletter made up largely of articles written by students enrolled in the program (see Figure 13.2). The teacher reports that student work makes parents look forward to upcoming issues. "Once I have their eyes and ears, I can share with them some of the things they can do at home to promote their children's learning."

Newsletters should be personal and informative. The personal touch is best achieved by including student work or descriptions of individual students' accomplishments. The informative is achieved by including information that assists parents in helping their children read. Book lists, instructional ideas and strategies, answers to questions that parents frequently ask, news about upcoming meetings and speakers, and practical tips will help many parents better meet the reading needs and interests of their children.

Make sure your newsletters avoid talking down to parents. Many parents complain that they feel intimidated or are made to feel inadequate at their children's schools. Newsletters should be informal and conversational, highlighting the notion of partnerships between home and school. (See Appendix G for an example of an introductory letter to parents.)

In addition to communication from school to home, teachers need to foster ongoing communication from home to school. Parents know a lot about their children—their likes and dislikes, as well as how they respond to at-school instruction. Effective teachers not only make it a point to inform parents about what is going on in school and how they can help but they also regularly ask parents to share information about their children that may

FIGURE 13.2 Reading Newsletter

#4 Hayes School **March 2003**

READING

Published by the parents, students, and Mrs. Liu Hayes School

LITTLE GIANTS OF READING NEWSLETTER

Right to Read Week
March 3 - 7

A POTPOURRI OF READING

A Parent's Response

As a parent of a child in Chapter I reading, I have taken the opportunity to check out some of the reading material Mrs. Liu has available for parents. One of the books I have read is titled "Read to Me: Raising Kids Who Love to Read" by Bernice Cullinan. This book shares with parents the importance of reading aloud to kids. It explains how reading aloud helps teach children to love books. It includes tips for how to expand a child's imagination through reading, how to use television wisely, and how to interest children in writing. I would recommend this book to parents so they recognize how reading aloud to kids influences their motivation to read.

Sincerely

Cheryl

Mom & Johnathan

AUTHOR, AUTHOR!

Author Amy D will present an evening program for Chapter I students and their parents on March 1st. Students and parents will have an opportunity to do creative writing together.

Books written by Amy include "Me and My Friends," "The Ghost Man," "The Squirrel's Dinner," "No Homes," and others.

(continues)

FIGURE 13.2 Reading Newsletter *(Continued)*

The Moral of the Story is . . .

The farmer and the little boy think that nothing ever happens in the stories of *Hill of Fire* and *The Boy Who Cried Wolf*. The farmer and the little boy were bored. In the *Hill of Fire* there was a big explosion. In *The Boy Who Cried Wolf* the wolf came to eat the sheep for lunch. The people in the village got away to safety but the wolf ate the boy's sheep. I liked *The Boy Who Cried Wolf* the best because it was funny and the boy tricked the fisherman and the hunters.

by Rosa

I will never tell a lie so that I won't get in trouble because it is not fun.

Heidi

Nobody believed the boy when he cried "wolf." The hunters and the fisherman believed him at first but after they were tricked and there really was a wolf, the sheep were eaten.

by Robert

It is better to tell the truth because people will believe what you say when you tell the truth.

by Jo

FIGURE 13.2   Reading Newsletter *(Continued)*

A POTPOURRI OF READING

FUN READING
I Love A Story

Mouse Soup by Jacob S.

The mouse was reading a book under a tree. A wolf was behind a tree and caught the mouse and brought it home. The wolf put the mouse in a cage to save for supper. The mouse told the wolf four stories. The wolf believed the stories and got into trouble. The mouse got away.

The story was make-believe. The wolf should not have listened to the mouse.

George and Martha

The best part of the story was story number three. The Tub. George peeked in on Martha. It was funny.

By Kanika

KIDS ARE AUTHORS
I'm an Author
COMPETITION

Dreams
Hold fast to dreams
For if dreams die
Life is a broken-winged bird
That cannot fly.
Hold fast to dreams
for when dreams go
Life is a barren field
Covered with snow.

Langston Hughes

Poetry Surprise

I like to go sledding in the middle of winter.
Going down the hill at the cemetery, I hit the big snow ramp.
Elbows hitting the ground, I go up in the air—the best part.

Sijo —This verse pattern was developed in Korea. Its structure has three lines with 14 to 16 syllables to each line.

by Mathew

help them become better teachers. This may mean something as simple as a parent questionnaire that accompanies each report card or a periodic call to parents in order to ask how their children are responding at home to classroom reading instruction. When parents realize that the teacher values their opinions and their knowledge about their children, they are more likely to invest themselves in supporting school learning at home. When this happens, authentic partnerships develop.

ENCOURAGEMENT AND INCENTIVE PROGRAMS

We discussed some incentive programs in Chapter 4 as approaches to improving students' attitudes and motivation to read. The home is a great place to help nurture student reading, and incentive programs may offer a good connection between home and school.

A schoolwide project, called *Reading Millionaires* (O'Masta & Wolf, 1991) began when the staff at Diablo Elementary School in the Panama Region Department of Defense Schools wanted to increase students' out-of-school reading. They set a goal for students: a million minutes of reading by the end of the school year. An informational flier and newsletters about the program were sent to parents, who were asked to play an integral part in the project. Parents monitored children's reading at home, encouraged home reading, read to their children, and completed periodic reading logs of the number of minutes that children had read. Time spent reading to children also counted.

A display chart at school showed progress toward the reading goal. Teachers and the school principal constantly encouraged the children to read at home. In the end, they achieved their goal. Students felt a sense of community accomplishment, student reading at home increased and remained high throughout the school year, and parents felt better about helping their children in reading.

Similar programs have demonstrated similar results. Shanahan, Wojciechowski, and Rubik (1998) reported that their school's year-long program to encourage students to read for a million minutes at home resulted in more reading, better reading, more interest in reading for students, and parents' greater enthusiasm for reading at home. One parent wrote at the end of the program that her two children "read more this year than ever before. Their interest in books was greater as were the variety of books they chose. They read more challenging books and were eager to discuss the stories and authors who wrote them. They became so well versed in a topic that I felt I was actually learning from them. Please continue this program"(p. 96).

PAIRED READING

Paired Reading, a reading-support program, is described in Chapter 7. Although less able students can be matched with more proficient classmates, older students, teachers, parent volunteers, or other reasonably proficient readers, the program was initially intended for parents and children (Topping, 1987, 1995). In Paired Reading, parent and child sit side by side and read one text aloud together. (The child chooses the text.) The reading is done at a comfortable rate for the child, and either the parent or the child points to the text as he or she reads to draw both readers' attention to the print. In places where children feel comfortable reading alone, they signal parents nonverbally (perhaps with a nudge of an elbow). Parents stop reading aloud but continue to follow the reading and begin to read again if necessary. When children come to unfamiliar words and cannot decode them after a reasonable period, the parents simply say the words and the reading continues. Parents work with their children 5 to 10 minutes daily.

In England, where Paired Reading was first developed as a parent-involvement program, research shows it to be a powerful method for improving students' reading. Students engaged in Paired Reading made gains in word recognition and comprehension three to five times above previous gains. That is an impressive achievement, especially given the small amount of time involved in the program.

Several schools in North America have incorporated Paired Reading as a parent involvement program. At Robinson School, an inner-city school, parents are invited to learn about Paired Reading at the beginning of each year. Because Robinson has used the program for several years, parents know about it and are anxious to participate. The gymnasium is full when the Title I teachers Sandra, Gail, and Nancy introduce Paired Reading in an hour-long training session that includes a live demonstration, a videotaped description and demonstration, and an explanation of how the program works at Robinson. Parents try out Paired Reading with their children during this training session while the teachers provide feedback. Parents learn that students choose books to bring home. They also learn to work daily with their children; to maintain a monthly log of their Paired Reading; and to contact Sandra, Gail, or Nancy if they have questions about how Paired Reading works. Parents receive a packet of information about the program for future reference. They sign a contract in which they agree to do Paired Reading with their children throughout the school year. The contracts, along with photographs of the children and parents taken at this session, are displayed on a bulletin board in a prominent location in the school.

Sandra, Nancy, and Gail consider Paired Reading a parent-involvement program that actually works. Nancy says, "It works because parents know how they can help their children in a way that's easy, fun, and doesn't take the whole evening." Jackie, another veteran Title I teacher in the same school district, gives Paired Reading an enthusiastic and unconditional thumbs up: "Paired Reading and Reading Recovery are the best things to have happened in the remedial reading programs" (Rasinski & Fredericks, 1991, p. 515).

FAST START IN READING

Fast Start (Padak & Rasinski, 2005) is a program we developed at Kent State University for involving parents of young readers (kindergarten through grade 2) and struggling readers. In Fast Start, parents read short, highly predictable passages with their children. We have found that rhyming poetry, nursery rhymes, jokes and riddles for children, and short vignettes work well. Each day parents and their children spend about 15 minutes on one of the passages. What we ask of parents is specific and based on effective instructional principles:

1. The parent reads the passage to the child, and they both talk about its content.

2. The parent and the child read the passage together until the child is able to read it alone.

3. The parent listens to the child read and gives encouragement, support, and praise.

4. The parent and the child choose a word or two from the passage, write them on index cards, add them to their word bank, and engage in word play and word bank activities. (See Chapter 6 for a description of making and using word banks and word sorts.)

School personnel invite parents to attend Fast Start training sessions at the beginning of the school year. Several sessions are offered, morning and evening, so that parents can choose which session to attend. We have found that this active encouragement and flexible scheduling helps more parents attend the meetings. We consistently have 85 to 100 percent participation in the training/introductory sessions. Parents leave the sessions with informational packets, enough passages for one month, and log forms for recording their work with their children. Each month, from October through May, teachers send home new sets of readings and new log sheets. They also write and distribute a newsletter that answers common questions and concerns about the program, re-explains the program, describes other activities related to reading, and lists grade-appropriate books for children. Figures 13.3 and 13.4 show examples of Fast Start materials.

Parent participation in Fast Start has been exceptionally high, and student growth in reading is apparent and significant, especially among children who are most at risk for reading problems (Padak & Rasinski, 2004a, 2004b; Rasinski, 1995; Rasinski & Stevenson, 2005). In as little as one month, we have detected noticeable and significant improvement in students' reading and word recognition when compared with students not part of the Fast Start program but receiving extra tutoring in reading. In one study (Rasinski & Stevenson, 2005), the most at-risk first-graders using Fast Start with their parents over about three months made more than 50 percent greater gains in letter and word recognition and more than double the gain in reading fluency than students who received the same instruction in school but did not do Fast Start with their parents at home. By November of the school year, the Fast Start students had essentially met the reading fluency benchmark for January.

The program is relatively inexpensive and time efficient. The major cost is duplication, and the major time commitment for teachers is in the initial training sessions. Fast Start has demonstrated to us that parents really do want to help their children in reading. In many cases, they just need to know what to do or what materials and programs to choose. When schools involve parents in a systematic way, using effective methods of instruction and providing support, materials, and communication, children make substantial and significant progress as readers.

BACKPACK PROGRAMS

Providing books, materials, and activities is critical to successful parent involvement. Backpack programs, in which students bring the materials and activities home with them,

FIGURE 13.3   Fast Start in Reading Newsletter

Fast Start in Reading
Newsletter #1
Timothy Rasinski
Kent State University

Welcome to the **Fast Start in Reading** program. **Fast Start** is a simple yet effective way for parents to help their first grade children get off to a fast start in reading. Together with the instruction in reading your child receives in school, the Fast Start program helps to lay a solid foundation for continual growth and enjoyment in reading for your child. Parents are important, and in Fast Start parents are asked to work with their children a few minutes each day in a way that is enjoyable for both parents and children.

Fast Start employs short, highly readable passages that children will learn easily. Familiar rhymes, poetry, and other fun-to-read short passages form the core of materials that parents and children read in Fast Start.

The key activities in Fast Start are actually quite simple and easy to follow. We ask that you follow these four steps in every lesson.

1)   Read the passage to your child.
2)   Read the passage with your child.
3)   Listen to your child read to you.
4)   Choose and practice words from the passage.

This four-step procedure is extremely effective, in conjunction with regular classroom instruction, in helping children learn to read at an accelerated pace and diminishing the need for corrective or remedial instruction. Children who have been in the Fast Start program for as few as 4 weeks have demonstrated marked improvements in their reading as measured by various reading tests.

General Plan for Fast Start

In the Fast Start program, parents are asked to work with their children for about 10 minutes per day, every day. We realize that it isn't possible to work every single day with your child. Nevertheless, we want to set this as a goal and hope that all parents involved in Fast Start will be able to work with their first-grade child as much as possible.

We ask that you work with your child every day for about 10 minutes. The schedule for introducing new passages is as follows:

Monday: Introduce and read new reading passage or rhyme.
Tuesday: Introduce and read a second new passage.
Wednesday: Review and reread passages from Monday and Tuesday.
Thursday: Introduce and read a third new passage.
Friday: Introduce and read a fourth new passage.
Saturday and Sunday: Review passages introduced during the week.

We hope you will be able to keep as close to this schedule as possible throughout the year. Although you are asked to work each day with your child, the amount of time you need to devote to the Fast Start readings is only about 10 minutes. Remember, one of the most important aspects of this program—one that accounts for children's great progress in reading—is the consistent daily interaction between parent and child in reading.

In addition to doing the Fast Start program with your child throughout the school year, it is important that parents encourage and invite their children into reading in other ways as well. These other ways include reading interesting books to your child every day, making regular visits to the library to allow your child to choose books, having plenty of books and other reading materials around your home for you child to read, allowing your child to write by keeping a journal or diary, composing letters and notes to others, writing his or her own stories, providing your child with interesting experiences and discussing them with your child, and allowing your child to dictate stories to you that you then write down and read together. Above all, make sure your child knows that *you think reading is important and fun.* The best way to share your enthusiasm is to read to your child every day and talk about what you read together.

FIGURE 13.4   Daily Fast Start Lesson

Daily Fast Start Lesson

Parents: Please

1. Read the rhyme to your child.

2. Read it with your child.

3. Listen to your child read.

4. Word play—write interesting words from the rhyme on this sheet; expand to other related words (dock—sock, rock, block)

Hickory, dickory, dock,

The mouse ran up the clock.

The clock struck one,

The mouse ran down,

Hickory, dickory, dock.

capitalize on this characteristic. Ray Reutzel and Parker Fawson (1990) described a backpack program called *Traveling Tales*. Teachers develop backpacks that contain materials for writing, from various types of paper, to rulers and paper clips, to a letter of introduction and direction for parents (see Figures 13.5 and 13.6). The letter explains the program and invites parents to write a story with their children. It provides details for parents and children about the various stages of the writing process. When the writing is complete, parents come to school with their child and share the story. The backpack then goes home with the next child. Reutzel and Fawson found that parents were eager for specific guidance in working with their children and valued close working relationships with school personnel.

The Reutzel and Fawson model readily adapts for reading. Teachers decide what sort of activity to invite parents and children to do together, gather materials that allow parents and children to complete the activity successfully at home, provide parents with appropriate directions for the activity, and develop a management system that allows every family access to the backpack for enough time to complete the activity.

FIGURE 13.5   Traveling Tales Instructions

Traveling Tales Instructions

Dear Parent(s),

Home writing activities are a great way to improve your child's reading and writing development. Traveling Tales is a backpack that includes a variety of writing materials for you to use with your child. We encourage you to work together with your child to create a story that we can share and enjoy at school.

Your child has been given this backpack for two nights. If you need more time, please call us at 555-2836.

We hope these guidelines will help you have a successful and enjoyable Traveling Tales experience with your child.

1. With your child, brainstorm a list of ideas or topics for writing. Ask questions that will invite your child to express ideas, interests, feelings, and so on, about which he or she may wish to write. Stories about personal experiences (factual or fictional), information stories that tell of something your child finds interesting, stories about family members or others, and stories of science or history are great topics.

2. Next, help your child decide which of the writing materials included in the Traveling Tales backpack he or she will use to create the story. Suggest that the story may take several different forms. Some ideas include (a) poetry, (b) fold-out book, (c) a play or skit, (d) puppet play, (e) dialogue, (f) pocket book, (g) backward book, and (h) shape book.

3. Help your child plan the story before beginning writing. You may wish to write down some of the ideas your child expresses for him or her to use in writing the first draft.

4. Remember, your child's first draft is a rough draft. It is all right for it to contain misspellings, poor handwriting, and incomplete ideas. Be available to answer questions as your child works on the first draft. Be careful to encourage him or her to keep writing and not worry about spelling, punctuation, and the like. Ask your child just to do his or her best. Both of you can work on correctness later. Now is the time to develop ideas for writing.

5. Once the first draft is done, try to involve others at home by asking them to listen to it read aloud. Reading one's writing aloud helps writers determine the sense of the message. Be sure to tell those who listen to be encouraging rather than critical and to ask questions about ideas that were unclear or were poorly developed. Questions help a writer think about his or her writing without feeling bad.

6. Write out questions and suggestions made by the home audience. Talk with your child about how a second draft could use these suggestions to make the story easier to understand or more interesting. Remember to be supportive and encouraging! Offer your help, but encourage your child to make his or her best own efforts first.

7. After the second draft is completed, your child may want to read his or her writing to the family again for their response. If not, it is time to edit the writing. Now is the time to correct spellings, punctuation, and so on. Praise your child for his or her attempts and tell

(continues)

FIGURE 13.5 Traveling Tales Instruction *(Continued)*

your child that you want to help make his or her writing the best it can be. Show your child which words are misspelled and explain why. Do the same with punctuation and capitalization.

8. With the editing complete, the writing is ready to be revised for the final time. When writing the final draft, encourage your child to use neat handwriting. Feel free to help your child at any point during final revisions.

9. When finished, encourage your family to listen to the final story and respond positively. This practice will help instill confidence in your child as he or she shares his or her writing at school.

10. We invite you to come to school with your child, if possible, to share the writing you have done together. Your child will appreciate the support, and we would enjoy talking with you.

Thank you for your help. We appreciate your involvement. If you are unable to come to school with your child, please call us or send a note with your child. We will be glad to call back or visit with you. Thanks again for your support. We hope you enjoy writing with your child!

Sincerely,

Ms. Robinson

FIGURE 13.6 Contents of the Traveling Tales Backpack

Materials for the Traveling Tales Backpack

Instructions and ideas in a notebook	Small stapler	Yarn
	Water-base markers	Wallpaper for book covers
Plain, unlined paper	Colored pencils	Glue stick
Lined paper	Pencils	Tape
Construction paper— multiple colors	Felt-tip pens	Paperclips
	Scissors	Ruler
Drawing paper	Staples	Letter stencils
Poster paper	Brass fasteners	Examples of other books done by students and parents
Crayons	Card stock	
Watercolors	Hole punch	

Source: D. R. Reutzel and P. C. Fawson, "Traveling Tales: Connecting Parents and Children through Writing," *The Reading Teacher, 44* (1990):222–227.

Many teachers consider backpack programs a great way to introduce parents to more extensive parent-involvement activities. But even if this is the only parent involvement a teacher or school offers, everyone benefits. Parents have access to solid and enjoyable reading and writing activities as well as appropriate directions and materials. Children read and write in the warm, supportive environment of their home with their parents.

ELL FAMILIES

Families whose first language is not English can also participate in activities to support their children's growth in learning to read English. Knowing a bit about parents' or older siblings' English proficiency is helpful, for this knowledge allows teachers to adapt at-home materials so that everyone—parents and children—can be successful. Here are three adaptations that have been successful with Fast Start. With tweaking, they can work equally well with other at-home programs:

- Ask a classroom volunteer to audiotape the texts that parents and children will read. Two versions of each text will be best, one slow and deliberate, and the other a fluent rendition. To work with these texts at home, the parent and child could first look at the text and listen to the tape several times. Then they could read together along with the taped version. Finally, the child could read (or recite) the text by himself or herself.
- Family members may be learning English themselves. See how you can help both children and their families. For example, adults might practice the texts in their English classes so that they can read them at home with their children.
- Check with English language learner (ELL) teachers or tutors in your school. Because they will have knowledge about children's linguistic backgrounds, they may have more specific ideas for families. Share your home-involvement program with these teachers or tutors. Children can practice reading the texts in their ELL classes.

SOME FINAL THOUGHTS

Remember, too, that students' at-school reading and writing activities can also work at home with only minor modifications, if any, and with some support and direction from the teacher. For example, children can be expected to read at home daily for a designated period of time. Nursery rhymes and childhood songs and chants that develop phonemic awareness can be shared between children and their parents. Parents can take dictation (language experience activity) from their children, and children can read the collaborative composition with their parents. Parents can keep dialogue journals with their children. Parents and children can talk about the books or stories children read in school. We have found that parents will go far to help their children, if they have the support and encouragement of teachers.

Although parent involvement may not be a cure-all for every difficulty that children encounter in reading, we know that it does make a difference—in some cases, a huge difference. Whether you are a classroom teacher or a special reading teacher, we strongly recommend that you strive to involve parents actively in children's literacy development. The potential benefits are simply too great to pass up.

DISCUSSION QUESTIONS

Some of the discussion questions for each chapter ask you to think through your own work as a teacher. If you are not currently a practicing teacher, try to respond to these questions from your own school experience (either from when you yourself were a student or from visits to schools that you have made in your teacher education program).

1. What is the biggest challenge you face with parental involvement? Brainstorm some possible solutions with your colleagues.

2. Discuss ways to get ELL parents involved with their child's literacy if the parents speak little or no English.

3. If you could design the ideal parent lounge/library for your school, what would it look like? What materials would be there? When and how would it be used?

4. In addition to reading to children, list all the literacy activities that could take place in the home. Try to come up with as many as you can that on face value appear unrelated to school learning. What is the value of such activities?

5. Make a list of 10 tips for parents on how to help their struggling reader. Make each tip concise and jargon free. Share your tips with your colleagues.

Appendix A

POETRY AND RHYMES FOR READING

Adoff, Arnold. (1995). *Slowdance heartbreak blues.* New York: Macmillan.

Bagert, Brod. (1992). *Let me be the boss.* Honesdale, PA: Boyds Mills.

Bagert, Brod. (1999). *Rainbows, head lice, and pea-green tile: Poems from the voice of the class-room teacher.* Gainesville, FL: Maupin.

Bagert, Brod. (2002). *Giant children.* New York: Dial.

Benjamin, Alan. (1993). *A nickel buys a rhyme.* New York: Morrow.

Brown, Marc. (1980). *Pickle things.* New York: Putnam.

Carle, Eric. (1989). *Eric Carle's animals animals.* New York: Philomel.

Cofer, Judith O. (1995). *An island like you.* New York: Orchard.

Cole, Joanne, & Calmenson, Stephanie. (1995). *Yours till banana splits: 201 autograph rhymes.* New York: Beech Tree.

dePaola, Tomie. (1985). *Tomie dePaola's Mother Goose.* New York: Putnam.

dePaola, Tomie. (1988). *Tomie dePaola's book of poems.* New York: Putnam.

de Regniers, Beatrice S., Moore, Eva, & White, Mary M. (1969). *Poems children will sit still for.* New York: Citation.

de Regniers, Beatrice S., Moore, Eva, & White, Mary M. (1988). *Sing a song of popcorn: Every child's book of poems.* New York: Scholastic.

Dyer, Jane. (1996). *Animal crackers: A delectable collection of pictures, poems, and lullabies for the very young.* Boston: Little, Brown.

Fleischman, Paul. (1988). *Joyful noise: Poems for two voices.* New York: Harper & Row.

Fleming, Denise. (1996). *Where once there was a wood.* New York: Henry Holt.

Florian, Douglas. (1994). *Bing, bang, bong.* New York: Harcourt, Brace.

Florian, Douglas. (1994). *Beast feast.* New York: Harcourt Brace.

Goldstein, Bobbye. (1992). *What's on the menu?* New York: Viking.

Hale, Glorya. (1997). *Read-aloud poems for young people.* New York: Black Dog & Leventhal.

Hopkins, Lee Bennett. (Ed.). (1992). *Pterodactyls and pizza.* New York: Trumpet.

Hopkins, Lee Bennett. (1995). *Small talk: A book of short poems.* New York: Harcourt Brace.

Lansky, Bruce. (1994). *A bad case of the giggles.* New York: Meadowbrook Press.

Lansky, Bruce. (1996). *Poetry party.* New York: Meadowbrook Press.

Lewis, J. Patrick. (1998). *Doodle dandies: Poems that take shape.* New York: Atheneum.

Livingston, Myra C. (1987). *Cat poems.* New York: Holiday.

Livingston, Myra C. (1988). *Space songs.* New York: Holiday.

Lobel, Arnold. (1983). *The book of pigericks.* New York: Harper & Row.

Lobel, Arnold. (1986). *The Random House book of Mother Goose.* New York: Random House.

London, Jonathan. (1993). *Eyes of Grey Wolf.* San Francisco: Chronicle.

Martin, Rafe. (1996). *Mysterious tales of Japan.* New York: Putnam.

Medearis, Angela S. (1995). *Skin deep.* New York: Macmillan.

Moss, Jeff. (1989). *The butterfly jar.* New York: Bantam.

Moss, Jeff. (1991). *The other side of the door.* New York: Bantam.

Nye, Naomi S. (1995). *The tree is older than you are.* New York: Simon Schuster.

O'Neill, Mary. (1961). *Hailstones and halibut bones: Adventures in color.* Garden City, NY: Doubleday.

Opie, Iona. (Ed.). (1996). *My very first Mother Goose.* Cambridge, MA: Candlewick.

Opie, Iona, & Opie, Peter. (Eds.). (1992). *I saw Esau: The schoolchild's pocket book.* Cambridge, MA: Candlewick.

Patten, Brian. (1999). *The Puffin twentieth-century collection of verse.* London: Penguin.

Prelutsky, Jack. (Ed.). (1983). *The Random House book of poetry for children.* New York: Random House.

Prelutsky, Jack. (1984). *New kid on the block.* New York: Greenwillow.

Prelutsky, Jack. (Ed.). (1986). *Read-aloud rhymes for the very young.* New York: Knopf.

Prelutsky, Jack. (1986). *Ride a purple pelican.* New York: Greenwillow.

Prelutsky, Jack. (1990). *Something big has been here.* New York: Greenwillow.

Prelutsky, Jack. (1999). *The twentieth century children's poetry treasury.* New York: Knopf.

Silverstein, Shel. (1974). *Where the sidewalk ends.* New York: HarperCollins.

Silverstein, Shel. (1981). *A light in the attic.* New York: HarperCollins.

Slier, Deborah. (Ed.). (1991). *Make a joyful sound: Poems for children by African-American poets.* New York: Checkerboard.

Sword, Elizabeth Hauge. (1995). *A child's anthology of poetry.* Hopewell, NJ: Ecco Press.

Viorst, Judith. (1981). *If I were in charge of the world and other worries.* New York: Atheneum.

Wildsmith, Brian. (1964). *Brian Wildsmith's Mother Goose.* New York: Franklin Watts.

Appendix B

COMMON WORD FAMILIES

Teachers use word families (letter patterns or phonograms) as an alternative strategy for recognizing or decoding unknown words. One instructional approach is to focus on one or two word families at a time. Brainstorm short and long words that belong to the particular word families. List the words on chart paper and display the charts around the room for easy reading and spelling. When students come to unknown words, cue them to look for word families they know. Because words in word families rhyme, an excellent complement to word family instruction is reading and writing poetry.

ab: tab, drab
ace: race, place
ack: lack, track
ad: bad, glad
ade: made, shade
ag: bag, flag
age: page, stage
ail: mail, snail
ain: rain, train
ake: take, brake
alk: talk, chalk
all: ball, squall
am: ham, swam
ame: name, blame
amp: camp, clamp
an: man, span
and: land, gland
ane: plane, cane
ang: bang, sprang
ank: bank, plank

ant: pant, chant
ap: nap, snap
ape: tape, drape
ar: car, star
are: care, glare
ark: dark, spark
art: part, start
ash: cash, flash
ast: past, blast
at: fat, scat
ate: gate, plate
ave: gave, shave
aw: saw, draw
ay: hay, clay
eak: leak, sneak
eal: real, squeal
eam: team, stream
ean: mean, lean
ear: year, spear
eat: beat, cheat

eck: peck, check

ed: bed, shed

eed: need, speed

eel: feel, kneel

een: seen, screen

eep: keep, sheep

eet: feet, sleet

eg: leg, peg

ell: fell, swell

elt: felt, belt

en: Ben, when

end: tend, send

ent: sent, spent

ess: less, bless

est: rest, chest

et: get, jet

ew: flew, chew

ib: bib, crib

ice: rice, splice

ick: kick, stick

id: hid, slid

ide: wide, pride

ig: pig, twig

ight: tight, bright

ike: Mike, spike

ill: fill, chill

im: him, trim

in: tin, spin

ind: kind, blind

ine: mine, spine

ing: sing, string

ink: sink, shrink

ip: hip, flip

ipe: ripe, swipe

ire: tire, sire

ish: dish, swish

it: hit, quit

ite: bite, write

ive: five, hive

oat: boat, float

ob: job, throb

ock: lock, stock

og: fog, clog

oil: boil, broil

oke: woke, spoke

old: gold, scold

ole: hole, stole

oll: droll, roll

one: cone, phone

ong: long, wrong

ool: cool, fool

oom: room, bloom

oop: hoop, snoop

oot: boot, shoot

op: top, chop

ope: hope, slope

ore: bore, snore

orn: horn, thorn

ose: rose, close

oss: boss, gloss

ot: got, trot

ought: bought, brought

out: pout, about

ow: bow, throw

ow: how, chow

ox: fox, pox

oy: boy, ploy

ub: cub, shrub

uck: duck, stuck

ud: mud, thud

uff: puff, stuff

ug: dug, plug

um: sum, thumb

ump: bump, plump

un: run, spun

unch: bunch, scrunch

ung: hung, flung

unk: sunk, chunk

unt: hunt, grunt

ush: mush, crush

ust: dust, trust

ut: but, shut

~ *Appendix C*

THE ESSENTIAL PRIMARY GRADE
SIGHT WORD LIST

We developed this list of 400 essential words from the high-frequency word lists created by Dolch (1955), Fry (1980), and Cunningham and Allington (1999). It also includes words that represent the most common phonograms (Fry, 1998) and words selected by primary-grade teachers as words every student should recognize by sight and know by the end of third grade.

We recommend that primary-grade teachers in a school work together to determine the words that should be learned at each grade level. Kindergarten children might learn 25 words, and 125 words might be learned during each of the primary years, first, second, and third grade. The list could easily be covered in 25 weeks by presenting and teaching five words each week.

There is no best way to teach these words. They should be put on the class word wall and practiced regularly. Students can add them to their personal word banks and use them for practice and word games. Class word games work well in teaching these words. It is also a good idea to send the words home at the beginning of the school year and ask parents to regularly work with their children in helping them learn to know and recognize the words. Because these are high-frequency words, the absolute best way to provide plenty of exposure to them is through regular and wide reading.

about	both	even	hard	leave
above	bottom	every	has	left
add	boy	example	have	let
after	bring	eye	he	letter
again	brother	face	head	life
air	bug	fake	hear	lip
all	but	family	help	light
almost	buy	far	her	like
along	by	farm	here	line
also	call	fast	hill	list
always	came	father	him	little
am	can	favorite	high	live
America	can't	feed	his	lock
and	car	feet	hold	look
animal	carry	few	home	long
another	cat	find	hop	luck
answer	change	first	hot	made
any	chill	five	house	mail
are	children	fly	how	main
around	city	follow	hug	make
as	clean	food	hum	man
ask	close	for	hurt	many
at	cold	found	I	map
ate	come	four	idea	may
away	could	friend	if	me
back	country	from	important	mean
bag	crab	full	in	men
bank	cut	fun	into	might
be	dad	funny	is	mile
because	day	gave	it	mine
bed	did	get	its	miss
been	different	girl	it's	mom
before	do	give	jam	more
began	does	glow	job	most
begin	done	go	jump	mother
being	don't	goes	junk	mountain
bell	down	good	just	move
below	draw	got	keep	much
best	drink	grade	kind	must
better	drum	great	know	my
between	earth	green	land	myself
big	eat	group	large	name
black	eight	grow	last	near
blue	end	had	later	need
book	enough	hand	learn	new

never	point	sink	them	wash
next	pretty	sister	then	watch
new	pull	sit	there	water
nice	put	six	these	way
nine	ran	sleep	they	we
night	read	slow	they're	well
no	red	small	thing	went
not	really	so	think	were
now	ride	some	this	what
number	right	something	those	when
of	river	sometimes	thought	where
off	rock	song	three	which
often	round	soon	through	while
old	run	sound	time	white
on	said	spell	to	who
once	same	stand	today	why
one	saw	start	together	win
only	say	state	too	will
open	school	still	took	wish
or	sea	stop	top	with
other	second	store	tree	without
our	see	story	try	write
out	seed	study	turn	wrong
over	seem	such	two	won't
own	sentence	take	under	word
page	set	talk	until	work
paper	seven	tap	up	world
part	shall	teacher	upon	would
people	she	tell	us	write
pick	show	ten	use	year
picture	should	than	very	yellow
place	shout	thank	walk	yes
plant	sick	that	want	you
play	side	the	warm	young
please	sing	their	was	your

Appendix D

SOURCES OF INFORMATION ON WORD HISTORIES AND WORD PLAY

Allington, Richard. (1990). *Reading and science words.* Austin, TX: Raintree Steck-Vaughn. ISBN: 081722498X.

Almond, Jordan. *Dictionary of word origins: A history of the words, expressions, and cliches we use.* Secaucus, NJ: Carol Publishing. ISBN: 0-80651-713-1.

Ayto, John. (1998). *Oxford dictionary of slang.* Oxford, UK: Oxford University Press. ISBN: 019863157X.

Bromberg, Murray, & Liebb, Julius. (2005). *601 words you need to know to pass your exam.* Barrons Educational Series. ISBN: 0-81209-645-2.

Dalzell, Tom. (1996). *Flappers 2 rappers: American youth slang.* Springfield, MA: Merriam–Webster. ISBN: 0-87779-612-2.

Ehrlich, Ida. (1968). *Instant vocabulary.* New York: Simon & Schuster. ISBN: 0-671-67727-6.

Flavell, Linda, & Flavell, Roger. (1992). *Dictionary of idioms and their origins.* London: Kyle Cathie. ISBN: 1856261298.

Fry, Edward; Kress, Jacqueline; & Fountoukidis, Dona Lee. (1997). *The reading teacher's book of lists.* Upper Saddle River, NJ: Prentice Hall. ISBN: 0-13-0348937.

Funk, Charles. (1950). *Thereby hangs a tale: Stories of curious word origins.* New York: Harper & Row. ISBN: 0-06272-049-Y.

Funk, Charles. (1955). *Heavens to Betsy! And other curious sayings.* New York: HarperCollins. ISBN: 0060913533.

Gwynne, Fred. (1970). *The king who rained.* New York: Simon & Schuster. ISBN: 0-440-84127-5.

Gwynne, Fred. (1976). *A chocolate moose for dinner.* New York: Simon & Schuster. ISBN: 0-440-84330-8.

Gwynne, Fred. (1988). *A little pigeon toad.* New York: Simon & Schuster. ISBN: 0-440-84798-2.

Hendrickson, Robert. (1997). *The facts on file encyclopedia of word and phrase origins, revised and expanded edition.* New York: Facts on File. ISBN: 0-81603-266-1.

Hoad, T. F. (1996). *Oxford concise dictionary of English etymology.* Oxford, UK: Oxford University Press. ISBN: 019861182X.

Kennedy, John. (1996). *Word stems: A dictionary.* New York: Soho Press. ISBN: 1569470510.

Knowles, Elizabeth (Ed.). (1997). *The Oxford dictionary of phrase, saying, and quotation.* Oxford: Oxford University Press. ISBN: 0-19-886229-7.

Lederer, Richard. (1988). *Get thee to a punnery.* Charleston, SC: Wyrick. ISBN: 0440204992.

Lederer, Richard. (1991). *The play of words: Fun and games for language lovers.* New York: Pocket Books. ISBN: 0671689088.

Lederer, Richard. (1996). *Pun and games.* Chicago: Chicago Review Press. ISBN: 1556522649.

Moore, Bob, & Moore, Maxine. (1997). *NTC's dictionary of Latin and Greek origins.* Chicago: NTC Publishing. ISBN: 0844283215.

Muschell, David. (1996). *What in the word? Origins of words dealing with people and places.* Bradenton, FL: McGuinn & McGuire. ISBN: 1-88111-714-6.

Simon, Seymour. (1995). *Earth words: A dictionary of the environment.* New York: Harpercrest. ISBN: 0-06020-234-3.

Terban, Marvin. (1988). *Guppies in tuxedos: Funny eponyms.* New York: Houghton Mifflin. ISBN: 0-89919-509-1.

Terban, Marvin. (1982). *Eight ate: A feast of homonym riddles.* New York: Houghton Mifflin. ISBN: 0-89919-086-3.

Terban, Marvin. (1983). *In a pickle: And other funny idioms.* New York. Houghton Mifflin. ISBN: 0-60600-812-8.

Terban, Marvin. (1984). *I think I thought: And other tricky verbs.* New York: Houghton Mifflin. ISBN: 0-89919-290-4.

Terban, Marvin. (1985). *Too hot to hoot: Funny palindrome riddles.* New York: Houghton Mifflin. ISBN: 0-89919-320-X.

Terban, Marvin. (1986). *Your foot's on my feet: And other tricky nouns.* New York: Houghton Mifflin. ISBN: 0-89919-413-3.

Terban, Marvin. (1987). *Mad as a wet hen: And other funny eponyms.* New York: Houghton Mifflin. ISBN: 0-89919-479-6.

Note: A good dictionary and thesaurus are absolutely essential among any list of resources for word study.

Appendix E

MEANINGFUL PREFIXES, SUFFIXES, AND WORD PARTS

Latin-Greek Roots for the Primary Grades

Note: Order of roots is not sequential.

Prefixes

co-, con-	with, together
de-	own, off of
ex-	out
in-	not ("*negative*")
pre-	before
re-	back, again
sub-	under, below
un-	not ("*negative*")

Bases

audi-, audit-	hear, listen
graph-, gram-	write, draw
mov-, mot-, mobil-	move
port-	carry
vid-, vis-	see

Numerical Bases
(appear at beginning of words)

bi-	two
tri-	three

Suffixes

-able, ible	can, able to be done
-er,	more
-est	most
-ful	full of
-less	without

Latin-Greek Roots for the Upper Elementary Grades

Prefixes

a-, ab-, abs-	away, from
di-, dif-, dis-	apart, in different directions, not
pro-,	forward, ahead
tra-, tran-, trans-	across, change

Assimilating Prefixes

ad-	to, toward, add to
con-, com-, col-	with, together
in-, im-, il-	in, on, into (*directional*)
in-, im-, il-	not (*negative*)

Parallel Latin and Greek Prefixes

Latin	Greek	
contra-, contro-, counter-	anti-	against
circu-, circum-	peri-	around
multi-	poly-	many
super-, sur-	hyper-	over
sub-	hypo-	under, below

Bases

cred-, credit-	believe
cur-, curs-, cours-	run, go
dict-	say, tell, speak
duc-, duct-	lead
mis-, mit-	to send
pon-, pos-, posit-	put, place
scrib-, script	write
terr-	earth
fac-, fic-, fact-, fect-	do, make

Parallel Latin and Greek Bases

Latin	Greek	
aqua -	hydro-	water
ped-	pod-	foot, feet

Suffixes

-arium, -orium	place for, container for
-ify	to make
-or, -er	one who does
-ose, -ous, -eous, -ious	full of

Latin-Greek Roots for the Middle Grades

Prefixes

auto-	self
inter-	between, among
post-	after
ob- (assimilates)	up against, in the way
per-	through, thorough
tele-	from afar

Bases

solv-, solut-	free, loosen
sent-, sens	think, feel
tend-, tens-, tenu-	stretch, thin
trac-, tract	pull, draw, drag
ven-, vent-	come
volu-, volut-, volv-	roll

Parallel Latin and Greek Bases

Latin	Greek	
am(a)-, amat-	bi(o)-	live, life
fort-, forc-	dynamo-	power, strong
lumen-, luc-	gen-, gener-	be born, give birth, produce
nat-, natur-	neo-	new
nov-	pan(t)-	all, every
omni-	phil(o)-	love
spec-, spect	phon-	voice, call
viv-, vit	photo-	light
voc-, vok-, voice	scop-	look at, watch

"Flexing" Suffixes

-ate	do
-ation	state or condition
-ant, -ent	in the process, having the characteristics of
-ance, -ancy, -ence, -ency	state or quality
-crat,	ruler
-cracy	one who believes in rule by
-ologist	one who studies
-olgy	study of
-phobe,	one who fears
-phobia	fear

Sources: Adapted from Padak, Newton, Rasinski, and Newton (2008) and Rasinski, Padak, Newton, and Newton (2008).

❧ *Appendix F*

BOOKMAKING IDEAS

Basic Materials

Paper & Covers	Fasteners	Tools
heavy cardboard	metal rings	scissors
boxes	yarn, thread	glue
oak tag	ribbon, twine	1" and 2" tape
newspaper	staples	paper cutter
construction paper	brass fasteners	needles
newsprint	nuts, bolts, & washers	stapler
manila paper	elastic bands	
wallpaper sample books		
flat boxes		
paper towel tubes		
clear contact paper		
tie-dye, batik		

Large Class Books

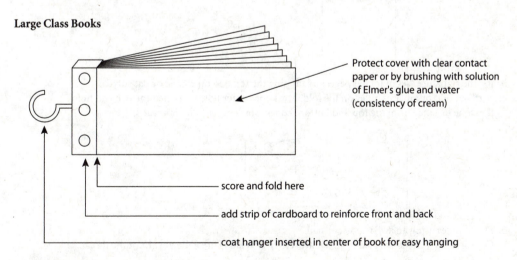

Protect cover with clear contact paper or by brushing with solution of Elmer's glue and water (consistency of cream)

score and fold here

add strip of cardboard to reinforce front and back

coat hanger inserted in center of book for easy hanging

— cut heavy cardboard covers to suit large sheets of paper.
    — punch holes and fasten with nuts, washers, and bolts.
      (These can easily be removed to add pages.)

Saddle Stitch Signature

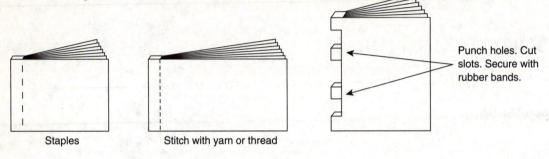

Staples   Stitch with yarn or thread

Punch holes. Cut slots. Secure with rubber bands.

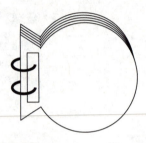

Apply Scotch tape to front and back covers. Punch holes through tape. Fasten with rings, brass fasteners, twists from plastic bags, shoe laces, etc.

Small Books for Individual Use

1. Fold paper in half.
2. Bone (sharpen) fold using a folding bone or blunt stick.

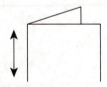

3. Jog the signature (set of folded pages) by tapping the top end on a table or flat surface.
4. Mark an odd number of holes on the fold. Mark the center hole first, then the two end holes the same distance from the top and bottom edges. Mark other holes if needed.

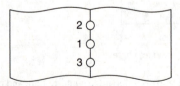

5. Punch holes using an awl, needle, or nail.
6. Cut thread 2 times longer than the signature. Wax thread. Thread needle. Knot the thread.

7. Sew signature pages together using a saddle stitch. Begin sewing in the center hole of the folio.

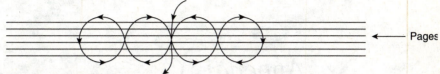

← Pages

8. On the third time through the center hole, loop thread under the beginning stitch and then go back through the center hole.

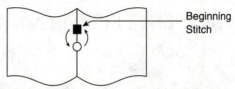

Beginning Stitch

9. Tie a knot and clip extra thread. The knot will be on the inside of the book.

Creative Blank Books

Pages that have holes of varying sizes and numbers
Pages that are shaped
Pages that have different textures
Pages that fold out
Pages that have windows and doors
Pages that indicate direction (up-down-over-in)
Pages that progress in color (light-bright-dark-dull)
Pages that pop up

Experiment with Lettering

❧ *Appendix G*

SAMPLE LETTER TO PARENTS

This letter should be sent at the beginning of the school year.

Dear Parents:

One of the most important things we know about how children learn to read is that children who read the most tend to be the best readers. The more you read, the better reader you become! For this reason I am asking you to take a few minutes (15–20 would be great) each day to read to or with your child.

The time you give to reading will allow your child to practice reading strategies and skills he or she will be learning here at school. More important, however, is the message you will send to your child. Through your actions you will say that reading is important in your life and in your child's life and that you want him or her to become the best reader possible.

You can read to or with your child in many ways. Here are a few suggestions:

Have your child sit next to you or on your lap as you read a good story to him or her. Be sure to read with an expressive voice and make sure your child can see the words and pictures.

Read together. Sitting side by side, read aloud together a story that your child has chosen. Let your voices blend together to create a real partnership in reading. If your child can read a section on his or her own without trouble, allow your voice to fade. On those sections that challenge your child, let your voice lead the way by reading slightly louder and ahead of your child. This has proven to be a superb way to improve children's reading.

Echo reading. Allow your child to read back, phrase for phrase, a short text that you read to him or her.

Alternate reading. Switch who does the reading after every page or paragraph.

Repeat reading. Read a short story or poem to your child. (You can read the passage several times if you like, over several days.) Then allow your child to read the same passage to you.

Spend your time together quietly reading material of your own choosing. Although your child may be reading on his or her own, the fact that you are in the same room reading sends a strong message to your child about the importance of reading.

Try to read with your child every day. Develop a routine for reading that will last a lifetime. Be sure to praise your child for good reading. And when he or she struggles over a word or phrase while reading, simply say the unknown word and continue. Don't make a lesson out of every mistake. (You can go back to the word after you've read.) Finally, don't just read—talk about the stories you read together and discuss your own reading habits and interests with your child. He or she needs to know that reading is an important part of everyday life.

Thank you for your help in making this year a successful one for your child in reading. Working together, we can help your child become a successful and lifelong reader.

Sincerely,

Ms. Summers, Teacher

∾ *References*

Adams, M. J. (1990). *Beginning to read: Thinking and learning about print.* Cambridge, MA: MIT Press.

Allington, R. L. (1977). If they don't read much, how they ever gonna get good? *Journal of Reading, 21,* 57–61.

Allington, R. L. (1978, March). *Are good and poor readers taught differently? Is that why poor readers are poor readers?* Paper presented at the meeting of the American Educational Research Association, Toronto.

Allington, R. L. (1980). Teacher interruption behaviors during primary grade oral reading. *Journal of Educational Psychology, 72,* 371–377.

Allington, R. L. (1983). Fluency: The neglected reading goal. *The Reading Teacher, 36,* 556–561.

Allington, R. L. (1984). Content coverage and contextual reading in reading groups. *Journal of Reading Behavior, 26,* 85–96.

Allington, R. L. (1987, July/August). Shattered hopes: Why two federal reading programs have failed to correct reading failure. *Learning, 87,* 60–64.

Allington, R. L. (1994). The schools we have. The schools we need. *The Reading Teacher, 48,* 14–29.

Allington, R. L. (2000). *What really matters for struggling readers: Designing research-based programs.* New York: Longman.

Allington, R. L. (2002). What I've learned about effective reading instruction. *Phi Delta Kappan, 83,* 740–747.

Allington, R. L., & McGill-Franzen, A. (1989). Different programs, indifferent instruction. In A. Gardner & D. Lipsky (Eds.), *Beyond separate education.* New York: Brookes.

Allington, R. L., Stuetzel, H., Shake, M., & Lamarche, S. (1986). What is remedial reading? A descriptive study. *Reading Research and Instruction, 24,* 15–30.

Allington, R. L., & Walmsley, S. A. (Eds.) (1995). *No quick fix: Rethinking literacy programs in America's elementary schools.* New York: Teachers College Press.

Alvermann, D. E. (1991). The discussion web: A graphic aid for learning across the curriculum. *The Reading Teacher, 45,* 92–99.

American Library Association. (1989). *American Library Association Presidential Committee on Information Literacy.* Chicago: Author.

Ames, C. (1992). Classrooms: Goals, structures, and student motivation. *Journal of Educational Psychology, 84,* 261–271.

Anderson, R. C., & Freebody, P. (1981). Vocabulary knowledge. In J. Guthrie (Ed.), *Comprehension and teaching: Research reviews* (pp. 77–117). Newark, DE: International Reading Association.

Anderson, R. C., Hiebert, E., Scott, J., & Wilkinson, I. (1985). *Becoming a nation of readers.* Washington, DC: U.S. Department of Education.

Armbruster, B., Lehr, F., & Osborn, J. (2001). *Put reading first.* Washington, DC: U.S. Department of Education.

Atwell, N. (1987). *In the middle: Writing, reading, and learning with adolescents.* Portsmouth, NH: Heinemann.

August, D., & Shanahan, T. (Eds.). (2006). *Developing literacy in second language learners: Report of the National Reading Panel on language-minority children and youth.* Mahwah, NJ: Erlbaum.

Baildon, R., & Baildon, M. (2008). Guiding independence: Developing a research tool to support student decision making in selecting online information sources. *The Reading Teacher, 61,* 636–647.

Baker, L., Afflerbach, P., & Reinking, D. (Eds.). (1996). *Developing engaged readers in school and home communities.* Mahwah, NJ: Erlbaum.

Ball, E., & Blachman, B. A. (1991). Does phoneme awareness training in kindergarten make a difference in early word recognition and developmental spelling? *Reading Research Quarterly, 26,* 49–66.

Barksdale–Ladd, M. A., & Nedeff, A. R. (1997). The worlds of a reader's mind: Students as authors. *The Reading Teacher, 50,* 564–573.

Baumann, J., & Duffy, A. (1997). *Engaged reading for pleasure and learning: A report from the National Reading Research Center.* Athens, GA: National Reading Research Center.

Baumann, J., Edwards, E., Boland, E., Olejnik, S., & Kame'enui, E. (2003). Vocabulary tricks: Effects of instruction in morphology and context on fifth-grade students' ability to derive and infer word meanings. *American Educational Research Journal, 40,* 447–494.

Baumann, J., Hooten, H., & White, P. (1999). Teaching comprehension through literature: A teacher-research project to develop fifth graders' reading strategies and motivation. *The Reading Teacher, 53,* 38–51.

Baumann, N. (1995). Reading millionaires—It works! *The Reading Teacher, 48,* 730.

Bear, D. R., Invernizzi, M., Templeton, S., & Johnston, F. (2007). *Words their way* (4th ed.). Upper Saddle River, NJ: Prentice-Hall.

Beck, I. L. (2006). *Making sense of phonics: The hows and whys.* New York: Guilford.

Beck, I. L., & McKeown, M. G. (2007). Increasing young low-income children's oral vocabulary repertoires through rich and focused instruction. *Elementary School Journal, 108,* 97–113.

Beck, I., McKeown, M.G., & Kucan, I. (2002). *Bringing words to life: Robust vocabulary instruction.* New York: Guilford.

Biemiller, A., & Boote, C. (2006). An effective method for building meaning vocabulary in primary grades. *Journal of Educational Psychology, 98,* 44–62.

Biggs, M., Homan, S., Dedrick, R., & Rasinski, T. (2008). Using an interactive singing software program: A comparative study of middle school struggling readers. *Reading Psychology, An International Quarterly, 29,* 195–213.

Billmeyer, R., & Barton, M. (1998). *Teaching reading in the content areas* (2nd ed.). Aurora, CO: Mid-Continent Regional Educational Laboratory.

Blachowicz, C., & Fisher, P. (2004). Vocabulary lessons. *Educational Leadership, 61,* 66–69.

Blachowicz, C., & Fisher, P. (2005). *Teaching vocabulary in all classrooms* (3rd ed.). Upper Saddle River, NJ: Prentice-Hall.

Bleich, D. (1978). *Subjective criticism.* Baltimore: Johns Hopkins University Press.

Block, C., & Israel, S. (2004). The ABCs of performing highly effective think-alouds. *The Reading Teacher, 58,* 154–167.

Block, C., & Mangieri, J. (2002). Recreational reading: Twenty years later. *The Reading Teacher, 55,* 572–580.

Booker, K., Invernizzi, M., & McCormick, M. (2007). "Kiss your brain": A closer look at flourishing literacy gains in impoverished elementary schools. *Reading Research and Instruction, 46,* 315–339.

Borman, G. D., Slavin, R. E., Cheung, A. C. K., Chamberlain, A. M., Madden, N. A., & Chambers, B. (2007). Final reading outcomes of the national randomized field trial of Success for All. *American Educational Research Journal, 44,* 701–731.

Boulware-Gooden, R., Carreker, S., Thornhill, A., & Malatesha, J. R. (2007). Instruction in metacognitive strategies enhances reading comprehension and vocabulary achievement of third-grade students. *The Reading Teacher, 61,* 70–77.

Brabham, E. G., Murray, B. A., & Hudson, S. (2001, December). *Effects of interactive reading aloud and multimedia interactions with alphabet books on phoneme awareness, letter knowledge, and vocabulary.* Paper presented at the annual meeting of the National Reading Conference, San Antonio, TX.

Bracey, G. (2007). *The evolution of the schools suck bloc.* Available: www.huffingtonpost.com/gerald-bracey/the-evolution-of-the-scho_b_48464.html.

Bromley, K. (2007). Nine things every teacher should know about words and vocabulary instruction. *Journal of Adolescent and Adult Literacy, 50,* 528–537.

Brown-Chidsey, R., & Steege, M. W. (2005). *Response to intervention: Principles and strategies for effective practice.* New York: Guilford.

Burke, J. (2002). The Internet reader. *Educational Leadership, 60*(3), 38–42.

Callaghan, M. (1935). All the years of her life. *New Yorker, 11*(17), 17–19.

Cambourne, B. (1995). Towards an educationally relevant theory of literacy learning: Twenty years of inquiry. *The Reading Teacher, 49,* 182–190.

Carbo, M. (1978). Teaching reading with talking books. *The Reading Teacher, 32,* 267–273.

Catts, H. W. (1991). Early identification of reading disabilities. *Topics in Language Disorders, 12,* 1–16.

Cazden, C. (1981). Social context of learning to read. In J. Guthrie (Ed.), *Comprehension and teaching: Research reviews* (pp. 118–139). Newark, DE: International Reading Association.

Clarke, L., & Holwadel, J. (2007). "Help! What is wrong with these literature circles and how can we fix them?" *The Reading Teacher, 61,* 20–29.

Clarke, L. (1988). Invented versus traditional spelling in first graders' writing: Effects on learning to spell and read. *Research in the Teaching of English, 22,* 281–309.

Clay, M. M. (1985). *The early detection of reading difficulties* (3rd ed.). Portsmouth, NH: Heinemann.

Clay, M. M. (1993). *Reading Recovery: A guidebook for teachers in training.* Portsmouth, NH: Heinemann.

Clymer, T. (1996). The utility of phonics generalizations in the primary grades. *The Reading Teacher, 50,* 182–187 (originally published in *The Reading Teacher, 16,* 1963).

Cohen, D. (1968). The effect of literature on vocabulary and reading achievement. *Elementary English, 45,* 209–213, 217.

Coiro, J. (2003). Reading comprehension on the Internet: Expanding our understanding of reading comprehension to encompass new literacies. *The Reading Teacher, 56,* 458–464.

Commission on Chapter I. (1993). *Making schools work for children of poverty: A new framework*. Washington, DC: Author.

Connor, C., Morrison, F., & Petrella, J. (2004). Effective comprehension instruction: Examining child X instruction interactions. *Journal of Educational Psychology, 96*, 682–698.

Cooper, H. (1977). Controlling personal rewards: Professional teachers' differential use of feedback and the effects of feedback on the students' motivation to perform. *Journal of Educational Psychology, 69*, 419–427.

Coyne, M. D., Simmons, D. C., Kame'enui, E. J., & Stoolmiller, M. (2004). Teaching vocabulary during shared storybook readings: An examination of differential effects. *Exceptionality, 12*, 145–162.

Cunningham, A. E., & Stanovich, K. E. (1998). What reading does for the mind. *American Educator, 22*, 8–15.

Cunningham, P. M. (2006). High-poverty schools that beat the odds. *The Reading Teacher, 60*, 382–385.

Cunningham, P. M., & Cunningham, J. W. (1992). Making words: Enhancing the invented spelling–decoding connection. *The Reading Teacher, 46*, 106–115.

Cunningham, P. M., Hall, D. P., & Defee, M. (1991). Nonability grouped, multilevel instruction: A year in a first-grade classroom. *Reading Teacher, 44*, 566–571.

Cunningham, P. M., Hall, D. P., & Defee, M. (1998). Nonability-grouped, multilevel instruction: Eight years later. *The Reading Teacher, 51*, 652–664.

Daane, M. C., Campbell, J. R., Grigg, W. S., Goodman, M. J., & Oranje, A. (2005). *Fourth-grade students reading aloud: NAEP 2002 special study of oral reading*. Washington, DC: U.S. Department of Education, Institute of Education Sciences.

Dahl, K., & Scharer, P. (2000). Phonics teaching and learning in whole language classrooms: New evidence from research. *The Reading Teacher, 53*, 584–594.

Daniels, H. (2002). *Literature circles: Voice and choice in book clubs and reading groups* (2nd ed.). Portland, ME: Stenhouse.

Daniels, H., & Steineke, N. (2004). *Mini-lessons for literature circles*. Portsmouth, NH: Heinemann.

Davidson, J. (1982). The group mapping activity for instruction in reading and thinking. *Journal of Reading, 26*, 52–56.

Davidson, J. (1986). The teacher–student generated lesson: A model for reading instruction. *Theory into Practice, 25*, 84–90.

Davidson, J. (1987, June). *Writing across the curriculum*. Paper presented at the meeting of the Language Experience Special Interest Council, DeKalb, IL.

Davis, F. B. (1944). Fundamental factors of comprehension in reading. *Psychometrika, 9*, 185–197.

Doiron, R. (1994). Using nonfiction in a read-aloud program: Letting the facts speak for themselves. *The Reading Teacher, 47*, 616–624.

Dowhower, S. L. (1987). Effects of repeated reading on second-grade transitional readers' fluency and comprehension. *Reading Research Quarterly, 22*, 389–407.

Dowhower, S. L. (1994). Repeated reading revisited: Research into practice. *Reading and Writing Quarterly, 10*, 343–358.

Dugan, J. (1997). Transactional literature discussions: Engaging students in the appreciation and understanding of literature. *The Reading Teacher, 51*, 86–96.

Duke, N. K., Pressley, M., & Hilden, K. (2004). Difficulties in reading comprehension. In C. A. Stone, E. R. Silliman, B. J. Ehren, & K. Apel (Eds.), *Handbook of language and literacy: Development and disorders* (pp. 501–520). New York: Guilford.

Durkin, D. (1966). *Children who read early*. New York: Teachers College Press.

Durkin, D. (1979). What classroom observations reveal about reading comprehension. *Reading Research Quarterly, 14*, 481–533.

Dymock, S. (2007). Comprehension strategy instruction: Teaching narrative text structure. *The Reading Teacher, 61*, 161–167.

Ebbers, S. M., & Denton, C. A. (2008). A root awakening: Vocabulary instruction for older students with reading difficulties. *Learning Disabilities Research and Practice, 23*, 90–102.

Edwards, P. (1995). Combining parents' and teachers' thoughts about storybook reading at home and school. In L. M. Morrow (Ed.), *Family literacy: Connections in schools and communities* (pp. 54–69). Newark, DE: International Reading Association.

Ehri, L. C. (1994). Development of the ability to read words: Update. In R. Ruddell, M. Ruddell, & H. Singer (Eds.), *Theoretical models and processes of reading* (pp. 323–358). Newark, DE: International Reading Association.

Eldredge, J. L., & Baird, J. E. (1996). Phonemic awareness training works better than whole language instruction for teaching first graders how to write. *Reading Research and Instruction, 35*, 193–208.

Elley, W. (1992). *How in the world do students read?* Hamburg, Germany: International Association for the Evaluation of Educational Achievement.

Epstein, J. L., Sanders, M. G., Simon, B. S., Salinas, K. C., Jansorn, N. R., & Van Voorhis, F. L. (2002). *School, community, and community partnerships: Your handbook for action* (2nd ed.). Thousand Oaks, CA: Corwin Press.

Ericson, L., & Juliebo, M. F. (1998). *The phonological awareness handbook for kindergarten and primary teachers*. Newark, DE: International Reading Association.

Esquith, R. (2004). *There are no shortcuts*. New York: Pantheon.

Esquith, R. (2007). *Teach like your hair's on fire*. New York: Viking.

Evans, C. (1984). Writing to learn in math. *Language Arts, 61*, 828–835.

Fan, X. T., & Chen, M. (2001). Parental involvement and students' academic achievement: A meta-analysis. *Educational Psychology Review, 13*, 1–22.

Fernald, G. M. (1943). *Remedial techniques in basic school subjects*. New York: McGraw-Hill.

Fielding–Barnsley, R. (1997). Explicit instruction in decoding benefits children high in phonemic awareness and alphabet knowledge. *Scientific Studies of Reading, 1,* 85–98.

Fisher, B. (1991). *Joyful learning.* Portsmouth, NH: Heinemann.

Fisher, D., & Frey, N. (2007). Implementing a schoolwide literacy framework: Improving achievement in an urban elementary school. *The Reading Teacher, 61,* 32–43.

Fitzharris, L., Jones, M. B., & Crawford, A. (2008). Teacher knowledge matters in supporting young readers. *The Reading Teacher, 61,* 384–394.

Flynt, S. E., & Brozo, W. G. (2008). Developing academic language: Got words? *The Reading Teacher, 61,* 500–502.

Flynt, E. S., & Cooter, R. (2005). Improving middle grades reading in urban schools: The Memphis comprehension framework. *The Reading Teacher, 58,* 774–780.

Fountas, I., & Pinnell, G. S. (2001). *Guiding readers and writers.* Portsmouth, NH: Heinemann.

Fox, B. J. (2004). *Word identification strategies: Phonics from a new perspective* (3rd ed). Upper Saddle River, NJ: Merrill Prentice-Hall.

Fry, E. (1998). The most common phonograms. *The Reading Teacher, 51,* 620–622.

Fuchs, D., Fuchs, L. S., & Vaughn, S. (2008). *Response to intervention: A framework for reading educators.* Newark, DE: International Reading Association.

Furr, D. (2003). Struggling readers get hooked on writing. *The Reading Teacher, 56,* 518–525.

Gambrell, L. (1996). Creating classroom cultures that foster reading motivation. *The Reading Teacher, 50,* 14–25.

Gambrell, L. (1998, November). *Motivating readers.* Paper presented at the annual Kent State University Reading Conference, Kent, OH.

Gamse, B. C., Bloom, H. S., Kemple, J. J., Jacob, R. T., Boulay, B., Bozzi, L., Caswell, L., Horst, M., Smith, W. C., St. Pierre, R. G., & Unlu, F. (2008). *Reading First impact study: Interim report.* Washington, DC: U.S. Department of Education.

Garner, J., & Bochna, C. (2004). Transfer of a listening comprehension strategy to independent reading in first-grade students. *Early Childhood Education Journal, 32,* 69–74.

Gaskins, I. W. (1998). There's more to teaching at-risk and delayed readers than good reading instruction. *The Reading Teacher, 51,* 534–547.

Gaskins, I. W. (2005). *Success with struggling readers: The Benchmark School approach.* New York: Guilford.

Gaskins, I. W., Ehri, L. C., Cress, C., O'Hara, C., & Donnelly, K. (1997). Procedures for word learning: Making discoveries about words. *The Reading Teacher, 50,* 312–327.

Gentry, J. R. (2005). Instructional techniques for emerging writers and special needs students at kindergarten and grade one levels. *Reading and Writing Quarterly, 21,* 113–134.

Gere, A. (Ed.). (1985). *Roots in the sawdust: Writing to learn across the disciplines.* Urbana, IL: National Council of Teachers of English.

Gersten, R., Baker, S., Shanahan, T., Linan-Thompson, S., Collins, P., & Scarcella, R. (2007). *Effective literacy and English language instruction for English learners in the elementary school.* Washington, DC: Institute of Education Sciences. Retrieved July 22, 2007 from http://ies.ed.gov/ncee/pdf/20074011.pdf.

Gillet, J., & Kita, M. (1979). Words, kids, and categories. *The Reading Teacher, 32,* 538–542.

Goldenberg, C. (2008). Teaching English language learners: What the research does—and does not—say. *American Educator, 32,* 8–19, 22–23, 42–44.

Good, R. H., & Kaminski, R. (2001). *Dynamic indicators of basic early literacy skills.* Eugene, OR: University of Oregon Center on Teaching and Learning.

Good, T. (1987). Two decades of research on teacher expectations: Findings and future directions. *Journal of Teacher Education, 38,* 32–47.

Goodman, Y. (1985). Kidwatching: Observing children in the classroom. In A. Jaggar & M. T. Smith-Burke (Eds.), *Observing the language learner* (pp. 9–18). Newark, DE: International Reading Association.

Goodman, Y. (1989). Evaluation of students: Evaluation of teachers. In K. S. Goodman, Y. M. Goodman, & W. J. Hood (Eds.), *The whole language evaluation book* (pp. 3–14). Portsmouth, NH: Heinemann.

Goodman, Y., & Watson, D. (1977). A reading program to live with: Focus on comprehension. *Language Arts, 54,* 868–879.

Graves, D. (1983). *Writing: Teachers and children at work.* Portsmouth, NH: Heinemann.

Graves, D., & Stuart, V. (1985). *Write from the start.* New York: Dutton.

Griffith, L. W., & Rasinski, T. V. (2004). A focus on fluency: How one teacher incorporated fluency with her reading curriculum. *The Reading Teacher, 58,* 126–137.

Griffith, P., & Klesius, J. P. (1990, November). *The effect of phonemic awareness ability and reading instructional approach on first grade children's acquisition of spelling and decoding skills.* Paper presented at the annual meeting of the National Reading Conference, Miami, FL.

Griffith, P., & Olson, M. (1992). Phonemic awareness helps beginning readers break the code. *The Reading Teacher, 45,* 516–523.

Guthrie, J., & Davis, M. (2003). Motivating struggling readers in middle school through an engagement model of classroom practice. *Reading and Writing Quarterly, 19,* 59–85.

Guthrie, J., Schafer, W., Wang, Y., & Afflerbach, P. (1995). Relationships of instruction to amount of reading: An exploration of social, cognitive, and instructional connections. *Reading Research Quarterly, 30,* 8–25.

Haager, D., Klingner, J., & Vaughn, S. (2007). *Evidence-based reading practices for response to intervention.* Baltimore, MD: Brookes.

Hansen, J. (1987). *When writers read.* Portsmouth, NH: Heinemann.

Hanser, C. (1986). The writer's inside story. *Language Arts, 63,* 153–159.

Harmon, J. M., Hedrick, W. B., & Wood, K. D. (2005). Research on vocabulary instruction in the content areas: Implications for struggling readers. *Reading & Writing Quarterly, 21,* 261–280.

Harp, B. (Ed.). (1994). *Assessment and evaluation for student-centered learning.* Norwood, MA: Christopher–Gordon.

Hart, B., & Risley, T.R. (2003). *The early catastrophe: The 30 million word gap by age 3.* Available online: www.aft.org/pubs-reports/american_educator/spring2003/catastrophe.html.

Harris, T., & Hodges, R. (Eds.). (1995). *The literacy dictionary.* Newark, DE: International Reading Association.

Harste, J. C. (1989). *New policy guidelines for reading: Connecting research and practice.* Urbana, IL: National Council of Teachers of English.

Hartman, D., & Hartman, J. (1993). Reading across texts: Expanding the role of the reader. *The Reading Teacher, 47,* 202–211.

Hasbrouck, J. E., & Tindal, G. (1992). Curriculum-based oral reading fluency forms for students in grades 2 through 5. *Teaching Exceptional Children, 24*(3), 41–44.

Hasbrouck, J. E., & Tindal, G. A. (2006). Oral reading fluency norms: A valuable assessment tool for reading teachers. *The Reading Teacher, 59,* 636–644.

Haynes, J. (2007). *Getting started with English language learners.* Alexandria, VA: Association for Supervision and Curriculum Development.

Heald–Taylor, B. G. (1996). Three paradigms for literature instruction in grades 3 to 6. *The Reading Teacher, 49,* 456–466.

Heap, J. (1980). What counts as reading: Limits to certainty in assessment. *Curriculum Inquiry, 10,* 265–292.

Heckelman, R. G. (1969). A neurological impress method of reading instruction. *Academic Therapy, 4,* 277–282.

Henk, W., & Melnick, S. (1995). The Reader Self-Perception Scale (RSPS): A new tool for measuring how children feel about themselves as readers. *The Reading Teacher, 48,* 470–482.

Henk, W., & Melnick, S. (1998). Upper elementary-aged children's reported perceptions about good readers: A self-efficacy influenced update in transitional literacy contexts. *Reading Research and Instruction, 38,* 57–80.

Herber, H. (1978). *Teaching reading in content areas* (2nd ed.). Englewood Cliffs, NJ: Prentice-Hall.

Heritage, M. (2007). Formative assessment: What do teachers need to know and do? *Phi Delta Kappan, 89,* 140–145.

Herman, P. A. (1985). The effect of repeated readings on reading rate, speech pauses, and word recognition accuracy. *Reading Research Quarterly, 20,* 553–564.

Heyman, R. (1983). Clarifying meaning through classroom talk. *Curriculum Inquiry, 13,* 23–42.

Hiebert, E. H., Pearson, P. D., Taylor, B. M., Richardson, V., & Paris, S. G. (1998). *Every child a reader: Concepts of print, letter naming, and phonemic awareness.* Ann Arbor, MI: Center for the Improvement of Early Reading Achievement.

Hiebert, J., & Wearne, D. (1993). Instructional tasks, classroom discourse, and students' learning in second grade arithmetic. *American Educational Research Journal, 30,* 393–425.

Hirsh, E. D. (2003). Reading comprehension requires knowledge—Of words and the world. *American Educator, 27*(1), 10–13, 16–22, 28–29, 48.

Hoffman, J. (1992). Critical reading/thinking across the curriculum: Using I-charts to support learning. *Language Arts, 69,* 121–127.

Holdaway, D. (1979). *The foundations of literacy.* Sydney, Australia: Ashton Scholastic.

Holdaway, D. (1981). Shared book experience: Teaching reading using favorite books. *Theory into Practice, 21,* 293–300.

Howe, K. B., & Shinn, M. M. (2001). *Standard reading assessment passages (RAPS) for use in general outcome measurements: A manual describing development and technical features.* Eden Prairie, MN: Edformations.

Hui-Tzu, M. (2008). EFL vocabulary acquisition and retention: Reading plus vocabulary enhancement activities and narrow reading. *Language Learning, 58,* 73–115.

Invernizzi, M., & Hayes, L. (2004). Developmental-spelling research: A systematic imperative. *Reading Research Quarterly, 39,* 216–228.

Ivey, G., & Broaddus, K. (2001). "Just plain reading": A survey of what makes students want to read in middle school classrooms. *Reading Research Quarterly, 36,* 350–377.

Jacobson, D. (1989). The evaluation process—In process. In K. S. Goodman, Y. M. Goodman, & W. J. Hood (Eds.), *The whole language evaluation book* (pp. 177–188). Portsmouth, NH: Heinemann.

Jewell, T., & Pratt, D. (1999). Literature discussions in the primary grades: Children's thoughtful discourse about books and what teachers can do to make it happen. *The Reading Teacher, 52,* 842–850.

Jimerson, S. R., Burns, M. K., & VanDerHeyden, A. M. (2007). *The handbook of response to intervention: The science and practice of assessment and intervention.* New York: Springer.

Kajder, S., & Bull, G. (2003). Scaffolding for struggling students: Reading and writing with blogs. *Learning and Leading with Technology, 31*(2), 32–35.

Kamil, M. L. (2004). Vocabulary and comprehension instruction: Summary and implications of the National Reading Panel findings. In P. McCardle & V. Chhabra (Eds.), *The voice of evidence in reading research* (pp. 213–234). Baltimore, MD: Brookes.

Keene, E., & Zimmermann, S. (2007). *Mosaic of thought* (2nd ed.). Portsmouth, NH: Heinemann.

Kitagawa, M. M. (1989). Guise, son of the shoemaker. In K. S. Goodman, Y. M. Goodman, & W. J. Hood (Eds.), *The whole language evaluation book* (pp. 101–109). Portsmouth, NH: Heinemann.

Koch, K. (2000). At play with words. *American Educator, 24*(3), 11–15.

Kohn, A. (2008, January). Do kids read less for fun? *District Administrator*, p. 58.

Koskinen, P. S., & Blum, I. H. (1984). Repeated oral reading and the acquisition of fluency. In J. A. Niles & L. A. Harris (Eds.), *Changing perspectives on research in reading/language processing and instruction. Thirty-third yearbook of the National Reading Conference* (pp. 183–187). Rochester, NY: National Reading Conference.

Koskinen, P. S., & Blum, I. H. (1986). Paired repeated reading: A classroom strategy for developing fluent reading. *The Reading Teacher, 40,* 70–75.

Koskinen, P. S., Blum, I. H., Bisson, S. A., Phillips, S. M., Creamer, T. S., & Baker, T. K. (1999). Shared reading, books, and audiotapes: Supporting diverse students in school and at home. *The Reading Teacher, 52,* 430–444.

Krashen, S. *Free voluntary reading: New research, applications, and controversies.* Available: www.sdkrashen.com/articles/singapore/index.html, accessed 6/14/08.

Kuhn, M., & Stahl, S. (2000). *Fluency: A review of developmental and remedial reading practices.* CIERA Report #2–008. Ann Arbor, MI: University of Michigan, Center for the Improvement of Early Reading Achievement.

Lancia, P. (1997). Literary borrowing: The effects of literature on children's writing. *The Reading Teacher, 50,* 470–475.

Lederer, R. (1987). *Anguished English: An anthology of accidental assaults upon our language.* Charleston: Wyrick.

Lehman, B., & Scharer, P. (1996). Reading alone, talking together: The role of discussion in developing literary awareness. *The Reading Teacher, 50,* 26–35.

Lewis, M., & Samuels, S. J. (2003). *Read more—Read better? A meta-analysis of the literature on the relationship between exposure to reading and reading achievement.* Available: www.tc.umn.edu/∼samue001/publications.htm.

Lubliner, S., & Smetana, L. (2005). The effects of comprehensive vocabulary instruction on Title I students' metacognitive word-learning skills and reading comprehension. *Journal of Literacy Research, 37,* 163–200.

Malloy, J., & Gambrell, L. (2006). Approaching the unavoidable: Literacy instruction and the Internet. *The Reading Teacher, 59,* 482–484.

Martinez, M., Roser, N. L., & Strecker, S. (1999). "I never thought I could be a star": A reader's theater ticket to reading fluency. *The Reading Teacher, 52,* 326–334.

Marzano, R. (2004). *Building background knowledge for academic achievement.* Alexandria, VA: Association for Supervision and Curriculum Development.

Marzano, R., Pickering, D., & Pollock, J. (2001). *Classroom instruction that works: Research-based strategies for increasing student achievement.* Alexandria, VA: Association for Supervision and Curriculum Development.

Maxim, D., & Five, C. L. (1997). Classroom practices that monitor and inform learning. *School Talk, 3*(2), 1.

McCandliss, B., Beck, I. L., Sandak, R., & Perfetti, C. (2003). Focusing attention on decoding for children with poor reading skills: Design and preliminary tests of the word building intervention. *Scientific Studies of Reading, 7,* 75–102.

McCormick, S. (1994). A nonreader becomes a reader: A case study of literacy acquisition by a severely disabled reader. *Reading Research Quarterly, 29,* 156–176.

McCormick, S. (1995). *Instructing students who have literacy problems.* Upper Saddle River, NJ: Prentice-Hall.

McDermott, R. (1978). Pirandello in the classroom: On the possibility of equal educational opportunity in American culture. In M. Reynolds (Ed.), *Futures of exceptional children: Emerging structure* (pp. 41–64). Reston, VA: Council for Exceptional Children.

McGee, L., & Schickendanz, J. (2007). Repeated interactive read-alouds in preschool and kindergarten. *The Reading Teacher, 60,* 742–751.

McKenna, M., & Kear, D. (1990). Measuring attitude toward reading: A new tool for teachers. *The Reading Teacher, 43,* 626–629.

McKeon, C. (1999). The nature of children's e-mail in one classroom. *The Reading Teacher, 52,* 698–706.

McMahon, S., & Raphael, T. (1997). *The book club connection: Literacy learning and classroom talk.* New York: Teachers College Press.

Menon, M., & Mirabito, J. (1999). "Ya' mean all we hafta do is read?" *The Reading Teacher, 53,* 190–196.

Merriam, S. B. (1998). *Qualitative research and case study applications in education* (2nd ed.). San Francisco: Jossey-Bass.

Miller, S. (2003). How high- and low-challenge tasks affect motivation and learning: Implications for struggling readers. *Reading and Writing Quarterly, 19,* 39–57.

Moats, L. C. (1998). Teaching decoding. *American Educator, 22,* 42–49, 95.

Moffett, J., & Wagner, B. (1992). *Student-centered language arts, K–12* (4th ed.). Portsmouth, NH: Boynton/Cook.

Moore, P. W., & Moore, S. A. (1986). Possible sentences. In E. K. Dishner, T. W. Bean, J. E. Readence, & P. W. Moore (Eds.), *Reading in the content areas: Improving classroom instruction* (2nd ed., pp. 174–179). Dubuque, IA: Kendall/Hunt.

Morgan, D., Mraz, M., Padak, N., & Rasinski, T. (2009). *Independent reading: Strategies for K–3 classrooms.* New York: Guilford.

Morris, D. (1998, December). *Research address: Preventing reading failure in the primary grades.* Paper presented at the annual meeting of the National Reading Conference, Austin, TX.

Morris, D. (2008). *Diagnosis and correction of reading problems.* New York: Guilford.

Morris, D., & Nelson, L. (1992). Supported oral reading with low-achieving second graders. *Reading Research and Instruction, 31,* 49–63.

Moss, B., & Hendershot, J. (2002). Exploring sixth-graders' selection of nonfiction trade books. *The Reading Teacher, 56,* 6–17.

Mountain, L. (2005). ROOTing out meaning: More morphemic analysis for primary pupils. *The Reading Teacher, 58,* 742–749.

Mullis, I. V. S., Martin, M. O., Kennedy, A. M., & Foy, P. (2007). *IEA's Progress in International Reading Literacy Study in primary school in 40 countries.* Chestnut Hill, MA: TIMSS & PIRLS International Study Center, Boston College.

Nagy, W. E. (1988). *Teaching vocabulary to improve reading comprehension.* Urbana, IL: National Council of Teachers of English.

National Assessment of Educational Progress. (2000). Available online at http://nces.ed.gov/nationsreportcard/reading.

National Center for Education Statistics. (2001). *Fourth-grade reading highlights 2000.* Washington, DC: U.S. Department of Education, Office of Educational Research and Improvement.

National Middle School Association. (2003). *This we believe: Successful schools for young adolescents.* Westerville, OH: Author.

National Reading Panel. (2000). *Report of the National Reading Panel: Teaching children to read. Report of the subgroups.* Washington, DC: U.S. Department of Health and Human Services, National Institutes of Health.

Nelson, J. R., & Stage, S. A. (2007). Fostering the development of vocabulary knowledge and reading comprehension through contextually-based multiple meaning vocabulary instruction. *Education and Treatment of Children, 30,* 1–22.

Nicholson, T. (1998). The flashcard strikes back. *The Reading Teacher, 52,* 188–192.

Noe, K., & Johnson, N. (1999). *Getting started with literature circles.* Norwood, MA: Christopher Gordon.

Nolen, S. (2007). Young children's motivation to read and write: Development in social contexts. *Cognition and Instruction, 25,* 219–270.

Ogle, D. (1986). K–W–L: A teaching model that develops active reading of expository text. *The Reading Teacher, 38,* 564–570.

Oldfather, P., & Wigfield, A. (1996). Children's motivations for literacy learning. In L. Baker, P. Afflerbach, & D. Reinking (Eds.), *Developing engaged readers in school and home communities* (pp. 89–113). Mahwah, NJ: Erlbaum.

O'Masta, G. A., & Wolf, J. A. (1991). Encouraging independent reading through the Reading Millionaires project. *The Reading Teacher, 44,* 656–662.

Opitz, M. F., & Rasinski, T. V. (1998). *Good-bye Round Robin: 25 effective oral reading strategies.* Portsmouth, NH: Heinemann.

Padak, N. (1987). *Reading placement and diagnosis: A guide for elementary teachers.* Springfield: Illinois State Board of Education.

Padak, N., Newton, E., Rasinski, T., & Newton, R. (2008). Getting to the root of word study: Teaching Latin and Greek word roots in elementary and middle grades. In A. Farstrup & S. J. Samuels (Eds.), *What research has to say about vocabulary instruction* (pp. 6–31). Newark, DE: International Reading Association.

Padak, N., & Rasinski, T. (2004a). Fast Start: Successful literacy instruction that connects homes and schools. In J. Dugan, P. Linder, M. B. Sampson, B. Brancato, & L. Elish-Piper (Eds.), *Celebrating the power of literacy, 2004 College Reading Associa-* tion Yearbook (pp. 11–23). Logan, UT: College Reading Association.

Padak, N., & Rasinski, T. (2004b). Fast Start: A promising practice for family literacy programs. *Family Literacy Forum, 3*(2), 3–9.

Padak, N., & Rasinski, T. (2005). *Fast Start for early readers: A research-based, send-home literacy program.* New York: Scholastic.

Palincsar, A. S., & Brown, A. L. (1984). Reciprocal teaching of comprehension-fostering and comprehension-monitoring activities. *Cognition and Instruction, 2,* 117–175.

Palmer, B., Codling, R., & Gambrell, L. (1994). In their own words: What elementary students have to say about motivation to read. *Reading Teacher, 48,* 176–178.

Palmer, R., & Stewart, R. (2005). Models for using nonfiction in the primary grades. *The Reading Teacher, 58,* 426–434.

Patton, M. Q. (1990). *Qualitative evaluation methods* (2nd ed.). Newbury Park, CA: Sage.

Pearson, P. D., Hiebert, E. H., & Kamil, M. L. (2007). Vocabulary assessment: What we know and what we need to learn. *Reading Research Quarterly, 42,* 282–296.

Pikulski, J. J. (1994). Preventing reading failure: A review of five effective programs. *The Reading Teacher, 48,* 30–39.

Pinnell, G. S. (1989). Reading Recovery: Helping at-risk children learn to read. *Elementary School Journal, 90,* 161–183.

Pinnell, G. S., Fried, M. D., & Estice, R. M. (1990). Reading Recovery: Learning how to make a difference. *The Reading Teacher, 43,* 282–295.

Pinnell, G. S., Pikulski, J. J., Wixson, K. K., Campbell, J. R., Gough, P. B., & Beatty, A. S. (1995). *Listening to children read aloud.* Washington, DC: U.S. Department of Education, Office of Educational Research and Improvement.

Postlethwaite, T. N., & Ross, K. N. (1992). *Effective schools in reading: Implications for educational planners.* The Hague: International Association for the Evaluation of Educational Achievement.

Potenza-Radis, C. (2008). *A study examining how struggling third grade readers, as members of a guided reading group, experienced peer-led literature discussions.* Unpublished doctoral dissertation, Kent State University.

Prescott, J. O. (2003). The power of reader's theater. *Instructor, 112*(5), 22–26+.

Pressley, M. (2001). *Effective beginning reading instruction.* Executive Summary and Paper Commissioned by the National Reading Conference. Chicago: National Reading Conference. Available online at http://nrconline.org.

Pressley, M. (2005). *Reading instruction that works.* New York: Guilford.

Pressley, M., Allington, R., Wharton-McDonald, R., Block, C., & Morrow, L. (2001). *Learning to read: Lessons from exemplary first grades.* New York: Guilford.

Primavera, J. (2000). Enhancing family literacy competence through literacy activities. *Journal of Prevention and Intervention in the Community, 20,* 85–101.

Public Law 107–110, 107th Congress. Available online: www.ed .gov/nclb/landing.html.

RAND Reading Study Group. (2002). *Reading for understanding: Toward an R&D program in reading comprehension.* Santa Monica, CA: RAND.

Rasinski, T. V. (1989). Fluency for everyone: Incorporating fluency in the classroom. *The Reading Teacher, 42,* 690–693.

Rasinski, T. V. (1990). *The effects of cued phrase boundaries in texts.* Bloomington, IN: ERIC Clearinghouse on Reading and Communication Skills (ED 313 689).

Rasinski, T. V. (1992). Promoting recreational reading. In K. Wood (Ed.), *Exploring literature in the classroom: Content and methods* (pp. 85–109). Norwood, MA: Christopher-Gordon.

Rasinski, T. V. (1994). Developing syntactic sensitivity in reading through phrase-cued texts. *Intervention in School and Clinic, 29,* 165–168.

Rasinski, T. V. (1995). Fast Start: A parent involvement reading program for primary grade students. In W. Linek & E. Sturtevant (Eds.), *Generations of literacy: 17th Yearbook of the College Reading Association* (pp. 301–312). Harrisonburg, VA: College Reading Association.

Rasinski, T. V. (1999). Making and writing words. *Reading Online,* an electronic journal of the International Reading Association. www.readingonline.org/articles/art_index.ap?HREF=/articles/ words/rasinski_index.html.

Rasinski, T. V. (2003). *The fluent reader: Oral reading strategies for building word recognition, fluency, and comprehension.* New York: Scholastic.

Rasinski, T. V. (2006). Reading fluency instruction: Moving beyond accuracy, automaticity, and prosody. *The Reading Teacher, 59,* 704–706.

Rasinski, T. V., & Fredericks, A. D. (1991). The Akron Paired Reading project. *The Reading Teacher, 44,* 514–515.

Rasinski, T. V., & Hoffman, J. V. (2003). Theory and research into practice: Oral reading in the school literacy curriculum. *Reading Research Quarterly, 38,* 510–522.

Rasinski, T. V., & Padak, N. D. (1998). How elementary students referred for compensatory reading instruction perform on school-based measures of word recognition, fluency, and comprehension. *Reading Psychology: An International Quarterly, 19,* 185–216.

Rasinski, T. V., & Padak, N. (2005a). *Three minute reading assessments: Word recognition, fluency, and comprehension for grades 1–4.* New York: Scholastic.

Rasinski, T. V., & Padak, N. (2005b). *Three minute reading assessments: Word recognition, fluency, and comprehension for grades 5–8.* New York: Scholastic.

Rasinski, T. V., Padak, N. D., Linek, W. L., & Sturtevant, E. (1994). Effects of fluency development on urban second-grade readers. *Journal of Educational Research, 87,* 158–165.

Rasinski, T., Padak, N., Newton, R., & Newton, E. (2008). *Greek & Latin roots: Keys to building vocabulary.* Huntington Beach, CA: Shell.

Rasinski, T., Reutzel, D. R., Chard, D., & Linan-Thompson, S. (in press). Reading fluency. In M. L. Kamil, P. D. Pearson, E. B. Moje, & P. Afflerbach (Eds.). *The handbook of reading research IV.*

Rasinski, T., & Stevenson, B. (2005). The effects of Fast Start Reading, a fluency based home involvement reading program, on the reading achievement of beginning readers. *Reading Psychology: An International Quarterly, 26,* 109–125.

Rasinski, T. V., & Zutell, J. B. (1996). Is fluency yet a goal of the reading curriculum? In E. G. Sturtevant and W. M. Linek (Eds.), *Growing literacy: 18th Yearbook of the College Reading Association* (pp. 237–246). Harrisonburg, VA: College Reading Association.

Read, C. (1971). Pre-school children's knowledge of English phonology. *Harvard Educational Review, 41,* 1–34.

Reutzel, D. R., & Fawson, P. C. (1990). Traveling Tales: Connecting parents and children through writing. *The Reading Teacher, 44,* 222–227.

Rhodes, L., & Dudley-Marling, C. (1988). *Readers and writers with a difference.* Portsmouth, NH: Heinemann.

Rhodes, L., & Shanklin, N. (1993). *Windows into literacy.* Portsmouth, NH: Heinemann.

Richek, M. A., & McTague, B. K. (1988). The "Curious George" strategy for students with reading problems. *The Reading Teacher, 42,* 220–226.

Rose, M. (1995). *Possible lives.* Boston: Houghton Mifflin.

Rosenblatt, L. (1938). *Literature as exploration.* New York: Modern Language Association.

Rosenblatt, L. (1978). *The reader, the text, and the poem.* Carbondale, IL: Southern Illinois University Press.

Rothstein-Fisch, C., & Trumbull, E. (2008). *Managing diverse classrooms: How to build on students' cultural strengths.* Alexandria, VA: Association for Supervision and Curriculum Development.

Rupley, W. H., & Nichols, W. D. (2005). Vocabulary instruction for the struggling reader. *Reading and Writing Quarterly, 21,* 239–260.

Rupley, W., Wise, B., & Logan, J. (1986). Research in effective teaching: An overview of its development. In J. Hoffman (Ed.), *Effective teaching of reading: Research and practice* (pp. 3–36). Newark, DE: International Reading Association.

Samuels, S. J. (1979). The method of repeated readings. *The Reading Teacher, 32,* 403–408.

Schmitt, N. (2008). Instructed second language vocabulary learning. *Language Teaching Research, 12,* 329–363.

Schnorr, R., & Davern, L. (2005). Creating exemplary literacy classrooms through the power of teaming. *The Reading Teacher, 58,* 494–506.

Scholastic 2008 Kids and Family Reading Report. (2008) Available online: www.scholastic.com/readingreport.

Schreiber, P. A. (1980). On the acquisition of reading fluency. *Journal of Reading Behavior, 12,* 177–186.

Schreiber, P. A. (1991). Understanding prosody's role in reading acquisition. *Theory into Practice, 30,* 158–164.

Schwartz, R., & Raphael, T. (1985). Concept of definition: A key to improving students' vocabulary. *The Reading Teacher, 39,* 198–205.

Schwartz, R. M. (2005). Literacy learning of at-risk first-grade students in the reading recovery early intervention. *Journal of Educational Psychology, 97,* 257–267.

Scott, C. (2006). *Keeping watch on Reading First.* Washington, DC: Center on Education Policy. Retrieved November 13, 2007 from www.cep-dc.org/document/docWindow.cfm?fuseaction= document.viewDocument&documentid=34&documentFor matId=491.

Shanahan, S., Wojciechowski, J., & Rubik, G. (1998). A celebration of reading: How our school read for one million minutes. *The Reading Teacher, 52,* 93–96.

Shanahan, T. (2000, November). *The literacy teaching framework.* Paper presented at the annual Kent State University Reading Conference, Kent, OH.

Shanahan, T. (2006). Developing fluency in the context of effective literacy instruction. In T. Rasinski, C. L. Z. Blachowicz, & K. Lems (Eds.), *Fluency instruction: Research-based best practices* (pp. 21–38). New York: Guilford.

Shimron, J. (1994). The making of readers: The work of Professor Dina Feitelson. In D. Dickinson (Ed.), *Bridges to literacy* (pp. 80–99). Cambridge, MA: Blackwell.

Silvers, P. (1986). Process writing and the reading connection. *The Reading Teacher, 39,* 684–688.

Slavin, R., & Madden, N. (2001). *One million children: Success for All.* Thousand Oaks, CA: Corwin.

Slavin, R. E., Madden, N. L., Karweit, N. L., Dolan, L., & Wasik, B. A. (1992). *Success for All: A relentless approach to prevention and early intervention in elementary schools.* Arlington, VA: Educational Research Service.

Smith, J., & Elley, W. (1997). *How children learn to read: Insights from the New Zealand experience.* Katonah, NY: Richard C. Owen.

Smolkin, L., & Donovan, C. (2003). Supporting comprehension acquisition for emerging and struggling readers: The interactive information book read-aloud. *Exceptionality, 11*(1), 25–38.

Snow, C. (2002). *Reading for understanding: Toward an R&D program in reading comprehension.* Santa Monica, CA: RAND.

Snow, C. E., Burns, M. S., & Griffin, P. (1998). *Preventing reading difficulties in young children.* Washington, DC: National Academy Press.

Spurlin, J., Dansereau, D., Larson, C., & Brooks, L. (1984). Cooperative learning strategies in processing descriptive text: Effects of role and activity level of the learner. *Cognition and Instruction, 1,* 451–463.

Stahl, S. A. (1986). Three principles of effective vocabulary instruction. *Journal of Reading, 29,* 662–671.

Stahl, S. A. (1992). Saying the "p" word: Nine guidelines for exemplary phonics instruction. *The Reading Teacher, 45,* 618–625.

Stahl, S. A., & Clark, C. H. (1987). The effects of participatory expectations in classroom discussion on the learning of science vocabulary. *American Educational Research Journal, 24,* 541–556.

Stahl, S. A., Duffy-Hester, A. M., & Stahl, K. A. (1998). Everything you wanted to know about phonics (but were afraid to ask). *Reading Research Quarterly, 33,* 338–355.

Stahl, S. A., & Heubach, K. (2005). Fluency-oriented reading instruction. *Journal of Literacy Research, 37,* 25–60.

Stahl, S. A., Heubach, K., & Cramond, B. (1997). *Fluency-oriented reading instruction.* Reading research report no. 79. Athens, GA and College Park, MD: National Reading Research Center.

Stahl, S. A., & Kapinus, B. A. (1991). Possible sentences: Predicting word meanings to teach content vocabulary. *The Reading Teacher, 45,* 36–43.

Stahl, S. A., & Vancil, S. J. (1986). Discussion is what makes semantic maps work in vocabulary instruction. *The Reading Teacher, 40,* 62–69.

Stanovich, K. E. (1986). Matthew effects in reading: Some consequences of individual differences in the acquisition of literacy. *Reading Research Quarterly, 21,* 360–407.

Stanovich, K. E. (1994). Romance and reality. *The Reading Teacher, 47,* 280–289.

Stauffer, R. (1980). *The language-experience approach to the teaching of reading* (2nd ed.). New York: Harper & Row.

Sullivan, J. (1998). The electronic journal: Combining literacy and technology. *The Reading Teacher, 52,* 90–93.

Sweet, A., & Guthrie, J. (1996). How children's motivations relate to literacy development and instruction. *The Reading Teacher, 49,* 660–662.

Tancock, S. M. (1994). A literacy lesson framework for children with reading problems. *The Reading Teacher, 48,* 130–140.

Tapscott, D. (1998). *Growing up digital.* New York: McGraw-Hill.

Taylor, B., Frye, M., & Maruyama, K. (1990). Time spent reading and reading growth. *American Educational Research Journal, 27,* 351–362.

Taylor, B., Pearson, P. D., Clark, S., & Walpole, S. (2000). Effective schools and accomplished readers: Lessons about primary-grade reading instruction in low-income schools. *Elementary School Journal, 101,* 121–165.

Templeton, S., & Morris, D. (1999). Questions teachers ask about spelling. *Reading Research Quarterly, 34,* 102–112.

Tierney, R. (1998). Literacy assessment reform: Shifting beliefs, principled possibilities, and emerging practices. *The Reading Teacher, 51,* 374–390.

Topping, K. (1987). Paired Reading: A powerful technique for parent use. *The Reading Teacher, 40,* 608–614.

Topping, K. (1989). Peer tutoring and Paired Reading: Combining two powerful techniques. *The Reading Teacher, 42,* 488–494.

Topping, K. (1995). *Paired reading, spelling, and writing.* New York: Cassell.

Turner, J., & Paris, S. (1995). How literacy tasks influence children's motivation for literacy. *The Reading Teacher, 48,* 662–673.

U.S. Department of Education, National Center for Educational

Statistics. (1996, 2000). *Almanac: Reading.* Washington, DC: Author.

Vacca, R. T., & Vacca, J. L. (2008). *Content area reading* (9th ed.). Boston: Allyn & Bacon.

VanDeWeghe, R. (2007). What about vocabulary instruction? *English Journal, 97,* 101–114.

Van Voorhis, F. L. (2003). Interactive homework in middle school: Effects on family involvement and science achievement. *The Journal of Education Research, 96,* 323–338.

Vygotsky, L. (1962). *Thought and language.* Cambridge, MA: MIT Press.

Vygotsky, L. (1978). *Mind in society.* Cambridge, MA: Harvard University Press.

Walker, B. (2005). Thinking aloud: Struggling readers often require more than a model. *The Reading Teacher, 58,* 688–692.

Watson, B., & Konicek, R. (1990). Teaching for conceptual change: Confronting children's experience. *Phi Delta Kappan, 71,* 680–685.

Watson, D. (1987). *Ideas and insights.* Urbana, IL: National Council of Teachers of English.

Weiner, B. (1979). A theory of motivation for some classroom experiences. *Journal of Educational Psychology, 71,* 3–25.

Wells, G. (1986). *The meaning makers.* Portsmouth, NH: Heinemann.

Werderich, D., & Pariza, J. (2007). Teaching the love of reading. *Illinois Reading Council Journal, 35*(2), 22–31.

Wigfield, A., & Asher, S. (1984). Social and motivational influences on reading. In R. Barr, M. Kamil, P. Mosenthal, & P. D. Pearson (Eds.), *Handbook of reading research* (Vol. 1, pp. 423–452). New York: Longman.

Winograd, P., & Smith, L. (1987). Improving the climate for reading comprehension instruction. *The Reading Teacher, 41,* 304–310.

Wolf, M., Crosson, A., & Resnick, L. (2005). Classroom talk for rigorous reading comprehension instruction. *Reading Psychology, 26,* 27–53.

Worthy, J., & Prater, K. (2002). "I thought about it all night": Reader's theater for reading fluency and motivation. *The Reading Teacher, 56,* 294–297.

Yopp, H. (1992). Developing phonemic awareness in young children. *The Reading Teacher, 45,* 696–703.

Yopp, H. K. (1995a). A test for assessing phonemic awareness in young children. *The Reading Teacher, 49*(1), 20–29.

Yopp, H. K. (1995b). Read-aloud books for developing phonemic awareness: An annotated bibliography. *The Reading Teacher, 48,* 538–543.

CHILDREN'S BOOKS CITED IN THE TEXT

Bridwell, N. (1985). *Clifford the big red dog.* New York: Scholastic.

Brown, M. W. (1949/1999). *The important book.* New York: HarperCollins.

Cameron, P. (1961). *"I can't," said the ant.* New York: Coward-McCann.

Cowley, J. (1999). *Mrs. Wishy Washy.* DeSoto, TX: Wright Group/McGraw Hill.

Curtis, C. P. (1999). *Bud, not Buddy.* New York: Scholastic.

dePaola, T. (1982). *Strega Nona's magic lessons.* New York: Harcourt Brace Jovanovich.

Fleischman, P. (1985). *I am Phoenix: Poems for two voices.* New York: Harper & Row.

Fleischman, P. (1988). *Joyful noise: Poems for two voices.* New York: Harper & Row.

Fleischman, P. (1993). *Bull Run.* New York: HarperCollins.

Fleischman, P. (1997). *Seedfolks.* New York: HarperCollins.

Fleischman, P. (2000). *Big talk: Poems for four voices.* Cambridge, MA: Candlewick Press.

Fleischman, J. (2007). *Black and white airmen: Their true history.* Boston: Houghton Mifflin.

Hall, D. (1994). *I am the dog, I am the cat.* New York: Dial.

Hoberman, M. A. (2001). *You read to me, I'll read to you.* Boston: Little, Brown.

Hunt, I. (1970). *No promises in the wind.* Chicago: Follet.

Johnson, A. (1989). *Tell me a story Mama.* New York: Orchard.

Lansky, B. (1996). *Poetry party.* New York: Meadowbrook Press.

Lansky, B. (2006). *Oh my darling, porcupine: And other silly sing-a-long songs.* New York: Simon and Schuster.

Martin, B., Jr. (1983). *Brown bear, brown bear, what do you see?* New York: Holt, Rinehart and Winston.

Numeroff, L. (2005). *If you give a mouse a cookie.* New York: HarperCollins.

Paulsen, G. (1999). *Hatchet.* New York: Aladdin.

Rey, H. A., & Rey, M. (1941). *Curious George.* Boston: Houghton Mifflin.

Seuss, Dr. (1963). *ABC.* New York: Beginner Books.

Silverstein, S. (1974). *Where the sidewalk ends.* New York: HarperCollins.

Silverstein, S. (1981). *A light in the attic.* New York: HarperCollins.

Steig, W. (1986). *Caleb and Kate.* New York: Farrar, Straus and Giroux.

Taback, S. (2002). *This is the house that Jack built.* New York: G. P. Putnam's Sons.

Viorst, J. (1981). *If I were in charge of the world and other worries.* New York: Atheneum.

Waber, B. (1972). *Ira sleeps over.* Boston: Houghton Mifflin.

White, E. B. (1952). *Charlotte's web.* New York: Harper.

Williams, S. (1989). *I went walking.* San Diego: Harcourt Brace Jovanovich.

Yolen, J. (1988). *The devil's arithmetic.* New York: Viking.

Zion, G. (1956). *Harry, the dirty dog.* New York: Harper.

Zolotow, C. (1980). *Say it!* New York: Greenwillow.

❧ Name Index

〜 Subject Index